DATE DUE

# PAPERS

OF THE

## PEABODY MUSEUM OF AMERICAN ARCHAEOLOGY
## AND ETHNOLOGY, HARVARD UNIVERSITY

Vol. XIII. — No. 1

# MAYA–SPANISH CROSSES
# IN YUCATAN

BY

## GEORGE DEE WILLIAMS

CAMBRIDGE, MASSACHUSETTS, U.S.A.

PUBLISHED BY THE BUREAU OF INTERNATIONAL RESEARCH

OF HARVARD UNIVERSITY AND RADCLIFFE COLLEGE

## FOR THE MUSEUM

1931

PRINTED AT THE HARVARD UNIVERSITY PRESS

CAMBRIDGE, MASS., U. S. A.

# PREFACE

THE following report is based upon field work in physical anthropology carried on by me in the state of Yucatan, Mexico, from February to October, 1927. Mrs. Williams acted as my assistant both in the field and in the later treatment of the data. The work was done under a grant made by the Bureau of International Research of Harvard University and Radcliffe College. I wish here to indicate my indebtedness to the Bureau and its chairman, Professor G. G. Wilson. To Professor E. A. Hooton, to whom the grant was made, and under whose direction the work was done, I owe thanks for advice and guidance; and to him, to Professor A. M. Tozzer, and to Professor R. J. Terry I am indebted for counsel in the preparation of the manuscript.

To the Carnegie Institution of Washington, and to its president, Dr. John C. Merriam, to Dr. S. G. Morley, director of the Chichen Itza Project, and to Dr. F. G. Benedict, director of the Nutrition Laboratory in Boston, I desire at this time to express my appreciation and thanks for coöperation in the work. I owe special thanks for assistance to the governor of the state of Yucatan, Sr. Dr. Alvaro Torre Diaz, and to Sr. Professor Bartolome Garcia Correa, who was acting governor in the absence of Dr. Torre Diaz.

The field work would have been doubly arduous and many times impossible without the aid, advice, friendship, and hospitality of many persons in Yucatan, among whom are: Sr. A. Vales S., Director General of the Ferrocarriles Unidos de Yucatan, S.A., who placed facilities for travel at our disposal; Sr. Alonso Patron Espada, Sr. Dr. Rafael Cervera L., Sr. Fernando Cervera G. R., Sr. Arturo Ponce C., the brothers Gamboa A., Don Luis, Don Alfredo, Don Octavio, and their nephew Don Camilo, all owners of henequen plantations where valuable data were obtained; Sr. Dr. Guillermo Vega L. and Sr. Dr. Eduardo Urzaiz R., who made the patients of their hospitals available to me; Sr. Dr. Narciso Souza N., whose technical aid in roentgen-ray work and whose advice were invaluable; Miss Eunice Blackburn, director of the Turner-Hodge Colegio Americano, who permitted me to examine the children of her school; Mr. A. A. Voganitz, American Consul; Mr. Arthur P. Rice; Sres. Juan and Eduardo Martinez; Sr. Vicente Molina; Sr. Pedro P. Castillo C.; Sr. Tranquilino Perez C.; Sr. Delio Zaldivar; Sr. A. Burgos C.   Finally I wish to thank for assistance Dr. W. L. Moss of Harvard Medical School, Mr. Franklin M. Kellogg of the Munson Line; and the Plymouth Cordage Company of Plymouth, Massachusetts.

The publication of this work has been made possible by a grant from the Bureau of International Research of Harvard University and Radcliffe College and by the further financial assistance of the Peabody Museum.

Many obligations were incurred by me other than the ones named. None can be adequately repaid. I can only acknowledge my indebtedness.

G. D. W.

SCHOOL OF MEDICINE
WASHINGTON UNIVERSITY, ST. LOUIS

# CONTENTS

|  | PAGE |
|---|---|
| INTRODUCTION | xiii |
| HABITAT | 1 |
| The Maya Region | 1 |
| Topography | 1 |
| Climate | 2 |
| Flora | 3 |
| Fauna | 3 |
| HISTORY | 4 |
| Pre-Columbian History | 4 |
| Post-Columbian History | 6 |
| Population: General | 8 |
| Population: The Spanish Element | 9 |
| THE PROBLEM | 12 |
| SORTING: ITS TECHNIQUE AND THE THEORY OF ITS APPLICATION TO THE STUDY OF RACE MIXTURE | 16 |
| Apparatus and Technique | 16 |
| THEORY OF SORTING IN RACE MIXTURE: GENERAL | 18 |
| Hair Texture | 34 |
| Hair Form | 34 |
| Pigmentation | 34 |
| Epicanthic (or Mongoloid) Fold | 35 |
| Prognathism | 35 |
| Nose Form | 35 |
| Lip Thickness | 35 |
| THEORY AND PRACTICE OF SORTING IN YUCATECAN RACE MIXTURE | 41 |
| LENGTH DIMENSIONS OF THE BODY | 49 |
| Stature | 49 |
| Acromial and Sternal Heights | 55 |
| Relative Shoulder Height | 56 |
| Sitting Height | 57 |
| Tibiale-sphyrion | 59 |
| Relative Sitting Height | 59 |
| Span | 63 |
| Relative Span and Relative Total Arm Length | 63 |
| Acromion-radiale and Radiale-dactylion | 66 |
| Intermembral Index | 66 |

SHOULDERS AND HIPS . . . . . . . . . . . . . . . . . . . 68
    Biacromial Diameter and Relative Shoulder Breadth . . . . . 68
    Bi-iliac Diameter and Hip-shoulder Index . . . . . . . . . 71
THE THORAX . . . . . . . . . . . . . . . . . . . . . . . 73
    Chest Breadth . . . . . . . . . . . . . . . . . . . . 73
    Chest Depth . . . . . . . . . . . . . . . . . . . . . 74
    Thoracic Index . . . . . . . . . . . . . . . . . . . . 75
    Chest Girth (at rest) . . . . . . . . . . . . . . . . . 76
    Relative Chest Girth . . . . . . . . . . . . . . . . . 78
    Vital Capacity . . . . . . . . . . . . . . . . . . . . 79
BODY BUILD . . . . . . . . . . . . . . . . . . . . . . . 79
    Weight . . . . . . . . . . . . . . . . . . . . . . . 81
    Indices of Build . . . . . . . . . . . . . . . . . . . 83
PHYSIOLOGICAL OBSERVATIONS . . . . . . . . . . . . . . . . 85
    Blood Pressure . . . . . . . . . . . . . . . . . . . . 85
    Pulse Rate . . . . . . . . . . . . . . . . . . . . . 89
    Hand Squeeze . . . . . . . . . . . . . . . . . . . . 90
    Basal Metabolism . . . . . . . . . . . . . . . . . . . 94
THE HEAD . . . . . . . . . . . . . . . . . . . . . . . . 98
    Head Length . . . . . . . . . . . . . . . . . . . . . 98
    Head Breadth . . . . . . . . . . . . . . . . . . . . 101
    Cephalic Index . . . . . . . . . . . . . . . . . . . 104
    Head Height . . . . . . . . . . . . . . . . . . . . 108
    Length-height Index . . . . . . . . . . . . . . . . . 108
    Breadth-height Index . . . . . . . . . . . . . . . . . 111
THE FACE . . . . . . . . . . . . . . . . . . . . . . . . 112
    Radiometric Measurements . . . . . . . . . . . . . . . 112
    Bizygomatic Diameter . . . . . . . . . . . . . . . . . 124
    Cephalo-facial Index . . . . . . . . . . . . . . . . . 129
    Bigonial Diameter . . . . . . . . . . . . . . . . . . 129
    Minimum Frontal Diameter . . . . . . . . . . . . . . . 131
    Fronto-parietal Index . . . . . . . . . . . . . . . . 134
    Zygo-frontal Index . . . . . . . . . . . . . . . . . . 134
    Fronto-gonial Index . . . . . . . . . . . . . . . . . 134
    Zygo-gonial Index . . . . . . . . . . . . . . . . . . 136
    Face Height . . . . . . . . . . . . . . . . . . . . . 139
    Upper Face Height . . . . . . . . . . . . . . . . . . 140
    Facial Index . . . . . . . . . . . . . . . . . . . . 142
    Upper Facial Index . . . . . . . . . . . . . . . . . . 144
THE NOSE . . . . . . . . . . . . . . . . . . . . . . . . 147
    Nose Height . . . . . . . . . . . . . . . . . . . . . 147
    Nose Breadth . . . . . . . . . . . . . . . . . . . . 149
    Nasal Index . . . . . . . . . . . . . . . . . . . . . 149
    Observations on Nasal Wings . . . . . . . . . . . . . . 151
    Other Observations on the Nose . . . . . . . . . . . . . 153

# CONTENTS

THE EAR . . . . . . . . . . . . . . . . . . . . . . . . . 161
   Ear Length and Ear Breadth . . . . . . . . . . . . . 161
   Auricular Index . . . . . . . . . . . . . . . . . . . 162
   Ear Protrusion . . . . . . . . . . . . . . . . . . . 164
   Roll of Helix . . . . . . . . . . . . . . . . . . . . 165
   Attachment of Ear Lobes . . . . . . . . . . . . . . 165

CERTAIN SUBJECTIVELY OBSERVED TRAITS . . . . . . . . . 166
   The Hair and Beard . . . . . . . . . . . . . . . . . 166
   Pigmentation . . . . . . . . . . . . . . . . . . . . 169
   Eye-folds . . . . . . . . . . . . . . . . . . . . . . 178

BLOOD GROUPING . . . . . . . . . . . . . . . . . . . . . 180

SOCIAL PHENOMENA . . . . . . . . . . . . . . . . . . . . 184
   Occupation . . . . . . . . . . . . . . . . . . . . . 184
   Birthplace . . . . . . . . . . . . . . . . . . . . . 186
   Birthplace Compared with Residence . . . . . . . . . . 188
   Marriage . . . . . . . . . . . . . . . . . . . . . . 190
   The Family: Its Size and Constitution . . . . . . . . . . 197
   The Family: Modifying Factors of its Size and Constitution . . 208

VARIABILITY . . . . . . . . . . . . . . . . . . . . . . . 214

CONCLUSION . . . . . . . . . . . . . . . . . . . . . . . 228

APPENDIX . . . . . . . . . . . . . . . . . . . . . . . . 237

BIBLIOGRAPHY . . . . . . . . . . . . . . . . . . . . . . 249

# LIST OF TABLES

1. Provenience of some of Cortes' companions in the conquest of Mexico . . . . . . . . . . . . . . . . . . . . . . . . . . . . . 10
2. Tests of amount of association existing between certain qualitative and quantitative traits . . . . . . . . . . . . 24
3. Definition of Group A . . . . . . . . . . . . . . . . . . 44
4. Definition of traits for Whiter subgroups of the Yucatecan mixture . . . . . . . . . . . . . . . . . . . . . . . . . 47
5. Definition of Group E . . . . . . . . . . . . . . . . . . 49
6. Stature . . . . . . . . . . . . . . . . . . . . . . . . . . 50
7. Acromial height . . . . . . . . . . . . . . . . . . . . . 54
8. Sternal height . . . . . . . . . . . . . . . . . . . . . . 55
9. Relative shoulder height . . . . . . . . . . . . . . . . . 56
10. Sitting height . . . . . . . . . . . . . . . . . . . . . . 57
11. Tibiale-sphyrion . . . . . . . . . . . . . . . . . . . . . 59
12. Relative sitting height . . . . . . . . . . . . . . . . . . 60
13. Span . . . . . . . . . . . . . . . . . . . . . . . . . . . 62
14. Total arm length and relative total arm length . . . . . . 64
15. Relative span . . . . . . . . . . . . . . . . . . . . . . 65
16. Acromion-radiale . . . . . . . . . . . . . . . . . . . . 66
17. Radiale-dactylion . . . . . . . . . . . . . . . . . . . . 67
18. Intermembral Index . . . . . . . . . . . . . . . . . . . 67
19. Biacromial diameter . . . . . . . . . . . . . . . . . . . 69
20. Relative shoulder breadth . . . . . . . . . . . . . . . . 70
21. Bi-iliac diameter . . . . . . . . . . . . . . . . . . . . . 71
22. Hip-shoulder Index . . . . . . . . . . . . . . . . . . . 72
23. Chest breadth . . . . . . . . . . . . . . . . . . . . . . 73
24. Chest depth . . . . . . . . . . . . . . . . . . . . . . . 74
25. Thoracic Index . . . . . . . . . . . . . . . . . . . . . . 75
26. Chest girth (at rest) . . . . . . . . . . . . . . . . . . . 76
27. Relative chest girth . . . . . . . . . . . . . . . . . . . 77
28. Vital capacity . . . . . . . . . . . . . . . . . . . . . . 78
29. Weight . . . . . . . . . . . . . . . . . . . . . . . . . . 80
30. Index of bodily fullness . . . . . . . . . . . . . . . . . 81
31. Index of build . . . . . . . . . . . . . . . . . . . . . . 82
32. Index of robustness . . . . . . . . . . . . . . . . . . . 84
33. Blood pressure in relation to age . . . . . . . . . . . . . 86
34. Blood pressure — systolic . . . . . . . . . . . . . . . . 88
35. Blood pressure — diastolic . . . . . . . . . . . . . . . . 88
36. Pulse pressure . . . . . . . . . . . . . . . . . . . . . . 89
37. Hand squeeze . . . . . . . . . . . . . . . . . . . . . . 91
38. Basal metabolism . . . . . . . . . . . . . . . . . . . . . 96

39. Head length . . . . . . . . . . . . . . . . . . . . . . . . .   99
40. Head breadth . . . . . . . . . . . . . . . . . . . . . . .  102
41. Cephalic Index . . . . . . . . . . . . . . . . . . . . .  105
42. Head height . . . . . . . . . . . . . . . . . . . . . . .  109
43. Length-height Index . . . . . . . . . . . . . . . . . .  110
44. Breadth-height Index . . . . . . . . . . . . . . . . . .  111
45. Average protrusion indices of cephalic and facial points . . .  113
46. Prominence of brow-ridges . . . . . . . . . . . . . . .  115
47. Amount of alveolar prognathism . . . . . . . . . . . .  117
48. Thickness of membranous lips . . . . . . . . . . . . .  119
49. Chin prominence . . . . . . . . . . . . . . . . . . . . .  121
50. Average angular location of cephalic and facial points . . .  123
51. Bizygomatic diameter . . . . . . . . . . . . . . . . . .  125
52. Malar prominence . . . . . . . . . . . . . . . . . . . .  127
53. Cephalo-facial Index . . . . . . . . . . . . . . . . . .  128
54. Bigonial diameter . . . . . . . . . . . . . . . . . . . .  130
55. Prominence of gonial angles . . . . . . . . . . . . . .  131
56. Minimum frontal diameter . . . . . . . . . . . . . . .  132
57. Fronto-parietal Index . . . . . . . . . . . . . . . . . .  133
58. Zygo-frontal Index . . . . . . . . . . . . . . . . . . .  135
59. Fronto-gonial Index . . . . . . . . . . . . . . . . . . .  136
60. Zygo-gonial Index . . . . . . . . . . . . . . . . . . . .  137
61. Face height . . . . . . . . . . . . . . . . . . . . . . . .  138
62. Upper face height . . . . . . . . . . . . . . . . . . . .  141
63. Facial Index . . . . . . . . . . . . . . . . . . . . . . .  143
64. Upper facial Index . . . . . . . . . . . . . . . . . . . .  145
65. Nose height . . . . . . . . . . . . . . . . . . . . . . . .  146
66. Nose breadth . . . . . . . . . . . . . . . . . . . . . . .  148
67. Nasal Index . . . . . . . . . . . . . . . . . . . . . . . .  150
68. Shape of nasal wings . . . . . . . . . . . . . . . . . . .  152
69. Shape of nasal profile . . . . . . . . . . . . . . . . . .  153
70. Amount of nasal root depression . . . . . . . . . . . .  154
71. Height of nasal root . . . . . . . . . . . . . . . . . . .  155
72. Breadth of nasal root . . . . . . . . . . . . . . . . . . .  156
73. Shape of nasal tip . . . . . . . . . . . . . . . . . . . .  157
74. Nostril shape . . . . . . . . . . . . . . . . . . . . . . .  158
75. Frontal visibility of nostrils . . . . . . . . . . . . . . .  159
76. Lateral visibility of nostrils . . . . . . . . . . . . . . .  160
77. Ear length . . . . . . . . . . . . . . . . . . . . . . . . .  161
78. Ear breadth . . . . . . . . . . . . . . . . . . . . . . . .  162
79. Auricular Index . . . . . . . . . . . . . . . . . . . . . .  163
80. Amount of ear protrusion . . . . . . . . . . . . . . . .  164
81. Roll of helix . . . . . . . . . . . . . . . . . . . . . . . .  165
82. Attachment of ear lobes . . . . . . . . . . . . . . . . .  166
83. Hair form . . . . . . . . . . . . . . . . . . . . . . . . .  167
84. Hair texture . . . . . . . . . . . . . . . . . . . . . . . .  168
85. Beard (and moustache) . . . . . . . . . . . . . . . . . .  169

86. Hair color . . . . . . . . . . . . . . . . . . . . . . . 170
87. Grayness . . . . . . . . . . . . . . . . . . . . . . 171
88. Eye color . . . . . . . . . . . . . . . . . . . . . . 172
89. Homogeneity of iris . . . . . . . . . . . . . . . . 174
90. Skin color . . . . . . . . . . . . . . . . . . . . . 176
91. Freckles . . . . . . . . . . . . . . . . . . . . . . 178
92. Eye-folds . . . . . . . . . . . . . . . . . . . . . 179
93. Blood groups . . . . . . . . . . . . . . . . . . . 181
94. Occupation . . . . . . . . . . . . . . . . . . . . 185
95. Birthplace . . . . . . . . . . . . . . . . . . . . 187
96. Birthplace compared with residence . . . . . . . . . . 189
97. Marriage as related to racial subgroups . . . . . . . . 191
    I. Haciendas and villages . . . . . . . . . . . . . . 191
    II. Haciendas . . . . . . . . . . . . . . . . . . . 191
    III. Villages . . . . . . . . . . . . . . . . . . . 192
98. Marriage as related to skin color . . . . . . . . . . . 195
    I. Haciendas and villages . . . . . . . . . . . . . . 195
    II. Haciendas . . . . . . . . . . . . . . . . . . . 195
    III. Villages . . . . . . . . . . . . . . . . . . . 195
99. Families of rural Yucatan . . . . . . . . . . . . . . . 198
100. Age of mother at birth of first child . . . . . . . . . . 204
101. Twenty years' deaths in sub-department of Dzitas, Yucatan 209
102. State of Yucatan: births, stillbirths, and deaths . . . . . . 211
103. Important causes of death in Yucatan . . . . . . . . . . 212
104. Important causes of infant death in Yucatan . . . . . . . 213
105. Standard deviations of certain measurements in various
     human groups . . . . . . . . . . . . . . . . . . . 216
106. Comparison of coefficients of variation of certain groups and
     subgroups with those of the unit group of Total Yucatecans 219
107. Comparison of means of certain groups and subgroups with
     those of the unit group of Total Yucatecans . . . . . . 231

## APPENDIX TABLES

1. Denture measurements . . . . . . . . . . . . . . . . . 240
2. Teeth missing . . . . . . . . . . . . . . . . . . . . 243
3. Missing teeth and cavities . . . . . . . . . . . . . . 244
4. Wear of teeth . . . . . . . . . . . . . . . . . . . . 246
5. Shovel incisors . . . . . . . . . . . . . . . . . . . 247

# LIST OF PLATES

1. Map of the state of Yucatan showing birthplace of members of the Yucatecan male series
2. Record blank
3. Map of the Spanish peninsula showing the provenience of some of Cortes' companions in the conquest of Mexico
4. Sorting card
5. Figures from Spinden's *A Study of Maya Art*
6. Stature — frequency curves
7. Biacromial diameter — frequency curves
8. Weight — frequency curves
9. Index of build — frequency curves
10. Head length — frequency curves
11. Head breadth — frequency curves
12. Cephalic Index — frequency curves
13. Head height — frequency curves
14. Radii used in calculation of protrusion indices of cephalic and facial points
15. Bizygomatic diameter — frequency curves
16. Cephalo-facial Index — frequency curves
17. Face height — frequency curves
18. Facial Index — frequency curves
19. Nose height — frequency curves
20. Nose breadth — frequency curves
21. Nasal Index — frequency curves
22. Family questionnaire
23. Group A types, males
24. Group B types, males
25. Group C types, males
26. Group D types, males
27. Group E types, males
28. Group A types, females
29. Group B types, females
30. Group C types, females
31. Group D types, females
32. Group E types, females
33. Typical rural Yucatecan families
34. A rural Yucatecan family; a Yucateco-Mexican family
35. Hacienda laborers; hacienda woman
36. A village church; a hacienda chapel
37. Street of a Yucatecan town; hacienda street

38. A hacienda laborer's house; houses of villagers
39. *Casa principal* of a hacienda; mayor and school teachers of a Yucatecan town
40. A village school; a hacienda school
41. Water storage tank on a hacienda; irrigation system for a hacienda garden
42. Village women at a well; a hacienda well
43. Pulling water from a well by horse power; a Yucatecan beehive
44. Cutting henequen; drying henequen fibre
45. Making twine from henequen fibre; making rope from henequen fibre
46. Thatching; masons at work
47. Baking wheat bread; washing clothes

# INTRODUCTION

In February, 1927, the writer and his wife were sent to Yucatan, a southern state of Mexico in the peninsula of Yucatan, by the Bureau of International Research of Harvard University and Radcliffe College. The purpose of the expedition was to collect data relating to the physical anthropology of the Maya Indians of that region and to study the physical effects of race mixture between the Maya Indians and their conquerors. Although great progress has been made in the study of the archaeology of the Maya area, little accurate information is available concerning the physical characteristics of the descendants of those who were responsible for the great civilization for which that country is famous. Furthermore, the present population of Yucatan represents the result of race mixture which occurred, in the preponderant majority of cases, between only two distinct racial stocks who have interbred in comparative isolation. The opportunity to study such a comparatively simple case of race mixture is rather unusual.

For several years the Carnegie Institution of Washington has maintained an archaeological station at the ruins of the ancient city of Chichen Itza, in Yucatan. Between Dr. E. A. Hooton of Harvard University, who represented the Bureau of International Research for our work, and Dr. S. G. Morley, in charge of the Carnegie Chichen Itza Project, an arrangement was made whereby we acted as temporary members of the Carnegie expedition and began our study of the physical characters of the population of Yucatan with data collected from the native laborers employed at Chichen Itza. The work here and at the neighboring village of Pisté consumed two months of our time. Through our acquaintance so acquired in the region and through the good offices of Dr. Morley, we were able to move for our work to Xocenpich, a village a few miles from Chichen Itza. Dzitas, the nearest railway station to Chichen Itza, became our next headquarters. The work at this town of approximately fourteen hundred people occupied several weeks of our time. Work was done also at the following haciendas: Dziuche near Izamal, Sacapuc near Motul, Canicab near Acanceh, Cacao and Yaxcopoil, both near Chochola. Dr. Guillermo Vega L. of the Hospital O'Horan of Merida and Dr. Eduardo Urzaiz R. of the Asilo Ayala of the same city kindly permitted us to examine the patients in their hospitals in the interims between our hacienda visits.

The work at all these various locations required about eight months. It is needless to say that without the coöperation of the subjects themselves, and the advice and aid of the gentlemen mentioned in the preface, twenty-five hundred men, women, and children could not have been examined in that space of time. Of these twenty-five hundred subjects, only eight hundred and eighty male and six hundred and ninety-four female adults, born in Yucatan of racially mixed Indian-White parents, are to be considered in this study. As the map concerning birthplace of these subjects shows, our sample is a cross-section of the hacienda and village population of the country. (Plate 1.)

Besides the ordinary anthropological measurements and observations, we made observations concerning certain physiological characters, e. g. blood pressure, pulse, and basal metabolism. The latter data were collected by means of a portable machine furnished by Dr. F. G. Benedict of the Carnegie Institution of Washington Nutrition Laboratory. A period was spent in learning the technique of the machine in Dr. Benedict's laboratory before the departure for Yucatan.

The author wished to make some psychological tests on the Yucatecans but was advised by good authority that such tests had not yet reached the necessary perfection and that no accurate interpretation could be made from them. Two sets of data of psychological nature were obtained. One set was based on a test for color-blindness; the other was concerned with musical ability. All the latter data were collected in the Turner-Hodge Colegio Americano through its head, Miss Eunice Blackburn. The subjects for this Seashore test were pupils of the school and therefore non-adults. The results do not concern us in the present study.

The governor of the state of Yucatan, Dr. Alvaro Torre Diaz, was kind enough to permit the writer to send back to the Peabody Museum of Harvard University one hundred skeletons from the cemetery of the city of Merida. These will be studied at a later time and the data be added to those presented here.

About eight hundred and fifty blood samples were taken at Chichen Itza, at the two hospitals in the city of Merida and at the Haciendas Sacapuc and Canicab. These were sent as soon as collected to Dr. W. L. Moss of Harvard Medical School. About seven hundred and fifty of the samples withstood the journey to Boston without breakage or deterioration and were subsequently typed for isoagglutinins by Dr. Moss.

Certain sociological data were collected in each of the places visited. The material refers to the size of families, education, age at marriage and at childbirth. These findings are presented in this paper. Plate 2 gives a sample of the blanks used in collecting the physical data.

# MAYA–SPANISH CROSSES
# IN YUCATAN

## HABITAT

**The Maya Region.** The region in which remains of the pre-Columbian Maya civilization are found corresponds closely with that still inhabited by Indians speaking dialects of the Maya linguistic stock. Roughly it lies between eighty-seven degrees and ninety-four degrees west longitude and fourteen degrees and twenty-two degrees north latitude. More exactly it comprises, in Mexico, the states of Tabasco and Chiapas and the peninsula of Yucatan (with the states of Campeche and Yucatan and the territory of Quintana Roo), in addition to the whole of British Honduras and two-thirds of Guatemala lying north of the Motagua River, and a considerable portion of Honduras.

The Maya area, as above defined, contains three principal subdivisions. The first of these comprises the peninsula of Yucatan; the second, the great central valley; the third, the cordilleran plateau on the south and west. It is a part of the first of these natural subdivisions, the state of Yucatan, that is here interesting as the habitat of a human group.

**Topography.** The peninsula of Yucatan is generally level, with slight elevations. Owing to the formation of the country, the hydrographic conditions of Yucatan are peculiar. It is only in the extreme south of the peninsula that rivers are found. The limestone formation is said to be mainly Tertiary, but partially of the Cretaceous period. It admits of numerous underground streams. Natural sink-holes, called *cenotes*, are found everywhere throughout the peninsula. These *cenotes* were the source of water supply for the pre-Columbian population. The Spanish taught the Indians to dig wells and many of these are in use today. More commonly, at present, windmills, rather than hand power, lift the water to the surface. Mérida, the capital, when seen from an elevation, is a veritable forest of windmills.

The northern part of the Yucatecan peninsula, instead of having the luxuriant tropical vegetation often found in countries of low latitude, is in reality a great semi-arid plain.  The forests, nowhere dense, dwindle away in parts to a stunted "brush" barely supported by the scanty soil which only partially covers the underlying lime-stone rock.  It is indeed to the porous character of this rock and the absence of pronounced relief, rather than to a deficiency in the rainfall, that the aridity must be chiefly ascribed.

The great plain of northern Yucatan extends southward from the Gulf of Mexico as a gentle, even slope, at an average increase in elevation of about one foot per mile.  The coast itself is low.  To the southward of Mérida, the capital, about fifty miles from the sea, the land rises in the form of a series of low hills which have a general trend from northwest to southeast.  Their average height is four hundred or five hundred feet.  Between Mérida and the coast, the general surface appears to be almost as flat and level as a floor.  South of Mérida, however, the dissection of the plain has progressed further, and the surface topography is much more ir-regular.

**Climate.**  The climate of the Maya area as a whole is tropical; that of the state of Yucatan has been described as sub-tropical. The duration of the rainy season is less in Yucatan than in other regions of the general Maya area of greater land relief.  The rainy season lasts from June or July to September or October.  During the remainder of the year the rainfall is small, although there may be occasional thunder showers.  The semi-arid character of the soil is especially marked during the dry season, when many of the trees lose their leaves and the general appearance of the vegetation reminds one of more northerly regions in early spring or late fall. The climate of Yucatan, being dryer, is on the whole healthier than the neighboring regions.  Especially in the dry season, the nights are often cool.  The northern part of the peninsula is much healthier than most countries lying so well within the tropics, and lacks almost entirely the terrors of the *tierra caliente* of Mexico proper.  The temperature ranges from seventy-five to ninety-eight degrees Fahrenheit in the shade, but the heat is modified by sea winds which prevail day and night throughout the greater part of the year.  Occasional *temporales* or northers sweep down over the gulf and over the open region.  The hottest months appear to be March and April, when the heat is increased by the burning of the cornfields.

**Flora.** All the northern districts are destitute of large trees. Cole (1910) notes that "the failure of the soil to retain moisture also limits very closely the kinds of crops that can be cultivated successfully. It is true that during the rainy season many garden crops may be grown successfully, but the two most important products of the country are corn and henequen." It should be mentioned that the large haciendas or plantations are owned by landlords who live in the capital city of Mérida, and who generally delegate the immediate supervision of the work to major-domos. These large tracts of land are devoted almost exclusively to the growing of henequen, and the preparation of the fibre for the market. Much of the product reaches the United States and is used here in the form of binder twine. Sugar cane is cultivated to some extent, especially in the south of the state. The Indian of the hacienda does not do agricultural work for himself. Corn, one of the principal articles of diet, is bought for these laborers and in many cases comes from the United States. The village Indian represents a second type of agricultural laborer. He works for himself generally in growing his own corn. In the off season, he often does some other work for pay, but he is first and last an independent farmer.

The method of raising corn employed by the natives is dependent upon weather conditions, and is very impoverishing to the soil. At the close of the dry season, the Indian prepares his *milpa* or cornfield by burning the timber from a tract of land, which is then planted to corn when the rains begin. A good crop is dependent on plenty of rain. Corn is the staple food, and a scarcity of this cereal, due to a bad season, is a serious matter. It is common for village Indians to farm adjoining plots of a tract close to the village or even as far distant as ten miles. (The latter condition results from the necessity of constantly using new lands.) They are thus able to assist each other in the work. Beans and squashes are also raised. The corn is generally eaten in the form of *tortillas* or unleavened pancakes, which are prepared from lye-soaked corn, ground formerly by hand on stone *metates*, but now by means of hand food-choppers or power mills.

**Fauna.** The raising of cattle is limited by the scarcity of forage. The leaves of the *ramon* trees have to be gathered for the horses in place of hay. The writer recalls a hacienda where two men were employed for the sole purpose of procuring branches of such trees as food for the live stock. Chickens and tame turkeys are raised everywhere.

Deer, jaguars, pumas, and large rodents called *tipisquintli* are found in the stunted *monte* or "brush" which rims the cultivated portion of the state on the south and east. *Sopalotes* or scavenger buzzards abound. Wild turkeys, deer, and *tipisquintli* are eaten when procurable. Snakes are comparatively rare, but iguanas are a common sight. Tapirs, peccaries, monkeys, and a great variety of birds are not seen within the confines of the state of Yucatan. Wild animal life in general is more abundant and prolific in the better watered regions to the west, south, and east.

## HISTORY [1]

**Pre-Columbian History.** It seems safe to assume that by the beginning of the Christian era the Maya civilization was fairly started. How long a time had been required for the development of the complex calendar and hieroglyphic system to the point of graphic record, it is impossible to say, and any estimate can be only conjectural. But by the end of the second century A.D. there began an extraordinary development. City after city sprang into prominence throughout the southern part of the Maya territory.[2] Little more than the material evidences of architecture and sculpture have survived the ravages of the destructive environment in which this culture flourished, and it is chiefly from these remnants of ancient Maya art that the record of progress has been partially reconstructed.

This period of development lasted upward of four hundred years or until about the close of the sixth century. Judging from the dates inscribed upon their monuments, all the great cities of the south flourished during this period: Palenque and Yaxchilan in what is now southern Mexico; Piedras Negras, Seibal, Tikal, Naranjo, and Quirigua in the present Guatemala; and Copan in the present Honduras. All these cities rose to greatness and sank into insignificance, if not indeed into oblivion, before the close of this Golden Age.

[1] In the historical sketch here given, I have drawn freely upon the following authorities: Spinden, 1913 and 1928; Tozzer, 1907; Morley, 1915. Although most of the sketch consists of direct transcription, quotation marks have not been placed, for the sake of clarity.

[2] See THE MAYA REGION, p. 1.

The causes which led to the decline of civilization in the south
are unknown. The following theories have been put forward:

1. The Maya were driven from their southern homes by stronger peoples
pushing in from farther south and from the west. — Morley, 1915.

2. The Maya civilization, having run its natural course, collapsed through
sheer lack of inherent power to advance. — Morley, 1915.

3. The discovery and colonization of the southern part of Yucatan about
the middle or close of the fifth century doubtless hastened the general decline
of the cities of the south, if it did no more. — Morley, 1915.

4. Production of food did not keep pace with the growth of population, so
that emigration to fresh lands became necessary. — Morley quoted by Huntley, 1928.

5. Disease epidemics, probably of yellow fever, have been suggested as
causes of the decline. — Spinden, 1921.

6. The geological record shows a progressive tilting of the land from the
south, which has raised the surface above the permanent water-table in the
cavernous limestone bedrock, draining the lakes and *cenotes* from the bottom
progressively northward, until there are only remnants of their number remaining. With the diminution of the water supply, and a large population, the
nature of these stagnant pools remaining, plus the lack of knowledge of sanita-
tion on the part of the people, might easily have caused epidemics. The inhabitants moved always northward in the direction of Yucatan. The numbers
and virility of the people were thus depleted by both lack of food sources and
epidemics. — Huntley, 1928.

"There seems to be no reason for believing," contradicts Cole
(1910) "that the climatic conditions in Yucatan were any different
at the time the Maya civilization was at its height than they are
today."

The occupation and colonization of Yucatan marked the dawn
of a new era for the Maya, although their renaissance did not take
place at once. There seems to have been a feeling of unrest in the
new land, a shifting of homes and a testing of localities, all of which
retarded the development of architecture, sculpture, and other
arts. The opening of the eleventh century witnessed important and
far-reaching political changes in Yucatan. Chichen Itza (founded
long before) was reoccupied, and about this time the cities of
Uxmal and Mayapan seem to have been founded. In the year 1000
these three cities formed a confederacy in which each was to share
equally in the government of the country. Under the peaceful conditions which followed the formation of this confederacy, for the

next two hundred years the arts blossomed forth anew. When these and other cities were in their prime, the country must have been one great beehive of activity, for only a large population could have left remains so extensive.

This era of universal peace was abruptly terminated about 1200 A.D. Civil war broke out between the cities of Chichen Itza and Mayapan. The leader of Mayapan called to his aid the Mexican Toltecs, who had settlements in Tabasco, and utterly routed his opponent. There is strong evidence that Mayapan became the most important city in the land. It is not improbable that Chichen Itza was turned over to the Mexican allies, perhaps in recognition of their timely assistance. It is certain that sometime during its history Chichen Itza came under a strong Toltec influence. Several groups of buildings show in their architecture and bas-reliefs that they were undoubtedly inspired by foreign rather than by Maya ideals.

According to Spanish historians, the fourteenth century was characterized by increasing arrogance and oppression on the part of the rulers of Mayapan, who found it necessary to surround themselves with Mexican allies in order to keep the rising discontent of their subjects in check. This unrest finally reached its culmination about the middle of the fifteenth century, when the Maya nobility, unable longer to endure such tyranny, banded themselves together under the leadership of the lord of Uxmal, sacked Mayapan, and slew its ruler.

There can be but little doubt that this event sounded the death knell of Maya civilization. With the destruction of Mayapan, the country split into a number of warring factions. Soon the land was rent with strife. Presently, to the horrors of civil war were added those of famine and pestilence, each of which visited the peninsula in turn, carrying off great numbers of people.

This, briefly, is the history of Yucatan up to the arrival of the Spaniards.

**Post-Columbian History.** In 1502, on the fourth and last voyage of Columbus, when the expedition was in the Gulf of Honduras, an Indian canoe was encountered which had probably put out from the shores of Yucatan. In 1511, a ship was wrecked on the coast of Yucatan. Geronimo de Aguilar and Gonzalo Guerrero survived, and later Aguilar became an interpreter for Cortés. In 1517, Francisco de Cordoba landed the first Spanish expedition on the shores of Yucatan. The natives were so hostile, however, that he returned to Cuba, having accomplished little more than the discovery of the country. In the following year, Juan de Grijalva descended on the peninsula, but he, too, met with so determined a resistance that he sailed away, having gained little more than hard knocks for his pains. In the next year (1519), Hernando Cortés landed on the northeast coast, but reëmbarked in a few days for Mexico, again leaving the courageous natives to themselves. In 1526, Francisco Montejo, having been granted the title of Adelantado of Yucatan, set about the conquest of the country in earnest. Spinden notes that the number of early historical references to the Maya Indians is small, partly due to the fact that the principal theatre of action for the Spaniards lay in the Valley of Mexico. The early lack of interest of the Spaniards in Yucatan was probably contingent on the fact that that peninsula had no mineral wealth to exploit as had Mexico proper.

Montejo sailed with three ships and five hundred men for Yucatan. He first landed on the island of Cozumel, but soon proceeded to the mainland and took formal possession in the name of the King of Spain. This empty ceremony soon proved to be but the prelude to a sanguinary struggle, which broke out almost immediately and continued with extraordinary ferocity for many years, the Maya fighting desperately in defense of their homes. It was not until fourteen years later, in 1541, that the Spaniards, having defeated a coalition of Maya chieftains near the city of Ichcanizihoo, finally brought the conquest to a close and accomplished the pacification of the country. With this event ends the independent history of the Maya.

There was no large attempt made at Christianizing the natives until the year 1546, when one hundred and fifty missionaries were sent over from Spain. Villalpando settled at about this time at Campeche, where he founded a convent, and later at Mérida, where another convent was established.

In the year 1548 the province of Yucatan was made subject to Mexico.

About 1551 Diego de Landa was sent to Yucatan as a missionary. He later was made Bishop of Mérida. His account of the customs and ceremonies of the natives at the time of the Conquest is the best that we possess. Bernal Diaz del Castillo, a companion of Cortés, is another historian who wrote in this century.

The first half of the seventeenth century is marked by the number of Spaniards who visited Yucatan and the country to the south. Many of these men came to Yucatan and Tabasco as missionaries. Diego Lopez de Cogolludo, a Spanish Franciscan, spent the second quarter of the century in Yucatan. His *Historia de Yucatan* is the best authority on the early history of the country down to 1655. The best of the more recent books is one written by a native of Yucatan, Don Juan F. Molina y Solis, *Historia del descubrimiento y conquista de Yucatan con una reseña de la historia antigua.*

It is interesting to note that Montejo, in his conquest, had succeeded in establishing Spanish rule over barely one half of the peninsula. The eastern and southern parts of the peninsula were not conquered. The terrible War of the Castes was precipitated by the sending of several shiploads of Maya Indians to Cuba as slaves. This war broke out in 1848 and resulted in abandonment by White landowners of much of eastern and central Yucatan. A nominal treaty of peace was concluded in 1853, but those parts afterwards pacified were never able to retrieve the earlier prosperity. Quintana Roo was separated from the state of Yucatan in 1902 and received a territorial government under the immediate supervision of the national executive. Practical independence has always been maintained by the Indians of this region, and their unfriendliness has retarded thorough exploration of the area.

**Population: General.** The total population of the state of Yucatan was given, in the official census of 1910, as 339,613; in the official census of 1921, as 345,991. The statistical sample which serves for discussion in this paper comes from this total population, but concerns only adults.

Spinden (1928) remarks that the increase in population for all Mexico since the 1803 estimate of Humboldt is about one hundred and fifty per cent. The Indian part of the total Mexican population seems to have held its own or perhaps to have gained, if we eliminate immigrants. The Maya territory, Spinden states, in the peninsula of Yucatan, is an exception to the general advance. Humboldt, about 1803, gives the population of the political district of Mérida (which seems to have included Campeche) as 465,800 and that of Valladolid as 476,400, making a total of 942,200 for the

Mexican part of the peninsula. This may have been an overestimate, but a very great falling off resulted from the War of the Castes. Official figures for 1921 for the state of Campeche are 76,419; for the territory of Quintana Roo, 6956. These, therefore, plus the population of Yucatan above given, make the 1921 census for the Mexican part of the peninsula 429,366.

Spinden (1928) makes a "conservative minimum estimate of 26,000,000 for the red race at the present time. The chronological evidence indicates the greatest aboriginal population of America about 1200 A.D., this being a halcyon epoch of far-flung trade at the maximum expansion of wetland cultures. The numbers of the red race at that time may then have amounted to two or three times the present numbers, or say 50,000,000 to 75,000,000 souls." Yucatan was of course participating in this period of florescence. It is evident, therefore, that the Maya branch of the aboriginal American race has declined greatly in numbers since A.D. 1200, when its culture was at its peak.

**Population: the Spanish Element.** Estimates of the numbers of pure- or mixed-blood Mayas at any period since the Conquest are worthless. We may be certain, however, that race mixture has been prevalent in Yucatan since the days of the conquest. In this connection it is interesting that Stephens (1843, Vol. I, p. 350) notes that in the village of Nohcacab, near the ruins of Kabah, "the most backward and thoroughly Indian of any village we had visited, many of the white people could not speak Spanish, and the conversation was almost exclusively in the Maya language."

Since Spain is not a racially homogeneous nation, it is important to know from what part of Spain the majority of Spanish emigrants to Mexico came. We have been told that most of the emigration from Spain to Mexico has been from the central and southern parts of the former country. Accurate information on this point seems hard to get. We have, however, in the writings of one of Cortés' captains (see bibliography under Diaz del Castillo) a chapter which states the places of origin in Spain of some of the captains and soldiers of Cortés. Bernal Diaz del Castillo accompanied Cortés through the latter's adventures in the New World and devotes the chapter above mentioned of his history to interesting personal facts concerning various members of the companions of Cortés who were engaged in the conquest of Mexico. As to the Spanish and

Old World provenience of these soldiers and captains, we find the following:

TABLE 1

| | | | |
|---|---|---|---|
| "Old Castile" | 4 | | |
| Valladolid | 9 | | |
| Salamanca | 4 | | |
| Leon | 3 | | |
| Avila | 5 | | |
| Burgos | 3 | | |
| Segovia | 1 | | |
| Palencia | 3 | | |
| CASTELLANA SUPERIOR | | 32 | 38.6% |
| Badajos | 7 | | |
| Caceres | 4 | | |
| Toledo | 1 | | |
| "Estremadura" | 2 | | |
| CASTELLANA INFERIOR | | 14 | 16.9% |
| Sevilla | 9 | | |
| Huelva | 10 | | |
| Malaga | 1 | | |
| Cadiz | 2 | | |
| ANDALUCIA BAJA | | 22 | 26.5% |
| Granada | 4 | | |
| Almeria | 1 | | |
| ANDALUCIA ALTA | | 5 | 6.0% |
| GALAICA | | 2 | 2.4% |
| VALENCIANA | | 2 | 2.4% |
| Soria | 1 | | |
| Guadalajara | 1 | | |
| ARAGONESA | | 2 | 2.4% |
| ISLAS BALEARES | | 1 | 1.2% |
| BASQUES | | 3 | 3.6% |
| ALL SPAIN | | 83 | |
| PORTUGAL | | 8 | 8.7% of Grand Total |
| LEVANT | | 1 | 1.0% of Grand Total |
| GRAND TOTAL | | 92 | |

It is of course a small sample that Diaz gives considering that there were many more than ninety-two men in Cortés' expedition. But the historian has given us unique data, and we should thank rather than criticize him. He himself came from Valladolid. Since the largest proportion of the men mentioned came from that part of Spain, it may be said that Diaz knew more of the men from that part of the country, or wished his portion of Spain to appear as the land of the conquerors of the New World. Such a view is uncharitable to say the least.

It does not follow, furthermore, that the provinces that gave birth to the *conquistadores* were the same provinces that later sent emigrants to the New World. Yet in Diaz' data we have at least a rough index of the kind of Spaniard who came to the New World (and incidentally to Yucatan), and who was one of the parties involved in the race mixture that took place there.

A glance at the table and the map prepared from Diaz' data shows that the western half of Spain and also Portugal furnished the great majority of the adventurers listed by the historian. More came from the region of Spain termed by Oloriz (see Barras, 1925) "Castellana Superior" than from any other district. The importance of this knowledge lies in the fact that a fair cross section of the various Spanish types is represented in Diaz' group (Plate 3).

Aranzadi and Hoyos Sainz (1894a) tell us that "blue eyes cross Spain like a slanting ridge (from Vizcaya to Portugal) over a coat of arms, the upper left field representing the chestnut-brown, the lower right field the honey-colored, eye. Leptorrhiny, in the form of "aristocratic," Basque-like, or Old Castilian noses — or large, long noses, tends to be associated with the blue eyes. The Arab nose is an eagle nose, and the honey-colored and gray-brown eyes, of African origin, belong with mesorrhine and strongly dolichocephalic skulls. The gray-blue eyes north of the blues certainly contain a strong chestnut-brown influence which shows European (and Asiatic) relations."

If one accepts the statements of Aranzadi and Hoyos Sainz and the conclusions drawn from Diaz' data, it seems likely that all the various racial elements that make up the Spanish nation contributed to the Spanish emigration to the New World and consequently to the White side of the mixture of races. Thus, although dark eyes and hair characterize a large part of the Spanish population, depths of color of eyes and hair comparable to those of the Indians are not to be expected, for the Aranzadi and Hoyos Sainz classification of dark eyes includes such colors as black, dark chestnut, dark gray, and dark honey-colored. Such eye colors are found in the Andalucias and in northwest and northeast Spain in proportions of the population ranging from eighty per cent to eighty-six per cent. On the other hand, the Basque provinces and Navarra, with Aragonesa, are reported by Aranzadi and Hoyos Sainz as having about thirty-five per cent of blue or gray-blue eyes; southeastern Castellana Superior and northern Castellana Inferior as having twenty-one per cent; and Caceres and Badajos as having about fifteen per cent.

It may be concluded, then, that all the various racial elements of the Spanish nation were involved in the race mixture with Indians that took place after discovery of the New World.

## THE PROBLEM

One series of eight hundred and eighty men and another of six hundred and ninety-four women of the hemp plantations, towns, and cities of Yucatan have served as subjects for a somatological investigation, the data of which form the material of this monograph. These men and women represent the progeny of crosses between the indigenous Maya population and White conquerors and immigrants. The mixture has continued over a period of some three hundred and fifty years. The Whites have been for the most part of Spanish nationality. The Indian participants have always been numerically predominant. In comparative isolation these two stocks (and practically no others) have interbred during a sufficiently long period of time to have produced a great many of the various types possible.

The opportunity for study of race mixture presented by the Maya-White cross is unique in some ways. In all parts of the world race mixture has occurred, but the student of physical anthropology usually encounters certain obstacles in attempting to study the phenomena of miscegenation. These are specifically: (1) the difficulty of analyzing mixtures which have taken place between secondary or derived races; (2) lack of geographical isolation, involving the addition of new racial or environmental factors subsequent to the primary cross. In the case of the Yucatecans, the White group is itself the result of race mixture, but between White sub-races which are all distinctly different from the Maya group.

Before considering the particular problem of Maya-White mixture, it will be necessary to set forth certain existing conditions that affect the approach and method of solution of any investigation of race mixture.

There are differences among men in size of body and body parts. Two kinds of factors operate to effect these differences: racial or hereditary, and environmental ones, such as nutrition and disease. Where the effect of one kind of factor ceases and the other begins, it is often difficult to determine. Indicial or proportional differences are racially important; yet, since they are calculated from expressions of size, they are not free from certain environmental effects. Environment affects to greater or less extent every human individual, and races are collections of such individuals.

What parts of the individual does the environment affect? Are all organs and tissues equally influenced by a given environmental factor? After consideration of a large number of environmental factors, does there remain a single part, organ, or tissue that has not been markedly affected? In the present state of our knowledge, such questions can not be answered with certainty, and an open mind must be maintained.

Following the discoveries of Pasteur, the medical profession, in its study of the human body and its affections, has devoted itself almost exclusively to the investigation of environmental causes and effects. As the result of this line of attack upon the nature of disease, medicine has made remarkable progress. Likewise, students of man's social life have demonstrated the great part that environment plays in that field. In the face of these great contributions to our knowledge of human life, certain over-zealous individuals have nevertheless made ill-advised statements regarding the influence of heredity on man, and in consequence have brought down upon themselves and unfortunately also upon their more cautious co-workers a certain degree of distrust of the claims made for the importance of the hereditary factor.

It is unfortunate, too, that some of the students of race seem at times to have forgotten what they were studying, and have introduced confusion into the biological definition by indicating national, linguistic, religious, and geographical "races." Today investigators are adhering more strictly to the biological conception of race. With this more general realization that race is a biological term has come an appreciation of the fact that the relation of man to his heredity and to his environment is very complicated. With it has come the conclusion that a great deal will have to be learned before the problems that arise can be thoroughly understood. It is certain, however, that some human traits are less susceptible to ordinary environmental influences than others. Such non-adaptive traits appear generation after generation, relatively unchanged, unless there is mixture with another race. This provision concerning miscegenation brings us to another important consideration.

A widely prevalent feeling today is that there is little utility in the study of race. The protagonists of this view state correctly that race mixture has continued at least throughout the historical period and is going on now; therefore, pure races as entities are non-existent. Draper (1924, p. 36) says, "It may well be that the conception of race as we have so far held it is no longer tenable on account of the almost universal admixture which modern means of transportation have brought about. The increasing facilities for migratory movements during the last hundred years have forever shattered the biologic isolation of the subspecies of man." It is the contention of this monograph that such a view as Draper's too readily abandons hope of a way out of the difficulties involved in the study of race mixture. If there are traits relatively unaffected by environment, those traits must be non-functional or relatively so. These comparatively useless traits are then inherited according to genetic laws. If the characteristics of this kind that are found in the parent races are known, genetic principles can be applied to the study of the offspring and the investigator can deal, not with what appears to be a "melting pot," but with groups segregated according to the laws of genetics and according to an acceptable definition of race. The following definition of the term "race", by Hooton (1926), has been selected as the best so far proposed: "A race is a great division of mankind, the members of which, though individually varying, are characterized as a group by a certain combination of morphological and metrical features, principally non-adaptive, which have been derived from their common descent."

How these segregated groups can be derived from a seemingly inextricable mélange is one of the important problems of this monograph. The shortness of the memory of man and the well-known inadequacy of his systems of recording births prevent in most cases the availability of reliable genealogical data. It is mainly for this reason that, when racial data are derived, skeptics express such views as that of Draper quoted above.

Granted that it is possible to give a racial designation to any individual, of what value is that to humanity? As for contributions to human well-being, it is admitted that in comparison with the students of environment in medicine (such as the bacteriologist and the immunologist, who by the study of pathogenic organisms have kept us or made us well) and with the student of nutrition (who has demonstrated how to free us of such diseases as rickets, scurvy, and pellagra), the student of race has so far contributed little. The study of environment has proved its utilitarian importance in the immediate, pressing problems of man. The study of race has not thus far demonstrated its practical use, partly because the laws it seeks to discover are, if more fundamental, less obvious and less susceptible to experimental test in man, and partly because the investigators of the attributes of race have in the past been misled into investigating the attributes of something else than race. Racial attributes will not be discovered if national or linguistic groups are studied in place of those biologically defined.

It is the contention of this monograph that no group but the biologic one can serve for an inquiry into racial characters and that no worthwhile data on racial attributes can be secured in the absence of a reliable technique for the isolation of racial types. It is fatuous to attempt a study of the varying mental or physical capacities of races when the investigator has neither a clear conception of what races are, nor any reliable methods of separating heterogeneous populations into racial types.

*The object of this study is to demonstrate the practicability of resolving a racially mixed and heterogeneous population into significantly differing subgroups which present a uniformity of physical characters, adaptive and non-adaptive, sufficient to justify the conclusion that relatively pure racial types have been distinguished.*

## SORTING: ITS TECHNIQUE AND THE THEORY OF ITS APPLICATION TO THE STUDY OF RACE MIXTURE

**Apparatus and Technique.** Race systematists in the past have been inclined to link the varieties of mankind with certain areas of the earth's surface, with nations, languages, and religions. They have assigned in certain cases a racial designation to some geographical or linguistic unit in spite of the obvious physical diversity of its population. The authors of these unnatural classifications have eventually found their systems involved in serious difficulties. Today no anthropologist should define a race on other criteria than physical ones nor should risk the definition of a subgroup by employing other sorts of criteria.

Those investigators, on the other hand, who have tried to classify man according to the biological concept of race have also met with difficulties. In some cases they have defined a racial type in such a way as to exclude from their classification all but a very few of a population assumed to be relatively homogeneous from the physical viewpoint. The systematist who classifies by the use of a single criterion, such as cephalic index, pigmentation, hair form, or facial angle, often finds that he has separated a complex group into subgroups which do not agree with his commonsense ideas as to their racial identification. The use of several or many characters in analyzing a mixed population undoubtedly offers the best approach to the discovery of the various types in the group. The principle of sorting for "a certain combination of morphological features, principally non-adaptive" is certainly correct if we adhere to the definition of race already quoted from Hooton. But if several criteria are regularly used for classification, the mechanical difficulties of such sorting by hand suddenly loom up as almost insuperable, and the investigator becomes lost in a complex maze. The method is correct but the mechanical difficulties must be overcome.

The difficulties involved in sorting can be overcome by use of machines of the type of Hollerith or of Powers. Sorting is their prime function. In the sorting done for the Yucatecan male series, a homemade sorter was used. A brief description of it and its method of functioning follows:

Stiff Manila cards, thirteen by nineteen inches, were perforated by machine in the manner of a candy punch board, with holes arrayed in forty columns of twenty-five holes each (Plate 4). The work was done with such mechanical precision that when a large number of the perforated cards are superimposed and held up to the light, each hole is as clearly defined as it is in a single card. Each hole on each card was designated by a printed number.

The use of such an apparatus for sorting may be explained in a simple manner by taking a very few physical traits as the criteria of group selection. Let us define the racial or subracial group which we want to segregate as being characterized by (1) straight hair, (2) black hair, (3) high-bridged ($++$ and $+++$) noses, and (4) prominent ($++$ and $+++$) malars. In the case of hair form, there are, according to the classification used, six possibilities of subcategories in this single trait: straight, low waves, deep waves, curly, frizzly, woolly. Therefore, six cards are necessary; one for each subcategory of the trait; the cards are properly designated. Next the data from the original field notes are transferred to the six cards. Guided by the data blanks, the investigator covers with an adhesive tab hole Number One on the card for straight hair, if data sheet Number One shows that individual to have straight hair. If the data sheet for individual Number Two shows him to possess curly hair, hole Number Two is covered on the card for curly hair, and so on through the list for each individual and for each desired trait. When he has finished, the investigator is able to see on any one of the six cards what individuals are characterized by the trait category represented by that card. If the investigator superimposes all the category cards for one trait, and holds them to the light, it is obvious that rays cannot penetrate at the site of a single hole. This is so because all the holes have been accounted for and are therefore covered. If he wishes to know what individuals have wavy hair (both low and deep waves), he has two options: (1) he can look directly for covered holes on the cards for low and deep waves, or (2) he can remove the two cards for low and deep waves from the total stack of hair-form cards, and by holding this incomplete stack to the light he is able to see through the same holes which are covered on the cards removed from the stack.

This negative demonstration of a positive fact can be carried out for groups of traits as well as for a single trait. Therefore, if one returns to the problem formulated on the preceding page — namely, to determine what individuals of a group are characterized by having (1) straight hair, (2) black hair, (3) $++$ and $+++$ heights of nasal bridge, and (4) $++$ and $+++$ malar prominence, one proceeds by laying aside from each stack of trait-category cards all cards representing those trait categories for which one wishes to sort. One then superimposes the remaining cards, holds the stack up to the light, and is able to identify by lighted holes the individuals who meet the stipulated requirements.

In this way multiple combinations of morphological features and metric features may be sorted out with absolute precision and with comparative ease.

### THEORY OF SORTING IN RACE MIXTURE: GENERAL

With a suitable sorting mechanism available, and the necessary data at hand, how does one proceed in resolving a racially mixed and heterogeneous population into truly racial subgroups? It is of course desired to break up the heterogeneous sample of Yucatecans who represent a variety of grades of mixture between Maya Indians and Spanish, into groups representing some of these grades.

What criteria shall be used in the sorting? It is unnecessary to say that upon the careful choice of the criteria depends the validity of the sorted groups. The belief in the usefulness of a sorting method for the purpose of separating into racial subgroups the heterogeneous progeny of a mixture that has occurred between primary races of mankind is based upon the convictions of Hooton concerning the distinction between adaptive and non-adaptive characters of man. It will be well to quote freely from Dr. Hooton's article concerning this subject (Hooton, 1926):

If race implies the common possession of certain variations as a result of the same ancestry, significant racial criteria should be based principally upon non-adaptive bodily characters. No bodily characters are absolutely unmodifiable, but certain organs are more or less stabilized in their functions, and the less important these functions are, the greater is the probability of hereditary variations manifesting themselves unimpeded and unmodified in such organs. Heredity runs riot in indifferent variations and atrophied organs. The very insignificance of certain features, such as the form of the hair or the thickness of the lips, insures their hereditary transmission in the absence of selected adaptive modifications that have survival value. The human foot, on the contrary, is rigorously adapted and modified for support and locomotion in all varieties of man, and the practically identical requirements of a functional nature tend to obscure and obliterate any racial variations which may have existed or to subordinate them to such variations as may be consequent upon the habits of going barefoot or shod.

I. I regard the following bodily characters as mainly non-adaptive variations: the form, color and quantity of the hair, and its distribution in tracts; the color of the eyes and the form of the eyelid skin-folds; the form of the nasal cartilages; the form of the lips and of the external ear, the prominence of the chin; the breadth of the head relative to its length; the length of the face; the sutural patterns, the presence or absence of a postglenoid tubercle and a pharyngeal fossa or tubercle, prognathism, the form of the incisor teeth; the form of the vertebral border of the scapula, the presence or absence of a supracondyloid process or foramen of the humerus, the length of the forearm relative to the arm; the degree of bowing of the radius and ulna; the length of the leg relative to the thigh. This list is not, of course, exhaustive. Many of the features enumerated above, and perhaps all of them, may be functionally modified, if the need for such modification arises. For example, the breadth of certain Eskimo skulls appears to have been constricted by the hypertrophy of the temporal muscles. Usually, these characters, however, show no apparent relationship to function, and seem to maintain themselves by the inertia of heredity, occurring sometimes as individual or family variations, and sometimes more widely distributed in racial stocks.

II. Another group of bodily characters includes those the distinctive variations of which may have originated in functional modifications, but which have become so stabilized as to persist in certain stocks even in contravention of their original function. These may also be utilized as racial criteria, subject to a precaution, viz., that they may be remodified in an opposite direction. Among these are pigmentation of the skin, breadth of the face, height and breadth of the nose, size and prominence of the malars, shape and proportions of the hard palate, height of the head, volume of the brain, proportions of the thorax, relative length of the lower extremities, relative length and angle of inclination of the heel-bone and size and development of the calf muscles.

III. Features that seem easily modifiable in the individual and in the group through the action of environmental factors, and especially by quality of nutrition, diet, gait and exercise, cannot be trusted as criteria of race, except in the absence of evidence for the operation of such environmental causes. These include stature, weight, length of the upper extremity, proportions of the hand, most variations of the bones of the arm, degree of lumbar curvature and pelvic inclination, most of the variations in the long bones of the lower extremity, including femoral torsion, bowing, pilaster, platymeria, variations of the articular surfaces of the tibia and of the shape of the tibial shaft.

What are some of the characteristics of such non-adaptive variations? It is interesting to note that of a considerable number of traits offered as relatively non-adaptive, a very great proportion refer to characteristics of the head, as opposed to other body parts. It is also noteworthy that most of these head characters are non-mensurable, at least with techniques now in vogue.

With the use of sorting methods, in which there must be several categories for each trait, or several class intervals for each measurement, traits or observations are much more easily graded into categories than are continuously distributed measurements or indices. For example, the grades of cephalic index have been expressed by the terms dolicho-, meso-, and brachycephalic. The exact place in the continuous distribution where a head ceases to be dolicho- and becomes mesocephalic has not always been agreed upon. When a choice for such a point is made, that choice is conscious and perhaps a reasoned one.

If instead of cephalic index, the categories of hair form are the objects of designation, it seems likely that several observers are more apt to agree than in the former case. No conscious decision as to whether the hair is straight, wavy, curly, frizzly, or woolly is made by the practised observer; rather the verdict is thrust upon him and the judgment is mechanical. It is true that in the judgment of hair color or eye color, a distinction made between dark brown and light brown is arbitrary. In such a case, as in the case of hair form, convenient categories are ready-made for the sorter. In the case of color, as with cephalic index, there are intergrades. The distribution for hair color, as well as for cephalic index, is continuous. But the mechanical judgment of the competent observer is certainly more exact as to color than it would be in estimation of linear measurements or indicial values. The estimation of color values by the sense of sight makes colors of objects for practical purposes almost qualitative, even though the observer knows that the distribution is continuous.

It goes without saying that subjective observations involving judgment of color and estimation of the relative prominence or degree of development of a facial feature are less desirable for comparative purposes than are objective measurements of the same traits. Undoubtedly many traits which are now recorded as subjective observations will some day (and it is hoped, soon) be measured mechanically and may be recorded without the stigma of personal bias which is frequently attached to subjective observations. Adequate mechanical methods of this kind were not available to the author for the study of the Yucatecans. Consequently, subjective observations of many important facial features were made. Some of these observed characters are so important in racial diagnosis that, despite the fact that they were obtained subjectively, they cannot be disregarded or ignored as important factors in selection of racial subgroups.

The characters to be used in sorting subgroups from the heterogeneous general group should differ in their exhibition in the two parent races; the characters should be non-adaptive or relatively so and therefore governed to a much greater degree by heredity than by environment; the characters should be those which show evidence of linkage with certain traits, mensurable or non-mensurable, which in numerous studies have been found to vary definitely with race.

A fairly large number of such traits are available for the purpose in mind. Not all can be chosen. One investigator may use one group, another worker another group of traits. But it seems likely that if the traits chosen fulfil the above requirements, and a fair number of important characters are used, the groups selected in either case will exhibit in general the same sort of gradation from one parent group to the other. It is obvious that the group of characters finally selected for subdivision of the heterogeneous series of Yucatecans are not the only characters that can be used for that purpose. The criteria used represent one of several ways in which the sorting could be done, and the racial subgroups so delimited represent one particular application of the general method of statistical treatment of a miscegenetic population advanced in this monograph.

One of the measures of the suitability of an observational trait for racial sorting is the amount of linkage that exists between it and other characters known to vary to some extent with race. The first work done in such a search for suitable criteria consisted in sorting the numerically expressed quantities in the Yucatecan data of stature, head length, head breadth, bizygomatic diameter, and cephalic index with reference to the following non-mensurable and relatively non-adaptive characters of the Yucatecans:

| | |
|---|---|
| Hair form | Form of nasal profile |
| Hair texture | Amount of chin prominence |
| Amount of beard | Form of nasal wings |
| Hair color | Form of eye-folds |
| Eye color | Amount of nostril visibility—frontal |
| Skin color | Amount of nostril visibility—lateral |
| Presence or absence of freckles | Amount of nasal tip depression |

All of these traits pertain to the head or face. They are all relatively functionless, therefore relatively non-adaptive. Many of them have been used before as criteria in racial classification and others could have been added to the list. The above traits were chosen, however, as important among the relatively non-adaptive characters.

No one will dispute that there are racial differences in stature, head length, head breadth, bizygomatic diameter, and cephalic index. There are also, as is well known, racial differences in the expression of the fourteen traits above enumerated. What relations exist between these quantitative and qualitative characters, so far as the Yucatecan data are concerned? Is it expected in this particular case of race mixture that the straight hair of the Indian will be highly associated with the Indian's small stature? Is it anticipated that straight hair will be as strongly linked with broad bizygomatic diameter as with short stature? Is it probable that the typically Indian blackness of hair will be as highly correlated with the Indian's small stature as the equally typical straightness of hair? Before a combination of characters is chosen as typical of Maya Indians, or of Whites, it will be necessary to seek answers to the proposed questions, and to test individually the degree of association that exists between each of the fourteen descriptive traits and the five mensurable characters. Table 2 shows the results of such an examination.

*Explanation.* If one looks at the first square of the table representing the stature of individuals having straight hair form, one sees the expression " −7." This means that the mean stature of the subgroup of individuals having straight hair is less than the mean stature of the group as a whole of persons undifferentiated as to hair form by a difference (between the means) which is more than seven times the probable error of the difference between the means.[1]

---

[1] Pearson (1906) gives the probable error of the difference in type of the general sample and the sub-sample as:

Goring (1913, p. 33) states:

If the differences between the results compared are not greater than the probable error of these results, such differences may be regarded as insignificant; if the difference is not greater than twice the probable error, it may be regarded as *probably* insignificant; and if it is not greater than three times the probable error, it may be regarded as *possibly* insignificant. On the other hand, if any difference found is greater than three times the probable error, it is reasonable to assume that that difference is due to some definite influence over and above those causes which are inherent in the sampling process, for such cases will account for this amount of difference only once in 23 samplings.

There are in Table 2 data which show the distribution of certain traits within the general series, as may be seen from the relative numbers of the grades of the traits. An examination from this viewpoint is interesting in itself.

At present, however, it is of greater interest to see what significant differences from the means of the series as a whole occur, after categories of observational traits have been used singly to group their associated metrical characters. It is also important at this time to determine in what direction those mean differences show themselves. Only those differences will be considered as truly significant which are more than three times the probable error of the difference between the means of the whole group and any subgroup.

Examination of Table 2 demonstrates that there is good reason to believe that straight-haired people of the unselected group are shorter in stature, have shorter heads, and because of the latter fact, have higher cephalic indices. The converse is true for the other hair forms. Coarse hair, likewise, selects shorter heads and medium, longer. In the case of beard, it is noteworthy that beardless and scantily bearded individuals are smaller in breadth as well as in length diameters, while the more heavily bearded are larger in the same measurements. The obvious explanation of such a finding is that there is superimposed upon the racial difference an age effect. If beard amount is to be used as a differential racial

$$.67449 \sqrt{\frac{\sigma^2}{n} - \frac{2\sigma^2 - \Sigma^2}{N}} \bigg/ \sqrt{1 + \frac{\beta^2 n}{N(N-n)}}$$

where N and $\Sigma$ are number and standard deviation of the group as a whole, n and $\sigma$ are number and standard deviation of the subgroup, and $\beta$ the number of times the probable error of the difference that is necessary to indicate significance. (The expression $\sqrt{1 + \frac{\beta^2 n}{N(N-n)}}$ may be neglected when the number of the subgroup is less than half the number of the group as a whole.)

TABLE 2.   MEANS OF SUBGROUPS CLASSIFIED BY MORPHOLOGICAL
FEATURES IN TERMS OF DIFFERENCES FROM TOTAL MEANS
DIVIDED BY PROBABLE ERRORS OF SUCH DIFFERENCES

MALES

| | No. | Stature | Head length | Head breadth | Bizygomatic | Cephalic index |
|---|---|---|---|---|---|---|
| HAIR FORM | | | | | | |
| Straight .......... | 633 | −7 | − 6 | .. | .. | +4 |
| Low waves .......... | 32 | .. | .. | −2 | .. | −2 |
| Deep waves .......... | 170 | +6 | +5 | .. | .. | −2 |
| Curly .............. | 37 | +3 | +4 | .. | .. | −4 |
| Frizzly ............. | 1 | .. | .. | .. | .. | .. |
| HAIR TEXTURE | | | | | | |
| Coarse .............. | 781 | .. | −4 | .. | .. | .. |
| Medium.............. | 92 | +2 | +3 | +2 | .. | .. |
| BEARD | | | | | | |
| 0 ................... | 49 | −5 | −4 | .. | −3 | +3 |
| sm ................. | 542 | −4 | −5 | −2 | −2 | +2 |
| + ................... | 181 | +6 | +6 | .. | +4 | −2 |
| ++, +++ .......... | 58 | .. | +3 | .. | .. | −3 |
| HAIR COLOR | | | | | | |
| Black .............. | 789 | .. | .. | .. | .. | .. |
| Dark brown .......... | 80 | +3 | +2 | .. | .. | .. |
| Other .............. | 4 | .. | .. | .. | .. | .. |
| EYE COLOR | | | | | | |
| Black .............. | 459 | −5 | .. | .. | .. | .. |
| Dark brown ........ | 251 | +2 | .. | .. | .. | .. |
| Light brown ........ | 97 | .. | .. | .. | .. | ... |
| Green-brown ........ | 46 | .. | .. | .. | .. | −2 |
| Blue-brown .......... | 15 | .. | +3 | .. | .. | −2 |
| Other .............. | 5 | .. | .. | .. | .. | .. |
| SKIN COLOR (Von Luschan Scale) | | | | | | |
| White, 10, 11 ........ | 10 | .. | +2 | .. | .. | .. |
| 12, 13, 14 ........... | 68 | +4 | +3 | .. | −2 | −2 |
| 15 .................. | 44 | .. | .. | .. | .. | .. |
| 16 .................. | 41 | +2 | +2 | .. | .. | −2 |
| 17, 18 .............. | 38 | .. | .. | .. | .. | .. |
| 19, 20 .............. | 232 | .. | .. | .. | .. | .. |
| 21, 22 .............. | 380 | −4 | −2 | .. | .. | .. |
| 23, 24, 25 ........... | 60 | .. | .. | .. | +4 | .. |

TABLE 2. (*Continued*)

| FRECKLES | No. | Stature | Head length | Head breadth | Bizygo-matic | Cephalic index |
|---|---|---|---|---|---|---|
| 0 | 665 | .. | .. | .. | .. | .. |
| sm | 117 | .. | +3 | .. | .. | −2 |
| + | 47 | +3 | −2 | .. | .. | .. |
| ++, +++ | 18 | .. | .. | .. | .. | −2 |
| Mass [1] | 26 | .. | .. | .. | .. | .. |
| NASAL PROFILE | | | | | | |
| Convex | 671 | .. | .. | −3 | .. | .. |
| Concavo-convex | 89 | .. | .. | +3 | +2 | .. |
| Straight | 100 | .. | .. | +2 | .. | .. |
| Concave | 13 | .. | .. | .. | −2 | .. |
| CHIN PROMINENCE | | | | | | |
| sm | 212 | −4 | −6 | −2 | .. | +3 |
| + | 305 | −3 | −3 | −2 | −2 | .. |
| ++ | 346 | +3 | +8 | +4 | .. | −2 |
| +++ | 10 | .. | .. | .. | .. | .. |
| NASAL WINGS | | | | | | |
| Compressed | 37 | +4 | .. | −2 | −2 | −4 |
| Medium | 260 | .. | .. | −3 | −2 | .. |
| Flaring | 576 | −4 | .. | +3 | +3 | .. |
| EYE-FOLDS | | | | | | |
| Mongoloid | 12 | .. | .. | .. | .. | .. |
| Epicanthic | 478 | −5 | −7 | −3 | −2 | −2 |
| No fold | 341 | +4 | +6 | .. | .. | −2 |
| External | 42 | +2 | +2 | .. | .. | .. |
| NOSTRILS — FRONTAL VISIBILITY | | | | | | |
| 0 | 9 | .. | .. | .. | .. | .. |
| sm | 122 | +3 | +2 | .. | .. | −2 |
| + | 341 | .. | .. | +2 | .. | +2 |
| ++ | 339 | .. | .. | .. | .. | .. |
| +++ | 62 | .. | .. | .. | .. | .. |
| NOSTRILS — LATERAL VISIBILITY | | | | | | |
| 0 | 2 | .. | .. | .. | .. | .. |
| sm | 80 | +3 | .. | .. | .. | .. |
| + | 332 | .. | +3 | +2 | .. | .. |
| ++ | 381 | −2 | .. | −2 | .. | .. |
| +++ | 78 | .. | .. | .. | .. | .. |
| NASAL TIP DEPRESSION | | | | | | |
| Depression ++, +++ | 463 | .. | −5 | .. | .. | .. |
| Depression sm, + | 298 | .. | +3 | .. | .. | −3 |
| Horizontal | 10 | .. | .. | .. | .. | .. |
| Elevation sm, + | 95 | .. | .. | +4 | +2 | .. |
| Elevation ++, +++ | 7 | .. | .. | .. | .. | .. |

[1] Mass freckling refers to a class of cases in which the cheeks show an area of deeper pigmentation than that of the surrounding skin, the deeper coloring being the brown of ordinary freckling. Discrete spots resembling freckles do not appear.

factor, the age complication must be remembered and care should be taken that selection is being made for race, not for youth.

It seems clear that the few dark-brown-haired individuals are taller than the remainder of the series and that certain of the lighter-eyed are longer-headed, while the stature of the black-eyed is less. In the same way, lighter skin color seems linked with taller statures and longer heads, and darker, with shorter lengths. There is also evidence that the darker-skinned tend to have broader cheek bones. Freckling is associated with greater stature and head length.

The data on nasal profile do not tell much that is helpful; convex, concavo-convex, and straight noses occur in both Whites and Indians. In regard to head breadth, convex noses are associated with narrower, and concavo-convex noses with broader heads. Chin prominence [1] tells an entirely different story; less prominent chins belong to individuals having lesser lengths, the more prominent chins to individuals having greater lengths and greater head breadths. In other words, the latter are larger people. There is no reason to believe that age here exerts such an influence as seen in the case of beard amount. The characteristic feature of the retreating chin (exaggerated to the eye to some extent, probably by prominence of the lips) is easily recognized in ancient Maya art and seen very frequently in the Maya of today.

It is to be noted in the case of such a trait as hair form, and in others in which age has no effect, that lengths are much more affected than breadths. In such a hybrid group, where breadths are less highly correlated with observational traits than lengths, great breadths must have been, during the long period of race mixture, somewhat independently impressed upon the bulk of the population. If the heads of the population as a whole are inclined to be broad, no matter what the degree of mixture, variations in breadth can then occur and not be of great significance, while greater variations are occurring at the same time in lengths. Thus it is seen in the case of retreating (sm) chins that the mean of head length is smaller than the mean of the group as a whole, and that cephalic index shows in the case of sm chins a significantly higher mean index, in spite of the fact that there is a possibly significant de-

---

[1] The subjective observation on chin prominence refers to relative protrusion of the chin anteriorly in comparison with protrusion of the other parts of the facial profile, and especially of the lips and alveolar region.

crease in head breadth. In the case of prominent (+ +) chins, both the head length and head breadth means are significantly greater than the means of the unselected group. However, the significance of the increase of head length is much larger than that for head breadth (eight as compared with four times the probable error of the difference between the means). It is therefore not unexpectedly that individuals with prominent chins show a probably significant decrease in cephalic index.

Individuals of the general series who show compressed nasal wings are taller and have smaller cephalic indices. Those having medium wings possess significantly narrower heads, while the flaring nosed have smaller stature, and broader heads and faces. Correlated somewhat with the flare of nasal wings are the observations on nostril visibility — both frontal and lateral. The less flare there is, the less visibility, and the lesser degrees of visibility are linked with taller stature and longer heads.

As to the data on nasal tip depression, it seems very probable from the numbers involved that great depression of the tip and great flare of nasal wings are closely associated, and, judging from experience, that is a relation to be expected. Experience in observation of Yucatecans leads one to believe that greatly depressed tips and flaring nasal wings both are to be found in people having marked visibility of the nostrils. The data from all four types of observations point to the same conclusions: that compressed nasal wings with small nostril visibility and only slight tip depression, or even tip elevation, go with greater size in stature and head length, smaller cephalic index, and unpredictable variability in breadths; that flaring wings with great nostril visibility and greatly depressed tips are found in people who are smaller in stature and in head length, have a possibly significant tendency toward greater cephalic index, and no certain selection one way or the other as to head breadth.

Selection of the series according to the variety of eye folds shows that those with epicanthic folds are smaller people in all the dimensions considered, but the possibly significant upward deviation of cephalic index suggests, as in the case of chin prominence, that the decrease in head length is greater than in head breadth. The individuals having no folds, or external ones, are taller and have longer heads.

From inspection of Table 2 it appears that certain observed traits, some of which have long been used as criteria of race, can, acting singly, effect significant selective action on certain mensurable traits, which have also been considered to vary on the average with race. It is not correct to say that all the black-haired people of the group of unselected Yucatecans in question are pure or almost pure Maya Indians. It is enough at the moment to realize that each one of several traits has categories, which, when used for selection against certain measurements, actually do select groups whose means vary significantly from the mean of the measurement representing the unselected group. The direction of the variation when present is in general the same for White categories of traits and opposite for Indian categories. One is justified in using for racial selection combinations of those traits that have shown such definite association.

One realizes that in making unconscious guesses as to the racial provenience of a man passed in the street, that his eyes take in more than a single trait, such as skin color; that the eyes, through long experience, see, besides the color of the skin, perhaps color of hair or color of eyes, the amount of beard, the form of the nose, the form of the eyelid folds. After a glance, one concludes, "There is a Negro." There is no conscious use of reasoning faculties in making this classification; the verdict is rather thrust upon the observer. Furthermore, the judgment made probably tells little (and likely nothing) of the subject's cultural status, of his national affiliation, of his place of birth, of the language he speaks, of the religion he professes. Since this is so, the classification made of the subject's race is truly biological, therefore truly racial. The Negro subject may be of Mexican nationality, may speak Spanish and profess the Roman Catholic faith, and not be distinguishable from an American Negro who speaks English and is a Baptist.

If after collection of a series of anthropological observations and measurements, it is desired to assign to each individual of a group a racial status (reliable data on the genealogies of the subjects being lacking, as is so often the case) why should not the investigator imitate the daily utilized method of guessing at diagnosis of race from the composite picture that comes to his eyes? If there are available rather complete observational data, collected consciously and methodically, rather than casually; if there is at hand a sorting apparatus, the student of race mixture can select subgroups characterized by various combinations of traits. Certain objections may be put forward against such a procedure. It may be urged that individual variations within biological races would invalidate the method; to which the author replies that the traits assumed as characteristic of the biological group are selected with a view to avoidance of such a number and such character of the criteria that in combination they would give to a person his individual appearance. Rather are the proper traits such that they create "a vague physical background, usually more or less obscured or overlaid by individual variations in single subjects, and realized best in a composite picture."[1]

The author admits that occasional inaccurate observations may have been recorded for individuals. As a result, certain individuals may be classified incorrectly as to the subgroup to which they belong. That the author strove constantly for accuracy need not be said. The incidence of such inaccuracies is surely small. Occasional errors in classification of individuals due to this factor are of little moment when it is considered that the vast majority of the members of such a subgroup undoubtedly do possess in common a number of hereditary characteristics and that such a majority by its preponderance in numbers impresses its characteristics upon the whole subgroup.

The principle of sorting a racially heterogeneous group into subgroups having been accepted, pertinent questions immediately arise: What is the nature of the common tie that binds the members into any one subgroup? What relation do the subgroups bear to one another? The answers to these questions clearly depend on the criteria used in the sorting. The nature of the relation existing between the members of a sorted subgroup should be, if the subgroups are racial ones, a genetic relation. This is necessarily so, for a race is a human group characterized by "a certain combination of morphological and metrical features, principally non-adaptive, *which have been derived from their common descent.*" (Hooton, 1926.) If individuals are under examination concerning their fitness for membership in a *pure* racial group, their common descent must be from members of only that pure race. But if the persons being examined are progeny of race mixture, their common descent is from

[1] Hooton, 1926.

members of two or more of the races which contributed to the mixture.  In the case of the Yucatecans, only two races were to any extent involved in the miscegenation — (Maya) Indians and (Spanish) Whites.

Herskovits, in his interesting study, *The American Negro* (1928), found the amounts of variability of that mixed group to be much smaller than the variability within families of that group.  This phenomenon he attributes to the fact that there is much inbreeding practised between the members of the American Negro group. "The pressure within the Negro community," says Herskovits, "as well as that of the larger community of which it forms a part, against sexual relations between Negroes and Whites, is of great importance in this connection."  Such social pressure undoubtedly plays a part in the problem with which Herskovits is engaged; but the author of this study does not believe that this factor is very important in the case of the Yucatecans.  Castle (1926) writes concerning race mixture in the United States:  "There is no strong social prejudice against the red man such as exists against the black man, recently a slave."  In Yucatan, prejudice against sexual relations between Whites and Indians and against backcrossing of the mixed-bloods with either Indians or Whites is negligible as compared with prejudice against similar procedures among the individuals involved in the Negro-White crosses of the United States.

Herskovits shares with Boas his belief in the advisability of studying variability within families of a mixed race as well as of examining the variability of the mixed group itself.  With this view, the author heartily concurs.  Boas has presented his ideas on the subject in his *Anthropology and Modern Life* (1928).  In that book, however, he makes certain statements and deductions with which the author does not agree.  Some of these statements are of such a nature that they seem directly to oppose certain assumptions on which this study is based.  It is necessary, therefore, to discuss at some length certain statements made by Boas in a chapter of his book entitled *The Problem of Race*.

Boas (1928) states:

The interest [of the anatomist, the physiologist, and the psychologist] centers always in the individual as a type. . . . To the anthropologist, on the contrary, the individual appears important only as a member of a racial or a social group. The distribution and range of differences between individuals and the characteristics as determined by *the group to which the individual belongs* [italics ours] are the phenomena to be investigated.

In this discussion relating to physical anthropology, *racial*, not social, groups are the objects of attention. The group to which the individual belongs is not a national group, nor a habitat group, nor a linguistic group, but a biological group. The author of this study proposes to show that an individual belongs to or is related to a biological group by virtue of his possession of certain non-adaptive characters found in that group and by virtue of his common descent with the members of that group from common ancestors.

Deniker (1900) may here be quoted with profit to the discussion. He concludes:

On examining attentively the different "ethnic groups" commonly called "peoples," "nations," "tribes," etc., we ascertain that they are distinguished from each other especially by their language, their mode of life, and their manners; and we ascertain besides that the same traits of physical type are met with in two, three, or several groups, sometimes considerably removed the one from the other in point of habitat. On the other hand, we almost always see in these groups some variations of type so striking that we are led to admit the hypothesis of the formation of such groups by the blending of several distinct somatological units.

It is to these units that we give the name "races," using the word in a very broad sense, different from that given to it in zoölogy and zoötechnics. It (a race) is a sum-total of somatological characteristics once met with in a real union of individuals, now scattered in fragments of varying proportions among several "ethnic groups" from which it can no longer be differentiated except by a process of delicate analysis.

Returning to Boas, one finds:

A knowledge of all the bodily traits of a particular individual from Denmark does not enable us to identify him as a Dane. If he is tall, blond, blue-eyed, long-headed and so on he might as well be a Swede. . . . Identification of an individual as a member of a definite, local race is not possible.

The author quite agrees with Boas that the hypothetical Dane mentioned "might as well be a Swede," since the reasons for his being classified as a member of a national group do not depend upon his physical attributes. Those attributes mark him as a member of the Nordic race, whatever may be his nationality, and wherever he may live.

Boas appears to treat as equivalents the act of residing within Swedish or Danish domains and membership in "a definite, local race." Before easy and swift methods of communication and transportation had made their appearance, the relation of geographical grouping of peoples to racial grouping was somewhat stronger than at present. Deniker expresses this idea in the following language:

Ordinarily, the more peoples are civilized the more they are intermixed within certain territorial limits. Thus the number of "somatological units" is so much the greater when the "ethnic groups" are more civilized, and it is only among entirely primitive peoples that one may hope to find coincidence between the two terms.

It would appear that if the group whose characteristics are to be investigated in this day of easy migration is a racial one, habitat should not be used as definitive criterion.

Boas, continuing to identify habitat groups with racial ones, writes:

We also find individuals of the same bodily form in Germany, in France, and we may even find them in Italy. . . . Whenever these conditions prevail, we cannot speak of racial heredity. In a strict sense racial heredity means that *all* the members of the race partake of certain traits, — such as the hair, pigmentation and nose form of the Negro, as compared to the corresponding features among the North European. . . . The children of a given family represent the hereditarily transmitted qualities of their ancestors. Such a group of brothers and sisters is called a fraternity. We cannot speak of racial heredity if the fraternities are different, so that the distribution of forms in one family is different from that found in another one. . . . In addition to this we may observe that a fraternity found in one race may be duplicated by another one in another race; in other words, that the hereditary characteristics found in one race may not belong to it exclusively, but may belong also to other races.

This idea Boas illustrates by demonstrating that there is no racial unity and no racial heredity in either the habitat groups of New York or of France. He concludes:

Individuals of the same bodily appearance, if sprung from populations of distinct type, are functionally not the same. For this reason it is quite unjustifiable to select from a population a certain type and claim that it is identical with the corresponding type of another population. Each individual must be studied as a member of the group from which he has sprung.

This discussion deals with the idea of race. It is only fair to the reader to repeat Hooton's definition of the term "race," which is the definition accepted in this monograph. It reads as follows:

A race is a great division of mankind, the members of which, though individually varying, are characterized as a group by a certain combination of morphological and metrical features, principally non-adaptive, which have been derived from their common descent. A primary race is one which has been modified only by the operation of evolutionary factors. A secondary or composite race is one in which a characteristic and stabilized combination of morphological and metrical features has been affected by a long continued intermixture of two or more primary races within an area of relative isolation.

Boas states that in contrast to the lack of racial unity and of racial heredity in the habitat groups of New York and France, matters are different in old, inbred communities such as those of the Eskimos of North Greenland. "The people all bear a considerable likeness," he says. This group of Eskimos is an example of a racial group, for the group meets the two requirements of Hooton's definition; namely, possession in common of a certain combination of non-adaptive features, and common descent. It is universally recognized that movements of peoples, with subsequent intermarriage between invaders and invaded, has characterized the entire historical era. It is a part of the business of the anthropologist to study such movements of populations. It is known that African Negroes were brought to Mexico a few hundred years ago as slaves and that intermixture took place between the Negroes and other inhabitants. If today one finds in Mexico an individual some of whose non-adaptive characteristics resemble or are identical with several of those of the general racial group of African Negroes, and also if one knows that African Negroes once were sent to Mexico, is there not good reason to believe that such an individual is related in some degree to the general racial group of African Negroes? Are not the two requirements of Hooton's definition fulfilled when there is shown to exist between the individual and the African group resemblance or identity of several (not one) non-adaptive characters, as well as historical evidence of the possibility of common descent?

The differences in opinion between Boas and the author of this paper can be traced to one fact; namely, that their definitions of race are not the same.

The subgroups to be sorted from the racially mixed group of Yucatecans will be racial in character because the members of each subgroup will resemble each other in certain non-adaptive traits, which have been derived through the agency of common descent; that is to say, through the agency of heredity.

It will be necessary, if knowledge of heredity enters into the problem, to inspect the opinions and observations of some of the men who have studied the behavior of certain human traits from the standpoint of heredity.

**Hair Texture.** Bean (1911) states that in a mixture between Chinese and Filipinos, coarse hair seemed to be dominant.

**Hair Form.** Davenport (1913) quotes E. Fischer as having said:

In the bastards of Rehoboth the hair appears as a compromise between the Dutch and the negro. It is almost never entirely smooth, but almost never a close spiral "peppercorn" hair like the Hottentots. It is of intermediate length, usually has an open curl, or shows a narrow wave.

Dunn (1928) says:

Seventeen, or 60 per cent, of Hawaiian-Chinese hybrids had straight hair, while of the remaining eleven individuals, ten had wavy or curly hair of the Hawaiian type, while one had wiry hair. The genetic relationship between straight Mongoloid hair and the wavy European type has not been established, although the evidence of Bean and other observers makes it appear probable that the Mongoloid type behaves as a dominant trait in inheritance. Our evidence partially corroborates this assumption. . . .

Again Dunn (1923, p. 122) states:

Either dominance is incomplete or more than one factor is necessary for the expression of straight hair. . . . But [p. 124] it is probably a dominant.

**Pigmentation.** Castle (1920) concludes:

The lighter shades of hair color are recessive in relation to the darker shades. . . . It seems probable that the segregation of skin pigmentation in mulattoes is either incomplete or rarely complete, because multiple or modifying factors are involved. Davenport has concluded that there are two gametic (four somatic) factors for black in negro skin pigmentation (Davenport, 1913). This leads us to expect one in sixteen $F_2$ mulattoes to show skin as white as a European.

In the same book (p. 272) Castle states that dark skin and hair are dominant, and blond and albino recessive, the process being probably governed by multiple allelomorphs; also that black or brown eyes are dominant to blue eyes.

Hooton (1923) states:

Tanning and freckling are probably race mixture phenomena resulting from crosses of blonds and brunettes or heavily pigmented races. I do not believe that a pure blond freckles or tans. When a lightly pigmented race crosses with a heavily pigmented race, the resulting offspring may be intermediate in skin pigmentation but certain individuals often tan or become progressively pigmented to a shade much darker than that characteristic of the more heavily pigmented parent racial stock. I am credibly informed that such is the case with many Hottentot-Boer hybrids in German Southwest Africa. . . .

### Epicanthic (or Mongoloid) Fold. Dunn (1928, p. 140) asserts:

The presence of the Mongolian or epicanthic fold is certainly established in a majority of the $F_1$ hybrids (Hawaiian-Chinese) and it is therefore inherited as a dominant trait.

### Again (1923, p. 122) he further qualifies:

Those hybrids in which it does not occur are probably the offspring of parents which did not possess it. Although expressed in the hybrid, dominance is probably not perfect since in four of the hybrids the Mongolian fold was less marked than in the typical Chinese. Even among the Chinese, however, there is considerable variation in the fold.

### Prognathism. Hooton (1923) tells us:

It therefore seems fair to assume that prognathism is a functionally unstable character. This being the case it is very natural that crosses between prognathous and orthognathous races invariably result in a pronounced decrease of prognathism in the hybrid and often in a complete disappearance of this protrusion.

### Nose Form. Hooton (1923) says:

Any considerable mixture of White blood (with Negro), usually brings about a relatively high and narrow upper bridge of the nose. But the middle portion of the nose is likely to retain a Negroid breadth. In most instances there are Negro reminiscences in the thickness and lateral flare of the alae, the relatively vertical plane of the nostrils, and the convexity of the septum. But recessive individuals with predominantly European nose form occur.

### Lip Thickness. Hooton (1923) says:

The thickening of the integumental lips, and the puffiness and eversion of the membranous lips characteristic of full-blood negroes are rapidly modified by an admixture of European blood.

Certain definite hereditary tendencies have been pointed out. Other findings relating to human heredity now claim our attention. An interesting and important statement by Hooton (1923) is that:

It seems probable that in the case of race mixtures morphological features are inherited by the offspring in small units from both parent stocks. Often one type of feature in an organ seems to survive consistently at the expense of another.

Castle (1920) says:

The well-known lack of correlation between skin color and hair form in mulattoes of $F_2$ or later generations certainly indicates the existence of independent factors affecting these characters.

As to inheritance of simple Mendelian traits, Sinnott and Dunn (1925, p. 381) state:

It is evident that an individual showing a recessive character must be homozygous for it, but that one showing a dominant trait may be (and in a mixed population often is) heterozygous. A group of individuals displaying a given recessive trait is therefore pure genetically, as far as that trait is concerned, whereas among the members of a group showing a dominant character there may be many who are carrying a factor for its recessive allelomorph.

But it is to be remembered that few human traits behave as simple dominants or recessives. Sinnott and Dunn (1925, p. 102) say:

It may be accepted as a general rule that the characters of a plant or animal depend on multiple and finely balanced interactions between a very large number of factors.

Again (p. 252) they state:

That most quantitative characters are controlled by a series of similar but independent and cumulative factors is the explanation which the multiple-factor hypothesis offers for the inheritance of such traits.

Castle (1920, p. 205) tells us:

One mechanism will now suffice for all kinds of inheritance, this mechanism being found in the chromosomes. In them, we may reasonably suppose, is found the material basis of every inherited character. When the inheritance is of the simplest kind, involving presence or absence of color or some similar character, we may assume that a genetic change has occurred in a single definite locus in a particular chromosome, and that this single change is responsible for the observed inherited variation. Other characters depend on *two or more genes*, which may lie at different loci in the same chromosome or in different chromosomes. Each of these factors or genes behaves as an *independent unit* in transmission.

If individuals differing in several unit characters are crossed, a complex situation arises, as viewed from the genetic standpoint. If four traits are involved, the $F_2$ generation will have theoretically only one in two hundred and fifty-six who will resemble one of the original parents in appearance and genotype. If individuals differing in only *one* trait, which is controlled, for example, by three independent, equal, and cumulative factors (according to the multiple-factor hypothesis), the parental type will reappear in $F_2$ generation in approximately one-sixty-fourth of the individuals. If six factors are concerned in the inheritance of one trait, only 1/4096 of the $F_2$ population will resemble one of the parent types.

In our present state of knowledge, it is useless to speculate on the expected proportions of phenotypes and genotypes that will arise in $F_2$ and later generations from a given human cross. Especially is this true if it is realized that several considerations besides the two mentioned in the previous paragraph almost invariably complicate human crosses. Some of them are: (1) in case of multiple-factor control, the factors may not be independent, equal, and cumulative, but may be independent and in control of various differing manifestations of a given trait, e. g. the color, the black, the extension, the agouti, and the intensity factors cited by Castle (1920, p. 205) for the gray coat of a rabbit; (2) independence of the factors may not be complete, as in the case of linkage, i. e. when certain of the multiple factors are borne in the chromosome so that the factors concerned tend to segregate in pairs or groups as introduced into the cross; (3) availability of a reservoir of either or both of the parental groups with whom the hybrids can backcross; (4) disproportion in numbers in the original cross in favor of one or the other parent group; (5) presence of social factors which favor crosses toward one or the other parental group.

It is extremely difficult to evaluate the effect of any one of these factors that come into play in many of the crosses between human races, so that it is almost useless to attempt to estimate the numerical ratio of the types originating from a cross. But it seems very likely that the chances are remote for the reappearance in $F_2$ or later generations of individuals having all the traits in the characteristic degrees of either of the parent groups.

If for sorted approximations to the pure parent groups the investigator requires for his statistical purposes only those individuals of $F_2$ or later generations who duplicate all the traits of such parent groups, is he not forgetting the fact of individual variation and the possibility that the parent groups may not be homozygous for the traits concerned? In the world today, how many races are truly primary ones? And how many are not stabilized remains of former hybridizations, long forgotten? It will be the part of common sense to be a little lenient in the requirements for admission to the various subgroups that can be selected from the $F_2$ or later descendants of a human racial cross.

It is evident that there are several complex genetic factors which under varying conditions come into play in race mixture. It has been noted that some few characters are inherited as simple dominants or recessives and that many others are controlled by multiple factors. In the face of these facts, we can make the following statements:

Suppose in a case of race mixture that one of the two parental groups is characterized by twelve non-adaptive traits, some of which are dominant, some of which are recessive, and some blending: (1) If an individual product of this case of race mixture possesses all twelve of the traits, he is certainly very closely related genetically to that parental group. (2) If a second individual of the mixed group has nine out of twelve of the parental traits, he is less closely related to the ancestral group in question than is the first individual, but he bears a certain definite kinship. (3) If a third product of the mixture varies in half or two-thirds of the given parental traits, he is less closely related to the specified group than either of the other two individuals. It is probable that all traits should not have equal value in segregating racial subgroups by sorting, but until more is known concerning such relative values, there is no remedy.

If a race is, as Hooton has defined it (1926), "a great division of mankind, the members of which, though individually varying, are characterized as a group by a certain combination of morphological and metrical features, principally non-adaptive, which have been derived from their common descent," then there can be no doubt concerning the statements made in the preceding paragraph.

Subgroups delimited by such a method as is suggested above may not be said to possess given absolute amounts of Indian or White blood, but they will bear to one another such relationships that the subgroups will grade more or less evenly from an approximation to one parent group to an approximation to the other. Two investigators using different criteria or different methods of handling criteria, will, providing the criteria used in each case are characteristic and non-adaptive, show very much the same gradation as evidenced by the physical characters of the subgroups.

It may be urged as an objection that such a method of selection of miscegenetic subgroups, as is here advocated, selects phenotypes, not genotypes. In such a complicated matter as human heredity, that person would be rash indeed who would agree to describe the unknown parents of a given known individual, or the children that he might beget. Certain single traits might be estimated with better than even chance of success, but the present knowledge of heredity is so far too fragmentary to be used as a secure foundation for prediction or a basis for genetic derivation. A case recently seen by the author serves as an illustration of the argument. In a well-known maternity hospital of St. Louis, during the course of delivery of a colored woman, the obstetrician was able to see (as is often the case) the head of the baby before it had entirely passed through the birth canal. He remarked that the hair of the baby was tow-colored. The writer examined the baby and mother three weeks after delivery. The mother had the depressed nasal root and nasal bridge of the Negro, flaring nostrils, Von Luschan skin color value of twenty-eight on the forehead and twenty-nine on the breast, black eyes, and hair black, coarse, and frizzly. She showed few if any signs of White admixture, and claimed to know of none. The baby had fine, straight, blond hair which showed a slight reddish tinge in good light. The eyes were blue-brown, the brown tending to be arranged in a zoned fashion in the iris. The skin was pallid, and as white as that of the average White child. The husband of the mother was described by an interne as being about as dark as she, but not quite so Negroid in cast of features. Even if one cannot be certain as to the paternity of the child (and the hospital attachés are inclined to believe the child legitimate) the phenomenon is a remarkable and unusual one. It is realized that the immaturity of the child makes description of its facial features useless. In this respect, the child was not remarkably different from any White child, but one cannot tell what changes maturity will bring. Again, years may produce deepened pigmentation. It may be remarked that the mother did not at first believe that the baby was hers, and that she willingly posed with the baby for a photograph.

If the workings of human heredity are sometimes as unpredictable as this case seems to show, is it not more practical, considering the paucity of extant knowledge concerning human genetics, and the occasional untrustworthiness from the genetic viewpoint of human genealogical data, to make as good a racial diagnosis of each individual concerned as is possible from suitable and evident data, than to search for genotypes in a world of miscegenation? If an individual has the traits of a racial group, he belongs to that group. The groups to which his (and his consort's) children belong do not directly affect the question.

Race mixture has probably always been and is today prevalent in the world. The static concept of race is that of the person who deals with ideal races, which may not even exist except in the mind of the conceiver. From unknown antecedents come the varied members of a group of people. They move into an unoccupied geographical territory. They intermarry, eat the same kind of food, live together in the same climate, share the same culture. Intermarriage, natural selection, and isolation tend to make them homogeneous. They become a new secondary race. It is possible that the race is not new; that a group with a similar combination of traits has existed before. A group of immigrants comes into the territory, characterized by a different combination of traits. They subdue the indigenous group or are subdued by them. In any case, mixture occurs between the two races. The process of genetic adjustment begins all over again; perhaps continues with isolation of the new group for a long time, but eventually the more or less stable equilibrium is again disturbed.

An essentially similar train of events, multiplied manyfold, probably tells the origin and history of each of many of the secondary races of today. Let the investigator, therefore, in identifying individuals with races, use the evidence of his senses and of pertinent historical facts and what knowledge he has of inheritance of traits. He will at least then have the satisfaction of dealing with tangibles. His groups live and breathe.

If a definite name is applied to a race, let the donor define the name in terms of physical traits, instead of permitting the term to drift free and to be applied in the particular way that any investigator wishes. If the bulk of a population cannot be placed in some racial subgroup, or an approximation to that subgroup, then the term "race" is of little significance. Race is defined in terms of the characteristics of members. Since, in the world as it is, individuals appear each generation who exhibit new and different as well as old and well-known combinations of traits, races change from generation to generation in the numbers of members, in reactions to environment, and, in case of miscegenation, in essential nature. The description of races at one particular period of history is like a group of still photographs, while description of races through several periods of history resembles a motion picture in which not only one, but many of the subjects of the still pictures participate.

This is not to say that races, being unstable, cannot be said to have attributes. The attributes of a race are in each case the resultant of a complex of traits of that race that are themselves unknown (and probably unseen) but which are correlated with other traits perceptible to man's senses. It follows that the stronger the correlation between these unknown and known traits, the stronger the causal connection between them (either as one depending upon the other or both depending upon a third common cause), the better will be that trait or group of traits for purposes of prediction or diagnosis.

To recapitulate, how can one resolve a racially mixed and heterogeneous population into truly racial subgroups? A method suggested is that of sorting the heterogeneous racial sample into subgroups by means of certain racial criteria. The criteria used should be non-adaptive, easily observed traits, which differ in their exhibition in the parent races. One is more certain than he otherwise might be of the usefulness of traits for racial sorting, if those traits exhibit strong linkage with other characters that vary with race, and if something is already known about the behavior of the traits in human inheritance.

## THEORY AND PRACTICE OF SORTING IN YUCATECAN RACE MIXTURE

Race mixture as a general problem has been considered. In the Yucatecan data lies an opportunity to apply specifically the theories and methods suggested in the preceding chapter.

Briefly, the predominant in number of the two groups which mixed to make the Yucatecans of today were the Maya Indians. The other party of smaller number was most commonly of Spanish nationality. The mixing has been going on for about three hundred and fifty years. Evidence of the physical characteristics of the Mayas of pre-Columbian times is limited to what can be gleaned from the representations of Maya art. Descriptions by the early Spanish conquerors are few and of little utility. Fray Alonso Ponce is quoted as saying, "The Indians of Acandon are very small." Charnay (1887), who visited the country in the later part of the nineteenth century, gives the following list of Maya physical traits:

| | |
|---|---|
| Heads round | Ears and mouths small |
| Noses arched | Eyes black |
| Jaws straight | Hair straight, coarse, and black |
| Chins round | Complexions reddish-brown |
| Teeth square and sound | Chests deep |

Joyce (1927), mentions the lack of body hair in the representations of art.

Plate 5, from Spinden's *A Study of Maya Art* (1913), shows some facial characters of the ancient Maya that are seen in Yucatan today. The nasal profile is represented as convex or straight, never concave; nasal wings are flaring; epicanthic eye-fold is often depicted; the chin invariably retreats, in contrast to the protruded lips; cheek bones are high; there is little depression of the nasal root; the forehead slopes (but from cranial evidence we know that this is a result of artificial deformation). It is always unsafe to accept representations in art of human physical characteristics as valid. The visitor to Yucatan is, however, frequently struck by the close resemblances between certain Indians and the representations of their ancestors in ancient Maya art.

Starr (1902) states:

The Mayas are of little stature, with not one tall subject in the series. Their arms are the longest observed, and the finger-reach index is the maximum, at 105.6. They are next to the maximum in shoulder-breadth index. Their facial indices are the largest of our list (of Southern Mexican tribes), and their cephalic index next to the maximum. They have been characterized elsewhere as "short, dark, and brachycephalic." Short and brachycephalic they certainly are, but hardly dark. The hair is black and straight; in six cases the color was lighter or gray, and in fifteen cases it showed a tendency toward wavy or curly. The beard was lighter in nineteen cases. The growth of the beard is moderately strong, and its distribution much as usual (for South Mexican Indians): scanty to medium on the upper cheeks, absent from the lower cheeks, scanty or medium upon the chin, and medium to full in the moustache.

The eyes are dark brown and widely separated; one-half the subjects presented a notable obliquity, though the character tends to disappear with age; in children it is almost universal and well marked. The nose is aquiline, though low, flat, and wide; the bridge is long, sometimes sinuous, and often projects as a central beak beyond the alae. Lips are of moderate thickness and do not project much.

Starr (1908) also writes:

Among the village police force (at Hacienda San Juan, near Tekax) one man had attracted our particular attention, as representing a type of face quite common among the Mayas, which we had called the serpent face. It is round and broad, *with retreating chin* and *receding forehead* and with curious, widely separated, expressionless eyes.

Most if not all of Starr's measurements seem to have been made in the vicinity of Tekax, in the southernmost part of the state of Yucatan.

From the foregoing paragraphs it appears that there are two sources of information concerning physical characteristics of the Maya Indians. They are (1) representations in art of the ancient Mayas and (2) more recent descriptions of travelers and anthropologists. In searching for traits suitable for definition of a pure Maya type, these sources were used, together with observations made by the writer in the course of his work in Yucatan. Of the total possibilities, those traits which are known to be non-adaptive, easily observed, and which tend toward a qualitative character were noted. Most of them had previously proved definite individual sorting power for race, as demonstrated in Table 2. The behavior of many of them in human inheritance is to some extent known.

*Group A*. Table 3 shows a list of trait categories which meet the above requirements for definite racial characteristics of the Maya Indians.

All of these traits excepting prominent malars and slight depression of the nasal root have been tested and proven for their selective properties on certain measurements in Table 2. Many of them are the same as those represented in ancient Maya art, and all will be noted as very prevalent by the traveler in the Indian villages of Yucatan. It is unfortunate that estimations of height and breadth of nasal bridge were not made, but in a general way, use of the data on nasal profile and on amount of depression of the

## TABLE 3

### (Definition of Group A)

In the list of traits and their grades given, those set in capitals and small capitals or placed in quotation marks are the ones used for separating, from the group of Yucatecans as a whole, a subgroup approximating the Maya type.

HAIR
> Form: STRAIGHT, low waves, deep waves, curly, frizzly.
> Texture: COARSE, medium, fine.
> Amount of beard (or moustache):[1] "0", "SM", "+", ++, +++.

PIGMENTATION
> Hair Color: BLACK, dark brown, light brown, reddish-brown, red, blond.
> Eye color: BLACK, DARK BROWN, light brown, yellow-brown, green-brown, blue-brown, blue.
> Skin color: Von Luschan's scale "25" to "15" inclusive; 14 to light grades not well represented on Von Luschan's scale.
> Freckles: "0", "MASS", sm, +, ++, +++.

VARIATIONS PRINCIPALLY BONY
> Nasal Profile: CONVEX, STRAIGHT, CONCAVO–CONVEX, concave.
> Nasal root depression: "0", "SM", "+", ++, +++.
> Chin prominence: "SM", "+", ++, +++.
> Malar prominence: sm, +, "++", "+++".

VARIATIONS OF SOFT PARTS
> Nasal Wings: Compressed, MEDIUM, FLARING.
> Eye-folds: MONGOLOID, EPICANTHIC, NO FOLD, external.

---

[1] (Table 3.) In the definition of the female Group A, the amount of beard and moustache is not to be used, of course, as a criterion.

nasal root supply the deficiency. Dark and medium-dark pigmentation, straight, coarse hair, with scanty beard, prominent cheekbones, and flaring nasal wings are accepted as general characteristics of most American Indians. Noses prominent generally and at the root, receding chins, and more than occasional prevalence of epicanthic eye-folds are suggested as specific traits. Absence of freckles, except of the "mass" variety, involves the negative use of a criterion which has been found to indicate some degree of mixture between a dark and a more lightly pigmented race, which is here the case. When beard amount was discussed with reference to Table 2 a guess was made that there might be in this case some correlation between amount of beard and age. Accordingly, the mean square contingency coefficient between these two was obtained; it showed a value of .399. Such a coefficient is not an extremely high one, but it is high enough to command respect and consideration. One should not use the possession of only a "sm" or slight amount of beard as a sorting criterion in this case. In order to make sure that the sorting method selects for race and not age, "+" or average amount of beard is included among the characters for Group A.

It has been remarked that persons who have Mongoloid or epicanthic folds in childhood tend to lose them or to show them in diminished degree as youth passes. It was necessary to find the amount of correlation existing between these variables among Yucatecans. The mean square contingency coefficient in this case proved to be .424. But Dunn (1923, p. 122) shows that not even all Chinese have such eye-folds, so that in the schedule for the Maya group the criteria were so defined as to include besides Mongoloid and epicanthic folds, the possession of no fold at all.

The traits enumerated in Table 3 represent in their number and quality *one* group which may be selected for characterization of a relatively pure Maya subgroup. In this and the following statements of subgroup criteria, it is to be borne in mind that the number of traits and the traits themselves might have been varied from the traits and their numbers which were selected. The selections here given are specific but, nevertheless, typical examples of the application of the theory of racial subgroup sorting advanced in this study.

Eight hundred and eighty adult males and six hundred and ninety-four adult females constitute for each sex the two series of unselected Yucatecans to be examined and sorted into racial subgroups. They shall henceforth be designated in this study, in the case of either sex, as Total Yucatecans. The intention is to select a series of phenotypical groups which grade from a subgroup of nearly pure Maya Indians to subgroups which have few Maya traits and many White characteristics. In the racial mixture which occurred in Yucatan, the Maya Indians entering into the cross greatly outnumbered the Whites. Consequently, it is not to be expected that the subgroups which possess the greater number of White traits are as closely related to pure Whites as the subgroups characterized by Indian traits are related to pure Indians.

Five subgroups were selected by sorting. The subgroup sorted according to the scheme of Table 3 represents the group which most closely approaches the Maya Indian phenotype. If that sub-group be designated Group A, then the others may be called Groups B, C, D, and E.

*Group B.* The individuals who are to constitute Group B have been selected by the following criterion: any person who has all of the characters determined upon for definition of Group A, with the exception of any one character; e.g. a person who has all the other Group A traits but has low-waved instead of straight hair, or an individual who is Maya in all traits except that he is freckled.

*Group C* will be defined later.

*Groups D and E* are to represent the Whiter grades of the progeny of the Maya-Spanish cross. It is obviously unjustifiable to use for the sorting of Groups D and E the categories of traits remaining in Table 3 after the Group A traits have been subtracted. The justification for assuming that a member of Group A belongs to that group is not that he has black hair, but that he has black hair *and* twelve other Maya Indian traits. Spanish Whites and Maya Indians possess several characteristics in common. It is the cumulative character of the possession of the traits which makes the members of Group A phenotypically Indian. All pure Maya Indians are said to have black hair; only some Spanish Whites have that characteristic. If, therefore, it is desired to sort out phenotypes which resemble the White side of the racial cross, the other colors of hair than black cannot be used as definitive criteria, for some Spanish Whites have black hair. If the possession of any other color of hair than black were used as a criterion in the sorting of an approximation to the White type, certain individuals of good Spanish type would thereby be unjustly denied admission to that group.

Several other of the trait groups in Table 3 are similarly unsuitable for selection of Groups D and E. Hair form falls in this classification, as do also eye color, presence or absence of freckles, form of nasal profile, amount of nasal root depression, chin prominence, and form of nasal wings. Five of the trait groups of Table 3 remain; namely, hair texture, amount of beard or moustache, skin color, amount of malar prominence, and character of eye-folds. (In sorting female members of Groups D and E, amount of beard or moustache can not serve, of course, as a sorting criterion.)

Trait groups having been selected, the next step in the process of selecting the members of Groups D and E will be the sorting out of a group, characterized by the criteria shown in the headings of Table 4. The group selected by means of those traits characterizes the members of both Groups D and E; it will therefore have a temporary existence under the designation of "the composite group DE."

A male individual is accepted for the composite group DE if he possesses three or more of the five traits shown in the table heading.

A female individual is accepted for the group if she possesses two or more of the four traits shown in the table heading. The following combinations are possible:

TABLE 4.

MALES

|  | Hair texture: medium or fine | Amount of beard and moustache: +, ++, +++ | Skin color: 14 (Von Luschan) or lighter | Malar prominence: sm, + | Eye-folds: no fold or external fold |
|---|---|---|---|---|---|
| 5/5 .... | X | X | X | X | X |
| 4/5 .... |  | X | X | X | X |
|  | X |  | X | X | X |
|  | X | X |  | X | X |
|  | X | X | X |  | X |
|  | X | X | X | X |  |
| 3/5 .... |  |  | X | X | X |
|  |  | X |  | X | X |
|  |  | X | X |  | X |
|  |  | X | X | X |  |
|  | X | X | X |  |  |
|  | X | X |  | X |  |
|  | X |  | X | X |  |
|  | X |  |  | X | X |
|  | X | X |  |  | X |
|  | X |  | X |  | X |

FEMALES

|  | Hair texture: medium or fine | Skin color: 14 (Von Luschan) or lighter | Malar prominence: sm, + | Eye-folds: no fold or external fold |
|---|---|---|---|---|
| 4/4 ............... | X | X | X | X |
| 3/4 ............... |  | X | X | X |
|  | X |  | X | X |
|  | X | X |  | X |
|  | X | X | X |  |
| 2/4 ............... |  |  | X | X |
|  |  | X |  | X |
|  |  | X | X |  |
|  | X |  |  | X |
|  | X | X |  |  |
|  | X |  | X |  |

It is important to consider in the selection of the members of the group DE: (1) that each of these individuals possesses both White and Indian blood; (2) that the number of Indian ancestors of the group of Total Yucatecans is undoubtedly larger than the number of Whites who have had a part in the cross; (3) that there is at least partial dominance in some of the Indian traits; (4) that linkage of genes may favor the persistence of certain Indian traits. The significance of these facts is that while Groups D and E more nearly approximate the White type than do Groups A and B, the former groups will still retain certain Indian characteristics. Because of the four facts just enumerated, it will not be stipulated in the sorting of the group DE that its members shall have *all* of the traits mentioned in the headings of Table 4, but rather that they shall have certain proportions of those traits.

In regard to the traits of Table 4, the objection might be raised that even though most Spanish Whites have "sm" or " + " malar prominence, a particular member of that group might be purely White and have at the same time very prominent malar bones. The use in sorting of only a proportion, and not all of the traits in Table 4 helps to provide against this objection: for if the individual in question is aberrant in only one trait, according to the provisions of Table 4 he still has four of five characteristics which place him in the racial subgroup to which he should by right belong.

*Group C.* Groups A and B, which approximate the Maya Indian type in appearance, and the composite group DE, which is characterized by possession of some White traits, each were sorted. With these three groups subtracted from the whole series of Total Yucatecans, the remainder which results is neither quite Indian nor quite White according to the selective characteristics chosen for use in this study. This residual subgroup will henceforth be known as Group C.

*Group E.* Spanish Whites belong of course to that large division of mankind called the White race. But the Spanish themselves are a nation and not a race or subrace. There are, however, subracial groups in the Spanish nation. Therefore, in breaking down the composite group DE into the subgroups D and E, it is logical that pigmentation should be one suitable criterion for differentiation. The composite group DE deviates more strongly from the Indian type than do Groups A and B, and approaches more nearly to the general White type than do those groups. Group E of the composite group DE is to differ theoretically, at least, from Group D only in possession of lighter pigmentation. However, since the criteria for differentiation of the group DE are not so numerous nor so definitive as the author might wish, it should be remarked that it is probable that the lighter traits of pigmentation of Group E are linked with other White characters; in which case it is likely that the members of Group E approximate more closely to the White side of their ancestry than do the members of Group D.

A male or female individual of the composite group DE is accepted as a member of Group E if he has two or more of the three traits of pigmentation shown in the table heading. The following combinations are possible:

TABLE 5

|  | Skin color (Von Luschan): 14 or lighter | Hair color: dark brown or lighter | Eye color: light brown or lighter |
|---|---|---|---|
| 3/3 .................... | × | × | × |
| 2/3 .................... | × | × |  |
|  |  | × | × |
|  | × |  | × |

*Group D.* Table 5 shows the method by which Group E is sorted from group DE. After Group E has been differentiated and subtracted from the composite group, the remainder represents Group D.

Definition of Groups D and E marks the completion of the task of resolution of the racially mixed series of Yucatecans into supposedly racial subgroups. It remains to be seen whether the sorted subgroups present a uniformity of physical characters, adaptive and non-adaptive, sufficient to justify the conclusion that relatively pure racial types have been distinguished.

## LENGTH DIMENSIONS OF THE BODY

**Stature.** In both males and females, the tables for stature indicate a clear-cut trend from lower values in the more Indian subgroups to higher ones in the Whiter descendants of the White-Indian racial cross of Yucatan. The differences that exist between the means of the subgroups and those of the Total Yucatecans are

### TABLE 6.   STATURE [1]

#### MALES

| Group | No. | Range | Mean | S.D. | V. | Significance with Total Yucatecans |
|---|---|---|---|---|---|---|
| Total Yucatecans .. | 865 | 137–176 | 156.43±.12 | 5.46±.09 | 3.49±.06 | |
| Group A ......... | 221 | 137–168 | 154.71±.22 | 4.88±.16 | 3.15±.10 | 8×pe D [2] |
| Group B ......... | 194 | 141–170 | 155.80±.24 | 5.04±.17 | 3.23±.11 | 2×pe D |
| Group C ......... | 359 | 141–176 | 157.23±.19 | 5.44±.14 | 3.46±.09 | 5×pe D |
| Group D ........ | 45 | 147–171 | 158.26±.62 | 6.12±.44 | 3.87±.28 | 3×pe D |
| Group E ......... | 46 | 148–174 | 159.15±.63 | 6.34±.45 | 3.98±.28 | 4×pe D |
| | | | | | | |
| Cacereños ........ | 20 | ... | 165.00±.51 | 3.39 | 2.05 | |
| Aranzadi, 1894b | | | | | | |
| | | | | | | |
| Andalusian Moors . | 28 | ... | 164.04±.58 | 4.59±.41 | 2.80±.25 | |
| Coon, 1929 | | | | | | |
| | | | | | | |
| Spanish (General) . | 1690 | ... | 162.10 | | | |
| Galaica ........... | 182 | ... | 160.00 | | | |
| Cantabrica ........ | 47 | ... | 161.90 | | | |
| Vasco-Navarra..... | 186 | ... | 162.60 | | | |
| Catalana ......... | 182 | ... | 163.60 | | | |
| Castellana Superior. | 179 | ... | 161.90 | | | |
| Aragonesa ........ | 92 | ... | 162.40 | | | |
| Valenciana ........ | 87 | ... | 161.40 | | | |
| Castellana Inferior . | 132 | ... | 162.20 | | | |
| Andalucia Alta .... | 447 | ... | 162.40 | | | |
| Andalucia Baja .... | 137 | ... | 161.80 | | | |
| Islas Baleares ..... | 13 | ... | 162.60 | | | |
| Islas Canarias ..... | 6 | ... | 161.00 | | | |
| Hoyos Sainz and Aranzadi, 1894a | | | | | | |
| | | | | | | |
| Spanish (General) . | 7396 | ... | 164.50 | | | |
| Deniker, 1900 | | | | | | |
| | | | | | | |
| Spanish (General) . | 6072 | ... | 162.00 | | | |
| Higher Professions . | 497 | ... | 163.90 | | | |
| Other Professional | | | | | | |
| Occupations ..... | 295 | ... | 161.10 | | | |
| Laborers (Outdoor). | 329 | ... | 160.70 | | | |
| Laborers (Indoor) . | 677 | ... | 159.80 | | | |
| Oloriz, 1896 | | | | | | |
| | | | | | | |
| Mexicans ......... | 48 | ... | 161.11 | 5.98±.41 | 3.71±.28 | |
| | | | | | | |
| Tzendals ......... | 100 | 140–172 | 155.71 | | | |
| Chols ............ | 100 | 144–167 | 155.79 | | | |
| Huaxtecs.......... | 100 | 141–169 | 157.03 | | | |
| Chontals ......... | 80 | 139–177 | 159.80 | | | |
| *Mayas* ........... | 100 | 145–168 | 155.24 | | | |
| Tzotzils .......... | 100 | 144–167 | 155.90 | | | |
| Starr, 1902 | | | | | | |

[1] Statistics in Tables 6–107 are by the author unless otherwise stated.
[2] Pearson's formula for probable error of difference between general sample and sub-sample is used in this paper to determine significant differences between means of subgroups and means of the general sample of Total Yucatecans. See p. 22, footnote, and also quotation from Goring (1913, p. 46).

TABLE 6. (*Continued*)

| Group | No. | Range | Mean | S. D. | V. | Significance with Total Yucatecans |
|---|---|---|---|---|---|---|
| Sioux, Pure........ | 537 | 152–190 | 172.40 | 5.64 | 3.27 | |
| Sioux, Half-Blood .. | 77 | 154–194 | 173.50 | 6.81 | 3.92 | |
| Sullivan, 1920 | | | | | | |
| Hawaiians, Pure ... | 70 | ... | $171.31 \pm .40$ | $5.00 \pm .29$ | $2.92 \pm .17$ | |
| F₁ Hawaiian, North | | | | | | |
| European ...... | 10 | 162–181 | $173.48 \pm 1.2$ | $5.72 \pm .86$ | 3.30 | |
| Dunn, Tozzer, 1928 | | | | | | |

FEMALES

| Group | No. | Range | Mean | S. D. | V. | Significance with Total Yucatecans |
|---|---|---|---|---|---|---|
| Total Yucatecans .. | 687 | 125–160 | $143.87 \pm .13$ | $5.20 \pm .09$ | $3.61 \pm .07$ | |
| Group A .......... | 152 | 130–158 | $142.76 \pm .27$ | $5.02 \pm .19$ | $3.52 \pm .14$ | $4 \times$pe D |
| Group B ......... | 228 | 131–156 | $142.88 \pm .21$ | $4.74 \pm .15$ | $3.32 \pm .10$ | $5 \times$pe D |
| Group C ......... | 199 | 125–160 | $144.38 \pm .24$ | $5.10 \pm .17$ | $3.53 \pm .12$ | $2 \times$pe D |
| Group D ......... | 62 | 135–160 | $146.47 \pm .42$ | $4.94 \pm .30$ | $3.37 \pm .20$ | $6 \times$pe D |
| Group E .......... | 46 | 133–156 | $146.76 \pm .55$ | $5.56 \pm .39$ | $3.79 \pm .27$ | $5 \times$pe D |
| Spanish .......... | 111 | ... | 153.05 | | | |
| Oloriz, 1896 | | | | | | |
| Mexicans ........ | 29 | 129–162 | $149.16 \pm .86$ | $6.88 \pm .61$ | $4.61 \pm .41$ | |
| *Mayas* .......... | 25 | 133–150 | 141.52 | | | |
| Huaxtecs.......... | 20 | 140–153 | 147.27 | | | |
| Tzendals ........ | 25 | 134–155 | 143.84 | | | |
| Chols ........... | 25 | 130–148 | 141.32 | | | |
| Chontals ........ | 25 | 138–156 | 148.06 | | | |
| Tzotzils ......... | 25 | 137–153 | 144.13 | | | |
| Starr, 1902 | | | | | | |
| Smith Coll. Students | 100 | 152–176 | $162.80 \pm .38$ | 5.56 | 3.42 | |
| Steggerda *et al.*,1929 | | | | | | |
| French............ ... | | ... | 157.00 | | | |
| Bertillon and MacAuliffe (Martin, 1914) | | | | | | |
| Aztecs ............ ... | | ... | 148.90 | | | |
| Hrdlička (Martin, 1914) | | | | | | |
| Sioux, Pure........ | 157 | 146–174 | 160.00 | 5.29 | 3.30 | |
| Sioux, Half-Blood .. | 19 | 152–172 | 161.20 | 5.79 | 3.59 | |
| Sullivan, 1920 | | | | | | |
| Hawaiians, Pure ... | 34 | 150–175 | 162.60 | | | |
| ¾ Hawaiian, ¼ North | | | | | | |
| European ....... | 12 | 154–172 | 161.90 | | | |
| F₁ Hawaiian, North | | | | | | |
| European ...... | 10 | 156–167 | 162.60 | | | |
| ¼ Hawaiian, ¾ North | | | | | | |
| European ....... | 6 | 159–171 | 164.70 | | | |
| Dunn, Tozzer, 1928 | | | | | | |

statistically significant. Group E's average for this measurement is less than that of any of the Spanish groups cited, but not much less. The male Spanish mean that approaches closest is that of Oloriz' indoor laborers. The stature of the average Mexican exceeds that of Group E by about the same margin as that subgroup is surpassed by the lowest Spanish group.

Starr's Mayas and Groups A and B compare well in stature. It would appear that Starr's subjects were probably rather Indian Yucatecans. His other tribes are also of the same small stature; the Huaxtecs alone approximate the standing height of Group C.

Sapper (1905) believed that middle Yucatan, as compared with the northern and southern parts of the peninsula, was the habitat of a taller variety of Maya Indian. If that was once true, it can not now be proven because of recently bettered facilities for population shifts and because of race mixture.

It will later be shown that the subgroups differ in the kinds of work that their members perform and that the individuals of the Whiter groups tend to engage in occupations that give them better chances for growth and more adequate nutrition. Sapper (1905) states: "The shortness of middle American tribes may be attributed to disease, insufficient nutrition, and too early marriage." The effect of the environmental factor on stature is difficult to evaluate accurately. It seems probable that the effect of both racial (or hereditary) and certain environmental factors is reflected in the subgroup differences shown in the tables.

There is also the effect of age upon stature to be considered. All subjects under the age of eighteen years were omitted from the total series for each sex. In age, the male group A differs from the average of the group as a whole (34.1) by −1.5 years, B by −2.8 years, C by +1.6 years, D by +3.9 years, and E by +3.2 years. The female subgroup differences are in alphabetical order: −0.3, +0.9, −0.9, +4.1, and −5.1. The age mean for the female Total Yucatecans is 35.3 years. The fact that both stature and age are lower than in the group as a whole in the male Groups A and B and higher in Groups D and E suggests two possibilities: viz., (1) that the lower age means of the male Groups A and B and the higher ones of Groups D and E may be merely accidental; and (2) that small stature may be correlated with youth. To find which of the two possibilities is the fact, coefficients of correlation between age and stature were obtained for each male subgroup and for the male group as a whole. The value of $r$ in the case of the male Total Yucatecans is $-.010 \pm .020$; and for the male subgroups in alphabetical order: $-.017 \pm .045$, $-.009 \pm .048$, $-.014 \pm .036$, $+.007 \pm .100$, and $-.032 \pm .100$. In view of the absence of correlation between age and stature in each of the groups and in the group as a whole, it is established that the effect of age upon stature is negligible in each of these groups.

The age means of the female subgroups are such that no suggestion of an age effect upon stature is given. Despite the fact that the age averages for the female Groups A, B, and C are almost equal, a constant rise in height occurs; and while Group D's age mean rises four years and Group E's drops five, the rise in average stature continues. It may be concluded that age is not a significant affective factor in the subgroup differences which are to be discussed throughout this study.

The seriation curves for stature (Plate 6) confirm the findings of the statistical tables and add to one's knowledge of the way in which the character is distributed within the groups. Bimodality seems to be characteristic of the D and E subgroups of both sexes. In the males, the taller modes for D and E are at about the same stature level as that of the Andalusian Moors, the only Spanish sample for which seriation data were available. The higher modes of the women fall short of the Smith College Students' mean but are immensely higher in centimeters than the modes for Groups A, B, or C.

Two other cases of race mixture are cited for comparison of results: the Sioux Indian-White mixture of Sullivan, and the Hawaiian-White cross of Dunn and Tozzer. The subgroup classification of the progeny in each of these cases was based wholly on genetic histories. Sullivan doubts that the average stature of the Whites who mixed with the Sioux was as great as the stature of those Indians; he is at a loss to explain the taller stature of the Half-Bloods. Dunn and Tozzer's $F_1$ Hawaiian males show heterosis, but the later female descendants of that cross are characterized by an increase in height roughly comparable with that observed in the means of the D and E women. Shapiro (1926) found heterosis in stature in his Norfolk Island hybrids. Sinnott and Dunn (1925) state: "Hybrid vigor is noticeable only in the

## TABLE 7.  ACROMIAL HEIGHT

### MALES

| Group | No. | Range | Mean | S. D. | V. | Significance with Total Yucatecans |
|---|---|---|---|---|---|---|
| Total Yucatecans .. | 828 | 115–148 | 129.46±.12 | 5.12±.08 | 3.95±.06 | |
| Group A ......... | 221 | 115–144 | 127.98±.21 | 4.66±.15 | 3.64±.12 | 7×pe D |
| Group B ......... | 188 | 117–142 | 129.00±.22 | 4.54±.16 | 3.52±.12 | 2×pe D |
| Group C ......... | 340 | 117–148 | 130.28±.19 | 5.20±.13 | 3.99±.10 | 5×pe D |
| Group D ........ | 40 | 120–143 | 130.30±.65 | 6.12±.46 | 4.70±.35 | 1×pe D |
| Group E ......... | 39 | 121–144 | 131.81±.62 | 5.70±.44 | 4.32±.33 | 3×pe D |
| Cacereños ........ Aranzadi, 1894b | 23 | ... | 135.56 | | | |
| Andalusian Moors . Coon, 1929 | 28 | ... | 134.11±.45 | 3.53±.32 | 2.63±.24 | |
| Chontals ......... | 80 | 114–149 | 132.50 | | | |
| Huaxtecs.......... | 100 | 115–139 | 129.63 | | | |
| *Mayas* ........... | 100 | 118–141 | 128.30 | | | |
| Tzotzils .......... | 100 | 116–142 | 129.10 | | | |
| Tzendals ......... | 100 | 115–150 | 128.67 | | | |
| Chols ............ Starr, 1902 | 100 | 118–142 | 128.84 | | | |
| Sioux, Pure........ | 534 | 124–162 | 142.70 | 5.03 | 3.52 | |
| Sioux, Half-Blood .. Sullivan, 1920 | 77 | 126–160 | 142.30 | 6.07 | 4.26 | |
| Hawaiians, Pure ... | 70 | ... | 140.12±.37 | 4.57±.26 | 3.26±.19 | |
| F₁ Hawaiian, North European ...... Dunn, Tozzer, 1928 | 10 | 133–150 | 142.61±1.05 | 4.93±.74 | 3.46 | |

### FEMALES

| Group | No. | Range | Mean | S. D. | V. | Significance with Total Yucatecans |
|---|---|---|---|---|---|---|
| Total Yucatecans .. | 630 | 105–136 | 118.86±.13 | 4.80±.09 | 4.04±.08 | |
| Group A .......... | 151 | 108–130 | 118.00±.25 | 4.54±.18 | 3.85±.15 | 3×pe D |
| Group B ......... | 215 | 105–131 | 118.14±.21 | 4.58±.15 | 3.88±.13 | 4×pe D |
| Group C ......... | 182 | 107–134 | 119.51±.24 | 4.86±.17 | 4.07±.14 | 3×pe D |
| Group D ......... | 45 | 113–136 | 121.41±.50 | 5.00±.36 | 4.12±.29 | 5×pe D |
| Group E ......... | 37 | 111–130 | 120.20±.53 | 4.74±.37 | 3.94±.31 | 2×pe D |
| *Mayas* ........... | 25 | 107–125 | 116.52 | | | |
| Huaxtecs.......... | 20 | 115–127 | 121.30 | | | |
| Tzendals ........ | 25 | 109–128 | 117.52 | | | |
| Chols ............ | 25 | 107–125 | 116.56 | | | |
| Chontals ........ | 25 | 113–130 | 121.86 | | | |
| Tzotzils .......... Starr, 1902 | 25 | 113–128 | 118.13 | | | |
| Smith Coll. Students Steggerda *et al.*, 1929 | 100 | 120–144 | 131.42±.35 | 5.12 | 3.90 | |
| Sioux, Pure........ | 157 | 120–150 | 132.50 | 4.89 | 3.69 | |
| Sioux, Half-Blood .. Sullivan, 1920 | 19 | 124–142 | 133.20 | 5.23 | 3.92 | |

first generation following the cross, and gradually disappears in later inbred generations." Race mixture between Maya Indians and Spanish Whites first occurred some three hundred years ago; exhibition of heterosis is not, therefore, now expected.

The trait of stature is not one of the easiest to study in case of race mixture. Standing height is not in itself a simple length. It is

TABLE 8. STERNAL HEIGHT

MALES

| Group | No. | Range | Mean | S. D. | V. | Significance with Total Yucatecans |
|---|---|---|---|---|---|---|
| Total Yucatecans .. | 865 | 112–145 | 128.16±.11 | 4.90±.08 | 3.82±.06 | |
| Group A ......... | 221 | 113–140 | 126.67±.21 | 4.56±.15 | 3.60±.12 | 8×pe D |
| Group B ......... | 194 | 115–140 | 127.52±.22 | 4.54±.16 | 3.56±.12 | 3×pe D |
| Group C ......... | 359 | 112–145 | 128.92±.17 | 4.80±.12 | 3.72±.09 | 5×pe D |
| Group D ........ | 45 | 119–142 | 129.94±.55 | 5.50±.39 | 4.23±.30 | 3×pe D |
| Group E ......... | 46 | 121–144 | 130.59±.56 | 5.59±.39 | 4.28±.30 | 4×pe D |

FEMALES

| Group | No. | Range | Mean | S. D. | V. | Significance with Total Yucatecans |
|---|---|---|---|---|---|---|
| Total Yucatecans .. | 687 | 101–134 | 117.90±.12 | 4.68±.09 | 3.97±.07 | |
| Group A ......... | 152 | 105–128 | 116.82±.24 | 4.36±.17 | 3.73±.14 | 5×pe D |
| Group B ......... | 228 | 105–129 | 117.20±.20 | 4.40±.14 | 3.75±.12 | 4×pe D |
| Group C ......... | 199 | 102–133 | 118.43±.23 | 4.76±.16 | 4.02±.14 | 2×pe D |
| Group D ........ | 62 | 109–134 | 119.73±.41 | 4.80±.29 | 4.01±.24 | 5×pe D |
| Group E ......... | 46 | 111–130 | 120.11±.47 | 4.70±.33 | 3.91±.28 | 4×pe D |

made up of several smaller segments which to some extent vary independently. The trait is also open to a certain amount of environmental influence, such as favoring conditions of growth. But despite these facts, there seems good reason to believe that the mixture of taller people of White blood with the Indians of Yucatan has resulted after many generations in stature differences which favor those descendants of the cross who possess White traits.

**Acromial and Sternal Heights.** The statements made concerning stature apply almost equally well to acromial height and to sternal height. That is not at all surprising in view of the high spurious correlation which exists between stature and acromial height. For the male group as a whole this coefficient is .950; for Groups A, B, C, D, and E respectively it is .949, .937, .952, .956, and .959.

Heterosis is again seen in the $F_1$ Hawaiian-White hybrids. The Half-Blood Sioux were taller than the Pure but their shoulder height is less. The explanation may lie in greater amount of shoulder slope in the Half-Bloods. Such an assumption is interesting, for there is some evidence that a similar condition appears to be present in Group D and to a less extent in Group E. The

TABLE 9. RELATIVE SHOULDER HEIGHT

MALES

| Group | No. | Range | Mean | S. D. | V. | Significance with Total Yucatecans |
|---|---|---|---|---|---|---|
| Total Yucatecans .. | 828 | 80–87 | 82.75 ± .02 | 1.04 ± .02 | 1.26 ± .02 | |
| Group A ......... | 221 | 80–86 | 82.72 ± .04 | 0.98 ± .03 | 1.19 ± .04 | None |
| Group B ......... | 188 | 81–87 | 82.74 ± .05 | 1.02 ± .04 | 1.23 ± .04 | None |
| Group C ......... | 340 | 80–86 | 82.82 ± .04 | 1.05 ± .03 | 1.27 ± .03 | 2×pe D |
| Group D ........ | 40 | 80–85 | 82.38 ± .12 | 1.16 ± .09 | 1.41 ± .11 | 3×pe D |
| Group E ......... | 39 | 81–86 | 82.87 ± .11 | 1.04 ± .08 | 1.25 ± .09 | None |
| Andalusian Moors . Coon, 1929 | 28 | ... | 81.89 ± .14 | 1.14 ± .10 | 1.39 ± .12 | |
| Hawaiians, Pure ... Dunn, Tozzer, 1928 | 70 | ... | 81.80 | | | |

FEMALES

| Group | No. | Range | Mean | S. D. | V. | Significance with Total Yucatecans |
|---|---|---|---|---|---|---|
| Total Yucatecans .. | 630 | 77–86 | 82.71 ± .03 | 1.17 ± .02 | 1.41 ± .03 | |
| Group A ......... | 151 | 81–85 | 82.66 ± .06 | 1.10 ± .04 | 1.33 ± .05 | None |
| Group B ......... | 215 | 79–85 | 82.73 ± .05 | 1.12 ± .04 | 1.35 ± .04 | None |
| Group C ......... | 182 | 79–86 | 82.75 ± .06 | 1.22 ± .04 | 1.47 ± .05 | None |
| Group D ........ | 45 | 77–86 | 82.80 ± .14 | 1.42 ± .10 | 1.72 ± .12 | None |
| Group E ......... | 37 | 79–85 | 82.57 ± .13 | 1.15 ± .09 | 1.39 ± .11 | 1×pe D |

differences between the means of acromial height and sternal height range for Groups A, B, and C from 1.31 to 1.48 cm. The difference for Group E is 1.22 and for Group D, 0.36 cm. It does not seem probable that the members of Group D have higher placed *manubria sterni*, so that it seems logical to surmise that their acromion processes lie at a relatively lower level. The females show a similar phenomenon, but with them it is Group E which shows the smallest difference between the means.

**Relative Shoulder Height.** This index states the relation existing between acromial height and stature. Its table gives evidence which tends to justify the conjectures in the preceding section on subgroup differences in shoulder slope. Members of Group D of the males have, on the average, shoulder heights which, in relation to vertex heights, are definitely lower than those of any other subgroup. The female Group E's value for this index is lower than the other means, but the difference from the Total Yucatecans is not significant.

**Sitting Height.** The rise in the means from Group A to Group E parallels the trend in stature. There is no doubt that this segment of the total length dimension of the body shows marked subgroup

## TABLE 10. SITTING HEIGHT

### MALES

| Group | No. | Range | Mean | S. D. | V. | Significance with Total Yucatecans |
|---|---|---|---|---|---|---|
| Total Yucatecans .. | 862 | 69–94 | 80.85 ±.08 | 3.44 ±.06 | 4.25 ±.07 | |
| Group A .......... | 221 | 69–90 | 80.03 ±.15 | 3.34 ±.11 | 4.17 ±.13 | 6×pe D |
| Group B .......... | 192 | 71–90 | 80.73 ±.15 | 3.14 ±.11 | 3.89 ±.13 | None |
| Group C .......... | 359 | 69–92 | 81.09 ±.12 | 3.47 ±.09 | 4.28 ±.11 | 2×pe D |
| Group D ......... | 45 | 75–88 | 81.77 ±.36 | 3.54 ±.25 | 4.33 ±.31 | 2×pe D |
| Group E .......... | 45 | 75–91 | 82.30 ±.35 | 3.52 ±.25 | 4.28 ±.30 | 4×pe D |
| Cacereños ........ Aranzadi, 1894b | 23 | ... | 84.19 | | | |
| Andalusian Moors . Coon, 1929 | 28 | ... | 85.00 ±.35 | 2.75 ±.25 | 3.24 ±.29 | |
| Mexicans ......... | 48 | ... | 83.12 ±.37 | 3.62 ±.26 | 4.36 ±.31 | |
| Tzentals .......... | 100 | 74–92 | 83.00 | | | |
| Chols ............ | 100 | 72–90 | 81.78 | | | |
| Chontals ........ | 80 | 73–90 | 82.54 | | | |
| Huaxtecs.......... | 100 | 74–92 | 83.08 | | | |
| Tzotzils .......... | 100 | 74–89 | 83.03 | | | |
| *Mayas* ........... Starr, 1902 | 100 | 76–89 | 80.37 | | | |
| Sioux, Pure........ | 538 | 70–98 | 88.50 | 3.50 | 3.95 | |
| Sioux, Half-Blood .. Sullivan, 1920 | 77 | 68–96 | 89.60 | 4.39 | 4.89 | |
| Hawaiians, Pure ... | 69 | ... | 90.11 ±.24 | 2.95 ±.17 | 3.27 ±.19 | |
| F₁ Hawaiian, North European ....... Dunn, Tozzer, 1928 | 10 | 83–94 | 90.69 ±.82 | 3.85 ±.58 | 4.24 | |

TABLE 10. *(Continued)*

FEMALES

| Group | No. | Range | Mean | S.D. | V. | Significance with Total Yucatecans |
|---|---|---|---|---|---|---|
| Total Yucatecans .. | 685 | 65–86 | 74.67 ±.08 | 3.04 ±.06 | 4.07 ±.07 | |
| Group A ......... | 151 | 68–82 | 73.92 ±.19 | 3.42 ±.13 | 4.63 ±.18 | 4×pe D |
| Group B ......... | 228 | 65–82 | 74.20 ±.13 | 2.80 ±.08 | 3.77 ±.12 | 4×pe D |
| Group C ......... | 199 | 65–86 | 74.99 ±.15 | 3.12 ±.11 | 4.16 ±.14 | 2×pe D |
| Group D ........ | 61 | 69–82 | 76.06 ±.23 | 2.62 ±.16 | 3.44 ±.21 | 6×pe D |
| Group E ......... | 46 | 69–83 | 76.28 ±.31 | 3.16 ±.22 | 4.14 ±.29 | 5×pe D |
| Mexicans ........ | 29 | 69–84 | 77.29 ±.42 | 3.34 ±.30 | 4.32 ±.38 | |
| *Mayas* .......... | 25 | 68–79 | 72.89 | | | |
| Huaxtecs.......... | 20 | 73–83 | 77.45 | | | |
| Tzendals ........ | 25 | 72–82 | 77.20 | | | |
| Chols ........... | 25 | 68–85 | 74.81 | | | |
| Chontals ........ | 25 | 75–86 | 78.80 | | | |
| Tzotzils .......... | 25 | 73–87 | 78.36 | | | |
|     Starr, 1902 | | | | | | |
| Smith Coll. Students | 100 | 80–93 | 86.84 ±.20 | 2.96 | 3.41 | |
|     Steggerda *et al.*, 1929 | | | | | | |
| Sioux, Pure........ | 156 | 70–94 | 82.10 | 3.49 | 4.25 | |
| Sioux, Half-Blood .. | 19 | 66–90 | 83.00 | 4.91 | 5.91 | |
|     Sullivan, 1920 | | | | | | |
| Hawaiians, Pure ... | 34 | 81–92 | 86.30 | | | |
| ¾ Hawaiian, ¼ North European ....... | 12 | 82–90 | 86.40 | | | |
| F₁ Hawaiian, North European ........ | 10 | 86–89 | 87.50 | | | |
| ¼ Hawaiian, ¾ North European ........ | 6 | 80–93 | 87.30 | | | |
|     Dunn, Tozzer, 1928 | | | | | | |

differences. This fact is more clearly demonstrated in the seriation curves, where bimodality is again seen as a characteristic of the male Groups D and E, and of the female Group E. The modes of highest frequency, as well as of highest value, of the male Groups D and E coincide with one of the Spanish peaks.

The approach of the Whiter averages to the Mexican and Spanish means is fairly close. Starr's values for the Mayas are about the same as for Groups A and B; the Mayas are distinctly shorter than any of the other tribes which he cites. Dunn and Tozzer's data for females and Sullivan's for both sexes indicate the same trend toward superior means as before.

**Tibiale-Sphyrion.** No direct measurement of total length of the lower extremity was made in this study. However, a good estimate of the values for the subgroups can be obtained by subtracting in each case the mean for sitting height from that of

TABLE 11.   TIBIALE–SPHYRION

MALES

| Group | No. | Range | Mean | S. D. | V. | Significance with Total Yucatecans |
|-------|-----|-------|------|-------|-----|------------------------------------|
| Total Yucatecans .. | 492 | 30–41 | 35.82 ±.06 | 2.01 ±.04 | 5.61 ±.12 | |
| Group A ......... | 128 | 30–41 | 35.52 ±.12 | 1.97 ±.08 | 5.55 ±.23 | 2 ×pe D |
| Group B ......... | 108 | 30–41 | 35.44 ±.12 | 1.91 ±.09 | 5.39 ±.25 | 3 ×pe D |
| Group C ......... | 198 | 30–41 | 36.10 ±.09 | 1.97 ±.07 | 5.46 ±.18 | 3 ×pe D |
| Group D ......... | 32 | 32–41 | 35.97 ±.26 | 2.22 ±.19 | 6.17 ±.52 | None |
| Group E ......... | 26 | 32–40 | 36.19 ±.26 | 1.94 ±.18 | 5.36 ±.50 | 1 ×pe D |
| Cacereños ........ | 23 | ... | 38.69[1] | | | |
| Aranzadi, 1894b | | | | | | |

[1] *Höhe des Unterschenckels.*

stature. For males, the results are (in alphabetical order): 74.68, 75.07, 76.14, 76.49, and 76.85; for females: 68.84, 68.68, 69.39, 70.41, and 70.48. The tendency toward rise in the Whiter means is manifested here as in sitting height. Since no statistical constants are available for determination of the significance of the differences, no definite statements can now be made as to whether there are proportional differences between the groups in relative length of trunk and lower extremity.

Data for tibiale-sphyrion length were obtained for males only. The evidence for significance of differences is not as clear-cut as in the case of sitting height, but real subgroup differentiation does occur. The table showing the proportion of trunk height to body height should next be considered.

**Relative Sitting Height.** In neither sex are found significant differences in mean relative sitting height. The Maya Indians are short people and the segments of stature are short in comparison with those of the Whiter progeny of the cross. But the proportion of trunk to stature and of total lower extremity length to stature does not significantly vary.

## TABLE 12. RELATIVE SITTING HEIGHT

### MALES

| Group | No. | Range | Mean | S. D. | V. | Significance with Total Yucatecans |
|---|---|---|---|---|---|---|
| Total Yucatecans .. | 861 | 45–57 | 51.73±.04 | 1.53±.02 | 2.96±.05 | |
| Group A ......... | 221 | 48–57 | 51.76±.07 | 1.53±.05 | 2.96±.10 | None |
| Group B ......... | 192 | 48–57 | 51.88±.07 | 1.50±.05 | 2.89±.10 | 2×pe D |
| Group C ......... | 359 | 45–55 | 51.65±.05 | 1.53±.04 | 2.96±.07 | 1×pe D |
| Group D ......... | 44 | 48–55 | 51.75±.17 | 1.70±.12 | 3.28±.24 | None |
| Group E ......... | 45 | 48–55 | 51.67±.16 | 1.55±.11 | 3.00±.21 | None |
| Andalusian Moors . Coon, 1929 | 28 | ... | 51.89±.17 | 1.35±.12 | 2.60±.23 | |
| Eskimo ........... | ... | ... | 51.40 | | | |
| Nahua ........... | ... | ... | 51.80 | | | |
| Shoshoni ......... | ... | ... | 52.20 | | | |
| Pima ............. | ... | ... | 52.90 | | | |
| Apache ........... | ... | ... | 53.20 | | | |
| Kalmucks ......... | ... | ... | 52.70 | | | |
| Yukuts ........... | ... | ... | 53.00 | | | |
| North Chinese .... | ... | ... | 53.70 | | | |
| Masai ........... (Martin, 1914) | ... | ... | 48.90 | | | |
| Mexicans ......... | 48 | ... | 51.75±.16 | 1.62±.12 | 3.13±.23 | |
| Chontals ........ | 80 | 47–55 | 51.60 | | | |
| Huaxtecs.......... | 100 | 50–56 | 52.80 | | | |
| *Mayas* ........... | 100 | 48–54 | 51.70 | | | |
| Tzotzils ......... | 100 | 49–58 | 53.20 | | | |
| Tzendals ........ | 100 | 51–59 | 53.30 | | | |
| Chols ............ Starr, 1902 | 100 | 49–56 | 52.40 | | | |
| Sioux, Pure........ | 536 | 46–56 | 51.40 | 1.68 | 3.26 | |
| Sioux, Half-Blood .. Sullivan, 1920 | 77 | 41–56 | 51.60 | 1.94 | 3.76 | |
| Hawaiians, Pure ... | 69 | ... | 52.61±.11 | 1.38±.08 | 2.62±.15 | |
| F₁ Hawaiian, North European ....... Dunn, Tozzer, 1928 | 10 | 50–54 | 52.28±.22 | 1.04±.16 | 1.99 | |

TABLE 12. (*Continued*)

FEMALES

| Group | No. | Range | Mean | S.D. | V. | Significance with Total Yucatecans |
|---|---|---|---|---|---|---|
| Total Yucatecans .. | 685 | 47–58 | 51.71±.02 | 0.78±.01 | 1.52±.03 | |
| Group A ......... | 151 | 47–57 | 51.61±.04 | 0.71±.03 | 1.38±.05 | 2×pe D |
| Group B ......... | 228 | 48–56 | 51.72±.03 | 0.78±.02 | 1.50±.05 | None |
| Group C ......... | 199 | 47–58 | 51.74±.04 | 0.84±.03 | 1.63±.06 | 1×pe D |
| Group D ........ | 61 | 47–56 | 51.76±.06 | 0.72±.04 | 1.38±.08 | None |
| Group E ......... | 46 | 48–56 | 51.74±.08 | 0.85±.06 | 1.64±.12 | None |
| Mexicans ........ | 29 | 49–56 | 51.78±.14 | 1.14±.10 | 2.20±.19 | |
| *Mayas* ........... | 25 | 48–55 | 51.50 | | | |
| Huaxtecs.......... | 20 | 50–54 | 52.50 | | | |
| Tzendals ........ | 25 | 51–56 | 53.60 | | | |
| Chols ........... | 25 | 46–64 | 52.80 | | | |
| Chontals ........ | 25 | 51–55 | 53.10 | | | |
| Tzotzils ......... | 25 | 51–60 | 54.20 | | | |
| Starr, 1902 | | | | | | |
| Smith Coll. Students | 100 | 49–56 | 53.28±.88 | 1.31 | 2.46 | |
| Steggerda *et al.*, 1929 | | | | | | |
| French............. | ... | ... | 53.60 | | | |
| Nahua ............ | ... | ... | 52.20 | | | |
| (Martin, 1914) | | | | | | |
| Sioux, Pure........ | 156 | 43–59 | 51.40 | 1.90 | 3.71 | |
| Sioux, Half-Blood .. | 19 | 41–54 | 51.40 | 2.75 | 5.35 | |
| Sullivan, 1920 | | | | | | |
| Hawaiians, Pure ... | 34 | 50–56 | 53.10 | | | |
| ¾ Hawaiian, ¼ North European ...... | 12 | 52–55 | 53.30 | | | |
| F₁ Hawaiian, North European ....... | 10 | 52–55 | 53.70 | | | |
| ¼ Hawaiian, ¾ North European ....... | 6 | 50–55 | 53.00 | | | |
| Dunn, Tozzer, 1928 | | | | | | |

If other peoples are compared with the Yucatecans, it is noted that, in comparison to standing height, the Yucatecans' sitting-height average is smaller than many. The converse of this statement is that, in comparison to stature, the total leg length of Yucatecans is greater. The relative shortness of trunk of Mayas

## TABLE 13.  SPAN

### MALES

| Group | No. | Range | Mean | S. D. | V. | Significance with Total Yucatecans |
|---|---|---|---|---|---|---|
| Total Yucatecans .. | 152 | 151–181 | 166.06 ±.34 | 6.24 ±.24 | 3.76 ±.15 | |
| Group A .......... | 61 | 155–181 | 165.04 ±.48 | 5.62 ±.34 | 3.41 ±.21 | 2 ×pe D |
| Group B .......... | 31 | 151–180 | 165.76 ±.84 | 6.98 ±.60 | 4.21 ±.36 | None |
| Group C .......... | 49 | 155–181 | 167.83 ±.58 | 6.02 ±.41 | 3.59 ±.24 | 3 ×pe D |
| Groups D and E ... | 11 | 155–176 | 165.50 ±.55 | 2.70 ±.39 | 1.63 ±.23 | None |
| Cacereños ........ Aranzadi, 1894b | 23 | ... | 168.80 | | | |
| Andalusian Moors . Coon, 1929 | 28 | ... | 172.11 ±.80 | 6.24 ±.56 | 3.63 ±.33 | |
| Chontals ........ | 80 | 142–182 | 164.86 | | | |
| Huaxtecs.......... | 100 | 148–179 | 163.00 | | | |
| Mayas ........... | 100 | 150–176 | 164.12 | | | |
| Tzotzils .......... | 100 | 145–172 | 160.34 | | | |
| Tzendals ........ | 100 | 142–183 | 161.33 | | | |
| Chols ............ Starr, 1902 | 100 | 129–178 | 161.40 | | | |
| Sioux, Pure........ | 535 | 156–202 | 181.40 | 7.03 | 3.87 | |
| Sioux, Half-Blood .. Sullivan, 1920 | 76 | 164–198 | 182.40 | 6.99 | 3.83 | |

### FEMALES

| Group | No. | Range | Mean | S. D. | V. | Significance with Total Yucatecans |
|---|---|---|---|---|---|---|
| Total Yucatecans .. | 107 | 135–166 | 151.69 ±.35 | 5.34 ±.25 | 3.52 ±.16 | |
| Group A .......... | 24 | 139–162 | 152.50 ±.57 | 4.12 ±.40 | 2.70 ±.26 | 1 ×pe D |
| Group B .......... | 35 | 141–166 | 152.07 ±.66 | 5.82 ±.47 | 3.83 ±.31 | None |
| Group C .......... | 41 | 135–164 | 150.82 ±.50 | 4.74 ±.35 | 3.14 ±.23 | 2 ×pe D |
| Group D ........ | 7 | 145–160 | 152.07 | | | |
| Group E .......... | No data | | | | | |
| Mayas ........... | 25 | 141–156 | 148.24 | | | |
| Huaxtecs.......... | 20 | 140–157 | 150.38 | | | |
| Tzendals ........ | 25 | 131–156 | 145.56 | | | |
| Chols ............ | 25 | 136–154 | 143.81 | | | |
| Chontals ........ | 25 | 141–161 | 150.36 | | | |
| Tzotzils .......... Starr, 1902 | 25 | 134–156 | 145.26 | | | |
| Smith Coll. Students Steggerda et al., 1929 | 100 | 148–176 | 164.02 ±.45 | 6.70 | 4.09 | |
| Sioux, Pure........ | 155 | 150–180 | 168.30 | 6.43 | 3.83 | |
| Sioux, Half-Blood .. Sullivan, 1920 | 19 | 156–180 | 167.40 | 6.79 | 4.05 | |

and Yucatecans in general seems to stand midway between the low averages of some Negroes and the higher of certain Europeans. This characteristic should be kept in mind in the later discussion of body breadths. The Yucatecan average compares well with Starr's Mayas and Chontals and Sullivan's Pure and Half-Blood Sioux. In neither Sullivan's nor Dunn and Tozzer's cases of race mixture between Whites and other peoples does alteration in average of relative sitting height occur.

**Span.** Span is an unsatisfactory measurement from the anthropological viewpoint, because it combines two independent variables — shoulder breadth and the two arm lengths. It is, however, highly correlated with stature. The coefficient of correlation existing between these two measurements for the male Total Yucatecans is .852. In view of the evidence for high correlation, it is remarkable that the trend toward higher stature in the Whiter groups is not mirrored in the data for span. It is true that Group C of either sex does vary somewhat from the Total Yucatecans (but in opposite directions for the sexes), and that the samples in Group D of either sex are small. Even so, the results are interesting; for Starr's Mayas, although the smallest in stature among the tribes cited, have the next to largest average in span.

**Relative Span and Relative Total Arm Length.** In comparison to stature, span of the Yucatecans is large. Groups C and D have smaller averages than the others, in both sexes, but the numbers of cases for the Groups D and E are too small for certain interpretation. Sullivan's male groups are indifferent in this index: his Half-Blood females react in much the same way as the Whiter Yucatecans.

Since span itself is a composite measurement, the question arises as to whether such a difference in proportion is due to the factor in span of arm length or to the factor of shoulder breadth.

The figures presented for total arm length were arrived at by addition in the case of each group of the averages of acromion-radiale and radiale-dactylion. Relative total arm length was then calculated by division of each sum by the appropriate mean stature. Groups E of both sexes are characterized by arms which are shorter in proportion to stature than is the case in the other groups. Again, Sullivan's two sets of males are alike, while his females differ. The latter variation is in the same direction as that

### TABLE 14.   ARM LENGTH

MALES

|  | TOTAL ARM LENGTH Mean | RELATIVE TOTAL ARM LENGTH (Calculated from means) Mean |
|---|---|---|
| Total Yucatecans | 69.66 | 44.5 |
| Group A | 68.94 | 44.6 |
| Group B | 69.28 | 44.5 |
| Group C | 70.10 | 44.6 |
| Group D | 70.37 | 44.5 |
| Group E | 70.08 | 44.0 |
| Sioux, Pure (535) | 77.00 | 44.6 |
| Sioux, Half-Blood (77) | 77.30 | 44.6 |
| Sullivan, 1920 | | |
| Hawaiians, Pure (69) | 77.76 | 45.3 |
| F$_1$ Hawaiian, North European (10) | 78.76 | 45.4 |
| Dunn, Tozzer, 1928 | | |
| French | ... | 44.8 |
| Japanese | ... | 43.2 |
| Buriat | ... | 44.5 |
| Fan | ... | 46.2 |
| Babinga | ... | 47.2 |
| Nunatagmiut Eskimo | ... | 44.1 |
| Shoshoni | ... | 44.6 |
| (Martin, 1914) | | |

FEMALES

|  |  |  |
|---|---|---|
| Total Yucatecans | 63.38 | 44.1 |
| Group A | 62.90 | 44.1 |
| Group B | 63.38 | 44.4 |
| Group C | 63.64 | 44.1 |
| Group D | 64.10 | 43.8 |
| Group E | 63.09 | 43.0 |
| Sioux, Pure (156) | 71.80 | 44.9 |
| Sioux, Half-Blood (19) | 71.00 | 44.1 |
| Sullivan, 1920 | | |
| Hawaiians, Pure | 72.07 | 44.3 |
| F$_1$ Hawaiian, North European | 70.10 | 43.1 |
| Dunn, Tozzer, 1928 | | |

TABLE 15. RELATIVE SPAN

MALES

| Group | No. | Range | Mean | S. D. | V. | Significance with Total Yucatecans |
|---|---|---|---|---|---|---|
| Total Yucatecans .. | 152 | 102–112 | 106.42 ±.12 | 2.12 ±.08 | 1.99 ±.08 | |
| Group A ......... | 61 | 102–112 | 106.62 ±.19 | 2.24 ±.14 | 2.10 ±.13 | 1×pe D |
| Group B ......... | 31 | 103–111 | 106.74 ±.25 | 2.03 ±.17 | 1.90 ±.16 | 1×pe D |
| Group C ......... | 49 | 102–111 | 106.10 ±.20 | 2.10 ±.14 | 1.98 ±.13 | 1×pe D |
| Groups D and E ... | 11 | 102–108 | 105.36 | | | |
| Swedes ............ | ... | ... | 104.00 | | | |
| French............. | ... | ... | 104.40 | | | |
| Chinese .......... | ... | ... | 102.10 | | | |
| Japanese ......... | ... | ... | 102.60 | | | |
| Koreans .......... | ... | ... | 104.00 | | | |
| Eskimo (Nunatagmiut) | | ... | 103.10 | | | |
| Athabascans (Tahltan) | | ... | 103.50 | | | |
| Bella Coola........ | ... | ... | 106.20 | | | |
| Iroquois .......... | ... | ... | 108.90 | | | |
| (Martin, 1914) | | | | | | |
| Chontals ........ | 80 | 98–110 | 103.10 | | | |
| Tzendals ........ | 100 | 98–109 | 103.40 | | | |
| Huaxtecs.......... | 100 | 99–109 | 103.70 | | | |
| Chols ........... | 100 | 98–109 | 103.80 | | | |
| *Mayas* ........... | 100 | 100–111 | 105.60 | | | |
| Starr, 1902 | | | | | | |
| Sioux, Pure........ | 531 | 95–112 | 105.20 | 2.41 | 2.29 | |
| Sioux, Half-Blood .. | 76 | 99–112 | 105.00 | 2.19 | 2.09 | |
| Sullivan, 1920 | | | | | | |

FEMALES

| | | | | | | |
|---|---|---|---|---|---|---|
| Total Yucatecans .. | 107 | 96–113 | 106.00 ±.17 | 2.55 ±.12 | 2.41 ±.11 | |
| Group A ......... | 24 | 103–109 | 106.04 ±.26 | 1.92 ±.19 | 1.81 ±.18 | None |
| Group B ......... | 35 | 100–112 | 106.54 ±.32 | 2.77 ±.22 | 2.60 ±.21 | 2×pe D |
| Group C ......... | 41 | 101–113 | 105.78 ±.24 | 2.27 ±.17 | 2.15 ±.16 | 1×pe D |
| Group D ......... | 7 | 96–109 | 104.43 | | | |
| Group E ......... | | No data | | | | |
| *Mayas* ........... | 25 | 99–111 | 104.70 | | | |
| Huaxtecs.......... | 20 | 98–106 | 102.00 | | | |
| Tzendals ........ | 25 | 96–107 | 101.10 | | | |
| Chols ........... | 25 | 95–107 | 101.70 | | | |
| Chontals ........ | 25 | 96–106 | 101.50 | | | |
| Tzotzils .......... | 25 | 95–105 | 100.70 | | | |
| Starr, 1902 | | | | | | |
| Smith Coll. Students | 100 | 94–101 | 99.41 ±1.0 | 1.48 | 1.49 | |
| Steggerda *et al.*, 1929 | | | | | | |
| Belgians .......... | ... | ... | 101.60 | | | |
| Nahua ............ | ... | ... | 104.70 | | | |
| (Martin, 1914) | | | | | | |
| Sioux, Pure........ | 156 | 97–111 | 105.30 | 2.32 | 2.11 | |
| Sioux, Half-Blood .. | 19 | 100–107 | 103.80 | 1.75 | 1.69 | |
| Sullivan, 1920 | | | | | | |

of the Yucatecans. In comparing the Mayas with twenty-two other Mexican groups, Starr states that their arms are the longest observed. It is not strange, then, that White admixture should modify this unusual trait. It will be interesting to compare the shoulder breadths of the various types of Yucatecans.

TABLE 16. ACROMION–RADIALE

MALES

| Group | No. | Range | Mean | S. D. | V. | Significance with Total Yucatecans |
|---|---|---|---|---|---|---|
| Total Yucatecans .. | 494 | 24–35 | 28.93 ±.06 | 1.85 ±.04 | 6.39 ±.14 | |
| Group A ......... | 129 | 24–33 | 28.61 ±.10 | 1.77 ±.07 | 6.19 ±.26 | 3×pe D |
| Group B ......... | 108 | 24–35 | 28.63 ±.12 | 1.83 ±.08 | 6.39 ±.29 | 2×pe D |
| Group C ......... | 198 | 24–35 | 29.18 ±.09 | 1.85 ±.06 | 6.34 ±.21 | 3×pe D |
| Group D ........ | 32 | 26–33 | 29.37 ±.22 | 1.83 ±.15 | 6.23 ±.53 | 2×pe D |
| Group E ......... | 27 | 24–32 | 29.04 ±.25 | 1.94 ±.18 | 6.68 ±.61 | None |
| Cacereños ........ | 23 | ... | 30.49 | | | |
| Aranzadi, 1894b | | | | | | |

FEMALES

| Group | No. | Range | Mean | S. D. | V. | |
|---|---|---|---|---|---|---|
| Total Yucatecans .. | 395 | 20–35 | 26.26 ±.06 | 1.64 ±.04 | 6.24 ±.15 | |
| Group A ......... | 94 | 22–29 | 25.97 ±.10 | 1.50 ±.07 | 5.78 ±.28 | 3×pe D |
| Group B ......... | 127 | 22–35 | 26.34 ±.10 | 1.66 ±.07 | 6.30 ±.27 | None |
| Group C ......... | 119 | 22–31 | 26.35 ±.10 | 1.62 ±.07 | 6.15 ±.27 | 1×pe D |
| Group D ........ | 31 | 24 31 | 26.63 ±.18 | 1.52 ±.13 | 5.71 ±.49 | 2×pe D |
| Group E ......... | 24 | 20–29 | 26.08 ±.29 | 2.08 ±.20 | 7.97 ±.78 | None |
| Smith Coll. Students | 100 | 25–33 | 29.16 ±.11 | 1.68 | 5.77 | |
| Steggerda et al., 1929 | | | | | | |

**Acromion-Radiale and Radiale-Dactylion.** The notable characteristic of the statistical tables for length of the two arm segments is that although step-like rises occur for each measurement in either sex through Groups A, B, C, and D, the means for Group E fail in continuation of the upward trend. This fact fits in nicely with the deduction made in the section on total arm length — that, in proportion to stature, arm length in Group E is less than in the others.

**Intermembral Index.** The proportion existing between length of the lower extremity and stature does not vary among the Yuca-

## TABLE 17. RADIALE–DACTYLION

### MALES

| Group | No. | Range | Mean | S. D. | V. | Significance with Total Yucatecans |
|---|---|---|---|---|---|---|
| Total Yucatecans . . | 494 | 36–46 | 40.73 ± .06 | 1.99 ± .04 | 4.88 ± .10 | |
| Group A . . . . . . . . . | 129 | 36–45 | 40.33 ± .12 | 1.96 ± .08 | 4.86 ± .20 | 3×pe D |
| Group B . . . . . . . . . | 108 | 36–46 | 40.65 ± .13 | 2.04 ± .09 | 5.02 ± .23 | None |
| Group C . . . . . . . . . | 198 | 36–46 | 40.92 ± .09 | 1.98 ± .07 | 4.83 ± .16 | 2×pe D |
| Group D . . . . . . . . | 32 | 38–45 | 41.00 ± .23 | 1.90 ± .16 | 4.63 ± .39 | 1×pe D |
| Group E . . . . . . . . . | 27 | 38–44 | 41.04 ± .21 | 1.65 ± .15 | 4.02 ± .37 | 1×pe D |
| Cacereños . . . . . . . . Aranzadi, 1894b | 23 | . . . | 43.12 | | | |

### FEMALES

| Total Yucatecans . . | 395 | 30–43 | 37.12 ± .07 | 1.96 ± .05 | 5.28 ± .13 | |
|---|---|---|---|---|---|---|
| Group A . . . . . . . . . | 94 | 30–43 | 36.93 ± .14 | 2.02 ± .10 | 5.47 ± .27 | 1×pe D |
| Group B . . . . . . . . . | 127 | 32–43 | 37.04 ± .11 | 1.88 ± .08 | 5.08 ± .21 | None |
| Group C . . . . . . . . | 119 | 32–43 | 37.29 ± .12 | 1.92 ± .08 | 5.15 ± .23 | 1×pe D |
| Group D . . . . . . . . | 31 | 34–43 | 37.47 ± .27 | 2.26 ± .19 | 6.03 ± .52 | 1×pe D |
| Group E . . . . . . . . . | 24 | 32–41 | 37.00 ± .26 | 1.86 ± .18 | 5.03 ± .49 | None |

## TABLE 18. INTERMEMBRAL INDEX

$$\frac{\text{(Acromion-Radiale} + \text{Radiale-Dactylion)}}{\text{(Stature} - \text{Sitting Height)}}$$

### MALES

| Group | No. | Range | Mean | S. D. | V. | Significance with Total Yucatecans |
|---|---|---|---|---|---|---|
| Total Yucatecans . . | 494 | 79–106 | 91.60 ± .10 | 3.45 ± .07 | 3.77 ± .08 | |
| Group A . . . . . . . . . | 129 | 84–104 | 91.97 ± .22 | 3.74 ± .16 | 4.07 ± .17 | 2×pe D |
| Group B . . . . . . . . . | 108 | 80–106 | 91.97 ± .22 | 3.43 ± .16 | 3.74 ± .17 | None |
| Group C . . . . . . . . . | 198 | 79–101 | 91.27 ± .15 | 3.16 ± .11 | 3.46 ± .12 | 2×pe D |
| Group D . . . . . . . . | 32 | 86–100 | 92.09 ± .39 | 3.29 ± .28 | 3.57 ± .30 | 1×pe D |
| Group E . . . . . . . . . | 27 | 84–101 | 91.37 ± .51 | 3.92 ± .36 | 4.29 ± .39 | None |

### FEMALES

| Total Yucatecans . . | 395 | 81–103 | 91.06 ± .12 | 3.63 ± .09 | 3.99 ± .10 | |
|---|---|---|---|---|---|---|
| Group A . . . . . . . . . | 94 | 84–100 | 90.92 ± .24 | 3.39 ± .17 | 3.73 ± .18 | None |
| Group B . . . . . . . . . | 127 | 81–103 | 91.68 ± .23 | 3.90 ± .17 | 4.25 ± .18 | 3×pe D |
| Group C . . . . . . . . . | 119 | 81–100 | 91.09 ± .22 | 3.49 ± .15 | 3.83 ± .17 | None |
| Group D . . . . . . . . | 31 | 82–97 | 89.81 ± .39 | 3.21 ± .27 | 3.57 ± .31 | 3×pe D |
| Group E . . . . . . . . . | 24 | 83–98 | 89.71 ± .47 | 3.42 ± .33 | 3.81 ± .37 | 2×pe D |

tecan types; the similar proportion of total arm length to stature does so vary. Intermembral index, which represents the ratio between length of upper and length of lower extremity, is thus expected to be, and is, smaller in the Whiter groups, especially the female. The deviation from the Total Yucatecans' mean is especially marked in the female Groups D and E. No male subgroup varies significantly in this index.

## SHOULDERS AND HIPS

**Biacromial Diameter and Relative Shoulder Breadth.** It has been noted that span fails to increase through the subgroups A to E as does stature. It has been pointed out that arm length, in comparison to stature, is less in the E groups of both sexes than in the others. The question arose as to whether shoulder breadth, being a part of the span measurement, is an important factor in the relative shortening of span in the Whiter types. The tabular data for biacromial diameter in the males indicate that from Groups A to C a rise in means occurs, such as is seen in stature, but it is not continued through Groups D and E. The seriation curves (Plate 7) tell the same story for Groups A, B, and C; and higher frequencies of low values are seen in Groups D and E. Among the female types, no truly significant variation in average appears. Group E's seriation curve is irregular, but the modal value is the same for all groups. The result is that the means for relative shoulder breadth are less in the Whiter female types, but of the same general magnitude in the subdivisions of the male Yucatecans. The low values for the Groups E in the relative span average, then, are principally due to smaller proportional length of arm in both sexes, and in the females partly also to relatively narrower shoulders. The sexual difference in reduction of relative shoulder breadth in Yucatecan race mixture reproduces a phenomenon noted by Sullivan in his Siouan case.

## TABLE 19.  BIACROMIAL DIAMETER

### MALES

| Group | No. | Range | Mean | S. D | V. | Significance with Total Yucatecans |
|---|---|---|---|---|---|---|
| Total Yucatecans .. | 494 | 32–42 | 37.59 ±.05 | 1.72 ±.04 | 4.58 ±.10 | |
| Group A .......... | 129 | 34–41 | 37.27 ±.10 | 1.67 ±.07 | 4.48 ±.19 | 3 ×pe D |
| Group B .......... | 108 | 33–42 | 37.43 ±.12 | 1.77 ±.08 | 4.73 ±.22 | 1 ×pe D |
| Group C .......... | 198 | 32–42 | 37.83 ±.08 | 1.69 ±.06 | 4.47 ±.15 | 3 ×pe D |
| Group D ......... | 32 | 35–41 | 37.72 ±.20 | 1.68 ±.14 | 4.45 ±.38 | None |
| Group E .......... | 27 | 35–41 | 37.96 ±.22 | 1.67 ±.15 | 4.40 ±.40 | 1 ×pe D |
| Andalusian Moors . Coon, 1929 | 28 | ... | 37.64 ±.25 | 1.97 ±.18 | 5.23 ±.47 | |
| Chontals ........ | 80 | 31–39 | 35.17 | | | |
| Huaxtecs.......... | 100 | 32–40 | 35.92 | | | |
| *Mayas* .......... | 100 | 32–39 | 36.21 | | | |
| Tzotzils ......... | 100 | 31–38 | 34.69 | | | |
| Tzendals ........ | 100 | 30–40 | 34.22 | | | |
| Chols ........... Starr, 1902 | 100 | 29–39 | 34.67 | | | |
| Sioux, Pure........ | 538 | 30–44 | 38.80 | 1.92 | 4.94 | |
| Sioux, Half-Blood .. Sullivan, 1920 | 76 | 32–42 | 38.90 | 1.89 | 4.83 | |

### FEMALES

| Group | No. | Range | Mean | S. D | V. | Significance with Total Yucatecans |
|---|---|---|---|---|---|---|
| Total Yucatecans .. | 395 | 26–39 | 34.31 ±.05 | 1.58 ±.04 | 4.61 ±.11 | |
| Group A .......... | 94 | 31–38 | 34.39 ±.09 | 1.34 ±.07 | 3.90 ±.19 | None |
| Group B .......... | 127 | 26–39 | 34.18 ±.10 | 1.63 ±.07 | 4.77 ±.20 | 1 ×pe D |
| Group C .......... | 119 | 31–38 | 34.50 ±.08 | 1.35 ±.06 | 3.91 ±.17 | 2 ×pe D |
| Group D ......... | 31 | 30–37 | 34.26 ±.19 | 1.56 ±.13 | 4.55 ±.39 | None |
| Group E .......... | 24 | 26–37 | 33.79 ±.37 | 2.66 ±.26 | 7.87 ±.77 | 1 ×pe D |
| *Mayas* .......... | 25 | 28–35 | 32.54 | | | |
| Huaxtecs.......... | 20 | 30–36 | 32.72 | | | |
| Tzendals ........ | 25 | 29–35 | 31.83 | | | |
| Chols ........... | 25 | 29–34 | 31.05 | | | |
| Chontals ........ | 25 | 30–35 | 32.64 | | | |
| Tzotzils .......... Starr, 1902 | 25 | 28–35 | 32.01 | | | |
| Smith Coll. Students Steggerda *et al.*, 1929 | 100 | 31–39 | 35.60 ±.10 | 1.51 | 4.24 | |
| Sioux, Pure........ | 157 | 30–40 | 35.50 | 2.09 | 5.91 | |
| Sioux, Half-Blood .. Sullivan, 1920 | 19 | 30–40 | 35.40 | 2.21 | 6.24 | |

## TABLE 20. RELATIVE SHOULDER BREADTH

MALES

| Group | No. | Range | Mean | S. D. | V. | Significance with Total Yucatecans |
|---|---|---|---|---|---|---|
| Total Yucatecans .. | 494 | 21–27 | 24.08±.03 | 1.02±.02 | 4.24±.09 | |
| Group A .......... | 129 | 22–26 | 24.15±.06 | 0.95±.04 | 3.93±.16 | 1×pe D |
| Group B ......... | 108 | 21–26 | 24.11±.07 | 1.04±.05 | 4.31±.20 | None |
| Group C .......... | 198 | 21–26 | 24.08±.05 | 1.02±.03 | 4.24±.14 | None |
| Group D ......... | 32 | 21–27 | 24.00±.13 | 1.06±.09 | 4.42±.37 | None |
| Group E .......... | 27 | 22–26 | 23.93±.15 | 1.12±.10 | 4.68±.43 | 1×pe D |
| Andalusian Moors . | 28 | ... | 22.93±.15 | 1.17±.10 | 5.10±.46 | |
| Coon, 1929 | | | | | | |
| French ............ | ... | ... | 18.90 | | | |
| Belgians ........... | ... | ... | 23.40 | | | |
| Yakuts ............ | ... | ... | 21.20 | | | |
| Kalmucks ......... | ... | ... | 24.50 | | | |
| Sudan Negroes..... | ... | ... | 21.80 | | | |
| Swahili ............ | ... | ... | 24.40 | | | |
| Athabascans (Tahltan) | | ... | 22.10 | | | |
| Eskimo (Nunatagmiut) | | ... | 22.60 | | | |
| Eskimo ............ | ... | ... | 24.30 | | | |
| Shoshoni ......... | ... | ... | 23.20 | | | |
| (Martin, 1914) | | | | | | |
| Sioux, Pure........ | 534 | 17–26 | 22.50 | 1.10 | 4.88 | |
| Sioux, Half-Blood .. | 77 | 19–24 | 22.40 | 1.01 | 4.51 | |
| Sullivan, 1920 | | | | | | |
| Chontals ........ | 80 | 19–24 | 21.90 | | | |
| Huaxtecs.......... | 100 | 21–25 | 22.80 | | | |
| *Mayas* ........... | 100 | 21–25 | 23.10 | | | |
| Tzotzils .......... | 100 | 20–24 | 22.20 | | | |
| Tzendals ......... | 100 | 20–24 | 21.90 | | | |
| Chols ............ | 100 | 20–25 | 22.10 | | | |
| Starr, 1902 | | | | | | |

FEMALES

| Group | No. | Range | Mean | S. D. | V. | Significance with Total Yucatecans |
|---|---|---|---|---|---|---|
| Total Yucatecans .. | 395 | 19–26 | 23.90±.04 | 1.09±.03 | 4.56±.11 | |
| Group A .......... | 94 | 22–26 | 24.13±.07 | 1.00±.05 | 4.14±.20 | 3×pe D |
| Group B ......... | 127 | 19–26 | 23.92±.06 | 1.04±.04 | 4.35±.18 | None |
| Group C .......... | 119 | 22–26 | 23.93±.06 | 1.03±.05 | 4.30±.18 | None |
| Group D ......... | 31 | 22–26 | 23.32±.14 | 1.12±.10 | 4.80±.41 | 4×pe D |
| Group E .......... | 24 | 19–26 | 23.46±.19 | 1.41±.14 | 6.01±.59 | 2×pe D |
| *Mayas* ........... | 25 | 21–25 | 22.90 | | | |
| Huaxtecs.......... | 20 | 21–23 | 22.10 | | | |
| Tzendals ......... | 25 | 20–24 | 22.00 | | | |
| Chols ............ | 25 | 20–24 | 21.90 | | | |
| Chontals ......... | 25 | 20–24 | 22.00 | | | |
| Tzotzils .......... | 25 | 20–24 | 22.10 | | | |
| Starr, 1902 | | | | | | |
| French ............ | ... | ... | 16.30 | | | |
| Topinard (Martin, 1914) | | | | | | |
| Germans (Baden) .. ... | | ... | 22.40 | | | |
| Nahua ............ | ... | ... | 21.60 | | | |
| (Martin, 1914) | | | | | | |
| Sioux, Pure........ | 157 | 20–26 | 22.40 | 1.20 | 5.36 | |
| Sioux, Half-Blood .. | 19 | 19–24 | 21.90 | 1.35 | 6.16 | |
| Sullivan, 1920 | | | | | | |

**Bi-Iliac Diameter and Hip-Shoulder Index.** Inspection of the data for males on breadth of the body at the iliac crests enables one to say: the larger the type of man, the wider his hips. That sort of statement was not found strictly applicable in regard to

TABLE 21. BI–ILIAC DIAMETER

MALES

| Group | No. | Range | Mean | S. D. | V. | Significance with Total Yucatecans |
|---|---|---|---|---|---|---|
| Total Yucatecans .. | 492 | 24–32 | 28.19±.04 | 1.44±.03 | 5.11±.11 | |
| Group A .......... | 129 | 24–31 | 27.77±.08 | 1.29±.05 | 4.65±.20 | 6×pe D |
| Group B .......... | 108 | 24–31 | 28.16±.10 | 1.58±.07 | 5.61±.26 | None |
| Group C .......... | 197 | 24–32 | 28.41±.07 | 1.40±.05 | 4.93±.17 | 4×pe D |
| Group D ......... | 32 | 25–32 | 28.28±.18 | 1.50±.13 | 5.30±.45 | None |
| Group E .......... | 26 | 27–32 | 28.65±.16 | 1.18±.11 | 4.12±.39 | 3×pe D |
| Andalusian Moors . Coon, 1929 | 28 | ... | 30.93±.29 | 2.25±.20 | 7.27±.66 | |

FEMALES

| Group | No. | Range | Mean | S. D. | V. | Significance with Total Yucatecans |
|---|---|---|---|---|---|---|
| Total Yucatecans .. | 104 | 24–36 | 27.94±.16 | 2.37±.11 | 8.48±.40 | |
| Group A .......... | 19 | 24–32 | 27.68±.34 | 2.20±.24 | 7.95±.87 | None |
| Group B .......... | 39 | 24–34 | 27.90±.25 | 2.33±.18 | 8.35±.64 | None |
| Group C .......... | 31 | 25–36 | 28.03±.32 | 2.63±.23 | 9.38±.80 | None |
| Group D ......... | 9 | 24–32 | 28.11 | | | |
| Group E .......... | 6 | 27–30 | 28.33 | | | |
| Smith Coll. Students Steggerda et al., 1929 | 100 | 24–32 | 28.55 | 1.56 | 5.43 | |
| Japanese, Hard-working ........ | | | 27.60 | after Ogato | | |
| Japanese, Leisure class ........ | | | 25.30 | after Ogato | | |
| Germans ................... (Martin, 1914) | | | 28.00 | after Martin | | |

shoulder breadth, so that in average hip-shoulder index, Group A has a probably significantly smaller mean, and Group E a probably greater. In other words, it is probable that, as compared to shoulder breadth, the more Indian Yucatecans have narrower hips than the Whiter ones.

The female data for hip breadth are scanty. It may be that the small number of cases of the extreme subgroups does not permit

significant differences to appear. However, the difference between
A and E means in the males is 0.88 cm.; the similar difference for
females is 0.65 cm. From averages of hip breadth and stature,
relative bi-iliac diameter was calculated for the Yucatecan subgroups. All of these values were found to greatly exceed that of the
Smith students, but the latter were not considered comparable
because of differences in age. Ogato's data for two social classes
of Japanese indicate the presence of another factor worthy of consideration — that of functional or environmental influence. It is

### TABLE 22.  HIP-SHOULDER INDEX

$$\frac{\text{Bi-iliac} \times 100}{\text{Biacromial}}$$

#### MALES

| Group | No. | Range | Mean | S. D. | V. | Significance with Total Yucatecans |
|---|---|---|---|---|---|---|
| Total Yucatecans .. | 492 | 65–88 | 75.07 ±.11 | 3.76 ±.08 | 5.01 ±.11 | |
| Group A ......... | 129 | 66–86 | 74.63 ±.22 | 3.73 ±.16 | 5.00 ±.21 | 2×pe D |
| Group B ......... | 108 | 65–88 | 75.19 ±.28 | 4.36 ±.20 | 5.80 ±.27 | None |
| Group C ......... | 197 | 66–85 | 75.22 ±.17 | 3.62 ±.12 | 4.81 ±.16 | 1×pe D |
| Group D ........ | 32 | 69–82 | 74.88 ±.34 | 2.84 ±.24 | 3.97 ±.32 | None |
| Group E ......... | 26 | 71–80 | 75.73 ±.31 | 2.38 ±.22 | 3.14 ±.29 | 2×pe D |
| Fan ................... | | | 65.30 | | | |
| Sudan Negroes............... | | | 74.60 | | | |
| Igorots (Lowland) ......... | | | 72.90 | | | |
| Germans (Baden) ......... | | | 75.80 | | | |
| Jews.................... | | | 74.20 | | | |
| Jews (Weissenberg)......... | | | 76.50 | | | |
| Igorots (Highland) ......... | | | 75.40 | | | |
| (Martin, 1914) | | | | | | |

#### FEMALES

| Group | No. | Range | Mean | S. D. | V. | Significance with Total Yucatecans |
|---|---|---|---|---|---|---|
| Total Yucatecans .. | 104 | 67–94 | 80.88 ±.40 | 6.04 ±.28 | 7.47 ±.35 | |
| Group A ......... | 19 | 71–92 | 80.76 ±1.1 | 7.08 ±.77 | 8.77 ±.96 | None |
| Group B ......... | 39 | 67–93 | 80.27 ±.65 | 6.04 ±.46 | 7.52 ±.57 | 1×pe D |
| Group C ......... | 31 | 75–94 | 81.18 ±.64 | 5.28 ±.45 | 6.50 ±.56 | None |
| Group D ........ | 9 | 71–94 | 82.39 | | | |
| Group E ......... | 6 | 73–88 | 81.50 | | | |
| Smith Coll. Students | 100 | 60–87 | 79.49 ±.28 | 4.11 | 5.17 | |
| Steggerda et al., 1929 | | | | | | |

probable that a tendency toward squatness of build, and that hard work and child-bearing are all responsible for the generally high indices of Yucatecan women. It is to be regretted that a larger number of these women was not measured so that it could be certainly determined whether or not the female Whiter Yucatecans differ significantly from the Indian women in this respect.

## THE THORAX

**Chest Breadth.** Coon's Andalusian Moors exceed the Total Yucatecan males in average stature by over seven and a half centimeters. The Spanish group's superiority in breadth of chest is only about four-tenths of a centimeter. Relative chest breadths for the two groups are roughly 18.19 for the Yucatecans and 17.56 for the Moors. It should be made clear that the relatively large chests

TABLE 23.   CHEST BREADTH

MALES

| Group | No. | Range | Mean | S. D. | V. | Significance with Total Yucatecans |
|---|---|---|---|---|---|---|
| Total Yucatecans .. | 153 | 25–32 | 28.45 ±.08 | 1.39 ±.05 | 4.89 ±.19 | |
| Group A ......... | 61 | 25–32 | 28.28 ±.13 | 1.49 ±.09 | 5.27 ±.32 | 1×pe D |
| Group B ......... | 31 | 26–31 | 28.23 ±.15 | 1.26 ±.11 | 4.46 ±.38 | 1×pe D |
| Group C ......... | 50 | 26–32 | 28.72 ±.12 | 1.28 ±.09 | 4.46 ±.30 | 2×pe D |
| Groups D and E ... | 11 | 27–32 | 28.91 ±.25 | 1.24 ±.18 | 4.29 ±.62 | 1×pe D |
| Andalusian Moors . Coon, 1929 | 28 | ... | 28.82 ±.26 | 2.04 ±.19 | 7.08 ±.65 | |
| African Negroes............... | | | 26.90 | | | |
| French..................... | | | 26.90 | | | |
| Navajo ..................... (Martin, 1914) | | | 29.70 | | | |

FEMALES

| | | | | | | |
|---|---|---|---|---|---|---|
| Total Yucatecans .. | 107 | 22–33 | 26.63 ±.14 | 2.10 ±.10 | 7.89 ±.36 | |
| Group A ......... | 24 | 23–30 | 26.83 ±.24 | 1.72 ±.17 | 6.41 ±.62 | None |
| Group B ......... | 35 | 23–30 | 26.03 ±.20 | 1.75 ±.14 | 6.72 ±.54 | 3×pe D |
| Group C ......... | 41 | 22–31 | 26.46 ±.21 | 2.03 ±.15 | 7.67 ±.57 | None |
| Group D ........ | 7 | 27–33 | 29.86 ±.58 | 2.29 ±.41 | 7.67 ±1.4 | 4×pe D |
| Group E ......... | No data | | | | | |
| Smith Coll. Students Steggerda et al., 1929 | 100 | 21–28 | 25.07 ±.08 | 1.30 | 5.19 | |

of the Mayas and Maya-Whites are not caused by living in a high altitude, for the whole peninsula of Yucatan lies near sea level. The male subgroups show no certainly significant differences in breadth of chest. The female Group D with its seven representa-

TABLE 24.   CHEST DEPTH

MALES

| Group | No. | Range | Mean | S. D. | V. | Significance with Total Yucatecans |
|---|---|---|---|---|---|---|
| Total Yucatecans .. | 153 | 14–22 | 18.74±.07 | 1.30±.05 | 6.94±.27 | |
| Group A ......... | 61 | 16–21 | 18.49±.10 | 1.14±.07 | 6.16±.38 | 3×pe D |
| Group B ......... | 31 | 14–22 | 18.52±.19 | 1.54±.13 | 8.32±.71 | 1×pe D |
| Group C ......... | 50 | 17–22 | 19.04±.11 | 1.18±.08 | 6.20±.42 | 3×pe D |
| Groups D and E ... | 11 | 17–21 | 19.54±.27 | 1.31±.19 | 6.70±.96 | 3×pe D |
| African Negroes............... | | | 19.50 | | | |
| French...................... | | | 19.40 | | | |
| Navajos ..................... | | | 21.60 | | | |
| (Martin, 1914) | | | | | | |

FEMALES

| Group | No. | Range | Mean | S. D. | V. | Significance with Total Yucatecans |
|---|---|---|---|---|---|---|
| Total Yucatecans .. | 107 | 15–24 | 18.45±.11 | 1.71±.08 | 9.27±.43 | |
| Group A ......... | 24 | 16–22 | 18.08±.20 | 1.47±.14 | 8.13±.79 | 1×pe D |
| Group B ......... | 35 | 15–22 | 18.23±.18 | 1.57±.13 | 8.61±.69 | 1×pe D |
| Group C ......... | 41 | 15–21 | 18.39±.15 | 1.41±.11 | 7.67±.57 | None |
| Group D ........ | 7 | 18–24 | 21.14±.60 | 2.36±.43 | 11.16±2.0 | 4×pe D |
| Group E ......... | No data | | | | | |
| Smith Coll. Students | 100 | 15–22 | 18.84±.07 | 1.10 | 5.81 | |
| Steggerda et al., 1929 | | | | | | |

tives has a high average because of two unusually high individual values. The women of Group B, for no known reason, have a significantly small average. It is, however, noteworthy that their mean is higher than that of the Smith students, who are much taller. Groups A, B, and C of both males and females are characterized by possession of high means in chest breadth. Since the number of cases for Groups D and E is so small, it is best to defer comparison in chest size of Indian with Whiter groups until discussion of chest girth.

**Chest Depth.** In contrast to breadth, chest depth in both male and female subgroups favors significantly the Whiter. For the women, however, the subgroup differences are small, the value for Group D females being based upon only seven cases. That the mean chest depths of the Yucatecan women are absolutely great is

### TABLE 25.   THORACIC INDEX

MALES

| Group | No. | Range | Mean | S. D. | V. | Significance with Total Yucatecans |
|---|---|---|---|---|---|---|
| Total Yucatecans .. | 153 | 129–196 | 151.88 ±.60 | 10.90 ±.42 | 7.18 ±.28 | |
| Group A ......... | 61 | 136–186 | 152.78 ±.85 | 9.82 ±.60 | 6.43 ±.39 | None |
| Group B ......... | 31 | 137–196 | 153.56 ±1.5 | 12.14 ±1.0 | 7.91 ±.68 | None |
| Group C ......... | 50 | 129–181 | 151.46 ±1.1 | 11.44 ±.77 | 7.55 ±.51 | None |
| Groups D and E ... | 11 | 135–165 | 149.68 ±1.8 | 9.08 ±1.3 | 6.07 ±.87 | None |
| African Negroes.............. | | | 138.00 | | | |
| Hova ..................... | | | 143.50 | | | |
| Navajo .................... | | | 137.50 | | | |
| French..................... | | | 138.60 | | | |
| Bugu ..................... | | | 124.00 | | | |
| (Martin, 1914) | | | | | | |

| Age | Europeans | Mean Negroes |
|---|---|---|
| 16–20 | | 139.00 |
| 21–25 | 134.00 | 142.00 |
| 26–30 | | 143.70 |
| 31–40 | 135.80 | 139.20 |
| 41–50 | | 137.50 |
| 51–60 | | 136.90 |
| 61–70 | | 136.00 |
| Over 70 | 129.20 | 138.90 |
| (Martin, 1914) | | |

FEMALES

| Group | No. | Range | Mean | S. D. | V. | Significance with Total Yucatecans |
|---|---|---|---|---|---|---|
| Total Yucatecans .. | 107 | 123–172 | 144.71 ±.65 | 9.96 ±.46 | 6.88 ±.32 | |
| Group A ......... | 24 | 129–166 | 148.75 ±1.2 | 8.84 ±.86 | 5.94 ±.58 | 3×pe D |
| Group B ......... | 35 | 123–162 | 143.04 ±1.0 | 9.20 ±.74 | 6.43 ±.52 | 1×pe D |
| Group C ......... | 41 | 123–172 | 144.23 ±1.1 | 10.16 ±.76 | 7.04 ±.52 | None |
| Group D ........ | 7 | 131–168 | 142.07 | | | |
| Group E ......... | | No data | | | | |
| Europeans ................... | | | 132.90 | | | |
| Negroes .................... | | | 139.80 | | | |
| (Martin, 1914) | | | | | | |

demonstrated by comparison with the Smith students. No such definite evidence is forthcoming in the case of the males, although their chest depths are by no means small.

**Thoracic Index.** The proportionately broader chests of Yucatecan males are indicated by comparison of the various subgroup means for thoracic index with those cited by Martin. The chests of Yucatecans are absolutely large, and especially so in the transverse diameter. Those of the females of all subgroups are proportionately much broader than those of the Smith women; this is expected in view of the previous discussion of absolute values.

**Chest Girth (at rest).** The male subgroups have been shown to differ insignificantly in breadth of chest, but significantly in favor of the Whiter groups in depth. In circumference, Group A has a

### TABLE 26. CHEST GIRTH

(At rest and at level of upper border of fourth chondro-sternal articulation)

#### MALES

| Group | No. | Range | Mean | S. D. | V. | Significance with Total Yucatecans |
|---|---|---|---|---|---|---|
| Total Yucatecans .. | 858 | 77–107 | 89.20 ± .12 | 5.04 ± .08 | 5.65 ± .09 | |
| Group A .......... | 221 | 77–102 | 88.36 ± .22 | 4.95 ± .16 | 5.60 ± .18 | 4 × pe D |
| Group B .......... | 193 | 77–105 | 88.83 ± .24 | 4.86 ± .17 | 5.47 ± .19 | 1 × pe D |
| Group C .......... | 359 | 77–106 | 89.79 ± .17 | 4.92 ± .12 | 5.48 ± .14 | 4 × pe D |
| Group D ......... | 40 | 79–117 | 90.72 ± .70 | 6.57 ± .50 | 7.24 ± .55 | 2 × pe D |
| Group E .......... | 45 | 79–108 | 89.40 ± .58 | 5.76 ± .41 | 6.44 ± .46 | None |
| Serbs ....................... | | | 80.00 | | | |
| Russians, Bulgarians ........... | | | 81.00 | | | |
| Bavarians ................... | | | 87.00 | | | |
| French...................... | | | 88.70 | | | |
| English ..................... | | | 88.70 | | | |

Martin, 1914 (Davenport and Love, 1921)

U. S. (Davenport and Love, 1921)

| | | | | | | |
|---|---|---|---|---|---|---|
| French (167 cm. Stature) ....... | | | 80.10 | | | |
| (170 cm. Stature) ....... | | | 84.40 | | | |
| (174 cm. Stature) ....... | | | 88.70 | | | |

(Martin, 1914)

#### FEMALES

| Group | No. | Range | Mean | S. D. | V. | Significance with Total Yucatecans |
|---|---|---|---|---|---|---|
| Total Yucatecans .. | 688 | 67–120 | 86.52 ± .18 | 7.11 ± .13 | 8.22 ± .15 | |
| Group A .......... | 152 | 73–109 | 86.71 ± .36 | 6.54 ± .25 | 7.54 ± .29 | None |
| Group B .......... | 229 | 70–109 | 86.37 ± .28 | 6.36 ± .20 | 7.36 ± .23 | None |
| Group C .......... | 199 | 67–120 | 86.89 ± .37 | 7.71 ± .26 | 8.87 ± .30 | 1 × pe D |
| Group D ......... | 62 | 70–108 | 86.44 ± .68 | 7.92 ± .48 | 9.16 ± .56 | None |
| Group E .......... | 46 | 69–111 | 85.09 ± .83 | 8.37 ± .59 | 9.84 ± .69 | 1 × pe D |
| Mexicans ......... | 29 | 73–96 | 82.47 ± .61 | 4.88 ± .43 | 5.92 ± .52 | |

definitely smaller mean, Group C a larger, and Group D a probably larger; Group E fails to follow the lead of Groups C and D toward greater average circumference.

Davenport and Love's Army measurements of chest girth were taken "over the nipples, and perpendicular to the axis of the trunk at this level." There is, no doubt, great personal error in this measurement, but the techniques of the Army measurers and that of the writer are on the average comparable. Comparison with the

TABLE 27.   RELATIVE CHEST GIRTH

MALES

| Group | No. | Range | Mean | S. D. | V. | Significance with Total Yucatecans |
|---|---|---|---|---|---|---|
| Total Yucatecans . . | 860 | 47–69 | 57.02 ±.07 | 3.21 ±.05 | 5.63 ±.09 | |
| Group A . . . . . . . . . | 221 | 50–64 | 57.08 ±.14 | 3.06 ±.10 | 5.36 ±.17 | None |
| Group B . . . . . . . . . | 193 | 50–68 | 57.03 ±.14 | 2.95 ±.10 | 5.17 ±.18 | None |
| Group C . . . . . . . . . | 358 | 47–69 | 57.08 ±.11 | 3.22 ±.08 | 5.64 ±.14 | None |
| Group D  . . . . . . . . | 43 | 51–68 | 57.12 ±.38 | 3.71 ±.27 | 6.50 ±.47 | None |
| Group E . . . . . . . . . | 45 | 49–68 | 56.22 ±.41 | 4.09 ±.29 | 7.27 ±.52 | 2×pe D |
| Belgians . . . . . . . . . . . . . . . . . . . . | | | 52.80 | | | |
| French. . . . . . . . . . . . . . . . . . . . . . | | | 53.70 | | | |
| Ba-Tua . . . . . . . . . . . . . . . . . . . . . | | | 47.30 | | | |
| Bushmen. . . . . . . . . . . . . . . . . . . . . | | | 49.00 | | | |
| Iroquois . . . . . . . . . . . . . . . . . . . . . | | | 55.70 | | | |
| Nahua  . . . . . . . . . . . . . . . . . . . . . | | | 56.00 | | | |
| Yaghan  . . . . . . . . . . . . . . . . . . . . . | | | 58.70 | | | |
| (Martin, 1914) | | | | | | |

FEMALES

| Group | No. | Range | Mean | S. D. | V. | Significance with Total Yucatecans |
|---|---|---|---|---|---|---|
| Total Yucatecans . . | 685 | 46–80 | 60.20 ±.13 | 5.02 ±.09 | 8.34 ±.15 | |
| Group A . . . . . . . . . | 151 | 51–75 | 60.76 ±.26 | 4.72 ±.18 | 7.77 ±.30 | 2×pe D |
| Group B . . . . . . . . . | 227 | 47–73 | 60.44 ±.20 | 4.49 ±.14 | 7.43 ±.24 | 1×pe D |
| Group C . . . . . . . . . | 199 | 48–80 | 60.43 ±.25 | 5.33 ±.18 | 8.82 ±.30 | 1×pe D |
| Group D  . . . . . . . . | 62 | 48–70 | 58.94 ±.43 | 5.07 ±.31 | 8.60 ±.52 | 3×pe D |
| Group E . . . . . . . . . | 46 | 46–74 | 58.04 ±.60 | 6.01 ±.42 | 10.35 ±.73 | 3×pe D |
| Belgians . . . . . . . . . . . . . . . . . . . . | | | 53.00 | | | |
| French. . . . . . . . . . . . . . . . . . . . . . | | | 52.70 | | | |
| Ba-Tua . . . . . . . . . . . . . . . . . . . . . | | | 46.70 | | | |
| Bushmen. . . . . . . . . . . . . . . . . . . . . | | | 46.30 | | | |
| (Martin, 1914) | | | | | | |

Army data indicates that all Yucatecans are, on the average, absolutely (and judging from stature, relatively) large-chested. Martin's values are not based on the same technique, for the measurements quoted from him were taken at a higher level of the chest than were those of the author or of the Army.

TABLE 28.  VITAL CAPACITY

MALES

| Group | No. | Range | Mean | S. D. | V. | Significance with Total Yucatecans |
|---|---|---|---|---|---|---|
| Total Yucatecans .. | 85 | 3000–5100 | 3957 ±39 | 533 ±28 | 13.47 ±.70 | |
| Group A ......... | 30 | 3000–4900 | 3843 ±63 | 510 ±44 | 13.27 ±1.2 | 2×pe D |
| Group B ......... | 22 | 3000–4900 | 3959 ±70 | 484 ±49 | 12.23 ±1.2 | None |
| Group C ......... | 26 | 3100–4900 | 4039 ±69 | 532 ±49 | 13.17 ±1.2 | 1×pe D |
| Groups D and E ... | 7 | 3000–5100 | 4064 ±168 | 658 ±119 | 16.19 ±2.9 | None |

French, age 20–25 years .......... (Martin, 1914)

$\left\{\begin{array}{l} 3529 \text{ (Stature 167 and Chest Circum. 80)} \\ 3868 \text{ (Stature 170 and Chest Circum. 84)} \\ 4351 \text{ (Stature 174 and Chest Circum. 89)} \end{array}\right.$

Filipinos .......... .. 2800–3000
Bobbit (Martin, 1914)

3727 Dreyer's Class A when Wt. = 54.5 k.
3403 Dreyer's Class B when Wt. = 54.5 k.
3183 Dreyer's Class C when Wt. = 54.5 k.

3300 Class A when Sitting Ht. = 80.8 cm.
3013 Class B when Sitting Ht. = 80.8 cm.
2818 Class C when Sitting Ht. = 80.8 cm.

4519 Class A when Chest Girth = 89.2 cm.
4126 Class B when Chest Girth = 89.2 cm.
3860 Class C when Chest Girth = 89.2 cm.
Dreyer, 1921

The Yucatecan female subgroups have no one mean that is significantly different from that of the whole group. As pointed out above, size of chest is absolutely great, and also relatively so, as is seen when the mean for Mexican females (also measured by the writer) is compared with the various averages for Yucatecans.

**Relative Chest Girth.** The index of relative chest girth is computed by dividing girth by stature. The implication that the relatively great size of chest in comparison with stature is an Indian characteristic is suggested by two facts: (1) Group E of the males and Groups D and E of the females have smaller chests relative to stature than do the remaining subgroups; (2) average relative chest girth is greater in American Indian groups than in any others cited by Martin.

**Vital Capacity.** No significant differences appear in the data for vital capacity. There is, however, statistical probability that Group A has a smaller mean than the whole group. The data for vital capacity in any case are not expected to be strictly parallel with those for chest measurements, because a psychological factor — that of the subject making his best effort — is intruded.

The data obtained for females are too scanty to justify presentation.

## BODY BUILD

The discussion of the physical characteristics of the Yucatecan subgroups has brought out the following facts:

1. Maya Indians are absolutely small in stature. The Whiter types of the race-mixture progeny are taller.

2. The relative shortness of trunk of the Mayas, and of Yucatecans in general, stands midway between the proportionately short trunks of most Negroes and the proportionately long ones of many Whites.

3. The arms of the Indians are absolutely long; those of the Whiter types are shorter.

4. Indian types of the Yucatecans have squarer shoulders than do the Whiter.

5. Yucatecans as a group have, in relation to stature, broader shoulders than most peoples. No significant subgroup differences are found among the males, but the shoulders of the Whiter women are proportionately narrower than are those of the Indian females.

6. The proportion of pelvic breadth to stature for Yucatecan males is not unusual; that index for females is higher than the values for European Whites and leisure-class Japanese, but compares well with the average figure for hard-working Japanese women.

7. Yucatecans in general have large chests relative to their stature. The Whiter of the miscegenetic progeny are less well endowed in this respect.

It would appear from the foregoing summary that Maya Indians are characterized by possession of short and broad trunks com-

### TABLE 29. WEIGHT (IN KILOGRAMS)

MALES

| Group | No. | Range | Mean | S. D. | V. | Significance with Total Yucatecans |
|---|---|---|---|---|---|---|
| Total Yucatecans .. | 576 | 41–99 | 54.49 ±.19 | 6.73 ±.13 | 12.35 ±.24 | |
| Group A ......... | 163 | 41–69 | 52.86 ±.32 | 6.08 ±.23 | 11.50 ±.43 | 5 ×pe D |
| Group B ......... | 133 | 42–77 | 54.32 ±.38 | 6.46 ±.27 | 11.89 ±.49 | None |
| Group C ......... | 233 | 41–99 | 55.03 ±.28 | 6.29 ±.20 | 11.43 ±.36 | 2 ×pe D |
| Group D ........ | 27 | 42–98 | 55.98 ±1.3 | 10.34 ±.95 | 18.47 ±1.7 | 1 ×pe D |
| Group E ......... | 20 | 48–80 | 59.40 ±1.2 | 7.86 ±.84 | 13.23 ±1.4 | 4 ×pe D |
| Polish Jews................ | | | 55.00 | | | |
| Roumanians ............... | | | 58.40 | | | |
| Annamese ................. | | | 51.30 | | | |
| Japanese ................. | | | 52.7–56.2 | | | |
| Koreans .................. | | | 56.40 | | | |
| Trumai ................... | | | 58.20 | | | |
| (Martin, 1914) | | | | | | |
| Mulattoes (American) ....... | | | 65.80 | | | |
| Iroquois................... | | | 73.80 | | | |
| Gould (Martin, 1914) | | | | | | |
| Belgians ................... | | | 65.00 | | | |
| Norwegians ................ | | | 66.00 | | | |
| (Martin, 1914) | | | | | | |
| U. S. Troops (Demobilization, 1919) | | | | | | |
| White ..................... | | | 65.86 | | | |
| Negro ..................... | | | 67.83 | | | |
| Indian (N. A.) ............. | | | 68.10 | | | |
| Chinese ................... | | | 67.56 | | | |
| Japanese ................. | | | 65.73 | | | |
| French.................... | | | 64.48 | | | |
| Italian ................... | | | 62.59 | | | |
| Davenport and Love, 1921 | | | | | | |
| Hawaiians, Pure ... ... ... | | | 77.00 | | | |
| F₁ Hawaiian, North European ....... | 9 | ... | 88.13 | | | |
| Dunn, Tozzer, 1928 | | | | | | |

FEMALES

| Group | No. | Range | Mean | S. D. | V. | Significance with Total Yucatecans |
|---|---|---|---|---|---|---|
| Total Yucatecans .. | 304 | 32–94 | 50.36 ±.35 | 8.91 ±.25 | 17.69 ±.49 | |
| Group A .......... | 66 | 35–70 | 49.99 ±.56 | 6.73 ±.40 | 13.46 ±.79 | None |
| Group B ......... | 101 | 32–74 | 48.87 ±.52 | 7.69 ±.36 | 15.74 ±.75 | 3 ×pe D |
| Group C ......... | 103 | 34–94 | 50.98 ±.65 | 9.85 ±.46 | 19.33 ±.91 | 1 ×pe D |
| Group D ......... | 19 | 34–86 | 53.62 ±1.8 | 11.96 ±1.3 | 22.31 ±2.4 | 1 ×pe D |
| Group E ......... | 15 | 34–78 | 55.74 ±1.9 | 10.76 ±1.3 | 19.31 ±2.4 | 2 ×pe D |
| Smith Coll. Students | 100 | 44–72 | 55.59 ±.82 | 12.10 | 21.77 | |
| Steggerda et al., 1929 | | | | | | |
| Hawaiians, Pure ... | 34 | 51–107 | 69.59 | | | |
| ¾ Hawaiian, ¼ North European ......·. | 12 | 43–90 | 71.73 | | | |
| ¼ Hawaiian, ¾ North European ....... | 6 | 50–62 | 57.45 | | | |
| Dunn, Tozzer, 1928 | | | | | | |

bined with long arms. The Maya Indian leaven in the mixture shows its effect in the build of the Whiter progeny in many respects, although segregation of a tendency toward relative spareness in the latter is also evident. Body weight may now be considered.

**Weight.** As in stature, so in weight: progression from the more Indian subgroups to the Whiter is marked by significant increase

TABLE 30.  INDEX OF BODILY FULLNESS

$$\frac{\text{Weight (Kilos)} \times 100}{\text{Stature (cm.) cubed}}$$

(Calculated from means)

| MALES | | FEMALES | |
|---|---|---|---|
| Group | Mean | Group | Mean |
| Total Yucatecans ........ | 1.42 | Total Yucatecans........ | 1.69 |
| Group A ............... | 1.43 | Group A ............... | 1.72 |
| Group B ............... | 1.44 | Group B ............... | 1.68 |
| Group C ............... | 1.42 | Group C ............... | 1.69 |
| Group D ............... | 1.41 | Group D ............... | 1.71 |
| Group E ............... | 1.47 | Group E ............... | 1.76 |
| Norwegians ............. | 1.29 | Hawaiians, Pure (34) ..... | 1.61 |
| Swiss (Schaffhausen) ...... | 1.35 | $\frac{3}{4}$ Hawaiian, $\frac{1}{4}$ North | |
| Japanese................. | 1.22 | European (12) ......... | 1.69 |
| Koreans ................ | 1.30 | $\frac{1}{4}$ Hawaiian, $\frac{3}{4}$ North | |
| North Chinese........... | 1.37 | European (6) .......... | 1.28 |
| Baluba (Africa).......... | 1.10 | Dunn, Tozzer, 1928 | |
| Trumai................. | 1.43 | | |
| (Martin, 1914) | | | |
| Hawaiians, Pure ........ | 1.53 | | |
| $F_1$ Hawaiian, N. European.. | 1.68 | | |
| U. S. Soldiers, 1917 ....... | 1.30–1.35 | | |
| Dunn, Tozzer, 1928 | | | |

in values. As pointed out previously in discussion of stature, there is no evidence for heterosis. The seriation curves (Plate 8) show the distribution of this character in the various subgroups in a way that the list of means can not. For comparison with the Yucatecan groups, no Spanish data were available; the curve used for comparison is that of another South European group — Italians of the U. S. Army in the World War. The trend of the means shows that the Whiter the subgroup, the greater the average weight; the trend of the modes indicates that the Whiter the sub-group, the greater the frequency of heavier individuals.

In comparison with other world peoples, Maya Indians are short, and are also seen to be lighter in weight. They fall in approximately the same weight class as the Annamese, Japanese, and Koreans, and are much lighter, on the average, than any of the U. S. troops

### TABLE 31.   INDEX OF BUILD

(The index here used is that used by Davenport and Love, 1921, p. 164.)

$$\frac{\text{Weight (pounds)} \times 1000}{\text{Height (inches) squared}}$$

#### MALES

| Group | No. | Range | Mean | S. D. | V. | Significance with Total Yucatecans |
|---|---|---|---|---|---|---|
| Total Yucatecans .. | 577 | 24–48 | 31.62 ±.09 | 3.12 ±.06 | 9.87 ±.20 | |
| Group A .......... | 164 | 24–38 | 31.38 ±.15 | 2.93 ±.11 | 9.34 ±.35 | 1 ×pe D |
| Group B .......... | 134 | 26–44 | 31.68 ±.18 | 3.02 ±.12 | 9.53 ±.39 | None |
| Group C .......... | 232 | 25–46 | 31.56 ±.13 | 2.99 ±.09 | 9.47 ±.30 | None |
| Group D ......... | 27 | 27–48 | 31.70 ±.57 | 4.43 ±.41 | 13.97 ±1.3 | None |
| Group E .......... | 20 | 28–43 | 33.50 ±.61 | 4.06 ±.43 | 12.12 ±1.3 | 3 ×pe D |
| English ..................... | | | 31.59 | | | |
| Scotch .................... | | | 31.41 | | | |
| Irish....................... | | | 31.41 | | | |
| German ................... | | | 32.31 | | | |
| French..................... | | | 32.28 | | | |
| Italian ................... | | | 32.63 | | | |
| Polish ..................... | | | 32.73 | | | |
| Hebrew ................... | | | 31.93 | | | |
| Indians (N. A.) ............. | | | 32.93 | | | |
| Chinese ................... | | | 32.82 | | | |
| Negro-Mulatto ............. | | | 32.63 | | | |
| Japanese .................. | | | 32.00 | | | |

Davenport and Love, 1921

#### FEMALES

| Group | No. | Range | Mean | S. D. | V. | Significance with Total Yucatecans |
|---|---|---|---|---|---|---|
| Total Yucatecans .. | 304 | 24–60 | 34.43 ±.21 | 5.42 ±.15 | 15.74 ±.43 | |
| Group A .......... | 66 | 25–46 | 33.68 ±.35 | 4.18 ±.25 | 12.41 ±.73 | 2 ×pe D |
| Group B ......... | 101 | 25–46 | 34.17 ±.31 | 4.64 ±.22 | 13.58 ±.64 | None |
| Group C .......... | 103 | 24–60 | 34.63 ±.42 | 6.30 ±.30 | 18.19 ±.85 | None |
| Group D ......... | 19 | 24–53 | 35.29 ±1.1 | 7.30 ±.80 | 20.69 ±2.3 | None |
| Group E .......... | 15 | 27–48 | 37.1 ±.88 | 5.06 ±.62 | 13.64 ±1.7 | 3 ×pe D |

cited, even including the better nourished Japanese of the U. S. World War Army.

**Indices of Build.** Three formulas for index of build were applied to the Yucatecan material. One of these, Rohrer's index of bodily fullness, was calculated from means. Concerning this formula, Martin (1914) states, "Die Körperfülle ist gleich dem prozentualen Verhältnis der Körpervolumens zum Längenwürfel ... Dies Formel lässt den Unterschied in der Entwicklung der Körperfülle am besten hervortreten." Comparison with Martin's list of average values for various peoples shows that the Yucatecan males have relatively heavy bodies for their stature. The male Group D has the smallest mean of all the subgroups, and Group C stands close, but Group E has the highest value of all. Among the female groups, much the same sort of situation obtains. The conclusions from these data are that bodily fullness is greatest in the E groups and least in the D group of both sexes. But in the summary at the beginning of this section, it was pointed out that the more Indian, not the Whiter of the Yucatecan progeny, have the proportionately broader shoulders and the larger chests. Perhaps the explanation of the paradox is that the nutrition of the Groups E is better than that of the other types; possibly the formula has faults.

Rohrer's index of bodily fullness considers the body as a cube. All bodies are therefore considered as of the same general shape. As a matter of fact, bodies are not cubes or spheres, and they do differ in shape. It may be well to consider the results of the application of another formula to the material at hand.

Davenport and Love (1921) recommend highly as an index of build the formula in which weight is divided by the second power of stature. They state that the formula fits natural conditions well because the form of the body lies between the two hypothetical conditions of a cylinder of equal dimensions and a cube or sphere. This index of build was calculated for each individual of the two Yucatecan series; means and their statistical constants were then calculated for the subgroups. The means for both sexes rise in steps in much the same manner as noted in stature and weight. The only truly significant subgroup differences, are, however, those of the Groups E, who have the highest values. The reason for this in both sexes is apparent on examination of the frequency curves for this index (Plate 9); larger minorities of persons heavy for their stature are found in the Groups E of both sexes than in any of the other types.

It should be remarked that such indices as those of bodily fullness and of body build consider the amount of total bulk that goes with a given stature. That bulk consists mainly of bony framework, musculature, and fat. In the cases of individuals of high indices, it is impossible to determine from the values alone which

TABLE 32. INDEX OF ROBUSTNESS

Stature in centimeters — (chest girth at rest in centimeters + weight in kilograms) [1]

(Calculated from means)

| MALES | | FEMALES | |
|---|---|---|---|
| Group | Mean | Group | Mean |
| Total Yucatecans ....... | 12.74 | Total Yucatecans......... | 6.99 |
| Group A .............. | 13.49 | Group A .............. | 6.06 |
| Group B .............. | 12.65 | Group B .............. | 7.64 |
| Group C .............. | 12.41 | Group C .............. | 6.51 |
| Group D .............. | 11.56 | Group D .............. | 6.41 |
| Group E .............. | 10.35 | Group E .............. | 5.93 |

[1] Pignet (1901) offers the following table of standards, by which one can interpret the results obtained by the formula (Davenport and Love, 1921):

Class A — Under 10: A very powerful constitution.
Class B — 11 to 20: Good constitution.
Class C — 21 to 25: Mediocre constitution.
Class D — 26 to 30: Weak constitution.
Class E — 31 to 35: Very weak constitution.
Class F — Over 36: Extraordinarily weak constitution.

ones of the three factors are responsible for the numerical result obtained. It would appear from the data of the table on index of build that the male groups A, B, C, and D rate slightly below the sparest groups of the United States Army, and that Group E possesses a slightly higher average. It will later be demonstrated that the men of Group E have better opportunities for good nutrition than those of at least Groups A, B, and C, and that their work is apt to be of a more sedentary nature. It is therefore possible that these men are fatter than the others.

But the possibility that the men of Group E are fatter does not mean that they have the stronger constitutions. The evidence from bony measurements seems rather to point to the opposite conclusion. Fortunately there is available a so-called index of robustness, devised by Pignet. It takes into account the factor of chest size (girth), as well as the factors of magnitude of stature and weight. The data presented in the table were calculated from means. Even with this imperfect method, the writer believes that the differences in results for the various subgroups are sufficiently great to warrant certain conclusions being drawn.

The average Yucatecan has, according to Pignet's classification, a good constitution. The fact that he is small of stature conduces toward rather than opposes such a result. In respect to bony body framework, the more Indian Yucatecans appear to be better equipped than many peoples; but better nutrition and greater freedom from hard work has probably allowed the individuals of Whiter type to better already good constitutions.

The women in all three indices possess higher values than the men. Most of them lead active lives, and the usual physiological changes peculiar to the sex, causing a tendency toward obesity, operate here as elsewhere. It was particularly noted by the writer that obese men are almost a rarity in Yucatan, but that heavy women, especially those of middle life, are by no means uncommon.

It may be concluded that the nutritive state of Yucatecans in general varies little from the human average, but that their natural endowment in bodily sturdiness is somewhat above that average.

## PHYSIOLOGICAL OBSERVATIONS

**Blood Pressure.** The data on blood pressure are of chief interest in comparison with the recently published work of C. P. Donnison, late Medical Officer of the East African Medical Service. Dr. Donnison studied the blood pressure of apparently healthy Kavirondo Negro males of ages varying from fifteen to seventy. Table 33 shows Donnison's findings, compared with Dally's blood-pressure estimate for normal Europeans and Americans, and the data for Yucatecans. It will be interesting to consider Donnison's comments on his own work:

The (Kavirondo) natives live under primitive conditions, that is, under conditions which have probably undergone no appreciable change for many centuries. . . . In two years' observation at a native hospital while eighteen hundred patients were seen, no case of raised blood pressure was encountered, though abnormally low were not uncommonly noted. On no occasion was a

## TABLE 33. BLOOD PRESSURE AND AGE

| Age | Yucatecans — Males | | | | Yucatecans — Females | | | | Kavirondo Negroes[2] | | | | Americans, Europeans[3] | | |
|---|---|---|---|---|---|---|---|---|---|---|---|---|---|---|---|
| | No. | Mean Sys. | Mean Dias. | Mean P.P.[4] | No. | Mean Sys. | Mean Dias. | Mean P.P. | No. | Mean Sys. | Mean Dias. | Mean P.P. | S | D | P.P. |
| 15–19[1] | 17 | 113.6 | 67.6 | 46.0 | 15 | 113.6 | 70.0 | 43.6 | 99 | 123.1 | 81.9 | 41.2 | 123 | 80 | 43 |
| 20–24 | 34 | 112.2 | 70.0 | 42.2 | 15 | 112.7 | 71.1 | 41.6 | 100 | 122.8 | 80.0 | 42.8 | 125 | 81 | 44 |
| 25–29 | 26 | 113.9 | 71.2 | 42.7 | 16 | 108.0 | 67.5 | 40.5 | 100 | 126.4 | 84.0 | 42.4 | 126 | 82 | 44 |
| 30–34 | 15 | 121.4 | 75.2 | 46.2 | 12 | 113.2 | 70.8 | 42.4 | 115 | 126.0 | 84.7 | 41.3 | 127 | 83 | 44 |
| 35–39 | 11 | 119.3 | 74.2 | 45.1 | 7 | 113.4 | 71.4 | 42.0 | 100 | 125.6 | 85.9 | 39.7 | 128 | 84 | 44 |
| 40–44 | 12 | 121.7 | 74.3 | 47.4 | 17 | 114.0 | 72.9 | 41.1 | 93 | 118.3 | 81.3 | 27.0 | 129 | 85 | 44 |
| 45–49 | 9 | 108.0 | 70.2 | 37.8 | 6 | 115.3 | 77.0 | 38.3 | 96 | 113.2 | 75.5 | 37.7 | 131 | 86 | 45 |
| 50–54 | 8 | 112.5 | 75.8 | 36.7 | 10 | 116.6 | 69.8 | 46.8 | 100 | 109.8 | 74.1 | 35.7 | 133 | 87 | 46 |
| 55–59 | 4 | 123.5 | 74.5 | 49.0 | 0 | .. | .. | .. | 100 | 106.6 | 69.6 | 37.0 | 135 | 88 | 47 |
| 60 and over | 11 | 115.4 | 71.8 | 43.6 | 7 | 124.1 | 68.3 | 55.8 | 97 | 105.8 | 67.0 | 38.8 | 140+ | 90+ | 50+ |

[1] Ages 18 to 19 instead of 15 to 19 for Yucatecans.
[2] Donnison, C. P., 1929.
[3] *Ibid.*, quoted from J. F. H. Dally, "High Blood Pressure."
[4] P. P. = Pulse pressure.

86

diagnosis of arteriosclerosis or chronic interstitial nephritis made. . . . Hyper-
trophied hearts, without intrinsic cardiac disease to account for the enlarge-
ment, are very rarely met with in the African. . . . Opportunities for carrying
out post-mortems have often occurred, and it has been noted that the native
African usually shows much less atheroma in the aorta than does an average
European of the same age.

The results of this investigation thus lend support to the view that hyperpiesia and arteriosclerosis are diseases associated with civilization. Hyperpiesia has been recorded as quite common in Egypt by Ismail, but this is a
country that has been considerably influenced by European and other civilizations, recent and remote. Furthermore, Ismail points out that the disease is
almost confined to middle, upper, and more educated classes and is rare
amongst hospital (lower class) patients. . . . The greater mental stress required
by the ordinary European citizen in his everyday life, as a result of the tendencies of modern civilization, has had its effect upon the physiology as well as
the pathology of the race.

In Donnison's table it is notable in the case of Europeans that
both systolic and diastolic blood pressures, as well as pulse pressure
(the difference between the two former), rise constantly with age.
In Kavirondo Negroes the values reach a peak about the age of
thirty-five, or earlier, and after that age decline. The male Yucatecans exhibit a similar tendency, while the means for the females
show no middle-age change. Four males whose ages range from
fifty-five to fifty-nine and seven females of more than sixty years
have higher average systolic pressures than do the younger age
groups; but in neither case do the averages top a systolic value of
125 mm. of mercury. The highest single systolic reading in the
case of either sex was 150 mm.; the maximum diastolic value for
males was 106, for females, 94 mm.

The numbers in the Yucatecan age groups are very small. In
all, one hundred and forty-seven males and one hundred and five
females were examined. For the group of males as a whole, the
average systolic pressure is 115.4 mm.; the average diastolic,
71.9 mm. Although the male and the female age-blood-pressure
curves for Yucatecans do not duplicate that of Donnison's Kavirondos, yet there is little doubt that essentially the same tendencies are
at work in the two groups. In comparison with the European and
American modes of life, the rural Yucatecan, like the Kavirondo,
lives simply. It may very well be true that, as Donnison indicates,
the Yucatecans and Kavirondos have really normal blood pressure
and that the more "civilized" Europeans are the abnormals.

### TABLE 34. BLOOD PRESSURE — SYSTOLIC

#### MALES

| Group | No. | Range | Mean | S. D. | V. | Significance with Total Yucatecans |
|---|---|---|---|---|---|---|
| Total Yucatecans . | 150 | 85–150 | 115.43±.78 | 14.01±.55 | 12.14±.48 | |
| Group A ........ | 60 | 88–144 | 117.20±1.2 | 13.71±.84 | 11.70±.72 | None |
| Group B ........ | 31 | 85–144 | 111.45±1.5 | 12.69±1.1 | 11.39±.98 | None |
| Group C ........ | 49 | 88–150 | 116.18±1.4 | 14.58±.99 | 12.55±.85 | None |
| Groups D and E .. | 10 | 96–142 | 117.70 | | | |
| Zuñi, age 50–70 ... | 65 | ... | 120–130 | | | |
| Zuñi, age 25–50 ... | 74 | ... | 110–125 | | | |
| Fleming, 1924 | | | | | | |

#### FEMALES

| Group | No. | Range | Mean | S. D. | V. | Significance |
|---|---|---|---|---|---|---|
| Total Yucatecans . | 106 | 82–159 | 113.91±.98 | 14.91±.69 | 13.09±.61 | |
| Group A ........ | 24 | 88–150 | 115.12±2.0 | 14.58±1.4 | 12.66±1.2 | None |
| Group B ........ | 34 | 82–153 | 113.00±1.7 | 15.06±1.2 | 13.33±1.1 | None |
| Group C ........ | 41 | 88–159 | 113.80±1.6 | 15.69±1.2 | 13.79±1.0 | None |
| Group D ........ | 7 | 100–129 | 114.71±2.4 | 9.33±1.7 | 8.13±1.5 | None |
| Group E ........ | No data | | | | | |

### TABLE 35. BLOOD PRESSURE — DIASTOLIC

#### MALES

| Group | No. | Range | Mean | S. D. | V. | Significance with Total Yucatecans |
|---|---|---|---|---|---|---|
| Total Yucatecans .. | 150 | 46–106 | 71.85±.50 | 8.97±.35 | 12.48±.49 | |
| Group A ........ | 60 | 46–106 | 72.55±.85 | 9.78±.60 | 13.48±.83 | None |
| Group B ........ | 31 | 58– 90 | 69.64±.99 | 8.19±.70 | 11.76±1.0 | None |
| Group C ........ | 49 | 58– 94 | 72.59±.75 | 7.80±.53 | 10.75±.73 | None |
| Group D ........ | 10 | 58– 88 | 71.90 | | | |
| Group E ........ | No data | | | | | |
| Zuñi, age 50–70 .... | 65 | ... | 58–85 | | | |
| Zuñi, age 25–50 .... | 74 | ... | 60–75 | | | |
| Fleming, 1924 | | | | | | |

#### FEMALES

| Group | No. | Range | Mean | S. D. | V. | Significance |
|---|---|---|---|---|---|---|
| Total Yucatecans .. | 106 | 34–96 | 71.14±.71 | 10.80±.50 | 15.18±.70 | |
| Group A ........ | 24 | 55–93 | 72.88±1.2 | 8.88±.86 | 12.18±1.2 | None |
| Group B ........ | 34 | 34–96 | 69.32±1.4 | 12.15±.99 | 17.53±1.4 | None |
| Group C ........ | 41 | 46–96 | 71.22±1.2 | 11.10±.83 | 15.58±1.2 | None |
| Group D ........ | 7 | 67–84 | 73.57±1.2 | 4.65±.84 | 6.32±1.1 | None |
| Group E ........ | No data | | | | | |

The discussion of blood pressure so far has considered the Yucatecans as a uniform group. The racial subgroups of the Yucatecans have been seen to differ significantly among themselves in certain measurements. In systolic blood pressure, no such difference appears; the numbers are probably too small for the statistical purpose in mind. Group A of the males shows higher value and Group B the lowest. Coincidence in Group B of low systolic,

TABLE 36. PULSE PRESSURE

MALES

| Group | No. | Range | Mean | S. D. | V. | Significance with Total Yucatecans |
|---|---|---|---|---|---|---|
| Total Yucatecans .. | 150 | 21–84 | 43.12± .65 | 11.80±.46 | 27.36±1.1 | |
| Group A ......... | 60 | 21–84 | 44.50± .98 | 11.26±.69 | 25.30±1.6 | None |
| Group B ......... | 31 | 21–80 | 41.08±1.37 | 11.34±.97 | 27.60±2.4 | None |
| Group C ......... | 49 | 21–80 | 42.91±1.22 | 12.68±.86 | 29.55±2.0 | None |
| Groups D and E ... | 10 | 25–68 | 42.50 | | | |

FEMALES

| Total Yucatecans .. | 106 | 13–72 | 42.54±.67 | 10.28±.48 | 24.17±1.1 | |
| Group A ......... | 24 | 21–60 | 43.00±1.3 | 9.48±.92 | 22.05±2.2 | None |
| Group B ......... | 34 | 25–72 | 43.20±1.3 | 11.32±.93 | 26.20±2.1 | None |
| Group C ......... | 41 | 13–64 | 42.11±1.1 | 10.12±.75 | 24.03±1.8 | None |
| Group D ........ | 7 | 29–56 | 40.22±2.0 | 7.96±1.4 | 19.79±3.6 | None |
| Group E ......... | No data | | | | | |

as well as low diastolic pressure, with a lower age mean than is seen in Groups C, D, and E suggests a correlation which is known ordinarily to exist; but Group A exhibits a higher systolic pressure than Group B and the former subgroup has the youngest mean age of the groups. It may be concluded that among racial subgroups, such as are seen among the Yucatecans, race as a factor affecting blood pressure is unimportant. The comparatively slow pace of life of Yucatecans gives a low average reading and appears to affect all alike.

**Pulse Rate.** Examination of pulse rate was made under two kinds of conditions: in the sitting posture at rest, and in the recumbent posture while the subjects were undergoing basal metabolism tests. Hrdlička (1908, p. 141) concludes, after presenting adequate data, that "the heart beat is decidedly slower in the Indian than in the White man." The mean rate of pulse (sitting) in one hundred and forty-eight Yucatecans is 73.6 beats per minute, a figure considerably above 62.3, the average for two hundred and eighty-two North American Indians of various tribes examined by Hrdlička.

The ascertaining of normal rate of heart beat is not the simple procedure that it may seem. Comparable figures are obtained only when the subject is in a normal physical condition, when he has been in a resting posture for at least five minutes, when he is not engaged in the digestive process, and probably most important of all, when nervousness, due to the fact that he knows he is under scrutiny, is not present. In examination of the Yucatecans, the first three conditions were probably fulfilled, but one can never be absolutely sure that the fourth element is not to some extent a disturbing factor.

On the other hand, the conditions under which pulse rate was counted during the metabolism tests were much better controlled. The average for thirty-two Yucatecan males is 54.7; that for one hundred and thirty-six White males measured in Boston by Benedict (1928) is 61. Such a finding is in accord with Hrdlička's pronouncement, but the data on Whites were obtained in a different climate — that of Boston. However, nine American Whites, whose metabolism rates were tested at Chichen Itza, showed an average heart rate of 60.3. Even with such small samples, one is justified in assuming the average pulse rate of Yucatecan Indian mixtures to be less than that of Whites, and to be in agreement with Hrdlička's previous finding for North American Indians.

With the small samples at hand, it is not possible to demonstrate a difference in pulse rate among the Yucatecan subgroups. As in the case of blood pressure, the factor of most importance in sustaining low values in pulse rate among Indians generally is probably freedom from the rush of "civilization," although, in the present state of knowledge, causes inherent in race itself cannot be summarily dismissed.

**Hand Squeeze.** Hand squeeze, as measured by use of a dynamometer, is an index of muscular strength. But the amount of pressure exerted also depends to a great extent upon a certain psychological quality: an ability to throw all available muscular power into an act at a given instant. Degree of mental alertness and habitual actions, then, influence any results relating to hand squeeze.

## TABLE 37. HAND SQUEEZE

### MALES

| Group | No. | Range | Mean | S. D. | V. | Significance with Total Yucatecans |
|---|---|---|---|---|---|---|
| Total Yucatecans .... | 646 | 23–64 | 39.64±.21 | 7.86±.15 | 19.83±.37 | |
| Group A ........... | 149 | 24–59 | 37.37±.38 | 6.80±.27 | 18.20±.71 | 6×pe D |
| Group B ........... | 146 | 24–59 | 39.02±.40 | 7.20±.28 | 18.45±.73 | 1×pe D |
| Group C ........... | 278 | 23–64 | 40.42±.34 | 8.40±.24 | 20.78±.59 | 3×pe D |
| Group D ......... | 37 | 24–59 | 39.98±.84 | 7.55±.59 | 18.88±1.48 | None |
| Group E ........... | 36 | 25–64 | 44.50±.89 | 7.95±.63 | 17.87±1.42 | 5×pe D |
| Andalusian Moors ... Coon, 1929 | 28 | ... | 36.82±1.30 | | | |

| Group | No. | Range | Mean | Age | Mean All ages | Mean Stature [1] |
|---|---|---|---|---|---|---|
| Maricopa ............ | 10 | 36–59 | 48.90 | 20–30 | 44.27 | 174.9 |
| | 15 | 32–61 | 44.90 | 30–40 | | |
| | 8 | 40–52 | 45.50 | 40–50 | | |
| | 7 | 26–48 | 34.90 | 50–60 | | |
| Yuma ............... | 13 | 31–60 | 44.70 | 20–30 | 42.92 | 172.2 |
| | 4 | 34–55 | 47.00 | 30–40 | | |
| | 8 | 30–47 | 38.80 | 40–50 | | |
| | 4 | 30–48 | 41.30 | 50–60 | | |
| Pima ............... | 13 | 34–48 | 41.70 | 20–30 | 37.10 | 171.8 |
| | 14 | 30–48 | 40.70 | 30–40 | | |
| | 12 | 30–43 | 36.30 | 40–50 | | |
| | 12 | 18–43 | 28.70 | 50–60 | | |
| Mohave ............. | 12 | 32–54 | 42.50 | 20–30 | 39.20 | 171.6 |
| | 8 | 32–58 | 45.90 | 30–40 | | |
| | 10 | 23–48 | 38.20 | 40–50 | | |
| | 8 | 22–42 | 28.80 | 50–60 | | |
| Apache (White Mt.) .... | 32 | 35–58 | 45.80 | 20–30 | 43.71 | 169.1 |
| | 6 | 35–50 | 43.50 | 30–40 | | |
| | 11 | 24–48 | 38.10 | 40–50 | | |
| | 1 | ... | 40.00 | 50–60 | | |
| Papago ............. | 28 | 26–50 | 38.90 | 20–30 | 38.92 | 170.9 |
| | 11 | 28–48 | 40.60 | 30–40 | | |
| | 8 | 31–41 | 36.70 | 40–50 | | |
| | 1 | ... | 39.00 | 50–60 | | |
| Cora ................. | 16 | 28–41 | 35.10 | 20–30 | 32.87 | 164.1 |
| | 8 | 26–41 | 33.60 | 30–40 | | |
| | 17 | 24–36 | 31.60 | 40–50 | | |
| | 8 | 24–35 | 30.40 | 50–60 | | |
| Hopi ............... | 26 | 25–56 | 42.10 | 20–30 | 38.91 | 164.5 [2] |
| | 14 | 34–48 | 40.20 | 30–40 | | |
| | 6 | 33–40 | 35.10 | 40–50 | | |
| | 12 | 24–42 | 32.40 | 50–60 | | |

Hrdlička, 1909 (Mean stature for the Yucatecans as a group is 156.43 cm.).
Mean of Pueblo Indians in general (Hrdlička, 1909).

TABLE 37. (*Continued*)

| Group | No. | Range | Mean | Age | Mean All ages | Mean Stature [1] |
|---|---|---|---|---|---|---|
| Laguna (Pueblos) . . . . . . | 20 | 26–58 | 41.80 | 20–30 | 39.16 | 164.5 [2] |
| | 17 | 36–54 | 43.40 | 30–40 | | |
| | 12 | 29–44 | 35.50 | 40–50 | | |
| | 9 | 18–38 | 30.20 | 50–60 | | |
| Zuñi . . . . . . . . . . . . . . . | 25 | 35–52 | 41.50 | 20–30 | 38.25 | 164.5 [2] |
| | 14 | 28–50 | 38.00 | 30–40 | | |
| | 8 | 32–52 | 39.70 | 40–50 | | |
| | 10 | 25–42 | 29.30 | 50–60 | | |
| Tarasco . . . . . . . . . . . . . | 25 | 29–44 | 35.70 | 20–30 | 33.78 | 163.1 |
| | 8 | 24–40 | 32.60 | 30–40 | | |
| | 8 | 27–34 | 32.90 | 40–50 | | |
| | 5 | 20–38 | 27.50 | 50–60 | | |
| Aztec . . . . . . . . . . . . . . | 18 | 26–38 | 31.20 | 20–30 | 28.50 | 164.3 |
| | 17 | 17–35 | 26.80 | 30–40 | | |
| | 8 | 20–38 | 27.60 | 40–50 | | |
| | 3 | 22–28 | 24.30 | 50–60 | | |
| Otomi . . . . . . . . . . . . . | 10 | 26–39 | 32.70 | 20–30 | 29.12 | 159.3 |
| | 6 | 30–39 | 34.80 | 30–40 | | |
| | 13 | 19–32 | 27.70 | 40–50 | | |
| | 17 | 16–34 | 26.10 | 50–60 | | |

Hrdlička, 1908

| | Age 20–30 | Age 30–40 | Age 40–50 | Age 50–60 |
|---|---|---|---|---|
| Mean of Taller Tribes: Maricopa, Yuma, Pima, Mohave, Apache, Papago . . . . . . . . . | 43.31 | 43.21 | 38.68 | 32.22 |
| Mean of Shorter Tribes: Hopi, Laguna, Zuñi, Cora, Tarasco, Aztec, Otomi. . . . . . . . . . . . | 37.93 | 36.03 | 32.44 | 28.92 |

[1] Hrdlička, 1909 (Mean stature for the Yucatecans as a group is 156.43 cm.).
[2] Mean of Pueblo Indians in general (Hrdlička, 1909).

FEMALES

| Group | No. | Range | Mean | S. D. | V. | Significance with Total Yucatecans |
|---|---|---|---|---|---|---|
| Total Yucatecans . . . . | 501 | 9–49 | 23.64 ±.18 | 6.10 ±.13 | 25.81 ±.55 | |
| Group A . . . . . . . . . . . | 118 | 9–49 | 22.46 ±.41 | 6.65 ±.29 | 29.60 ±1.3 | 3 ×pe D |
| Group B . . . . . . . . . . . | 163 | 9–39 | 23.35 ±.29 | 5.45 ±.20 | 23.34 ±.87 | 1 ×pe D |
| Group C . . . . . . . . . . . | 149 | 9–44 | 24.75 ±.33 | 6.00 ±.23 | 24.24 ±.95 | 3 ×pe D |
| Group D . . . . . . . . . | 40 | 10–39 | 22.88 ±.54 | 5.10 ±.38 | 22.30 ±1.7 | 1 ×pe D |
| Group E . . . . . . . . . . . | 31 | 9–39 | 25.22 ±.89 | 7.35 ±.63 | 29.14 ±2.5 | 1 ×pe D |
| Smith Coll. Students | 90 | 18–52 | 35.25 ±.51 | 6.99 | | |

Steggerda *et al.*, 1929

First of all it is apparent that for the Yucatecan subgroups, the values depend in a rather direct fashion on bodily size; larger men are able to squeeze more. This finding is seen to be all the more noteworthy when it is realized that significant differences appear between the groups in spite of the high variability exhibited by the coefficients of variation.

It is in the comparison of the Yucatecan data as a whole and of Group A with those for other American Indian tribes that one's interest becomes aroused. Hrdlička published in 1908 an invaluable study of the physiology of Indians of the southwestern United States and northern Mexico. For purposes of easier comparison, his data on hand squeeze have been regrouped and averaged. The first six taller tribes shown in the table have a mean squeeze (regardless of age) of 40.82 kilograms, which is approximately the same value as that for Total Yucatecans. Yet the compared tribes average very much taller than do the Yucatecans. It is possible that the Yucatecans possess more White blood than do the others. In such a case, it is more fitting to compare the average of these northern tribes with that of Group A. When this is done it is apparent that the difference in average squeeze is even more disproportionate to the difference in stature. The latter seven shorter tribes, whose data Hrdlička presents, show an average value of 34.79 kilograms. Even these Indians exhibit a mean stature which is considerably above that of either the Total Yucatecans or of Group A, but their average squeeze is definitely lower. To average the Pueblo groups with Cora, Tabasco, Aztec, and Otomi, however, is probably an incorrect procedure. The mean hand squeeze for the latter groups is only 31.10, while the three Pueblo groups average (without regard to age) 38.78 kilograms. Since the test of hand squeeze manifests not only amount of muscular strength but also ability to apply it efficiently, there is probably some justification in venturing the opinion that the Mayas and the Pueblo tribes reflect their demonstrated abilities to develop and maintain civilizations of their own in well-controlled use of their hands.

The findings for females parallel in general those for the males, but the data are not so trustworthy as are those for males, because the women often did not appear to make maximum efforts.

In summary, it may be said that various findings point toward superiority in physical efficiency of the Maya Indian and of his racially mixed relations. Some of them are: large chests and lungs, and broad shoulders in proportion to body size; general stockiness in build; an efficient cardiovascular system; and a notable degree of neuromuscular coördination.

**Basal Metabolism.** Probably the first published paper concerning the possibility of a relation existing between race and metabolism was that of MacLeod, Crofts, and Benedict (1925). Chinese and Japanese women living under the environmental conditions of American life were found to have a basal metabolism distinctly lower than the standards for American women of like age, weight, and height. This conclusion led to the suggestion that race is a specific factor influencing metabolism. As an outcome of this research, the Nutrition Laboratory of Carnegie Institution of Washington has undertaken a general study of racial metabolism. The data here presented are the results of collaboration between the Nutrition Laboratory, the Chichen Itza Project (both Carnegie organizations) and the Bureau of International Research of Harvard University and Radcliffe College. The location of an archaeological station at Chichen Itza presented an opportunity to study not only the metabolism of Yucatecans, but also that of American Whites living under identical climatic conditions. It was intended that the research should determine: (1) whether the environmental conditions of Yucatan (particularly climate, and to a certain extent, food) would alter the metabolism of the Whites from their standards at home, and (2) the metabolic rate of healthy Yucatecans.

The first question was not satisfactorily answered because of the shortness of the sojourn of most of the White subjects in the country before examination. Most of the measurements upon this group of White men were made less than four and one-half months after they had reached Yucatan, and it is a question whether there had been time enough for the change of locality to have any effect. Certain conclusions have already been drawn in a paper previously published (Williams and Benedict, 1928), which is here quoted:

The data are of interest chiefly because they indicate to what extent the metabolism of this group of White men varies from the probable metabolism of normal men in the northern part of the United States, as predicted from the Harris-Benedict formula for men. It is perhaps of significance that all the White men (nine in number) with the exception of subjects I and X, had a metabolism somewhat below the predicted value, — in two cases clearly ten per cent or more below. If the average deviation for the two experiments with subject I (+11.2 per cent) and the deviation of +5.3 per cent with subject X are included, the average apparent depression is lowered from −6.3 to −3.4 per cent. One would not expect to find such a large proportion of minus values with a group of White men selected at random in Boston or in the North. The evidence therefore seems positive that these men, on the whole, had a metabolism slightly below the predicted metabolism. Taking into consideration the shortness of the stay in Yucatan, however, we are not justified in interpreting this evidence as indicating that the differences in environment had any significant effect upon the basal metabolism.

The foregoing is pertinent to the present inquiry in that it presents metabolism values of a different race than the Mayas, who were living in the same climate as the native race. Further quotation from the same paper is necessary:

Of the greatest significance, of course, is the comparison between the actually measured metabolism of these Mayas and the metabolism predicted for White men by the Harris and Benedict formula. A large proportion of the men had a heat prediction measurably higher than the predicted metabolism. Thus, there are but twelve instances of minus values and thirty-eight of plus values. (The number of values mentioned refers to check tests as well as to original ones.) The average deviation of the actual from the predicted heat production for the entire group of thirty-two men is +5.2 per cent. The metabolism of these natives is therefore distinctly higher than that which would be expected for White men in the United States.

The definitely high level of heat production with this group of Mayas challenges attention. The fact that it cannot be the result of a febrile condition due to malaria or some other tropical disease is demonstrated by the records of the mouth temperature of the men, taken just prior to the metabolism measurements. Thus the maximum buccal temperature was 98.4 F. degrees, and the minimum 96.4 F., and the average for the entire group 97.2 F. degrees, values very close to the accepted normal of 98.6 F. degrees.

A tropical or subtropical climate has been commonly supposed to cause a low rather than a high metabolism. The recent observations on browns and blacks in Jamaica, however, suggest that climate probably does not have a marked influence (Steggerda and Benedict, 1928). The effect of climate is therefore ruled out.

Configuration (of the body) alone as judged from the "pelidisi" (of Pirquet) does not explain the high metabolism of these Mayas.

The measurements made upon this group of male Mayas differ from those made upon Whites in one particular. The Whites were, for the most part, studied in the early spring, in March and April. The majority of the Mayas were studied in July, although not an inconsiderable number of experiments were also made in the spring. Frequently measurements were made in March and April and again in July for comparison.

### TABLE 38.  BASAL METABOLISM

#### MALES

| | Serial No. | Oxygen per minute | | Percentage deviation from Harris-Benedict Prediction | |
|---|---|---|---|---|---|
| | | Test I | Test II | Test I | Test II |
| Group A (8)................ | 17 | 226 | 207 | +11.2 | + 7.2 |
| | 21 | 197 | 209 | + 2.4 | +10.0 |
| | 24 | 235 | (235)[1] | +14.5 | (+14.5) |
| | 28 | 230 | (230) | +13.7 | (+13.7) |
| | 53 | 237 | 238 | +13.7 | +14.1 |
| | 59 | 223 | (223) | +11.6 | (+11.6) |
| | 64 | 208 | 206 | − 0.3 | + 0.1 |
| | 118 | 239 | (239) | +15.2 | (+15.2) |
| Means ................ | | 224.4 | 223.4 | +10.2 | +10.8 |
| Group B (6)................ | 11 | 192 | 195 | + 0.1 | + 0.9 |
| | 35 | 202 | 191 | + 6.1 | + 3.9 |
| | 51 | 248 | 208 | +26.9 | +10.4 |
| | 67 | 192 | 191 | − 3.9 | − 5.3 |
| | 122 | 234 | 240 | +14.2 | +21.2 |
| | 160 | 244 | 218 | +14.4 | + 1.8 |
| Means................ | | 218.7 | 207.2 | + 9.6 | + 5.5 |
| Group C ................ | 57 | 203 | 211 | − 3.4 | + 1.6 |
| | 72 | 220 | (220) | + 3.5 | (+ 3.5) |
| | 105 | 235 | 200 | +10.6 | − 3.7 |
| | 117 | 207 | (207) | − 8.8 | (− 8.8) |
| | 167 | 164 | 188 | − 5.3 | + 8.6 |
| Group D.................... | 16 | 210 | 193 | + 6.4 | + 1.0 |
| Group E ................ | 15 | 215 | (215) | + 2.5 | (+ 2.5) |
| | 58 | 235 | (235) | + 5.5 | (+ 5.5) |
| Means................ | | 211.1 | 208.6 | + 1.4 | + 1.3 |
| Means: Group as a whole (22) . | | 218.0 | 213.6 | + 6.8 | + 5.9 |
| Means: Groups A+B (14)..... | | 222.0 | 216.5 | + 9.9 | + 8.5 |
| Means: Groups C+D+E (8) .. | | 211.1 | 208.6 | + 1.4 | + 1.3 |

[1] Parentheses indicate: No check test.

The average values for the measurements made on ten individuals in March or April, and again in July, are 217 cc. and 210 cc. respectively, a difference of 7 cc.  It hardly seems conceivable that this small difference can be justifiably ascribed to a seasonal effect.

Another possible explanation is that the high metabolism may be a reflection of the type of occupation.  These men were all engaged in fairly strenuous muscular work (as archaeological laborers) and might be considered as coming under the head of well-trained athletes or severe workers, more or less "hard" muscularly. In view of somewhat contradictory findings with athletes perhaps the safest conclusions to draw regarding the Mayas are: (1) that their metabolism on the average is distinctly above the predicted standard for northern White men; (2) that their customary life of hard labor may in part (not wholly) account for this elevated metabolism, but (3) that their diet is undoubtedly somewhat less stimulating to metabolism in so far as protein is concerned, than is that of the average White man in the north.

This leaves the racial factor to be considered. Of the total number of Yucatecans subjected to the metabolism test, there were some who, because of labor turnover, were not available for anthropological measurements. Others were immature, so that for consideration of racial status it is possible to present only twenty-two subjects. A summary of the findings is given in the table on Basal Metabolism.

Group A appears to have an average deviation from the Harris-Benedict prediction of from +10 to +11 per cent. The check tests, in all but one of the eight cases, compare well with the original examinations. With this doubtful case (Number 21) out of consideration, six-sevenths of the Test I cases of Group A are seen to show values of more than +10 per cent; of the Test II cases, six-sevenths top +7 per cent. Individual Number 64 of Group A shows values that agree almost exactly with the prediction, but with the exception of a −0.3 reading in this individual, there is not a single minus value in the Group A series.

The average of the first tests of Group B is higher than the average of the check tests, mainly because of the high reading for Number 51 on the original test. This is partially counteracted by Number 122's high second-test value. For Test I then, one-half of the Group B representatives show readings of more than +10 per cent, while for Test II, only one-third of them are so high. Two, and possibly three, exhibit ordinary metabolism values, and one is definitely below normal.

Group C is defined as possessing a considerable amount of White blood. The averages for this group are definitely below either of the means given for the previously considered more Indian groups. Only one examination, that of Test I on Number 105 lies above +10 per cent, and that high value was changed to a minus one on the second test.

The one case in Group D fails to show close agreement in his two tests.

Due precaution was taken, and there is no reason to believe that the metabolism tests here discussed were not made under basal conditions; that is to say, the results are not affected by the previous taking of food. This belief is, in part, substantiated by the values for the pulse rate, which are usually well within the normal limits and rarely are exceptionally high, which would be expected had food been taken.

It is realized that the number of cases discussed constitute a woefully inadequate set of cases from which to draw definite conclusions. The results here presented should be considered only as tentative. The fact that fourteen Yucatecans of predominately Maya Indian blood show an average deviation of eight or ten per cent more than the Harris-Benedict prediction, while eight other Yucatecans, who all possess distinctly White physical characteristics, exhibit no significant deviation from the same standard, is suggestive of the influence in this case of a racial factor in basal metabolism. It is the hope of the writer that the work can sometime be checked on a much larger scale so that definite answers can be given to the interesting questions that arise from the results here presented.[1]

## THE HEAD

**Head Length.** Group A shows the smallest mean value of the subgroups in length of head. The values increase steadily in alphabetical order and reach the maximum in Group E. Significant differences exist between the means of the several groups and that of the group as a whole. It would appear that the greater the amount of White admixture, the greater is the length of head. The phenomenon is similar to that seen in the case of stature. It is not unexpected, for generally a high correlation is found to exist between stature and head length in any group. There seems to be evidence here of the operation of a series of independent but cumulative factors, such as are supposed in the multiple-factor hypothesis. Heterosis is certainly not to be found in this case. Lack of heterosis is the expected finding, for this case of racial mixture is one of long standing and not one of recent origin.

Groups D and E approach but do not attain to the level of any

---

[1] These results have recently been confirmed in a paper by Morris P. Steggerda which is to be published soon.

## TABLE 39. HEAD LENGTH

### MALES

| Group | No. | Range | Mean | S. D. | V. | Significance with Total Yucatecans |
|---|---|---|---|---|---|---|
| Total Yucatecans .. | 880 | 164–208 | 182.64 ± .14 | 5.94 ± .10 | 3.25 ± .05 | |
| Group A ......... | 221 | 165–198 | 180.96 ± .27 | 5.92 ± .19 | 3.27 ± .10 | 7 ×pe D |
| Group B ......... | 199 | 167–194 | 181.87 ± .23 | 4.90 ± .17 | 2.69 ± .09 | 3 ×pe D |
| Group C ......... | 362 | 164–208 | 183.11 ± .21 | 5.83 ± .15 | 3.18 ± .08 | 2 ×pe D |
| Group D ........ | 52 | 174–205 | 186.04 ± .56 | 6.02 ± .40 | 3.24 ± .21 | 6 ×pe D |
| Group E ......... | 46 | 175–203 | 186.33 ± .70 | 7.00 ± .49 | 3.76 ± .26 | 5 ×pe D |
| Spanish ......... | 79 | 171–219 | 191.30 ± .57 | 7.56 ± .41 | 3.95 ± .21 | |
| Barras, 1928 | | | | | | |
| Cacereños ........ | 23 | ... | 192.80 | | | |
| Aranzadi, 1894b | | | | | | |
| Andalusian Moors . | 28 | ... | 194.50 ± .77 | 6.03 ± .54 | 3.10 ± .28 | |
| Coon, 1929 | | | | | | |
| Mexicans ......... | 48 | ... | 184.65 ± .60 | 6.21 ± .43 | 3.36 ± .23 | |
| Chontals ........ | 80 | 162–192 | 180.30 | | | |
| Huaxtecs.......... | 100 | 162–196 | 177.80 | | | |
| *Mayas* ........... | 100 | 165–197 | 181.80 | | | |
| Tzotzils .......... | 100 | 177–200 | 188.10 | | | |
| Tzendals ........ | 100 | 164–202 | 187.70 | | | |
| Chols ............ | 100 | 165–202 | 182.50 | | | |
| Starr, 1902 | | | | | | |
| Sioux, Pure........ | 539 | 164–218 | 194.90 | 6.16 | 3.16 | |
| Sioux, Half-Blood .. | 77 | 176–212 | 194.40 | 7.12 | 3.66 | |
| Sullivan, 1920 | | | | | | |
| Hawaiians, Pure ... | 74 | ... | 182.42 ± .70 | 8.90 ± .49 | 4.89 ± .27 | |
| F₁ Hawaiian, North | | | | | | |
| European ...... | 10 | 177–206 | 188.80 ± 1.87 | 8.78 ± 1.32 | 4.65 | |
| Dunn, Tozzer, 1928 | | | | | | |

### FEMALES

| Group | No. | Range | Mean | S. D. | V. | Significance with Total Yucatecans |
|---|---|---|---|---|---|---|
| Total Yucatecans .. | 694 | 155–196 | 175.56 ± .15 | 6.02 ± .11 | 3.43 ± .06 | |
| Group A ......... | 154 | 158–189 | 174.19 ± .32 | 5.82 ± .22 | 3.34 ± .13 | 4 ×pe D |
| Group B ......... | 231 | 161–191 | 175.60 ± .24 | 5.48 ± .17 | 3.12 ± .10 | None |
| Group C ......... | 201 | 155–195 | 175.51 ± .31 | 6.50 ± .22 | 3.70 ± .12 | None |
| Group D ........ | 62 | 167–192 | 177.34 ± .49 | 5.74 ± .35 | 3.24 ± .20 | 1 ×pe D |
| Group E ......... | 46 | 165–190 | 178.28 ± .66 | 6.60 ± .46 | 3.70 ± .26 | 4 ×pe D |

TABLE 39.  (*Continued*)

| Group | No. | Range | Mean | S. D. | V. | Significance with Total Yucatecans |
|---|---|---|---|---|---|---|
| Mexicans ......... | 30 | 165–200 | 177.83 ±.93 | 7.54 ±.66 | 4.24 ±.37 | |
| *Mayas* ........... | 25 | 167–183 | 174.90 | | | |
| Huaxtecs.......... | 20 | 155–180 | 169.40 | | | |
| Tzendals ........ | 25 | 171–197 | 180.70 | | | |
| Chols ........... | 25 | 167–188 | 177.10 | | | |
| Chontals ........ | 25 | 177–185 | 176.10 | | | |
| Tzotzils ......... | 25 | 172–191 | 179.70 | | | |
|    Starr, 1902 | | | | | | |
| Smith Coll. Students | 100 | 167–201 | 186.43 ±.38 | 5.60 | 3.00 | |
|    Steggerda *et al.*, 1929 | | | | | | |
| Sioux, Pure........ | 156 | 174–200 | 187.00 | 5.09 | 2.72 | |
| Sioux, Half-Blood .. | 19 | 176–192 | 187.30 | 4.17 | 2.22 | |
|    Sullivan, 1920 | | | | | | |
| Hawaiians, Pure ... | 34 | 162–198 | 178.80 | | | |
| ¾ Hawaiian, ¼ North | | | | | | |
|   European ....... | 12 | 164–182 | 174.60 | | | |
| F₁ Hawaiian, North | | | | | | |
|   European ....... | 10 | 164–189 | 173.60 | | | |
| ¼ Hawaiian, ¾ North | | | | | | |
|   European ....... | 6 | 171–187 | 178.80 | | | |
|    Dunn, Tozzer, 1928 | | | | | | |

of the Spanish groups cited in the table.  A clearer idea of the constitution of each of the subgroups may be gained by examination of the frequency curves for head length (Plate 10).  From Group A to Group D the major modes shift gradually toward higher values, and that of Group D coincides with that of Barras' Spanish. Group E is definitely bimodal; the major mode lies at the value of 184, the minor in the region of 194–196, which is very close to the highest mode shown in the Spanish series.

Group B has a mean value which is very close to that of Starr's Mayas, and which lies in the same general head-length group as do the Chontals, the Huaxtecs, and the Chols.  The Mexicans measured in Yucatan are an unselected group.  Their mean takes a place between that of Group C and those of Groups D and E.  The longer heads of this group may be explained in two ways: (1) the more northern Mexican Indians are longer-headed, and (2) White admixture is probably, on the average, greater in degree in Mexico north of Yucatan.

Sullivan's Half-Blood Sioux show no significant difference in mean from the value for the pure Sioux. In this case there is little difference in size between the two elements of the racial cross. The Dunn-Tozzer material tells a different story; here the participants in the mixture are different, and the $F_1$ male progeny exhibit definite lengthening of the head. This may also be ascribed to heterosis. The females show no heterosis, nor any definite trend. The numbers, however, are very small.

The female Yucatecan subgroups follow the trend of the males as to lengthened heads in the Whiter groups. Only Groups A and E differ significantly from the Total Yucatecans. The heads of the females are shorter than those of the males and the differences between the groups not so great. How short the heads really are is indicated by comparing any of the subgroups with the Smith College students. As in the case of the males, Starr's Mayas stand close to Groups A and B, while the Mexican women have a place near Groups D and E.

The frequency curves (Plate 10) tell much the same story for females as they do for males. By the evidence of the seriation curves, there seems to be no doubt that all of the subgroups, including D and E, have among their members some short-headed individuals who are typically Indian in respect to head length; but the Whiter groups have more longer-headed persons in their ranks than do the more Indian subgroups A and B.

**Head Breadth.** The trend toward higher values seen in the Whiter subgroups in head length is not evident in the case of head breadth. There are no significant differences between the subgroups. The length dimension of the head varies in accordance with the predictions of the multiple-factor hypothesis; but in this case the means of the groups give no evidence of the action of independent, cumulative factors. It may be assumed from this that a less pliable mechanism is at work in the heredity of breadth of head than in length. The actual means of the table indicate that the taller Whiter subgroups have slightly (although not significantly) broader heads. In no case is there a near approach to the lower Spanish means listed for comparison. Starr's Mayas are of

## TABLE 40.  HEAD BREADTH

### MALES

| Group | No. | Range | Mean | S. D. | V. | Significance with Total Yucatecans |
|---|---|---|---|---|---|---|
| Total Yucatecans . . | 880 | 139–173 | 155.59 ± .12 | 5.35 ± .09 | 3.44 ± .06 | |
| Group A . . . . . . . . . | 221 | 141–170 | 155.39 ± .24 | 5.38 ± .17 | 3.46 ± .11 | None |
| Group B . . . . . . . . . | 199 | 141–168 | 155.01 ± .25 | 5.30 ± .18 | 3.42 ± .12 | 2 ×pe D |
| Group C . . . . . . . . . | 362 | 143–173 | 155.81 ± .19 | 5.28 ± .13 | 3.39 ± .08 | 1 ×pe D |
| Group D . . . . . . . . | 52 | 139–171 | 156.62 ± .54 | 5.76 ± .38 | 3.68 ± .24 | 1 ×pe D |
| Group E . . . . . . . . . | 46 | 145–169 | 156.54 ± .54 | 5.46 ± .38 | 3.49 ± .25 | 1 ×pe D |
| Spanish . . . . . . . . . . . Barras, 1928 | 79 | 139–162 | 149.40 ± .36 | 4.72 ± .25 | 3.16 ± .17 | |
| Cacereños . . . . . . . . Aranzadi, 1894*b* | 23 | . . . | 149.40 | | | |
| Andalusian Moors . Coon, 1929 | 28 | . . . | 149.04 ± .65 | 5.09 ± .46 | 3.42 ± .31 | |
| Mexicans . . . . . . . . . | 48 | . . . | 149.77 ± .62 | 6.41 ± .44 | 4.25 ± .29 | |
| Chontals . . . . . . . . | 80 | 139–160 | 149.90 | | | |
| Huaxtecs . . . . . . . . . | 100 | 140–164 | 150.10 | | | |
| *Mayas* . . . . . . . . . . . | 100 | 135–168 | 154.10 | | | |
| Tzotzils . . . . . . . . . . | 100 | 135–156 | 144.60 | | | |
| Tzendals . . . . . . . . | 100 | 128–159 | 144.10 | | | |
| Chols . . . . . . . . . . . . Starr, 1902 | 100 | 134–159 | 147.50 | | | |
| Sioux, Pure . . . . . . . . | 539 | 134–182 | 155.10 | 5.39 | 3.47 | |
| Sioux, Half-Blood . . Sullivan, 1920 | 77 | 138–164 | 154.30 | 5.04 | 3.26 | |
| Hawaiians, Pure . . . F₁ Hawaiian, North | 74 | . . . | 152.03 ± .45 | 5.77 ± .32 | 3.80 ± .21 | |
| European . . . . . . . Dunn, Tozzer, 1928 | 10 | 138–167 | 156.60 ± 1.89 | 8.86 ± 1.34 | 5.66 | |

### FEMALES

| Group | No. | Range | Mean | S. D. | V. | Significance with Total Yucatecans |
|---|---|---|---|---|---|---|
| Total Yucatecans . . | 694 | 135–168 | 150.81 ± .13 | 4.94 ± .09 | 3.28 ± .06 | |
| Group A . . . . . . . . . | 154 | 138–168 | 151.18 ± .28 | 5.12 ± .20 | 3.39 ± .13 | 1 ×pe D |
| Group B . . . . . . . . . | 231 | 135–162 | 150.81 ± .20 | 4.40 ± .14 | 2.92 ± .09 | None |
| Group C . . . . . . . . . | 201 | 135–168 | 150.24 ± .25 | 5.34 ± .18 | 3.55 ± .12 | 2 ×pe D |
| Group D . . . . . . . . | 62 | 139–164 | 151.08 ± .42 | 4.88 ± .30 | 3.23 ± .20 | None |
| Group E . . . . . . . . . | 46 | 141–162 | 151.80 ± .48 | 4.78 ± .34 | 3.15 ± .22 | 2 ×pe D |

TABLE 40.  (*Continued*)

| Group | No. | Range | Mean | S. D. | V. | Significance with Total Yucatecans |
|---|---|---|---|---|---|---|
| Mexicans ......... | 30 | 131–164 | 145.17±.86 | 7.00±.61 | 4.82±.42 | |
| *Mayas* .......... | 25 | 141–161 | 148.70 | | | |
| Huaxtecs......... | 20 | 138–158 | 145.80 | | | |
| Tzendals ......... | 25 | 113–144 | 137.00 | | | |
| Chols ............ | 25 | 128–153 | 141.60 | | | |
| Chontals ........ | 25 | 132–153 | 144.50 | | | |
| Tzotzils ......... | 25 | 130–147 | 138.10 | | | |
| Starr, 1902 | | | | | | |
| Smith Coll. Students | 100 | 136–154 | 145.98±.29 | 4.36 | 2.99 | |
| Steggerda *et al.*, 1929 | | | | | | |
| Sioux, Pure........ | 157 | 140–162 | 150.90 | 4.83 | 3.20 | |
| Sioux, Half-Blood .. | 19 | 142–160 | 150.30 | 4.50 | 2.99 | |
| Sullivan, 1920 | | | | | | |
| Hawaians, Pure .... | 34 | 137–161 | 150.30 | | | |
| $\frac{3}{4}$ Hawaiian, $\frac{1}{4}$ North | | | | | | |
| European ....... | 12 | 138–156 | 144.20 | | | |
| F$_1$ Hawaiian, North | | | | | | |
| European ....... | 10 | 140 156 | 147.40 | | | |
| $\frac{1}{4}$ Hawaiian, $\frac{3}{4}$ North | | | | | | |
| European ....... | 6 | 130–151 | 143.00 | | | |
| Dunn, Tozzer, 1928 | | | | | | |

the same general magnitude of mean as are Groups A and B. His other groups have considerably smaller averages.

The seriation curves (Plate 11) help a little in explanation. The percentages of the subgroups A through E to Barras' Spanish, at head-breadth value of 150, are respectively: 5, 8, 8, 8, 9, 13; at breadth of 160 they are: 11, 12, 13, 9, 6, 0. Thus, a definite tendency is shown for the presence of a few more narrower heads in the Whiter groups, and a few more broader heads in the more Indian groups; but for all subgroups, the great majority of cases are found to lie between the two breadths of 150 and 160 mm. One reasons from this that there is at least partial dominance of the Indian broad-headedness in the Maya-Spanish cross, and that breadths behave quite differently from lengths in this case of racial mixture.

Sullivan's Sioux Half-Bloods have a smaller value for head breadth than his Full-Bloods; the difference is statistically insignificant. Dunn and Tozzer's $F_1$ males of the Hawaiian-North European cross seem to exhibit heterosis. The Sioux Half-Blood group contains individuals of $F_2$ and later generations as well as of $F_1$. They behave very much as do the Yucatecans.

The female Yucatecan groups have head breadths which are approximately five millimeters less than those of the males. Again, no significant differences are found between the subgroups. The breadth means for this study are slightly higher than those of Starr for the Mayas, but his Maya group overtops all the means which he presents for comparison. The Mexican females domiciled in Yucatan have much narrower heads than do the female Yucatecans — an expected finding; the Smith College students show a mean which is close to that of the Mexicans.

In considering the seriation curve for both male and female head breadth, no very definite tendencies appear, except possibly that Group E in the case of either sex shows a trend toward bimodality in which one mode lies at a value distinctly higher than the mode for any other subgroup. Is it possible that the partial dominance of the great head breadth of the Maya Indians has fixed itself in the germ plasm of practically all the descendants of the cross to such an extent that the larger of the progeny now tend to have broader heads than do the smaller?

Sullivan's Pure and Half-Blood Sioux females, like the males, do not differ significantly. But Dunn and Tozzer's females exhibit markedly smaller means in the Whiter groups than in the Pure Hawaiians. The Hawaiian Mixed-Bloods are certainly few in number, but it is very probable that the phenomenon is not accidental. One explanation of the difference in behavior between the Hawaiian and the Yucatecan mixtures as to breadth of head is: The Hawaiians are much taller and heavier than are any of the Yucatecans; yet the absolute values for head breadth are approximately equal. It is conceivable that such an extreme degree of broad-headedness as is possessed by Maya Indians might act more dominantly in case of racial mixture than the relatively milder degree of the Hawaiians.

**Cephalic Index.** The findings for head length and breadth tell what is to be expected in cephalic index. A definite and continuous drop occurs from Group A to Group E. Groups A, D, and E differ significantly. From the foregoing discussion, it is seen that the

## TABLE 41.  CEPHALIC INDEX

### MALES

| Group | No. | Range | Mean | S. D. | V. | Significance with Total Yucatecans |
|---|---|---|---|---|---|---|
| Total Yucatecans . . . . . | 880 | 75–95 | 85.21 ±.07 | 3.22 ±.05 | 3.78 ±.06 | |
| Group A . . . . . . . . . . . . . | 221 | 77–95 | 85.83 ±.14 | 3.14 ±.10 | 3.66 ±.12 | 5×pe D |
| Group B . . . . . . . . . . . . . | 199 | 75–95 | 85.25 ±.16 | 3.24 ±.11 | 3.80 ±.13 | None |
| Group C . . . . . . . . . . . . . | 362 | 75–95 | 85.14 ±.11 | 3.14 ±.08 | 3.69 ±.09 | None |
| Group D . . . . . . . . . . . | 52 | 77–91 | 84.00 ±.28 | 2.99 ±.20 | 3.56 ±.24 | 4×pe D |
| Group E . . . . . . . . . . . . | 46 | 77–91 | 84.17 ±.35 | 3.52 ±.25 | 4.18 ±.29 | 3×pe D |
| | | | | | | |
| All Spain. . . . . . . . . . . . . | 8368 | 63–94 | 77.74 ±.02 | 3.08 ±.02 | 3.96 ±.02 | |
| Cantabrica . . . . . . . . . . . | 463 | . . . | 80.27 | | | |
| Galaica . . . . . . . . . . . . . . | 330 | . . . | 78.80 | | | |
| Vasco-Navarra. . . . . . . . | 454 | . . . | 78.76 | | | |
| Catalana  . . . . . . . . . . . . | 574 | . . . | 78.07 | | | |
| Castellana Superior . . . . | 1315 | . . . | 77.79 | | | |
| Aragonesa . . . . . . . . . . . . | 805 | . . . | 77.40 | | | |
| Valenciana . . . . . . . . . . . | 502 | . . . | 76.84 | | | |
| Castellana Inferior . . . . | 1410 | . . . | 78.52 | | | |
| Andalucia Alta  . . . . . . . | 945 | . . . | 77.71 | | | |
| Andalucia Baja . . . . . . . | 751 | . . . | 79.01 | | | |
| Baleares  . . . . . . . . . . . . | 122 | . . . | 77.73 | | | |
| Madrid (Capital)  . . . . . | 697 | . . . | 77.87 | | | |
| Oloriz, 1894, p. 151 | | | | | | |
| | | | | | | |
| Andalusian Moors  . . . . | 28 | . . . | 76.54 ±.33 | 2.61 ±.24 | 3.41 ±.31 | |
| Coon, 1929 | | | | | | |
| | | | | | | |
| Spanish . . . . . . . . . . . . . | 79 | 69–86 | 78.25 ±.24 | 3.23 ±.17 | 4.13 ±.22 | |
| Barras, 1928 | | | | | | |
| | | | | | | |
| Spanish (Gen.). . . . . . . . | 206 | 71–96 | 79.05 ±.16 | 3.50 ±.12 | 4.43 ±.15 | |
| Cantabrica . . . . . . . . . . | 31 | . . . | 78.21 ±.54 | 4.42 ±.38 | 5.65 ±.48 | |
| Andalucia Baja . . . . . . . | 122 | . . . | 79.35 ±.22 | 3.57 ±.15 | 4.50 ±.15 | |
| Andalucia Alta  . . . . . . . | 36 | . . . | 79.28 ±.34 | 2.98 ±.24 | 3.76 ±.30 | |
| Castellana Inferior . . . . | 17 | . . . | 77.97 ±.53 | 3.26 ±.38 | 4.18 ±.48 | |
| Barras, 1923 | | | | | | |
| | | | | | | |
| Cacereños  . . . . . . . . . . | 23 | . . . | 77.50 ±.29 | 2.05 | 2.65 | |
| Aranzadi, 1894b | | | | | | |
| | | | | | | |
| Spanish Basques . . . . . . | 325 | . . . | 79.30 | | | |
| Deniker, 1900 | | | | | | |
| | | | | | | |
| Mexicans . . . . . . . . . . . | 48 | . . . | 81.17 ±.42 | 4.30 ±.30 | 5.30 ±.36 | |
| | | | | | | |
| Tzendals  . . . . . . . . . . . | 100 | 68–86 | 76.80 | | | |
| Chols  . . . . . . . . . . . . . . | 100 | 72–96 | 80.80 | | | |
| Chontals  . . . . . . . . . . . | 80 | 76–93 | 83.20 | | | |
| Huaxtecs. . . . . . . . . . . . | 100 | 76–96 | 84.40 | | | |
| *Mayas*  . . . . . . . . . . . . . | 100 | 75–95 | 85.00 | | | |
| Tzotzils  . . . . . . . . . . . . | 100 | 68–83 | 76.90 | | | |
| Starr, 1902 | | | | | | |
| | | | | | | |
| "Yucatecs of Mexico" . | 16 | . . . | 84.70 | | | |
| Deniker, 1900 | | | | | | |

TABLE 41. (*Continued*)

| Group | No. | Range | Mean | S.D. | V. | Significance with Total Yucatecans |
|---|---|---|---|---|---|---|
| Sioux, Pure | 537 | 70–95 | 79.60 | 3.20 | 4.03 | |
| Sioux, Half-Blood | 77 | 74–88 | 79.40 | 2.64 | 3.33 | |
| Sullivan, 1920 | | | | | | |
| | | | | | | |
| Hawaiians, Pure | 74 | ... | 83.44±.25 | 3.17±.17 | 3.80±.21 | |
| F₁ Hawaiian, North | | | | | | |
| European | 10 | 75–91 | 83.01±.95 | 4.46±.67 | 5.37 | |
| Dunn, Tozzer, 1928 | | | | | | |

| Group | No. | Dolicho- (− 74.9) | Meso- (75 − 79.9) | Brachycephalic (80 +) |
|---|---|---|---|---|
| Hawaiian Male and Female | 108 | 2.1% | 9.8% | 88.0% |
| F₁ Male and Female | 36 | 0.0% | 5.5% | 94.4% |
| F₂ Male and Female | 26 | 7.7%[1] | 34.6%[1] | 57.7% |
| Dunn, Tozzer, 1928 | | | | |

[1] The per cent of dolicho- and mesocephalic in F₂ as shown in the table is too low, since some of the subjects included were immature, and the index may be expected to fall somewhat with increasing age. — Note by Dunn.

FEMALES

| Group | No. | Range | Mean | S. D. | V. | Significance with Total Yucatecans |
|---|---|---|---|---|---|---|
| Total Yucatecans | 694 | 75–99 | 85.94±.08 | 3.28±.06 | 3.82±.07 | |
| Group A | 154 | 79–99 | 86.88±.18 | 3.22±.12 | 3.71±.14 | 6×pe D |
| Group B | 231 | 75–95 | 85.89±.14 | 3.06±.10 | 3.56±.11 | None |
| Group C | 201 | 75–96 | 85.67±.16 | 3.32±.11 | 3.88±.13 | 2×pe D |
| Group D | 62 | 75–94 | 85.21±.32 | 3.72±.23 | 4.37±.26 | 2×pe D |
| Group E | 46 | 77–90 | 85.20±.29 | 2.88±.20 | 3.38±.24 | 2×pe D |
| Mexicans | 30 | 73–92 | 81.90±.52 | 4.20±.37 | 5.13±.45 | |
| | | | | | | |
| *Mayas* | 25 | 78–89 | 85.00 | | | |
| Huaxtecs | 20 | 78–94 | 86.20 | | | |
| Tzendals | 25 | 66–82 | 75.90 | | | |
| Chols | 25 | 73–90 | 80.00 | | | |
| Chontals | 25 | 77–88 | 82.00 | | | |
| Tzotzils | 25 | 72–82 | 76.80 | | | |
| Starr, 1902 | | | | | | |
| | | | | | | |
| Smith Coll. Students | 100 | 71–85 | 78.50±.20 | 2.97 | 3.78 | |
| Steggerda *et al.*, 1929 | | | | | | |
| | | | | | | |
| Sioux, Pure | 156 | 72–87 | 80.50 | 2.68 | 3.33 | |
| Sioux, Half-Blood | 19 | 72–86 | 80.50 | 2.85 | 3.54 | |
| Sullivan, 1920 | | | | | | |
| | | | | | | |
| Hawaiians, Pure | 34 | 74–90 | 84.20 | | | |
| ¾ Hawaiian, ¼ North | | | | | | |
| European | 12 | 79–93 | 82.60 | | | |
| F₁ Hawaiian, North | | | | | | |
| European | 10 | 81–87 | 85.00 | | | |
| ¼ Hawaiian, ¾ North | | | | | | |
| European | 6 | 76–86 | 79.90 | | | |
| Dunn, Tozzer, 1928 | | | | | | |

difference in values is due to changes in the subgroups' means in length, rather than in breadth of head. Such a finding substantiates Hooton's (1923) statement that an index is not inherited directly but rather is the result of inheritance of the dimensions from which the index is calculated.

The Mayas are among the broadest-headed of the peoples of the world. Many groups have heads as short as they, but few of such small bodily size possess such absolutely broad heads. Brachycephals are found in Spain but they are comparatively few; the means indicate that the Spanish are predominately dolicho- and mesocephalic. The head lengths of the Whiter Yucatecan mixed-bloods have been seen to approach the Spanish mean; if head breadths had only responded similarly, the cephalic index means of Groups D and E would undoubtedly be much lower than they actually are.

The graphs of Plate 12 show unimodal curves except in the case of Group E. The minor mode of that curve has its peak at the index value of 78, which is also the Spanish mode. Groups D, C, B, and A have at the eighty-two index line the following percentages respectively: 23, 13, 9, and 10; at the eighty-eight line, respectively: 12, 16, 21, and 22. Even in the presence of partial dominance of the extreme head breadth of the Mayas, many low brachycephals and some mesocephals appear in the Whiter subgroups.

Sullivan's mixture occurred between races whose indices were not very different. The data from Dunn and Tozzer for males show only the $F_1$ progeny; in them occurs a slight drop in value. The percentage table on the Hawaiian mixture for both sexes tells approximately the same story as has been given above for the Yucatecans.

The Yucatecan females have, as is ordinarily found, slightly higher cephalic indices than do the males. Group A differs significantly from the group as a whole, but C, D, and E only probably so. The Maya and Huaxtec groups of Starr are the only ones which that author lists that nearly approach the Yucatecans' means.

The percentages at the value of eighty-two (on the graph) are for the subgroups alphabetically: 7, 8, 8, 16, and 15; at the indicial value of eighty-eight, 24, 23, 25, 11, and 17. The Group E curve is not bimodal in females as in males. As in the means, the females do not exhibit as much difference one from the other as do the males.

The female Half-Blood Sioux have the same mean as do the Full-Bloods; probably because the indices of the mixing groups are much alike. Dunn and Tozzer's females show segregation which is much more definite than that seen in the Yucatecans. An explanation for the difference in reaction of the two cases of mixture has already been put forward in discussion of head breadth.

**Head Height.** No significant differences occur in males or females in the means for height of head. The Spanish males cited from Coon, Barras, and Aranzadi all have heads much higher than any of the Yucatecan subgroups. The male Mexicans also have a higher average value, but the Mexican females' mean is approximately the same as that of the Yucatecan females. A partial dominance of low-headedness seems to be operative, possibly comparable with that for broad-headedness.

The seriation curves (Plate 13) indicate bimodality in the males for Groups D and E. Modal peaks at 128 and 130 millimeters, respectively, are seen. A's mode lies at 124, with Groups B and C at 126 millimeters. For the females, the modes of Groups A and B are at the value of 120; C reaches a peak of 122, and D at 124 (with a minor mode at 118). The curve for the female Group E has its highest peak at 120 millimeters. Twenty-two per cent of the group have heads of this height. The only way in which this subgroup differs from the others is that the minimum range is several millimeters higher than that of any of the remainder.

**Length-Height Index of the Head.** Head-length means have been found to vary with the subgroups; means of head height do not so vary. An index between these two dimensions is therefore expected to show subgroup differences. The length-height index in Groups D and E is practically the equivalent of the averages given by Barras and Coon. The more Indian subgroups have means quite like those of certain Swiss groups, Chinese, Buriats, and Kurds. Whatever may be the cause of that relation in those groups, in the Yucatecan subgroups a low index is produced by combination of moderate lowness with extreme shortness of head.

Little comment need be made on this index in the females. The subgroups vary just as do the males, but to a less marked degree.

## TABLE 42.  HEAD HEIGHT

### MALES

| Group | No. | Range | Mean | S. D. | V. | Significance with Total Yucatecans |
|---|---|---|---|---|---|---|
| Total Yucatecans .. | 880 | 108–140 | 123.65 ±.10 | 4.55 ±.07 | 3.68 ±.06 | |
| Group A .......... | 221 | 108–138 | 123.84 ±.22 | 4.75 ±.15 | 3.84 ±.12 | 1×pe D |
| Group B ......... | 199 | 113–134 | 123.29 ±.20 | 4.08 ±.14 | 3.31 ±.11 | 2×pe D |
| Group C ......... | 362 | 111–139 | 123.80 ±.16 | 4.52 ±.11 | 3.65 ±.09 | 1×pe D |
| Group D ......... | 52 | 113–132 | 123.27 ±.42 | 4.50 ±.30 | 3.65 ±.24 | None |
| Group E ......... | 46 | 110–135 | 123.24 ±.55 | 5.50 ±.39 | 4.46 ±.31 | None |
| Spanish .......... Barras, 1928 | 67 | 105–142 | 126.37 ±.67 | 8.14 ±.47 | 6.44 ±.38 | |
| Cacereños ........ Aranzadi, 1894b | 23 | ... | 130.20 | | | |
| Andalusian Moors . Coon, 1929 | 28 | ... | 129.50 ±.84 | 6.60 ±.60 | 5.10 ±.46 | |
| Mexicans ......... | 48 | ... | 126.92 ±.51 | 5.15 ±.36 | 4.22 ±.29 | |
| Batua .................... Czekanowski (Martin, 1914) | | | 118.00 | | | |
| Swiss (Safiental) ............. Wettstein (Martin, 1914) | | | 121.00 | | | |
| Tungus .................... Jochelson (Martin, 1914) | | | 123.00 | | | |
| Chinese ................... Koganei (Martin, 1914) | | | 124.00 | | | |
| South Chinese ............... Hagen (Martin, 1914) | | | 124.00 | | | |
| Buriats .................... Talko-Hryncewicz (Martin, 1914) | | | 127.00 | | | |

### FEMALES

| Group | No. | Range | Mean | S. D. | V. | Significance with Total Yucatecans |
|---|---|---|---|---|---|---|
| Total Yucatecans .. | 694 | 105–134 | 120.15 ±.12 | 4.58 ±.08 | 3.81 ±.07 | |
| Group A .......... | 154 | 107–130 | 119.97 ±.25 | 4.58 ±.18 | 3.82 ±.15 | None |
| Group B .......... | 231 | 107–134 | 120.47 ±.19 | 4.22 ±.13 | 3.50 ±.11 | 2×pe D |
| Group C .......... | 201 | 107–132 | 119.95 ±.22 | 4.70 ±.16 | 3.92 ±.13 | 1×pe D |
| Group D ......... | 62 | 105–124 | 119.76 ±.45 | 5.26 ±.32 | 4.39 ±.27 | None |
| Group E .......... | 46 | 111–134 | 120.63 ±.46 | 4.58 ±.32 | 3.80 ±.27 | 1×pe D |
| Mexicans ......... | 30 | 103–124 | 119.30 ±.66 | 5.40 ±.47 | 4.53 ±.39 | |
| Smith Coll. Students Steggerda et al., 1929 | 100 | 110–135 | 124.45 ±.34 | 5.00 | 4.02 | |

## TABLE 43.  LENGTH–HEIGHT INDEX

### MALES

| Group | No. | Range | Mean | S. D. | V. | Significance with Total Yucatecans |
|---|---|---|---|---|---|---|
| Total Yucatecans .. | 880 | 59–80 | 67.74±.06 | 2.84±.05 | 4.19±.07 | |
| Group A ......... | 221 | 61–75 | 68.51±.13 | 2.78±.09 | 4.06±.13 | 7×pe D |
| Group B ......... | 199 | 61–74 | 67.70±.11 | 2.36±.08 | 3.49±.12 | None |
| Group C ......... | 362 | 59–80 | 67.68±.10 | 2.86±.07 | 4.23±.11 | None |
| Group D ........ | 52 | 59–72 | 65.96±.26 | 2.74±.18 | 4.15±.27 | 7×pe D |
| Group E ......... | 46 | 60–73 | 65.87±.32 | 3.18±.22 | 4.83±.34 | 6×pe D |
| Spanish .......... Barras, 1928 | 67 | 55–78 | 66.04±.36 | 4.36±.25 | 6.60±.38 | |
| Spanish (Asturias).. Barras, 1923 | 31 | 51–91 | 65.56±.91 | 7.54±.65 | 11.50±.98 | |
| Andalusian Moors .. Coon, 1929 | 28 | ... | 66.68±.37 | 2.87±.26 | 4.30±.39 | |
| Swiss (Danis) ................ Reicher (Martin, 1914) | | | 66.70 | | | |
| Swiss (Safiental) .............. Wettstein (Martin, 1914) | | | 61.40 | | | |
| Kalmucks ................... Tschepourkovsky (Martin, 1914) | | | 64.10 | | | |
| Chinese ..................... Koganei (Martin, 1914) | | | 65.50 | | | |
| Armenians ................... Pittard (Martin, 1914) | | | 69.40 | | | |
| Buriats ..................... Iwanowski (Martin, 1914) | | | 69.50 | | | |
| Kurds ...................... Pittard (Martin, 1914) | | | 69.50 | | | |

### FEMALES

| Group | No. | Range | Mean | S. D. | V. | Significance with Total Yucatecans |
|---|---|---|---|---|---|---|
| Total Yucatecans .. | 694 | 59–78 | 68.51±.07 | 2.86±.05 | 4.17±.08 | |
| Group A ......... | 154 | 61–76 | 68.92±.15 | 2.80±.11 | 4.06±.16 | 1×pe D |
| Group B ......... | 231 | 63–77 | 68.72±.12 | 2.60±.08 | 3.78±.12 | 2×pe D |
| Group C ......... | 201 | 59–76 | 68.41±.15 | 3.14±.11 | 4.59±.15 | None |
| Group D ........ | 62 | 59–74 | 67.60±.23 | 2.74±.17 | 4.05±.25 | 3×pe D |
| Group E ......... | 46 | 59–74 | 67.80±.28 | 2.82±.20 | 4.16±.29 | 2×pe D |
| Smith Coll. Students Steggerda et al., 1929 | 100 | 59–73 | 66.59±.19 | 2.81 | 4.22 | |
| Swedes ...................... Valentin (Martin, 1914) | | | 60.10 | | | |
| Swiss (Danis) ................ Reicher (Martin, 1914) | | | 68.30 | | | |

TABLE 44. BREADTH–HEIGHT INDEX

MALES

| Group | No. | Range | Mean | S. D. | V. | Significance with Total Yucatecans |
|---|---|---|---|---|---|---|
| Total Yucatecans .. | 880 | 70–93 | 79.55±.07 | 3.20±.05 | 4.02±.06 | |
| Group A .......... | 221 | 70–88 | 79.78±.15 | 3.34±.11 | 4.19±.13 | 1×pe D |
| Group B .......... | 199 | 71–88 | 79.59±.14 | 2.90±.10 | 3.64±.12 | None |
| Group C .......... | 362 | 71–93 | 79.59±.11 | 3.24±.08 | 4.07±.10 | None |
| Group D ......... | 52 | 72–88 | 78.25±.27 | 2.86±.19 | 3.65±.24 | 4×pe D |
| Group E .......... | 46 | 73–88 | 78.80±.34 | 3.44±.24 | 4.37±.31 | 2×pe D |
| Spanish .......... Barras, 1928 | 67 | 71–93 | 84.25±.43 | 5.18±.30 | 6.15±.36 | |
| Andalusian Moors.. Coon, 1929 | 28 | ... | 86.96±.47 | 3.69±.33 | 4.24±.38 | |
| Swiss (Safiental) .............. Wettstein (Martin, 1914) | | | 75.30 | | | |
| Buriats ...................... Talko-Hryncewicz (Martin, 1914) | | | 79.40 | | | |
| Kurds ...................... Pittard (Martin, 1914) | | | 80.20 | | | |
| Armenians ................... Pittard (Martin, 1914) | | | 81.00 | | | |
| Chinese ..................... Koganei (Martin, 1914) | | | 81.60 | | | |

| FEMALES | | | | | | |
|---|---|---|---|---|---|---|
| Total Yucatecans .. | 694 | 69–92 | 79.71±.08 | 3.24±.06 | 4.06±.07 | |
| Group A .......... | 154 | 69–89 | 79.42±.18 | 3.36±.13 | 4.23±.16 | 1×pe D |
| Group B .......... | 231 | 71–92 | 79.95±.14 | 3.10±.10 | 3.88±.12 | 2×pe D |
| Group C .......... | 201 | 69–88 | 79.78±.15 | 3.22±.11 | 4.04±.14 | None |
| Group D ......... | 62 | 71–88 | 79.34±.28 | 3.28±.20 | 4.13±.25 | 1×pe D |
| Group E .......... | 46 | 71–86 | 79.63±.33 | 3.28±.23 | 4.12±.29 | None |
| Smith Coll. Students Steggerda et al., 1929 | 100 | 76–94 | 84.89±.24 | 3.48 | 4.10 | |

**Breadth-Height Index of the Head.** Group D varies significantly and Group E probably so, in the mean of this index, but in the direction away from the Spanish. The broad-headedness which is impressed upon all of the Yucatecan subgroups, and which appears to vary with bodily size, is undoubtedly the factor which causes this phenomenon. Again the females resemble the males of their respective groups, but the difference between their averages and those cited for comparison is less than in the case of the males.

## THE FACE

**Radiometric Measurements.** Before proceeding to the discussion of the more commonly used facial measurements and indices, it seems appropriate to consider first certain data relating to radiometric measurements of that part of the body.

In 1926 Dr. E. A. Hooton and the writer devised an instrument for the measurement of facial and cephalic angles and radii. The central point from which the radii are measured is tragion, which is the point on the living head corresponding to porion or superior border of the external auditory meatus of the skull. The angles are measured as deviations from the perpendicular to the Frankfort plane, which is automatically determined by the instrument. Records of the radial distance from tragion and of the angular deviation from the Frankfort plane can be made on the living head for various easily determined landmarks of the bony and soft parts. Some of these points [1] are (see Plate 14):

Opisthocranion: the most posterior projecting point of the posterior surface of the head.

Crinion: the hair line of the forehead.

Metopion: the point on the forehead in the middle line and at level of a horizontal line joining the two frontal bosses.

Glabella.

Nasion: the point on the skin overlying this bony point.

Nasal Depression: the most depressed point of the nasal root.

Prozygion: the most anteriorly projecting point on the face over the left zygomatic bone.

Rhinale: the point on the skin overlying the antero-inferior ends of the nasal bones.

Pronasale: the most anteriorly projecting point of the nasal tip.

Subnasale.

Labrale superior: the integumento-membranous junction of the upper lip.

Prosthion.

Labrale inferior: the integumento-membranous junction of the lower lip.

Inferior incisive point: the most depressed point between lower lip and promentale.

Promentale: the most anteriorly projecting point of the chin.

---

[1] All of these points are in the midline of the head or face except prozygion.

TABLE 45. AVERAGE PROTRUSION INDICES OF CEPHALIC
AND FACIAL POINTS

MALES

| Tragion | Group A (25) | Group B (17) | Group C (26) | Group DE (6) |
|---|---|---|---|---|
| Opisthocranion ................... | 104.9 | 102.2 | 104.2 | 110.3 |
| Crinion ........................ | 116.5 | 117.3 | 119.5 | 118.4 |
| Metopion ...................... | 109.8 | 110.8 | 111.8 | 112.7 |
| Glabella........................ | 105.8 | 106.2 | 106.1 | 107.6 |
| Nasal depression ................ | 97.8 | 97.7 | 97.7 | 97.8 |
| Prozygion ..................... | 75.7 | 76.1 | 75.2 | 73.8 |
| Rhinale ....................... | 106.4 | 106.4 | 106.4 | 105.8 |
| Subnasale...................... | 108.7 | 109.2 | 108.2 | 102.8 |
| Prosthion ...................... | 105.7 | 106.3 | 105.5 | 98.8 |
| Labrale superior................. | 117.8 | 118.7 | 118.1 | 111.2 |
| Pronasale ...................... | 121.0 | 121.7 | 121.6 | 117.7 |
| Labrale inferior ................. | 121.5 | 122.2 | 121.1 | 115.6 |
| Inferior incisive point ............ | 119.4 | 119.3 | 119.3 | 112.8 |
| Promentale .................... | 128.6 | 128.9 | 129.9 | 124.7 |

FEMALES

| Tragion | Group AB (15) | Group C (13) | Group DE (10) | Mexicans (6) |
|---|---|---|---|---|
| Opisthocranion ................... | 102.6 | 101.9 | 108.4 | 114.7 |
| Crinion ........................ | 125.2 | 124.0 | 126.0 | 127.9 |
| Metopion ...................... | 118.7 | 118.2 | 119.0 | 117.6 |
| Glabella ....................... | 108.0 | 107.1 | 107.6 | 106.7 |
| Nasal depression ................ | 97.6 | 97.7 | 97.2 | 97.8 |
| Prozygion ..................... | 80.3 | 77.7 | 77.8 | 79.0 |
| Rhinale ....................... | 104.5 | 103.8 | 102.8 | 103.4 |
| Subnasale...................... | 104.1 | 101.8 | 103.2 | 102.6 |
| Prosthion ...................... | 104.9 | 103.2 | 103.3 | 100.1 |
| Labrale superior ................ | 114.4 | 111.0 | 111.6 | 109.2 |
| Pronasale ...................... | 117.0 | 115.2 | 117.2 | 116.4 |
| Labrale inferior ................. | 119.0 | 116.9 | 116.2 | 114.1 |
| Inferior incisive point ............ | 117.7 | 115.7 | 114.7 | 114.1 |
| Promentale .................... | 126.6 | 124.7 | 126.0 | 123.1 |

Taking the tragion-nasion distance as a standard radius, indices
of protrusion for the various cephalic and facial parts were calculated for each individual by dividing a given radius by the tragion-
nasion radius of that person. Such indices answer the question:

In comparison to the perpendicular distance from nasion to a line joining the two points called tragion, how great is the proportional distance from the tragion line to a second given point on the head or face?

The technique involved in use of the instrument is difficult for the operator and trying to the subject. Consequently, the series of males and females measured is small. Only four females of Group A were examined; these were added to eleven women of Group B to form a group now to be known temporarily as Group AB. Groups D and E in the case of either sex were similarly combined. The average measurements of six Mexican women are listed for comparison. Table 45 shows the mean indices of protrusion, and Table 50 average angular locations of the various points for the subgroups of both sexes.

The radii and their angles will be discussed under the heads of the facial and cephalic points measured.

*Opisthocranion.* The Maya Indians are a very short-headed people. It was noted previously that the Whiter Yucatecan subgroups possessed head-length averages which were significantly greater than those of the remaining groups. Are those heads longer because of equal lengthening of both anterior and posterior segments or has one of the two segments increased more than the other? The average indices for tragion-glabella radius are slightly greater in the male DE group than in A and B; the female DE group has approximately the same value as the AB. But the average tragion-opisthocranion radii of both male and female Groups DE are markedly longer than in the more Indian groups. The relatively long-headed Mexican females have the highest value of all. It may be concluded that the increase in head length in the Whiter groups of the Yucatecans is to a greater extent due to lengthening of the posterior segment of the skull than to increased growth of the anterior segment.

*Crinion and Metopion.* In both males and females the radii from tragion to crinion and to metopion are longer in the DE groups than in the others. In slope of forehead a very definite sexual difference is observed; the females have much more protruding foreheads than do the males. Again the Mexican females have the highest average. One may summarize by stating that protuberance of the forehead is slightly greater in the Whiter than in the more

Indian groups, and that that feature is much more marked in females than in males.

*Glabella.* There is a slight superiority in value of this radius in DE males, but no difference that can be called significant appears in the female averages.

TABLE 46.  BROW–RIDGES

MALES

|  | sm | + | ++ | +++ | No. |
|---|---|---|---|---|---|
| Total Yucatecans | 67 | 434 | 312 | 15 | 828 |
|  | 8.1% | 52.4% | 37.7% | 1.8% |  |
| Group A | 27 | 125 | 68 | 1 | 221 |
|  | 12.2% | 56.6% | 30.8% | 0.4% |  |
| Group B | 19 | 101 | 65 | 3 | 188 |
|  | 10.1% | 53.7% | 34.6% | 1.6% |  |
| Group C | 21 | 171 | 138 | 10 | 340 |
|  | 6.2% | 50.3% | 40.6% | 2.9% |  |
| Group D | 1 | 17 | 22 | 0 | 40 |
|  | 2.5% | 42.5% | 55.0% | 0.0% |  |
| Group E | 0 | 19 | 19 | 1 | 39 |
|  | 0.0% | 48.7% | 48.7% | 2.6% |  |

FEMALES

|  | sm | + | ++ | +++ | No. |
|---|---|---|---|---|---|
| Total Yucatecans | 355 | 249 | 26 | 0 | 630 |
|  | 56.4% | 39.5% | 4.1% | 0.0% |  |
| Group A | 99 | 48 | 4 | 0 | 151 |
|  | 65.6% | 31.8% | 2.6% | 0.0% |  |
| Group B | 117 | 87 | 11 | 0 | 215 |
|  | 54.4% | 40.5% | 5.1% | 0.0% |  |
| Group C | 97 | 75 | 10 | 0 | 182 |
|  | 53.3% | 41.2% | 5.5% | 0.0% |  |
| Group D | 21 | 23 | 1 | 0 | 45 |
|  | 46.7% | 51.1% | 2.2% | 0.0% |  |
| Group E | 21 | 16 | 0 | 0 | 37 |
|  | 56.8% | 43.2% | 0.0% | 0.0% |  |

No radiometric measurement was made on the brow-ridges, but their prominence was subjectively graded. The results may be found in the percentage table for *prominence of brow-ridges.* The first fact of interest noted is that whereas a small proportion of the males have small ridges, more than half of each group of the females possess this trait. This agrees well with the finding from radiometry that females have more protruding foreheads than males. It is also found that the male Groups A, B, and C show six to twelve per cent of frequency of small ridges, while Groups D and E exhibit 0 to 2.5 per cent. In females, the difference between the two types is less, but again Group A leads in frequency of small brow-ridges. It may be concluded that the Whiter Yucatecans have on the average straighter foreheads and larger brow-ridges than the more Indian type.

*Nasal Depression.* The location of the point overlying the bony nasion is difficult but sufficiently accurate for comparison with points which are somewhat separated from nasion. The nasal depression point, however, lies very close to nasion, and comparison of the values of the tragion-nasion and the tragion-nasal depression radii should not be too critically made. No difference appears in the male subgroups. There is a suggestion of deeper depression in the DE females but no definite conclusions should be drawn from these data.

*Prozygion.* The measurement from tragion was in each case taken to a point not far distant from the lateral and inferior part of the maxillo-zygomatic suture. The zygomatic processes of the maxillae of the male Groups A, B, and C are thrust farther forward than those of Group DE to the extent of 1.4 to 2.3 index units. Among the female subgroups, Group C, as well as Group DE, lacks the amount of protrusion seen in Group A by 2.5 units. The Mexican women's mean lies between those of the contrasted groups.

*Rhinale.* The tragion-rhinale index represents to great extent the amount of slope toward the sagittal plane (as opposed to slope toward the frontal plane) in the frontal process of the maxilla, and in the nasal bones. The length of the nasal bones themselves constitutes a factor in this radius. Again Group DE in either sex exhibits slightly less protrusion. It may be said, therefore, that both the lateral and the medial wings of the maxillary bone appear to protrude farther anteriorly in the more Indian than in the Whiter subgroups of the Yucatecans.

*Subnasale.* The tragion-subnasale measurement, as compared to the tragion-nasion radius, indicates the thrust of the vomer bone from the sphenoidal body plus the added protrusion of the nasal spine of the maxilla. The farther forward the vomer pushes itself, the more anteriorly is carried the superior portion of the body of the maxilla which bears the anterior nasal spine.

In the males, Group DE's subnasale lies between 5.4 and 6.4 index units farther posteriorly than that point in Groups A, B, and C. The difference is considerably less in the females and is only doubtfully significant.

*Prosthion.* The anterior or posterior position of subnasale depends to great extent upon how much the vomer thrusts forward.

TABLE 47.  ALVEOLAR PROGNATHISM

MALES

|  | 0 | sm | + | ++ | +++ | No. |
|---|---|---|---|---|---|---|
| Total Yucatecans ....... | 154 | 301 | 311 | 61 | 1 | 828 |
|  | 18.6% | 36.4% | 37.6% | 7.4% | 0.1% | |
| Group A .............. | 26 | 75 | 88 | 32 | 0 | 221 |
|  | 11.8% | 33.9% | 39.8% | 14.5% | 0.0% | |
| Group B .............. | 18 | 61 | 96 | 13 | 0 | 188 |
|  | 9.6% | 32.4% | 51.1% | 6.9% | 0.0% | |
| Group C .............. | 71 | 140 | 114 | 14 | 1 | 340 |
|  | 20.9% | 41.2% | 33.5% | 4.0% | 0.3% | |
| Group D .............. | 22 | 12 | 6 | 0 | 0 | 40 |
|  | 55.0% | 30.0% | 15.0% | 0.0% | 0.0% | |
| Group E .............. | 17 | 12 | 8 | 2 | 0 | 39 |
|  | 43.6% | 30.8% | 20.5% | 5.1% | 0.0% | |

FEMALES

|  | 0 | sm | + | ++ | +++ | No. |
|---|---|---|---|---|---|---|
| Total Yucatecans ....... | 146 | 228 | 220 | 34 | 2 | 630 |
|  | 23.2% | 36.2% | 34.9% | 5.4% | 0.3% | |
| Group A .............. | 18 | 62 | 62 | 8 | 1 | 151 |
|  | 11.9% | 41.1% | 41.1% | 5.3% | 0.6% | |
| Group B .............. | 41 | 76 | 84 | 14 | 0 | 215 |
|  | 19.1% | 35.4% | 39.0% | 6.5% | 0.0% | |
| Group C .............. | 48 | 67 | 54 | 12 | 1 | 182 |
|  | 26.4% | 36.8% | 29.7% | 6.6% | 0.5% | |
| Group D .............. | 20 | 15 | 10 | 0 | 0 | 45 |
|  | 44.5% | 33.3% | 22.2% | 0.0% | 0.0% | |
| Group E .............. | 19 | 8 | 10 | 0 | 0 | 37 |
|  | 51.4% | 21.6% | 27.0% | 0.0% | 0.0% | |

But the forward or backward location of prosthion depends upon the factors that establish the position of the upper part of the maxilla, as well as upon the amount of anterior bending of the inferior portion of the body of that bone.

The male DEs show on the average less protrusion of prosthion than do Groups A, B, and C by a difference of from 6.7 to 7.5 units. The trend in the females follows that of the males but the subgroup

differences of the females are small. The Mexican women's prosthion is more retracted than any of those of the Yucatecan groups.
Since the male subgroup differences for prosthion protrusion are
greater than those for subnasale protrusion, it may be inferred that
there is more swinging forward of the tooth-bearing portion of the
maxillary bone in the more Indian groups than in the Whiter: in
other words, more alveolar prognathism.

Fortunately, there is an available check on the conclusion that
Maya Indian types are more prognathous than the Whiter. This
may be found in the percentage table for subjective observations
on *alveolar prognathism*. Examination of the table for males shows
that, while seventy-five to eighty-five per cent of the individuals of
Whiter type are graded as having slight protrusion of the upper
jaw or none, only forty-five to sixty of the more Indian subjects are so characterized. On the other hand, while fourteen per
cent of Group A has pronounced prognathism, not one of the other
subgroups exhibits half as much. Furthermore, considering moderate and pronounced prognathism together, it is seen that more than
half of Groups A and B were so classified; in contrast, Group C has
a little more than a third of its members in these grades, and
Groups D and E a quarter and less.

The females show less marked differences between subgroups.
In the extreme grades (none and pronounced prognathism) Groups
D and E vary from the other three in considerable degree; but
smaller subgroup differences are noted in slight and moderate
protrusion than among the males. These conclusions concerning
subjective observations on alveolar prognathism are substantiated
by the findings from mechanical (not subjective) radiometric measurements; in turn, the former substantiate the latter because they
are based upon a much greater number of observations.

*Labrale superior*. Bony alveolar prognathism has been established for the more Indian subgroups. It is therefore not surprising
to find the protrusion carried on to the fleshy parts. But examination of the percentage table for *membranous lip thickness* gives
some reason to believe that not only is the alveolar process of the
maxilla of the average Maya Indian thrust well forward, but also
that his labrale superior stands relatively farther away from tragion
than does prosthion. Such a surmise is made on the basis of greater
frequency of pronouncedly thick membranous lips in the more

Indian subgroups, both male and female, as shown in the tables for membranous lip thickness.

The point labrale superior lies just inferior to the anterior continuation of the line from tragion to prosthion. In Groups A, B, and C of the males, the point is located 6.6 to 7.5 index units farther

TABLE 48. MEMBRANOUS LIP THICKNESS

MALES

| | sm | + | ++ | +++ | No. |
|---|---|---|---|---|---|
| Total Yucatecans ............ | 86 10.4% | 347 41.9% | 383 46.3% | 12 1.4% | 828 |
| Group A ................... | 8 3.6% | 89 40.3% | 119 53.8% | 5 2.3% | 221 |
| Group B ................... | 20 10.6% | 63 33.5% | 100 53.2% | 5 2.7% | 188 |
| Group C ................... | 42 12.4% | 147 43.2% | 149 43.8% | 2 0.6% | 340 |
| Group D ................. | 7 17.5% | 28 70.0% | 5 12.5% | 0 0.0% | 40 |
| Group E ................... | 9 23.1% | 20 51.3% | 10 25.6% | 0 0.0% | 39 |

FEMALES

| | sm | + | ++ | +++ | No. |
|---|---|---|---|---|---|
| Total Yucatecans ............ | 59 9.3% | 233 37.0% | 330 52.4% | 8 1.3% | 630 |
| Group A ................... | 5 3.3% | 55 36.4% | 87 57.6% | 4 2.7% | 151 |
| Group B ................... | 17 7.9% | 68 31.6% | 127 59.1% | 3 1.4% | 215 |
| Group C ................... | 13 7.1% | 72 39.6% | 96 52.8% | 1 0.5% | 182 |
| Group D ................. | 13 28.9% | 19 42.2% | 13 28.9% | 0 0.0% | 45 |
| Group E ................... | 11 29.7% | 19 51.4% | 7 18.9% | 0 0.0% | 37 |

anteriorly than in the Group DE. This range of subgroup differences is the same as in the case of prosthion, which fact indicates that labrale superior does not protrude relatively farther than prosthion. Thus, in males, the two sets of data do not agree. Perhaps it is too much to expect the radiometric technique to measure so finely. However that may be, the difference between the indices for labrale superior and prosthion in females shows that the lip point of the more Indian type lies relatively farther forward than prosthion. In this case the objective and subjective data point to the same conclusion.

*Pronasale.* It was noted above that subnasale in the males lies 5.4 to 6.4 units farther anteriorly in Groups A, B, and C than in Group DE. But the difference at pronasale ranges on the average only from 3.3 to 4.0 units. In discussing the position of subnasale, it was also stated that antero-posterior length of the vomer, as well as length of the body of the sphenoid, may regulate protrusion of that point. In the case of pronasale, the perpendicular lamina of the ethmoid bone is even more responsible than is the vomer for protrusion or retraction. Other factors may be: length of the septal cartilage, size and shape of the lateral and greater alar cartilages, and especially the size and shape of the medial wing of the greater alar cartilage. Which one of these factors may be responsible it is impossible to determine with the technique used. Since lateral flare of the nasal wings is a typical Mayan characteristic, it may be ventured that the disposition of the cartilages of the nasal tip may have a great deal to do with the matter. The differences in the protrusion indices between pronasale and subnasale for the subgroups A, B, C, and DE are respectively: 12.3, 12.5, 13.4, and 14.9.

The female groups AB, C, and DE have respectively corresponding differences of 12.9, 13.4, and 14.0. The figure for the Mexicans is 13.8. Thus, as in the other cases, a trend is found in the female groups similar to that occurring in the males, but the differences between the female groups are less marked.

*Labrale inferior.* Unless there is great difference in shape or size of the upper and lower lips, it seems reasonable to assume that for proper occlusion of the teeth and lips, alveolar prognathism in the maxilla should be accompanied by protrusion in the superior part of the mandible as measured at labrale inferior. Protrusion of labrale inferior in both sexes correlates well with projection of labrale superior; if the upper lip is carried forward, the lower goes with it.

*Inferior incisive point* and *promentale.* Lack of prominence of the chin was chosen as one of the distinguishing characteristics of Maya Indians. The percentage table for *chin prominence* indicates that Group A of either sex was defined as including no individuals possessing prominent or very prominent ($++$ or $+++$) chins.

No stipulation regarding this character was made for the Whiter subgroups. The distribution for the various groups shows that, in comparison with the prominence of other parts of the facial profile (especially the region of the underlip and lips) the Whiter subgroups have much greater frequency of protuberant chins. It will

TABLE 49. CHIN PROMINENCE

MALES

| | sm | + | ++ | +++ | No. |
|---|---|---|---|---|---|
| Total Yucatecans | 213 | 306 | 349 | 11 | 879 |
| | 24.2% | 34.9% | 39.7% | 1.3% | |
| Group A | 99 | 121 | 0 | 0 | 220 |
| | 45.0% | 55.0% | 0.0% | 0.0% | |
| Group B | 57 | 71 | 70 | 1 | 199 |
| | 28.6% | 35.7% | 35.2% | 0.5% | |
| Group C | 51 | 90 | 214 | 7 | 362 |
| | 14.1% | 24.9% | 59.1% | 1.9% | |
| Group D | 3 | 12 | 35 | 2 | 52 |
| | 5.8% | 23.1% | 67.3% | 3.8% | |
| Group E | 3 | 11 | 31 | 1 | 46 |
| | 6.5% | 23.9% | 67.4% | 2.2% | |

FEMALES

| | sm | + | ++ | +++ | No. |
|---|---|---|---|---|---|
| Total Yucatecans | 293 | 316 | 84 | 1 | 694 |
| | 42.2% | 45.6% | 12.1% | 0.1% | |
| Group A | 75 | 79 | 0 | 0 | 154 |
| | 48.7% | 51.3% | 0.0% | 0.0% | |
| Group B | 109 | 105 | 17 | 0 | 231 |
| | 47.2% | 45.4% | 7.4% | 0.0% | |
| Group C | 90 | 72 | 38 | 1 | 201 |
| | 44.8% | 35.8% | 18.9% | 0.5% | |
| Group D | 11 | 34 | 17 | 0 | 62 |
| | 17.8% | 54.8% | 27.4% | 0.0% | |
| Group E | 8 | 26 | 12 | 0 | 46 |
| | 17.4% | 56.5% | 26.1% | 0.0% | |
| Mexicans | 3 | 10 | 17 | 0 | 30 |
| | 10.0% | 33.3% | 56.7% | 0.0% | |

be interesting to compare the findings derived from subjective observations with those obtained by mechanical radiometry.

It has already been established that the more Indian groups have facial prognathism. Among other points, labrale inferior is protruded farther in Groups A and B than in Group DE. If for each group the difference is taken between the protrusion index for promentale and the index for labrale inferior, it is found that the differences for the male subgroups A, B, C, and DE are as follows: 7.1, 6.7, 8.8, and 9.1. For the female subgroups AB, C, and DE the figures are: 7.6, 7.8, and 9.8; for the Mexicans, the difference is 9.0 units. Therefore in comparison with protrusion of the lower lip, the chins of the Whiter groups are projected farther anteriorly than those of the other groups.

Another method of evaluating the amount of chin prominence is that of obtaining the differences between the protrusion indices of promentale and those of inferior incisive point. In the male groups, promentale projects farther anteriorly than inferior incisive point by 9.2 units in Group A, 9.6 in Group B, 10.6 in Group C, and 11.9 in Group DE. The female groups AB, C, and DE show the following differences: 8.9, 9.0, and 11.3. The Mexican females have the same difference value as that of Group C. There seems to be no doubt that the chin is more prominent in the DE group of either sex, whether the relative protrusion is measured in comparison to that of the lower lip or estimated in relation to "the dip above the chin."

*Facial Angles.* If one examines carefully the table of facial angles in the males (Table 50), he finds no consistent differences between the subgroups in the angular locations of glabella, nasion, rhinale, and pronasale. But from subnasale inferiorly, Group DE has markedly lower averages for the various points than any of the other groups. A simple explanation of this phenomenon is as follows: The thrust from tragion to any of the points between subnasale and promentale is partly anteriorly and partly in an inferior direction. If prognathism is present, the thrust from tragion must have a greater anterior component than if prognathism is not present.

In the females, a different situation appears. Throughout the list of angles, there is continuous increase in value for the various points from Group AB through Group C to Group DE. The whole face of the average of the DEs seems to be lifted to a higher level in its relation to the eye-ear plane. These facts appear to be in direct opposition to the findings for the males. Prognathism is not lacking in the female DE group to the extent that it is in the similar group of the males, but still it is true that this female group has less prognathism than do Groups AB and C. If possession of a greater amount of orthognathism is causative of lower angles of the inferior part of the face in males, why do not the females show similar diminution in value of the angles? If one looks ahead to the tables on bizygomatic diameter and facial height, he sees that

TABLE 50.   AVERAGE ANGULAR LOCATION OF CEPHALIC
AND FACIAL POINTS (IN DEGREES)

(Angular averages are listed only for those points which
have very definite locations)

MALES

|  | Group A (25) | Group B (17) | Group C (26) | Group DE (6) |
|---|---|---|---|---|
| Glabella ......................... | 109.4 | 108.9 | 110.3 | 107.8 |
| Nasion........................... | 101.5 | 101.3 | 103.0 | 101.2 |
| Rhinale ......................... | 88.2 | 88.7 | 88.9 | 88.5 |
| Pronasale ....................... | 75.4 | 75.8 | 75.6 | 75.2 |
| Subnasale ....................... | 68.4 | 69.2 | 68.6 | 67.8 |
| Prosthion ....................... | 58.5 | 59.5 | 58.7 | 56.2 |
| Labrale superior .................. | 61.2 | 62.5 | 61.2 | 59.7 |
| Labrale inferior ................... | 53.5 | 54.4 | 54.3 | 51.3 |
| Inferior incisive point ............. | 47.2 | 48.7 | 48.2 | 44.3 |
| Promentale ...................... | 40.2 | 40.3 | 41.1 | 38.3 |

FEMALES

|  | Group AB (15) | Group C (13) | Group DE (10) | Mexicans (6) |
|---|---|---|---|---|
| Glabella ......................... | 111.3 | 111.2 | 111.5 | 108.3 |
| Nasion........................... | 103.1 | 104.2 | 105.3 | 102.7 |
| Rhinale ......................... | 88.9 | 89.8 | 91.8 | 90.0 |
| Pronasale ....................... | 75.5 | 77.2 | 78.6 | 78.8 |
| Subnasale ....................... | 67.3 | 69.5 | 69.7 | 69.3 |
| Prosthion ....................... | 59.1 | 60.2 | 61.1 | 60.5 |
| Labrale superior .................. | 60.5 | 62.8 | 63.7 | 61.3 |
| Labrale inferior ................... | 54.2 | 54.8 | 56.9 | 54.7 |
| Inferior incisive point ............. | 48.0 | 48.8 | 51.3 | 49.8 |
| Promentale ...................... | 39.9 | 41.8 | 44.1 | 42.0 |

in the males the facial breadth is less in Groups D and E than in the others to a degree that is probably significant; but facial height is possibly greater in the Whiter subgroups. On the other hand, these measurements in the female groups D and E are both significantly less than in the other subgroups; in other words, the faces of the Whiter women are smaller, less massive. The greatest subgroup differences in angular averages in the female groups occur in the angles to inferior incisor point and to promentale. This means that the chins of the DE women are smaller and less deep than those of the AB group. The condition of shortness of the face together with presence of a certain small amount of prognathism serves to explain the elevation of the angles of various points on the lower portion of the face of the Whiter group of females, as opposed to the depression of these angular values in the DE group of the males.

**Bizygomatic Diameter.** The extraordinary breadth diameter of head of the Maya Indians, it will be recalled, was not appreciably narrowed by White admixture. The averages of the subgroups for breadth of the face show that these two diameters do not behave exactly alike in the Yucatecan case of miscegenation. In the males, Group C has a mean which is probably significantly higher than the Group as a whole, while Group E's average in both sexes is probably significantly lower. The female Group D's lower value is undoubtedly significant. There is a definite approach in the D and E subgroups of both sexes toward the Mexican averages, but the mean face breadths of the Whites given for comparison are all much smaller than even those of the Whiter groups. The Tzendals and Chols have the narrowest faces of the tribes cited by Starr. The absolute values for Groups A and B are equivalent to those of the Eskimos of both sexes; the values are less than those of the generally larger Navajo and Shoshoni.

The seriation curves (Plate 15) for both sexes indicate a clear-cut bimodality in Groups D and E. These modes of lower value lie in the males between the two modes of the Spanish curve. Sullivan finds similar results in his Sioux Mixed-Bloods. He devotes considerable space to a discussion of the inheritance of face breadth. "In every case except the three-fourths Indians," he states, "the bimodal distribution is fairly clear. . . . It would seem that we are justified in concluding that face width is inherited in such a manner that either the Indian or White type of face is inherited." These findings fit in with those of the author regarding the Yucatecans. It should be recalled in this connection that while Groups A and B are theoretically regarded as representing rather pure Mayas, Groups D and E are not considered as pure Spanish

## TABLE 51. BIZYGOMATIC DIAMETER

### MALES

| Group | No. | Range | Mean | S. D. | V. | Significance with Total Yucatecans |
|---|---|---|---|---|---|---|
| Total Yucatecans .. | 880 | 127–165 | 142.30 ±.11 | 4.88 ±.08 | 3.43 ±.06 | |
| Group A . . . . . . . . . | 221 | 127–158 | 142.33 ±.21 | 4.56 ±.15 | 3.20 ±.10 | None |
| Group B . . . . . . . . . | 199 | 127–156 | 141.92 ±.23 | 4.84 ±.16 | 3.41 ±.12 | 1 ×pe D |
| Group C . . . . . . . . . | 362 | 127–165 | 142.69 ±.21 | 5.96 ±.15 | 4.18 ±.10 | 2 ×pe D |
| Group D . . . . . . . . | 52 | 131–155 | 141.69 ±.49 | 5.20 ±.34 | 3.67 ±.24 | 1 ×pe D |
| Group E . . . . . . . . . | 46 | 129–150 | 141.24 ±.52 | 5.20 ±.37 | 3.68 ±.26 | 2 ×pe D |
| Spanish . . . . . . . . . . | 78 | 117–150 | 133.29 ±.44 | 5.80 ±.31 | 4.35 ±.24 | |
| Barras, 1928 | | | | | | |
| Cacereños . . . . . . . | 23 | . . . | 133.80 | | | |
| Aranzadi, 1894b | | | | | | |
| Andalusian Moors . | 28 | . . . | 136.21 ±.55 | 4.29 ±.39 | 3.15 ±.28 | |
| Coon, 1929 | | | | | | |
| Mexicans . . . . . . . . | 48 | . . . | 139.98 ±.56 | 5.80 ±.40 | 4.14 ±.28 | |
| Chontals . . . . . . . . | 80 | 126–151 | 141.70 | | | |
| Huaxtecs. . . . . . . . . | 100 | 134–152 | 141.90 | | | |
| *Mayas* . . . . . . . . . . | 100 | 135–156 | 144.20 | | | |
| Tzotzils . . . . . . . . . | 100 | 130–156 | 140.90 | | | |
| Tzendals . . . . . . . . | 100 | 127–156 | 140.80 | | | |
| Chols . . . . . . . . . . . | 100 | 128–157 | 141.20 | | | |
| Starr, 1902 | | | | | | |
| Eskimo . . . . . . . . . . . . . . . . . . . . | | | 142.00 | | | |
| Duckworth (Martin, 1914) | | | | | | |
| Navajo . . . . . . . . . . . . . . . . . . . . | | | 147.00 | | | |
| Hrdlička (Martin, 1914) | | | | | | |
| Shoshoni . . . . . . . . . . . . . . . . . . | | | 147.00 | | | |
| Boas (Martin, 1914) | | | | | | |
| Sioux, Pure. . . . . . . | 538 | 134–168 | 149.10 | 5.45 | 3.65 | |
| Sioux, Half-Blood . . | 76 | 130–158 | 143.40 | 5.49 | 3.83 | |
| Sullivan, 1920 | | | | | | |
| Hawaiians, Pure . . . | 73 | . . . | 140.19 ±.65 | 8.25 ±.46 | 5.88 ±.39 | |
| F₁ Hawaiian, North | | | | | | |
| European . . . . . . . | 10 | 127–165 | 145.40 ± 2.2 | 10.35 ±1.56 | 7.12 | |
| Dunn, Tozzer, 1928 | | | | | | |

TABLE 51. *(Continued)*

FEMALES

| Group | No. | Range | Mean | S. D. | V. | Significance with Total Yucatecans |
|---|---|---|---|---|---|---|
| Total Yucatecans .. | 694 | 121–154 | 135.66±.12 | 4.86±.09 | 3.58±.06 | |
| Group A ......... | 154 | 123–148 | 136.27±.23 | 4.26±.16 | 3.13±.12 | 2×pe D |
| Group B ......... | 231 | 123–151 | 135.90±.20 | 4.60±.14 | 3.38±.11 | 1×pe D |
| Group C ......... | 201 | 121–153 | 135.81±.25 | 5.20±.17 | 3.83±.13 | None |
| Group D ........ | 62 | 121–148 | 133.60±.45 | 5.20±.31 | 3.89±.24 | 4×pe D |
| Group E ......... | 46 | 125–146 | 134.50±.50 | 4.98±.35 | 3.70±.26 | 2×pe D |
| Mexicans ........ | 30 | 117–144 | 130.03±.74 | 6.04±.53 | 4.64±.40 | |
| *Mayas* ........... | 25 | 130–145 | 136.90 | | | |
| Huaxtecs.......... | 20 | 129–143 | 134.20 | | | |
| Tzendals ........ | 25 | 126–137 | 131.10 | | | |
| Chols ........... | 25 | 122–139 | 130.20 | | | |
| Chontals ........ | 25 | 124–148 | 137.50 | | | |
| Tzotzils .......... | 25 | 124–144 | 132.70 | | | |
| Starr, 1902 | | | | | | |
| Smith Coll. Students | 100 | 122–140 | 130.46±.28 | 4.15 | 3.18 | |
| Steggerda *et al.*, 1929 | | | | | | |
| Eskimo ..................... | | | 136.00 | | | |
| Duckworth (Martin, 1914) | | | | | | |
| Navajo ..................... | | | 138.00 | | | |
| Hrdlička (Martin, 1914) | | | | | | |
| Shoshoni ................... | | | 137.00 | | | |
| Boas (Martin, 1914) | | | | | | |
| Sioux, Pure........ | 157 | 130–154 | 142.80 | 5.05 | 3.53 | |
| Sioux, Half-Blood .. | 19 | 134–146 | 139.30 | 3.70 | 2.65 | |
| Sullivan, 1920 | | | | | | |
| Hawaiians, Pure ... | 34 | 123–150 | 136.70 | | | |
| ¾ Hawaiian, ¼ North European ....... | 12 | 122–143 | 130.40 | | | |
| F₁ Hawaiian, North European ...... | 10 | 127–152 | 135.40 | | | |
| ¼ Hawaian, ¾ North European ....... | 6 | 117–137 | 129.50 | | | |
| Dunn, Tozzer, 1928 | | | | | | |

Whites but rather the nearest approximation to them that exists in the Yucatecan series.

Dunn and Tozzer's F₁ males show evidence of heterosis, but their females of later generations exhibit the same sort of alternating inheritance as is seen in the Siouan mixture and in the Yucatecans.

Subjective observations on malar prominence were used, it will be recalled, as sorting criteria. For membership in Group A of either sex it was required that each individual possess prominent

TABLE 52.   MALAR PROMINENCE

MALES

|  | sm | + | ++ | +++ | No. |
|---|---|---|---|---|---|
| Total Yucatecans ............ | 3 | 79 | 540 | 258 | 880 |
|  | 0.3% | 9.0% | 61.4% | 29.3% | |
| Group A .................... | 0 | 0 | 116 | 105 | 221 |
|  | 0.0% | 0.0% | 52.5% | 47.5% | |
| Group B .................... | 0 | 7 | 130 | 62 | 199 |
|  | 0.0% | 3.5% | 65.3% | 31.2% | |
| Group C .................... | 0 | 30 | 248 | 84 | 362 |
|  | 0.0% | 8.3% | 68.5% | 23.2% | |
| Group D  .................. | 1 | 27 | 18 | 6 | 52 |
|  | 1.9% | 51.9% | 34.6% | 11.5% | |
| Group E .................... | 2 | 18 | 25 | 1 | 46 |
|  | 4.3% | 39.1% | 54.3% | 2.2% | |

FEMALES

|  | sm | + | ++ | +++ | No. |
|---|---|---|---|---|---|
| Total Yucatecans ............ | 0 | 43 | 438 | 213 | 694 |
|  | 0.0% | 6.2% | 63.1% | 30.7% | |
| Group A .................... | 0 | 0 | 98 | 56 | 154 |
|  | 0.0% | 0.0% | 63.6% | 36.4% | |
| Group B .................... | 0 | 5 | 149 | 77 | 231 |
|  | 0.0% | 2.2% | 64.5% | 33.3% | |
| Group C .................... | 0 | 7 | 130 | 64 | 201 |
|  | 0.0% | 3.5% | 64.7% | 31.8% | |
| Group D  .................. | 0 | 19 | 32 | 11 | 62 |
|  | 0.0% | 30.7% | 51.6% | 17.7% | |
| Group E .................... | 0 | 12 | 29 | 5 | 46 |
|  | 0.0% | 26.1% | 63.0% | 10.9% | |
| Mexicans .................. | 2 | 12 | 13 | 3 | 30 |
|  | 6.7% | 40.0% | 43.3% | 10.0% | |

or very prominent (++ or +++) malars. Accordingly, the percentage table for *malar prominence* shows zero percentages for the Groups A in the *sm* and + grades. Among other possible stipulations for admission of individuals to Groups D or E, one was that they should have only slightly or moderately prominent malars. Since degree of malar prominence was used as one of the sorting

## TABLE 53.  CEPHALO–FACIAL INDEX

### MALES

| Group | No. | Range | Mean | S. D. | V. | Significance with Total Yucatecans |
|---|---|---|---|---|---|---|
| Total Yucatecans .. | 880 | 83–101 | 91.53±.06 | 2.80±.04 | 3.06±.05 | |
| Group A ......... | 221 | 85–100 | 91.64±.12 | 2.74±.09 | 2.99±.10 | 1×pe D |
| Group B ......... | 199 | 85–100 | 91.66±.14 | 3.00±.10 | 3.27±.11 | 1×pe D |
| Group C ......... | 362 | 83–101 | 91.69±.10 | 2.72±.07 | 2.97±.07 | 2×pe D |
| Group D ........ | 52 | 84– 96 | 90.69±.27 | 2.94±.19 | 3.24±.21 | 3×pe D |
| Group E ......... | 46 | 85– 96 | 90.11±.23 | 2.32±.16 | 2.57±.18 | 6×pe D |
| Spanish ........... Barras, 1928 | 56 | 77–100 | 89.46±.31 | 3.44±.22 | 3.85±.24 | |
| Andalusian Moors . Coon, 1929 | 28 | ... | 91.36±.41 | 3.25±.29 | 3.56±.32 | |
| Mexicans ......... | 48 | ... | 91.48±.32 | 3.28±.23 | 3.58±.35 | |
| Sioux, Pure........ | 536 | 76–110 | 96.10 | 3.22 | 3.35 | |
| Sioux, Half-Blood .. Sullivan, 1920 | 77 | 84–100 | 92.90 | 3.23 | 3.48 | |
| | | | *Crania* | | | |
| Eskimo (Nunatagmiut) ......... Boas (Martin, 1914) | | | 100.80 | | | |
| Chinese ..................... Reicher (Martin, 1914) | | | 95.10 | | | |
| Athabascans (Tahltan) ......... Boas (Martin, 1914) | | | 94.80 | | | |
| Swiss (Danis) ................ Reicher (Martin, 1914) | | | 89.90 | | | |
| Spanish ....................... Hoyos Sainz (Martin, 1914) | | | 91.50 | | | |
| Buriats ....................... Reicher (Martin, 1914) | | | 92.70 | | | |
| Japanese .................... Adachi (Martin, 1914) | | | 94.60 | | | |

### FEMALES

| Group | No. | Range | Mean | S. D. | V. | Significance with Total Yucatecans |
|---|---|---|---|---|---|---|
| Total Yucatecans .. | 694 | 79–98 | 89.95±.07 | 2.86±.05 | 3.18±.06 | |
| Group A ......... | 154 | 83–98 | 90.15±.14 | 2.56±.10 | 2.84±.11 | 1×pe D |
| Group B ......... | 231 | 83–98 | 90.09±.11 | 2.56±.08 | 2.84±.09 | 1×pe D |
| Group C ......... | 201 | 81–98 | 90.42±.14 | 3.04±.10 | 3.36±.11 | 3×pe D |
| Group D ........ | 62 | 79–94 | 88.47±.26 | 3.00±.18 | 3.39±.21 | 6×pe D |
| Group E ......... | 46 | 81–98 | 88.59±.32 | 3.22±.23 | 3.64±.26 | 4×pe D |
| Mexicans ......... | 30 | 85–98 | 89.70±.40 | 3.24±.28 | 3.61±.31 | |
| Eskimo (Nunatagmiut) ......... Boas (Martin, 1914) | | | 101.60 | | | |
| Athabascans (Tahltan) ......... Boas (Martin, 1914) | | | 94.40 | | | |
| Sioux, Pure........ | 156 | 87–105 | 94.70 | 3.22 | 3.40 | |
| Sioux, Half-Blood .. Sullivan, 1920 | 19 | 89–96 | 92.50 | 1.88 | 2.03 | |

criteria for subgroups, the general trend of the percentage table may be predicted. Because of this fact, discussion of frequency distributions, which in their construction were purposely biased, is not warranted. It needs only to be pointed out that Group E, which differs only from Group D in possessing lighter pigmentation, has a higher percentage of prominent ($+ +$) malars than Group D.

**Cephalo-Facial Index.** The tables for head breadth show practically no difference between the subgroups; those for face breadth give a smaller mean in Group E of both sexes that is probably significant and a definitely smaller average in the female Group D. The expected is therefore found in the table for cephalo-facial index when it is noted that Groups D and E of both males and females possess smaller values than do the other subgroups. Sullivan presents similar differences between his Sioux Pure- and Half-Bloods of the two sexes. In a White-Indian mixture it appears that the growth of the face in the lateral direction, in proportion to lateral growth of the head, does not occur in the Whiter progeny to the extent that it does in the less mixed Indian descendants.

The seriation curves for this index (Plate 16) require no comment.

**Bigonial Diameter.** The table relating to breadth of jaws at the gonial angles shows that the averages of the three Spanish groups listed for comparison do not agree. The Mexicans have broader jaws than any of the Mayan subgroups, and the averages for the latter are far inferior to those of the Yakuts and the Eskimo. No significant difference appears in the subgroups of either sex, except possibly in the females of Group C, whose mean diameter is slightly greater. Therefore no strong correlation with bodily size can be claimed. No rule of genetic behavior can be deduced, for the average diameter of Group A lies within the range of the various Spanish means. It seems possible, furthermore, that breadth of jaw is apt to be as much affected by functional factors (relating to the action of mastication) as by genetic ones.

At this point, the opportunity is presented of comparing data obtained by mensuration with data obtained by subjective observation: the findings for bigonial diameter may be compared with the percentage table for *prominence of gonial angles*. The only difference discernible in the percentage tables for either males or

## TABLE 54. BIGONIAL DIAMETER

MALES

| Group | No. | Range | Mean | S. D. | V. | Significance with Total Yucatecans |
|---|---|---|---|---|---|---|
| Total Yucatecans .. | 878 | 89–124 | 105.69±.12 | 5.47±.09 | 5.18±.08 | |
| Group A ......... | 220 | 91–122 | 105.37±.23 | 4.99±.16 | 4.74±.15 | 1×pe D |
| Group B ......... | 199 | 91–124 | 105.72±.26 | 5.46±.18 | 5.16±.17 | None |
| Group C ......... | 362 | 89–122 | 105.85±.20 | 5.66±.14 | 5.35±.13 | 1×pe D |
| Group D ......... | 51 | 96–120 | 105.42±.52 | 5.48±.37 | 5.20±.35 | None |
| Group E ......... | 46 | 96–123 | 106.24±.59 | 5.98±.42 | 5.63±.40 | None |
| Spanish .......... Barras, 1928 | 78 | 87–118 | 101.73±.46 | 5.96±.32 | 5.86±.32 | |
| Cacereños ....... Aranzadi, 1894b | 23 | ... | 106.50 | | | |
| Andalusian Moors . Coon, 1929 | 28 | ... | 103.39±.85 | 6.65±.60 | 6.43±.58 | |
| Mexicans ......... | 48 | ... | 106.65±.59 | 6.03±.42 | 5.66±.49 | |
| Fan .................. Poutrin (Martin, 1914) | | 89–106 | 99.00 | | | |
| Yakuts ..................... Mainow (Martin, 1914) | | | 115.00 | | | |
| Eskimo ..................... Duckworth (Martin, 1914) | | | 131.00 | | | |

FEMALES

| Group | No. | Range | Mean | S. D. | V. | Significance with Total Yucatecans |
|---|---|---|---|---|---|---|
| Total Yucatecans .. | 694 | 77–118 | 99.56±.14 | 5.42±.10 | 5.44±.10 | |
| Group A ......... | 154 | 78–114 | 99.49±.32 | 5.94±.23 | 5.97±.23 | None |
| Group B ......... | 231 | 82–118 | 99.45±.24 | 5.38±.17 | 5.41±.17 | None |
| Group C ......... | 201 | 83–118 | 100.01±.25 | 5.30±.18 | 5.30±.18 | 2×pe D |
| Group D ......... | 62 | 89–110 | 98.82±.41 | 4.78±.29 | 4.77±.29 | 1×pe D |
| Group E ......... | 46 | 91–110 | 99.46±.49 | 4.96±.35 | 4.99±.35 | None |
| Mexicans ......... | 30 | 87–110 | 98.63±.68 | 5.54±.48 | 5.62±.49 | |
| Smith Coll. Students Steggerda et al., 1929 | 100 | 90–110 | 100.37±.30 | 4.39 | 4.37 | |

females is that the Whiter groups have definitely smaller frequencies of extremely broad angles. One fact is brought out by the observations that is not made clear by the data from the measurements: it is that in proportion to the remainder of facial parts the jaws of all the males are in half the cases of the prominent (+ +)

variety; except in the case of Group E women, the females in the majority of cases are evenly divided between prominent gonial angles and those of average size. Summarizing the measured and observed material on gonial angles, it may be concluded that a large proportion of all Yucatecans possess broad jaws, and that there is little difference between the subgroups in this respect.

TABLE 55.  PROMINENCE OF GONIAL ANGLES

MALES

| | sm | + | ++ | +++ | No. |
|---|---|---|---|---|---|
| Total Yucatecans . . . . . . . . . . . . | 48 | 268 | 452 | 112 | 880 |
| | 5.4% | 30.4% | 51.4% | 12.7% | |
| Group A . . . . . . . . . . . . . . . . . . | 11 | 62 | 114 | 34 | 221 |
| | 5.0% | 28.0% | 51.6% | 15.4% | |
| Group B . . . . . . . . . . . . . . . . . . | 9 | 57 | 103 | 30 | 199 |
| | 4.5% | 28.6% | 51.8% | 15.1% | |
| Group C . . . . . . . . . . . . . . . . . . | 22 | 115 | 180 | 45 | 362 |
| | 6.1% | 31.8% | 49.7% | 12.4% | |
| Group D . . . . . . . . . . . . . . . . . | 4 | 17 | 29 | 2 | 52 |
| | 7.7% | 32.7% | 55.8% | 3.8% | |
| Group E . . . . . . . . . . . . . . . . . . | 2 | 17 | 26 | 1 | 46 |
| | 4.3% | 37.0% | 56.5% | 2.2% | |

FEMALES

| | sm | + | ++ | +++ | No. |
|---|---|---|---|---|---|
| Total Yucatecans . . . . . . . . . . . . | 101 | 278 | 286 | 29 | 694 |
| | 14.5% | 40.1% | 41.2% | 4.2% | |
| Group A . . . . . . . . . . . . . . . . . . | 18 | 64 | 61 | 11 | 154 |
| | 11.7% | 41.6% | 39.6% | 7.1% | |
| Group B . . . . . . . . . . . . . . . . . . | 35 | 83 | 105 | 8 | 231 |
| | 15.2% | 35.9% | 45.5% | 3.4% | |
| Group C . . . . . . . . . . . . . . . . . . | 31 | 81 | 81 | 8 | 201 |
| | 15.4% | 40.3% | 40.3% | 4.0% | |
| Group D . . . . . . . . . . . . . . . . . | 11 | 23 | 26 | 2 | 62 |
| | 17.8% | 37.1% | 41.9% | 3.2% | |
| Group E . . . . . . . . . . . . . . . . . . | 6 | 27 | 13 | 0 | 46 |
| | 13.0% | 58.7% | 28.3% | 0.0% | |

**Minimum Frontal Diameter.** The breadth between the zygomatic arches has been demonstrated as smaller in the Whiter of the subgroups. On each side of the skull, the superior of the two medial supports of the zygomatic bone is the zygomatic process of the frontal. The most medial points on the inferior temporal lines, and also on the zygomatic processes of the frontal bone, are the points from which the minimum frontal diameter is measured. The

### TABLE 56. MINIMUM FRONTAL DIAMETER

MALES

| Group | No. | Range | Mean | S. D. | V. | Significance with Total Yucatecans |
|---|---|---|---|---|---|---|
| Total Yucatecans .. | 880 | 89–118 | 105.79±.09 | 4.09±.07 | 3.87±.06 | |
| Group A .......... | 221 | 91–118 | 105.38±.18 | 4.02±.13 | 3.81±.12 | 2×pe D |
| Group B .......... | 199 | 89–116 | 105.57±.20 | 4.07±.14 | 3.86±.13 | 1×pe D |
| Group C .......... | 362 | 93–118 | 106.22±.15 | 4.12±.10 | 3.88±.10 | 3×pe D |
| Group D ......... | 52 | 97–117 | 105.35±.42 | 4.54±.30 | 4.31±.28 | 1×pe D |
| Group E .......... | 46 | 97–112 | 105.46±.33 | 3.32±.23 | 3.15±.22 | 1×pe D |
| Spanish ........... Barras, 1928 | 78 | 87–120 | 105.04±.43 | 5.67±.31 | 5.40±.29 | |
| Cacereños ........ Aranzadi, 1894b | 23 | ... | 105.70 | | | |
| Andalusian Moors . Coon, 1929 | 28 | ... | 106.11±.66 | 5.14±.46 | 4.84±.44 | |
| Mexicans ......... | 48 | ... | 106.28±.40 | 4.06±.28 | 3.82±.27 | |
| Chinese ..................... Koganei, Mondiere (Martin, 1914) | | | 104.00 | | | |
| Kalmucks ................... Worobjow (Martin, 1914) | | | 106.00 | | | |
| Tungus ..................... | | | 109.00 | | | |
| Buriats ..................... Talko-Hryncewicz (Martin, 1914) | | | 112.00 | | | |

FEMALES

| Group | No. | Range | Mean | S. D. | V. | Significance with Total Yucatecans |
|---|---|---|---|---|---|---|
| Total Yucatecans .. | 694 | 89–116 | 102.22±.10 | 3.94±.07 | 3.85±.07 | |
| Group A .......... | 154 | 89–112 | 101.81±.21 | 3.94±.15 | 3.87±.15 | 2×pe D |
| Group B .......... | 231 | 91–112 | 102.36±.17 | 3.88±.12 | 3.79±.12 | None |
| Group C .......... | 201 | 93–112 | 102.03±.19 | 4.02±.14 | 3.94±.13 | 1×pe D |
| Group D ......... | 62 | 93–116 | 102.73±.33 | 3.84±.23 | 3.74±.23 | 1×pe D |
| Group E .......... | 46 | 95–112 | 103.11±.38 | 3.84±.27 | 3.72±.26 | 2×pe D |
| Mexicans ......... | 30 | 93–110 | 102.10±.55 | 4.50±.39 | 4.41±.38 | |

tables for this measurement show anything but a tendency similar
to that of bizygomatic diameter; no correlation exists. The male
Group C's average is greater than that of any other; the female
Group A mean is possibly smaller and that of Group E possibly
larger than that of the female group as a whole. Although the

## TABLE 57. FRONTO–PARIETAL INDEX

MALES

| Group | No. | Range | Mean | S. D. | V. | Significance with Total Yucatecans |
|---|---|---|---|---|---|---|
| Total Yucatecans .. | 880 | 61–76 | 68.05 ± .06 | 2.79 ± .04 | 4.10 ± .07 | |
| Group A ......... | 221 | 61–74 | 67.88 ± .12 | 2.58 ± .08 | 3.80 ± .12 | 1 ×pe D |
| Group B ......... | 199 | 61–76 | 68.19 ± .14 | 2.99 ± .10 | 4.38 ± .15 | 1 ×pe D |
| Group C ......... | 362 | 61–76 | 68.22 ± .10 | 2.79 ± .07 | 4.09 ± .10 | 2 ×pe D |
| Group D ......... | 52 | 61–75 | 67.54 ± .26 | 2.77 ± .18 | 4.10 ± .27 | 2 ×pe D |
| Group E ......... | 46 | 63–71 | 67.48 ± .20 | 2.01 ± .14 | 2.98 ± .21 | 2 ×pe D |
| Spanish ........... Barras, 1928 | 57 | 61–82 | 70.73 ± .38 | 4.26 ± .29 | 6.02 ± .40 | |
| Spanish ........... Barras, 1923 | 206 | 59–87 | 71.00 ± .23 | 4.90 ± .16 | 6.90 ± .23 | |
| Andalusian Moors . Coon, 1929 | 28 | ... | 71.29 ± .42 | 3.28 ± .30 | 4.60 ± .42 | |
| Cacereños ........ Aranzadi, 1894b | 23 | ... | 70.80 | | | |
| | | | *Crania* | | | |
| Kalmucks .................... Reicher (Martin, 1914) | | | 64.50 | | | |
| Chinese ..................... Haberer (Martin, 1914) | | | 65.80 | | | |
| Swiss (Danis) ................ Reicher (Martin, 1914) | | | 66.90 | | | |
| Japanese .................... Baelz (Martin, 1914) | | | 67.60 | | | |
| Bretons .................... | | | 67.30 | | | |
| Parisians ................... Manouvrier (Martin, 1914) | | | 68.00 | | | |

FEMALES

| Group | No. | Range | Mean | S. D. | V. | Significance with Total Yucatecans |
|---|---|---|---|---|---|---|
| Total Yucatecans .. | 694 | 60–79 | 67.89 ± .07 | 2.65 ± .05 | 3.90 ± .07 | |
| Group A .......... | 154 | 60–77 | 67.47 ± .15 | 2.67 ± .10 | 3.96 ± .15 | 3 ×pe D |
| Group B .......... | 231 | 60–74 | 68.01 ± .11 | 2.58 ± .08 | 3.79 ± .12 | 1 ×pe D |
| Group C .......... | 201 | 60–77 | 68.01 ± .12 | 2.58 ± .09 | 3.79 ± .13 | 1 ×pe D |
| Group D ......... | 62 | 60–79 | 68.02 ± .24 | 2.79 ± .17 | 4.10 ± .25 | None |
| Group E .......... | 46 | 60–74 | 67.98 ± .29 | 2.88 ± .20 | 4.24 ± .30 | None |
| Mexicans ......... | 30 | 65–80 | 70.37 ± .38 | 3.12 ± .27 | 4.43 ± .39 | |
| | | | *Crania* | | | |
| Tyrolese ..................... Wacker (Martin, 1914) | | | 67.40 | | | |
| Australians .................. Schwalbe (Martin, 1914) | | | 77.40 | | | |

points of measurement are situated closely together, the diameters of breadth of forehead and breadth of face appear not to be interdependent. The tables on radiometry demonstrated that the Whiter males and females have more protuberant foreheads; the tables for minimum frontal diameter prove the presence of a tendency for Group A members of both sexes to possess narrower foreheads, in spite of the fact that these same individuals of Group A have wider faces.

**Fronto-Parietal Index.** No really significant differences appeared in the male means of the diameters from which this index was calculated. Consequently, no differences between male subgroups for the index are expected or found. In the females, however, although head breadth is possibly greater in Group E, minimum frontal breadth is probably significantly greater in Group E than in the group as a whole, and probably significantly less in Group A. These facts are the reasons for the significantly smaller value of fronto-parietal index in the female Group A; the Indian women have narrower foreheads in proportion to breadth of head than do the females of Whiter type.

**Zygo-Frontal Index.** If bizygomatic diameter tends to have a smaller value in the D and E groups, and minimum frontal breadth tends to vary in the opposite direction, then the index derived from these diameters should exhibit subgroup differences. Such variations in the indicial averages are found. The means differ greatly among the female groups, but to a much smaller degree among the males. This is mainly due to the fact that values for the diameters differ more in females than in males: among the women, the segregation seems to be of a more clear-cut type.

**Fronto-Gonial Index.** The bigonial diameter, a measure of breadth of jaw, does not vary significantly in the subgroups of either sex. There are but slight differences in forehead breadth among the males, and larger ones between the female groups. Between male subgroups, therefore, no differences in fronto-gonial index are expected. As pointed out under discussion of the radiometric data, the Whiter females have less massive faces than have the Indians. This applies to length and breadth of face and depth of lower jaw, but evidently not to forehead width. If the mandibles of the Whiter females are not as deep as those of the other groups, it might be reasonably expected that the bigonial diameter should

## TABLE 58. ZYGO–FRONTAL INDEX

### MALES

| Group | No. | Range | Mean | S. D | V. | Significance with Total Yucatecans |
|---|---|---|---|---|---|---|
| Total Yucatecans .. | 880 | 66–83 | 74.34 ± .06 | 2.67 ± .04 | 3.59 ± .06 | |
| Group A . . . . . . . . . | 221 | 69–83 | 74.06 ± .12 | 2.53 ± .08 | 3.42 ± .11 | 2×pe D |
| Group B . . . . . . . . . | 199 | 66–83 | 74.39 ± .14 | 2.88 ± .10 | 3.87 ± .13 | None |
| Group C . . . . . . . . . | 362 | 67–82 | 74.38 ± .10 | 2.70 ± .07 | 3.63 ± .09 | None |
| Group D . . . . . . . . | 52 | 69–82 | 74.40 ± .22 | 2.32 ± .15 | 3.12 ± .21 | None |
| Group E . . . . . . . . . | 46 | 69–80 | 74.83 ± .23 | 2.33 ± .16 | 3.11 ± .22 | 2×pe D |
| Spanish . . . . . . . . . . Barras, 1928 | 77 | 69–96 | 79.01 ± .33 | 4.30 ± .23 | 5.44 ± .30 | |
| Spanish . . . . . . . . . . Barras, 1923 | 206 | 67–99 | 81.09 ± .27 | 5.74 ± .19 | 7.08 ± .24 | |
| Andalusian Moors . Coon, 1929 | 28 | . . . | 77.96 ± .41 | 3.21 ± .29 | 4.12 ± .37 | |
| Mexicans . . . . . . . . . | 48 | . . . | 76.11 ± .29 | 2.93 ± .20 | 3.85 ± .27 | |
| | | | *Crania* | | | |
| Buriats . . . . . . . . . . . . . . . . . . . . . . Reicher (Martin, 1914) | | | 67.00 | | | |
| Kalmucks . . . . . . . . . . . . . . . . . . . Reicher (Martin, 1914) | | | 69.50 | | | |
| Eskimo . . . . . . . . . . . . . . . . . . . . . Oetteking (Martin, 1914) | | | 69.60 | | | |
| Chinese . . . . . . . . . . . . . . . . . . . . . Reicher (Martin, 1914) | | | 71.10 | | | |
| Swiss (Danis) . . . . . . . . . . . . . . . Reicher (Martin, 1914) | | | 74.60 | | | |
| Parisians . . . . . . . . . . . . . . . . . . . Manouvrier (Martin, 1914) | | | 74.90 | | | |
| Zulu . . . . . . . . . . . . . . . . . . . . . . . Shrubsall (Martin, 1914) | | | 89.80 | | | |

### FEMALES

| Group | No. | Range | Mean | S. D | V. | Significance with Total Yucatecans |
|---|---|---|---|---|---|---|
| Total Yucatecans .. | 694 | 66–85 | 75.39 ± .07 | 2.74 ± .05 | 3.64 ± .07 | |
| Group A . . . . . . . . . | 154 | 66–80 | 74.64 ± .14 | 2.52 ± .10 | 3.38 ± .13 | 6×pe D |
| Group B . . . . . . . . . | 231 | 69–83 | 75.39 ± .11 | 2.55 ± .08 | 3.38 ± .11 | None |
| Group C . . . . . . . . . | 201 | 66–83 | 75.19 ± .13 | 2.76 ± .09 | 3.67 ± .12 | 1×pe D |
| Group D . . . . . . . . | 62 | 72–85 | 77.02 ± .23 | 2.64 ± .16 | 3.43 ± .21 | 7×pe D |
| Group E . . . . . . . . . | 46 | 69–85 | 76.65 ± .31 | 3.12 ± .22 | 4.07 ± .29 | 4×pe D |
| Mexicans . . . . . . . . . | 30 | 73–82 | 78.50 ± .24 | 1.98 ± .17 | 2.52 ± .22 | |
| | | | *Crania* | | | |
| Swiss (Danis) . . . . . . . . . . . . . . . . Reicher (Martin, 1914) | | | 78.40 | | | |
| Australians . . . . . . . . . . . . . . . . . . Brackebusch (Martin, 1914) | | | 82.00 | | | |

also be less. Re-examination of the table for that measurement does show an absolutely smaller value for Group D than for any of the others, although the mean for Group E is almost exactly the same as the averages for Groups A and B. Turning to the data for fronto-gonial index, it is seen that the indicial percentages for Group D of the females is significantly smaller than that for the group as a

TABLE 59.  FRONTO–GONIAL INDEX

$$\frac{\text{Min. Frontal Diam.} \times 100}{\text{Bigonial Diam.}}$$

MALES

| Group | No. | Range | Mean | S. D. | V. | Significance with Total Yucatecans |
|---|---|---|---|---|---|---|
| Total Yucatecans .. | 878 | 84–119 | 99.96±.12 | 5.36±.09 | 5.36±.09 | |
| Group A .......... | 220 | 87–113 | 99.93±.24 | 5.35±.17 | 5.35±.17 | None |
| Group B .......... | 199 | 86–115 | 100.33±.25 | 5.22±.18 | 5.20±.18 | 1×pe D |
| Group C .......... | 362 | 85–116 | 99.70±.19 | 5.43±.14 | 5.45±.14 | 1×pe D |
| Group D ........ | 51 | 89–119 | 100.17±.52 | 5.46±.36 | 5.45±.36 | None |
| Group E .......... | 46 | 91–112 | 100.59±.46 | 4.62±.32 | 4.59±.32 | 1×pe D |
| Spanish ........... Barras, 1928 | 76 | ... | 96.56 | Calculated from means of Zygo-gonial and Zygo-frontal Indices | | |
| Spanish ........... Barras, 1923 | 206 | ... | 97.19 | | | |

FEMALES

| Group | No. | Range | Mean | S. D. | V. | |
|---|---|---|---|---|---|---|
| Total Yucatecans .. | 694 | 75–116 | 97.37±.13 | 5.06±.09 | 5.20±.09 | |
| Group A .......... | 154 | 75–116 | 97.72±.31 | 5.62±.22 | 5.75±.22 | 1×pe D |
| Group B ........ | 231 | 79–110 | 97.17±.24 | 5.32±.17 | 5.48±.17 | 1×pe D |
| Group C .......... | 201 | 79–113 | 97.93±.24 | 4.96±.17 | 5.06±.17 | 2×pe D |
| Group D ........ | 62 | 87–106 | 96.11±.40 | 4.72±.29 | 4.91±.30 | 3×pe D |
| Group E .......... | 46 | 83–108 | 96.41±.46 | 4.60±.32 | 4.77±.34 | 2×pe D |

whole, and that the mean for Group E is probably so. The slightly (though not significantly) broader foreheads and narrower jaws of the female Groups D and E have combined to give statistically significant differences from the group as a whole of the relation existing between these facial breadths.

Zygo-Gonial Index. Facial breadth is smaller in Groups D and E, and bigonial breadth about the same in all of the groups. The index between these widths of face is significantly larger in value

## TABLE 60. ZYGO–GONIAL INDEX

### MALES

| Group | No. | Range | Mean | S. D. | V. | Significance with Total Yucatecans |
|---|---|---|---|---|---|---|
| Total Yucatecans .. | 878 | 63–83 | 74.27 ± .08 | 3.54 ± .06 | 4.77 ± .08 | |
| Group A .......... | 220 | 63–83 | 74.08 ± .16 | 3.42 ± .11 | 4.62 ± .15 | 1 × pe D |
| Group B .......... | 199 | 63–83 | 74.36 ± .17 | 3.48 ± .12 | 4.68 ± .16 | None |
| Group C .......... | 362 | 64–82 | 74.18 ± .13 | 3.60 ± .09 | 4.85 ± .12 | None |
| Group D ........ | 51 | 67–81 | 74.45 ± .35 | 3.68 ± .25 | 4.94 ± .33 | None |
| Group E .......... | 46 | 68–83 | 75.28 ± .31 | 3.14 ± .22 | 4.17 ± .29 | 3 × pe D |
| Spanish .......... Barras, 1928 | 76 | 65–94 | 76.29 ± .36 | 4.66 ± .26 | 6.11 ± .33 | |
| Spanish .......... Barras, 1923 | 206 | 65–100 | 78.81 ± .27 | 5.73 ± .19 | 7.27 ± .24 | |
| Cacereños ........ Aranzadi, 1894b | 23 | ... | 78.80 | | | |
| Mexicans ........ | 48 | ... | 76.21 ± .33 | 3.37 ± .23 | 4.42 ± .30 | |
| | | | *Crania* | | | |
| Spanish .......... ........... Hoyos Sainz (Martin, 1914) | | | 76.50 | | | |
| Eskimo ..................... Oetteking (Martin, 1914) | | | 81.40 | | | |

### FEMALES

| | | | | | | |
|---|---|---|---|---|---|---|
| Total Yucatecans .. | 694 | 57–86 | 73.34 ± .09 | 3.69 ± .07 | 5.03 ± .09 | |
| Group A .......... | 154 | 57–86 | 72.90 ± .22 | 4.08 ± .16 | 5.60 ± .22 | 2 × pe D |
| Group B .......... | 231 | 60–86 | 73.20 ± .16 | 3.66 ± .11 | 5.00 ± .16 | 1 × pe D |
| Group C .......... | 201 | 63–86 | 73.57 ± .17 | 3.51 ± .12 | 4.77 ± .16 | 1 × pe D |
| Group D ........ | 62 | 66–80 | 73.97 ± .28 | 3.27 ± .20 | 4.42 ± .27 | 2 × pe D |
| Group E .......... | 46 | 66–80 | 73.78 ± .34 | 3.45 ± .24 | 4.68 ± .33 | 1 × pe D |
| Mexicans ........ | 30 | 69–84 | 75.90 ± .43 | 3.48 ± .30 | 4.58 ± .40 | |
| | | | *Crania* | | | |
| Spanish ..................... Hoyos Sainz (Martin, 1914) | | | 76.00 | | | |
| Tyrolese ..................... Frizzi (Martin, 1914) | | | 72.20 | | | |

in the Group E males, and tends to be so in the D and E groups of the other sex. The Whiter males make a good attempt at approach toward the Spanish averages, but not so close an approximation as is accomplished by the Mexicans.

## TABLE 61.  FACE HEIGHT

### MALES

| Group | No. | Range | Mean | S. D. | V. | Significance with Total Yucatecans |
|---|---|---|---|---|---|---|
| Total Yucatecans .. | 879 | 99–140 | 121.59 ±.14 | 6.22 ±.10 | 5.12 ±.08 | |
| Group A .......... | 221 | 105–136 | 120.93 ±.27 | 5.89 ±.19 | 4.87 ±.16 | 2×pe D |
| Group B ......... | 199 | 99–138 | 121.01 ±.30 | 6.36 ±.22 | 5.26 ±.18 | 2×pe D |
| Group C ......... | 361 | 103–140 | 122.24 ±.22 | 6.28 ±.16 | 5.14 ±.13 | 3×pe D |
| Group D ........ | 52 | 108–137 | 121.92 ±.61 | 6.56 ±.43 | 5.38 ±.36 | None |
| Group E ......... | 46 | 106–132 | 121.93 ±.59 | 5.98 ±.42 | 4.90 ±.34 | None |
| Spanish .......... Barras, 1928 | 56 | 103–141 | 120.27 ±.76 | 8.41 ±.54 | 6.99 ±.44 | |
| Andalusian Moors . Coon, 1929 | 28 | ... | 123.14 ±.75 | 5.88 ±.53 | 4.78 ±.43 | |
| Mexicans ......... | 48 | ... | 122.23 ±.51 | 5.22 ±.36 | 4.27 ±.29 | |
| Chontals ........ | 80 | 102–129 | 113.70 | | | |
| Huaxtecs.......... | 100 | 101–130 | 113.40 | | | |
| *Mayas* ........... | 100 | 99–124 | 110.60 | | | |
| Tzotzils .......... | 100 | 99–132 | 113.30 | | | |
| Tzendals ........ | 100 | 98–131 | 112.10 | | | |
| Chols ............ Starr, 1902 | 100 | 101–128 | 113.20 | | | |
| Shoshoni .................... Boas (Martin, 1914) | | | 119.00 | | | |
| Navajos .................... Hrdlicka (Martin, 1914) | | | 120.00 | | | |
| Nahuas...................... Ranke (Martin, 1914) | | | 120.00 | | | |
| Kalmucks .................. Worobjow (Martin, 1914) | | | 120.00 | | | |
| Germans (Baden) ............ Fischer (Martin, 1914) | | | 121.00 | | | |
| Germans .................... Weissenberg( Martin, 1914) | | | 123.00 | | | |
| Tyrolese (Walser) .. .... Wacker (Martin, 1914) | | 104–136 | 127.00 | | | |
| Eskimo .................... Duckworth (Martin, 1914) | | | 127.00 | | | |
| Chinese .................... Koganei (Martin, 1914) | | | 125.00 | | | |
| Sioux, Pure........ | 537 | 108–152 | 124.60 | 6.39 | 5.12 | |
| Sioux, Half-Blood .. Sullivan, 1920 | 77 | 106–140 | 121.50 | 6.36 | 5.23 | |
| Hawaiians, Pure ... | 74 | ... | 122.72 ±.57 | 7.22 ±.40 | 5.88 ±.39 | |
| $F_1$ Hawaiian, North European ....... Dunn, Tozzer, 1928 | 10 | 112–137 | 125.10 ±.36 | 6.39 ±.96 | 5.11 | |

TABLE 61.  (*Continued*)

FEMALES

| Group | No. | Range | Mean | S. D. | V. | Significance with Total Yucatecans |
|---|---|---|---|---|---|---|
| Total Yucatecans . . | 694 | 95–134 | 114.40±.15 | 6.04±.11 | 5.28±.10 | |
| Group A . . . . . . . . . | 154 | 99–129 | 114.49±.31 | 5.64±.22 | 4.93±.19 | None |
| Group B . . . . . . . . . | 231 | 101–130 | 114.65±.24 | 5.42±.17 | 4.73±.15 | 1×pe D |
| Group C . . . . . . . . . | 201 | 95–134 | 114.82±.33 | 6.92±.23 | 6.03±.20 | 1×pe D |
| Group D . . . . . . . . | 62 | 101–130 | 112.85±.52 | 6.06±.37 | 5.37±.33 | 3×pe D |
| Group E . . . . . . . . . | 46 | 101–124 | 113.15±.54 | 5.38±.38 | 4.76±.33 | 2×pe D |
| Mexicans . . . . . . . . . | 30 | 101–126 | 114.23±.79 | 6.44±.56 | 5.64±.49 | |
| Smith Coll. Students Steggerda *et al.*, 1929 | 100 | 98–122 | 111.99±.38 | 5.58 | 4.99 | |
| Shoshoni . . . . . . . . . . . . . . . . . . . Boas (Martin, 1914) | | | 109.00 | | | |
| Navajo . . . . . . . . . . . . . . . . . . . . Hrdlička (Martin, 1914) | | | 113.00 | | | |
| Nahua . . . . . . . . . . . . . . . . . . . . Ranke (Martin, 1914) | | | 112.00 | | | |
| Sioux, Pure. . . . . . . . | 157 | 100–130 | 117.40 | 6.18 | 5.26 | |
| Sioux, Half-Blood . . Sullivan, 1920 | 19 | 104–122 | 114.10 | 4.12 | 3.61 | |
| Hawaiians, Pure . . . | 34 | 101–125 | 116.20 | | | |
| ¾ Hawaiian, ¼ North European . . . . . . . | 12 | 99–122 | 112.50 | | | |
| F₁ Hawaiian, North European . . . . . . . | 10 | 110–126 | 116.60 | | | |
| ¼ Hawaiian, ¾ North European . . . . . . . Dunn, Tozzer, 1928 | 6 | 107–129 | 115.70 | | | |

**Face Height.** That head length is highly correlated with stature has long been recognized. It might be assumed that anatomical facial height is similarly related to stature, but if such correlation does exist, it must sometimes be of lower degree because of the action of certain modifying factors on the nasion-menton distance. In males, Groups A, B, and C show probably significantly lower averages than do Groups D and E. The female groups D and E, on the other hand, have smaller values than the others; that of

Group D is very definitely smaller. It will be recalled that the discussion of the radiometric and angular data showed very little prognathism to be present in the Whiter of the males, but that although there was less of that characteristic in the Whiter females than in the Indian women, they were not so free from it as were the men. It seems possible that the slightly longer faces of the male Groups D and E may be due, at least in part, to their freedom from prognathism. As has been stated before, the prognathous face expends more of its contour line in an anterior thrust than does the orthognathous one; consequently, of two faces of equal length of contour line, the orthognathous will have the greater nasion-menton length.

The seriation curves for facial height (Plate 17) are very irregular. In them are reflected the lack of precision of the measurement, as well as the multiplicity of factors that govern this length. Nothing of value can be added to the above discussion save that there seems to be indicated in the two Groups E a greater tendency than in the other subgroups toward segregation into longer- and shorter-faced types.

Starr's and the author's averages for this measurement cannot be compared; different identifications of the location of nasion probably explain the situation. Sullivan's Siouan Half-Bloods, both male and female, react as do the Mayan females. Unfortunately, Sullivan makes no statement concerning the amount of prognathism present in his material. Dunn and Tozzer's $F_1$ males exhibit what is probably heterosis, while the later generations in the females follow the example of the Sioux-White Mixed-Bloods in having shorter faces in the Whiter groups.

**Upper Face Height.** As in the case of the nasion-menton distance, the trends in the two sexes for the nasion-prosthion measurement are not exactly the same. No differences that are statistically significant appear among the male groups, but the female groups D and E have smaller averages than the compared subgroups. The differences in amount of prognathism may again be called upon for explanation of the situation. One may also suggest that the larger and taller D and E males have facial heights that average about the same as those of the smaller-bodied Indians; the Whiter women are shown to have definitely smaller faces than those of the Indian females.

### TABLE 62. UPPER FACE HEIGHT

MALES

| Group | No. | Range | Mean | S. D. | V. | Significance with Total Yucatecans |
|---|---|---|---|---|---|---|
| Total Yucatecans .. | 880 | 59–90 | 74.97±.10 | 4.63±.07 | 6.18±.10 | |
| Group A ......... | 221 | 61–88 | 74.84±.20 | 4.40±.14 | 5.88±.20 | None |
| Group B ......... | 199 | 59–86 | 74.80±.23 | 4.84±.16 | 6.47±.22 | None |
| Group C ......... | 362 | 59–90 | 75.20±.17 | 4.66±.12 | 6.20±.16 | 1×pe D |
| Group D ........ | 52 | 61–86 | 74.65±.41 | 4.42±.29 | 5.92±.39 | None |
| Group E ......... | 46 | 65–85 | 74.93±.47 | 4.73±.33 | 6.31±.44 | None |
| Spanish .......... Barras, 1928 | 79 | 61–96 | 72.92±.47 | 6.24±.34 | 8.56±.46 | |
| Andalusian Moors . Coon, 1929 | 28 | ... | 70.50±.51 | 3.99±.36 | 5.66±.51 | |
| Mexicans ........ | 48 | ... | 74.83±.38 | 3.91±.27 | 5.23±.36 | |
| Eskimo ............ Duckworth (Martin, 1914) | ... | ... | 73.00 | | | |
| Germans .......... Weissenberg (Martin, 1914) | ... | 62–89 | 76.00 | | | |
| Sioux, Pure........ | 43 | ... | 81.10 | 5.77 | 7.11 | |
| Sioux, Half-Blood .. Sullivan, 1920 | 13 | ... | 78.50 | 4.79 | 6.10 | |

FEMALES

| Group | No. | Range | Mean | S. D. | V. | Significance with Total Yucatecans |
|---|---|---|---|---|---|---|
| Total Yucatecans .. | 694 | 59–86 | 71.64±.12 | 4.58±.08 | 6.39±.12 | |
| Group A ......... | 154 | 59–85 | 71.97±.25 | 4.60±.18 | 6.39±.25 | 1×pe D |
| Group B ......... | 231 | 59–82 | 71.83±.19 | 4.24±.13 | 5.90±.19 | 1×pe D |
| Group C ......... | 201 | 59–86 | 71.80±.24 | 4.96±.17 | 6.91±.23 | None |
| Group D ........ | 62 | 59–82 | 70.73±.36 | 4.24±.26 | 6.00±.36 | 2×pe D |
| Group E ......... | 46 | 59–78 | 70.15±.42 | 4.24±.30 | 6.04±.43 | 3×pe D |
| Mexicans ........ | 30 | 57–78 | 70.23±.64 | 5.18±.45 | 7.38±.64 | |
| Sioux, Pure........ | 6 | ... | 77.30 | 2.86 | | |
| Sioux, Half-Blood .. Sullivan, 1920 | 4 | ... | 71.20 | 4.71 | | |

Sullivan's data further demonstrate that a similar mixture of massive-faced Indians with more delicate-faced Whites yields in the Whiter of the offspring a type of face like that of the White progenitors.

**Facial Index.** Facial breadth has been demonstrated to be somewhat narrower than in the group as a whole in the Group D and E males, and to be definitely so in the females of these subgroups. The nasion-menton distance is of about the same absolute magnitude in the male groups D and E as in the others, but the Whiter women have smaller values which differ significantly from the mean for Total Yucatecans. In other words, the male Ds and Es, in comparison to the whole group, have on the average narrower faces of about the same length, but the females of similar groups possess narrower and shorter faces.

The table for facial index bears out the conclusions that should be drawn from the preceding statements: Group A of the males has a smaller indicial value and Group E a larger one than the Total Yucatecans' average, the differences being probably significant. The females exhibit no real differences in their subgroup means.

The seriation curves (Plate 18) corroborate in part the evidence from the tables. Groups A, B, and C of both sexes possess essentially similar curves. The modes of Groups D and E of the males lie at the same higher value at which the Spanish male mode is placed. Group E of the females also has its mode at a higher indicial value than the others, while Group D of the women exhibits a lower incidence of the smaller indices.

The relatively longer faces of the Whiter males approach toward the average types of Spanish and Mexicans as well as the modal type of the Spanish. The means fail to indicate such a tendency in the Whiter subgroups of the females, but as stated above, the evidence from the seriation curves supports the view that an approximation toward the White Spanish type of face is a characteristic of Groups D and E in both sexes.

In Sullivan's example of White-Indian mixture, it is interesting that the Whiter male progeny, in comparison to the Pure Sioux, have relatively higher facial indices than do the Whiter female descendants. The behavior in the Siouan and Yucatecan cases of race mixture is very similar. Dunn and Tozzer's women show the trend that has been pointed out for the males of the other two examples of miscegenation. In the Hawaiian case, the reduction in bizygomatic diameter in the females of three-quarters White blood was very great, while the average for face height was but little

## TABLE 63.  FACIAL INDEX

### MALES

| Group | No. | Range | Mean | S. D. | V. | Significance with Total Yucatecans |
|---|---|---|---|---|---|---|
| Total Yucatecans .. | 879 | 70–102 | 85.50 ±.11 | 4.68 ±.08 | 5.47 ±.09 | |
| Group A . . . . . . . . . | 221 | 71– 94 | 85.00 ±.19 | 4.28 ±.14 | 5.04 ±.16 | 2×pe D |
| Group B . . . . . . . . . | 199 | 71–100 | 85.33 ±.22 | 4.62 ±.16 | 5.41 ±.18 | None |
| Group C . . . . . . . . . | 361 | 70– 96 | 85.67 ±.17 | 4.70 ±.12 | 5.49 ±.14 | 1×pe D |
| Group D . . . . . . . . | 52 | 75–102 | 86.27 ±.51 | 5.46 ±.36 | 6.33 ±.42 | 1×pe D |
| Group E . . . . . . . . . | 46 | 73– 96 | 86.59 ±.52 | 5.26 ±.37 | 6.07 ±.43 | 2×pe D |
| Spanish . . . . . . . . . Barras, 1928 | 77 | 73–114 | 89.37 ±.55 | 7.12 ±.39 | 7.97 ±.43 | |
| Andalusian Moors . Coon, 1929 | 28 | . . . | 90.79 ±.47 | 3.69 ±.33 | 4.06 ±.37 | |
| Mexicans . . . . . . . . . | 48 | . . . | 87.62 ±.43 | 4.39 ±.30 | 5.01 ±.34 | |
| Koriaks . . . . . . . . . . . . . . . . . . . . . Jochelson (Martin, 1914) | | | 85.50 | | | |
| Chinese . . . . . . . . . . . . . . . . . . . . . Koganei (Martin, 1914) | | | 87.00 | | | |
| Germans (Baden) . . . . . . . . . . . . . Fischer (Martin, 1914) | | | 85.80 | | | |
| Tungus . . . . . . . . . . . . . . . . . . . . . . Jochelson (Martin, 1914) | | | 84.40 | | | |
| Swiss (Safiental) . . . . . . . . . . . . . . Wettstein (Martin, 1914) | | | 93.30 | | | |
| Kamchadel . . . . . . . . . . . . . . . . . . | | | 83.30 | | | |
| Chukchi . . . . . . . . . . . . . . . . . . . . . Bogoras (Martin, 1914) | | | 88.00 | | | |
| Huaxtecs . . . . . . . . . . | 100 | 73–97 | 79.10 | | | |
| Chontals . . . . . . . . | 80 | 70–94 | 79.90 | | | |
| Chols . . . . . . . . . . . . | 100 | 71–91 | 80.40 | | | |
| Tzendals . . . . . . . . . | 100 | 66–94 | 81.60 | | | |
| *Mayas* . . . . . . . . . . . | 100 | 60–95 | 83.40 | | | |
| Tzotzils . . . . . . . . . . | 100 | 69–93 | 80.60 | | | |
| Starr, 1902 | | | | | | |
| Sioux, Pure . . . . . . . . | 534 | 68–100 | 83.60 | 4.84 | 5.78 | |
| Sioux, Half-Blood .. | 77 | 74–102 | 84.80 | 5.28 | 6.22 | |
| Sullivan, 1920 | | | | | | |
| Hawaiians, Pure . . . | 73 | . . . | 87.67 ±.41 | 5.18 ±.29 | 5.91 ±.33 | |
| F₁ Hawaiian, North European . . . . . . . | 10 | 79–95 | 86.29 ±1.04 | 4.89 ±.74 | 5.67 | |
| Dunn, Tozzer, 1928 | | | | | | |

TABLE 63. *(Continued)*

FEMALES

| Group | No. | Range | Mean | S. D. | V. | Significance with Total Yucatecans |
|---|---|---|---|---|---|---|
| Total Yucatecans .. | 694 | 71–101 | 84.37 ±.12 | 4.60 ±.08 | 5.45 ±.10 | |
| Group A .......... | 154 | 73– 95 | 84.07 ±.24 | 4.42 ±.17 | 5.26 ±.20 | 1×pe D |
| Group B ......... | 231 | 73–101 | 84.40 ±.20 | 4.42 ±.14 | 5.24 ±.16 | None |
| Group C .......... | 201 | 71–100 | 84.58 ±.24 | 5.10 ±.17 | 6.03 ±.20 | 1×pe D |
| Group D ......... | 62 | 73– 98 | 84.47 ±.35 | 4.08 ±.25 | 4.83 ±.29 | None |
| Group E .......... | 46 | 75– 94 | 84.11 ±.44 | 4.42 ±.31 | 5.26 ±.37 | None |
| Mexicans ......... | 30 | 75– 98 | 88.03 ±.75 | 6.12 ±.53 | 6.95 ±.61 | |
| Smith Coll. Students Steggerda *et al.*, 1929 | 100 | 74– 98 | 86.95 ±.33 | 4.93 | 5.67 | |
| Smith Coll. Students Wilder and Pfeiffer, 1924 (Steggerda *et al.*, 1929) | 50 | ... | 90.40 ±.51 | | | |
| Nahua ...................... Ranke (Martin, 1914) | | | 86.70 | | | |
| Trumai ..................... Ranke (Martin, 1914) | | | 88.80 | | | |
| Shoshoni .................... Boas (Martin, 1914) | | | 79.20 | | | |
| Sioux, Pure........ | 157 | 70–94 | 82.30 | 4.40 | 5.35 | |
| Sioux, Half-Blood .. Sullivan, 1920 | 19 | 72–86 | 82.20 | 3.27 | 3.97 | |
| Hawaiians, Pure ... | 34 | 76–92 | 85.10 | | | |
| ¾ Hawaiian, ¼ North European ....... | 12 | 78–92 | 86.30 | | | |
| F₁ Hawaiian, North European ....... | 10 | 80–97 | 86.30 | | | |
| ¼ Hawaiian, ¾ North European ....... Dunn, Tozzer, 1928 | 6 | 84–98 | 89.30 | | | |

changed. The Whiter Hawaiian women probably have greater amounts of White blood than either those of the Siouan or Yucatecan mixtures, and (which is probably more important) great breadth of face is probably not so constant a characteristic among Pure Hawaiians as in pure Mayas.

**Upper Facial Index.** The discussions concerning bizygomatic diameter and upper face height have prepared the reader for the

TABLE 64.  UPPER FACIAL INDEX

MALES

| Group | No. | Range | Mean | S. D. | V. | Significance with Total Yucatecans |
|---|---|---|---|---|---|---|
| Total Yucatecans .. | 880 | 40–66 | 52.72 ±.08 | 3.48 ±.06 | 6.60 ±.11 | |
| Group A ......... | 221 | 43–64 | 52.67 ±.15 | 3.28 ±.10 | 6.23 ±.20 | None |
| Group B ......... | 199 | 43–62 | 52.74 ±.16 | 3.40 ±.12 | 6.45 ±.22 | None |
| Group C ......... | 362 | 40–62 | 52.70 ±.12 | 3.45 ±.09 | 6.55 ±.16 | None |
| Group D ........ | 52 | 40–66 | 52.92 ±.40 | 4.23 ±.28 | 7.99 ±.53 | None |
| Group E ......... | 46 | 44–60 | 53.07 ±.41 | 4.10 ±.29 | 7.73 ±.54 | None |
| Spanish .......... Barras, 1928 | 78 | 45–72 | 54.65 ±.41 | 5.36 ±.29 | 9.81 ±.53 | |
| Andalusian Moors . Coon, 1929 | 28 | ... | 51.93 ±.43 | 3.34 ±.30 | 6.43 ±.58 | |
| Mexicans ........ | 48 | ... | 53.58 ±.31 | 3.16 ±.22 | 5.90 ±.41 | |
| | | | *Crania* | | | |
| Bohemians .................. Matiegka (Martin, 1914) | | | 51.30 | | | |
| Japanese ................... Adachi (Martin, 1914) | | | 53.60 | | | |
| Spanish .................... Hoyos Sainz (Martin, 1914) | | | 55.50 | | | |

FEMALES

| Group | No. | Range | Mean | S. D. | V. | Significance with Total Yucatecans |
|---|---|---|---|---|---|---|
| Total Yucatecans .. | 694 | 41–64 | 52.84 ±.09 | 3.46 ±.06 | 6.55 ±.12 | |
| Group A ......... | 154 | 43–62 | 52.80 ±.19 | 3.50 ±.13 | 6.63 ±.25 | None |
| Group B ......... | 231 | 43–62 | 52.92 ±.15 | 3.28 ±.10 | 6.20 ±.19 | None |
| Group C ......... | 201 | 43–64 | 52.90 ±.17 | 3.66 ±.12 | 6.92 ±.23 | None |
| Group D ........ | 62 | 41–62 | 52.89 ±.28 | 3.26 ±.20 | 6.16 ±.37 | None |
| Group E ......... | 46 | 43–60 | 52.20 ±.34 | 3.42 ±.24 | 6.55 ±.46 | 1×pe D |
| Mexicans ........ | 30 | 45–64 | 54.10 ±.55 | 4.44 ±.39 | 8.21 ±.71 | |
| | | | *Crania* | | | |
| Spanish .................... Hoyos Sainz (Martin, 1914) | | | 56.00 | | | |

findings in the upper facial index tables.  No significant differences appear in the means for either sex.  The female subgroups are therefore quite like one another in both facial and upper facial indices.  The extremes of the male groups differ in facial index to a probably significant degree; in upper facial index, no difference in the averages is apparent.  The probable explanation is that the

## TABLE 65. NOSE HEIGHT

### Males

| Group | No. | Range | Mean | S. D. | V. | Significance with Total Yucatecans |
|---|---|---|---|---|---|---|
| Total Yucatecans .. | 880 | 47–71 | 58.73 ±.09 | 3.80 ±.06 | 6.47 ±.10 | |
| Group A . . . . . . . . . . | 221 | 47–68 | 58.31 ±.17 | 3.70 ±.12 | 6.35 ±.20 | 2×pe D |
| Group B . . . . . . . . . | 199 | 47–68 | 58.55 ±.19 | 4.02 ±.14 | 6.87 ±.23 | 1×pe D |
| Group C . . . . . . . . . . | 362 | 47–71 | 58.36 ±.14 | 4.00 ±.10 | 6.85 ±.17 | 3×pe D |
| Group D . . . . . . . . | 52 | 48–67 | 59.12 ±.35 | 3.74 ±.25 | 6.33 ±.42 | 1×pe D |
| Group E . . . . . . . . . | 46 | 53–67 | 59.15 ±.32 | 3.24 ±.23 | 5.48 ±.39 | 1×pe D |
| Spanish . . . . . . . . . .<br>Barras, 1928 | 79 | 45–76 | 55.73 ±.38 | 5.06 ±.27 | 9.08 ±.49 | |
| Cacereños . . . . . . . .<br>Aranzadi, 1894*b* | 23 | . . . | 54.60 | | | |
| Andalusian Moors .<br>Coon, 1929 | 28 | . . . | 54.29 ±.47 | 3.66 ±.33 | 6.47 ±.61 | |
| Mexicans . . . . . . . . . | 48 | . . . | 57.46 ±.38 | 3.86 ±.27 | 6.72 ±.46 | |
| Chontals . . . . . . . . | 80 | 45–56 | 50.50 | | | |
| Huaxtecs. . . . . . . . . . | 100 | 43–56 | 48.90 | | | |
| *Mayas* . . . . . . . . . . . | 100 | 42–60 | 48.60 | | | |
| Tzotzils . . . . . . . . . . | 100 | 42–60 | 48.10 | | | |
| Tzendals . . . . . . . . . | 100 | 40–60 | 47.90 | | | |
| Chols . . . . . . . . . . . .<br>Starr, 1902 | 100 | 41–58 | 48.80 | | | |
| Sioux, Pure. . . . . . . . | 539 | 46–70 | 58.30 | 3.94 | 6.75 | |
| Sioux, Half-Blood . .<br>Sullivan, 1920 | 77 | 48–62 | 54.90 | 3.55 | 6.48 | |
| Hawaiians, Pure . . .<br>F₁ Hawaiian, North | 74 | . . . | 53.59 ±.32 | 4.12 ±.23 | 7.69 ±.43 | |
| European . . . . . . .<br>Dunn, Tozzer, 1928 | 10 | 46–61 | 53.80 ±.93 | 4.38 ±.66 | 8.14 | |

### Females

| Group | No. | Range | Mean | S. D. | V. | Significance with Total Yucatecans |
|---|---|---|---|---|---|---|
| Total Yucatecans .. | 694 | 43–68 | 55.26 ±.10 | 3.78 ±.07 | 6.84 ±.12 | |
| Group A . . . . . . . . . . | 154 | 45–65 | 55.73 ±.20 | 3.72 ±.14 | 6.68 ±.26 | 2×pe D |
| Group B . . . . . . . . . | 231 | 47–67 | 55.37 ±.16 | 3.50 ±.11 | 6.32 ±.20 | None |
| Group C . . . . . . . . . . | 201 | 43–68 | 55.16 ±.20 | 4.18 ±.14 | 7.58 ±.25 | None |
| Group D . . . . . . . . | 62 | 45–66 | 54.47 ±.33 | 3.84 ±.23 | 7.05 ±.43 | 2×pe D |
| Group E . . . . . . . . . | 46 | 47–60 | 54.54 ±.30 | 3.06 ±.22 | 5.61 ±.39 | 2×pe D |
| Mexicans . . . . . . . . . | 30 | 47–60 | 53.10 ±.33 | 2.70 ±.24 | 5.08 ±.44 | |

TABLE 65. (*Continued*)

| Group | No. | Range | Mean | S. D. | V. | Significance with Total Yucatecans |
|---|---|---|---|---|---|---|
| Smith Coll. Students | 100 | 42–58 | 50.51±.24 | 3.60 | 7.13 | |
| Steggerda *et al.*, 1929 | | | | | | |
| Smith Coll. Students | 100 | ... | 53.61 | | | |
| Wilder and Pfeiffer, 1924 | | | | | | |
| (Steggerda *et al.*, 1929) | | | | | | |
| Sioux, Pure........ | 157 | 46–62 | 55.20 | 3.51 | 6.35 | |
| Sioux, Half-Blood .. | 19 | 46–58 | 51.50 | 2.95 | 5.73 | |
| Sullivan, 1920 | | | | | | |
| Hawaiians, Pure ... | 34 | 43–58 | 51.20 | | | |
| $\frac{3}{4}$ Hawaiian, $\frac{1}{4}$ North | | | | | | |
| European ....... | 12 | 41–53 | 48.60 | | | |
| F₁ Hawaiian, North | | | | | | |
| European ....... | 10 | 46–56 | 52.40 | | | |
| $\frac{1}{4}$ Hawaiian, $\frac{3}{4}$ North | | | | | | |
| European ....... | 6 | 41–58 | 52.00 | | | |
| Dunn, Tozzer, 1928 | | | | | | |

distance from nasion to menton is longer than that from nasion to prosthion; that in such a greater distance, the differences in the projective interval due to a smaller amount of prognathism are more apt to manifest themselves than in the smaller distance from nasion to prosthion.

## THE NOSE

**Nose Height.** The so-called height of the nose from nasion to subnasale is a part of the distance measured in upper face height, which in turn forms a part of the larger measurement called anatomical face height. In consideration of the radiometric tables, subnasale, as well as prosthion, was found to be among the parts of the face responsible for the Indian's prognathism. The identity, in part, of the distance measured in the determinations of upper face height and nasal height, and the common participation of the two inferior points of both measurements in one or the other phenomena of prognathism or orthognathism gives great reason for supposing that the findings in the averages of one measurement might also aptly apply to the other. Comparison of the data for

### TABLE 66.   NOSE BREADTH

#### MALES

| Group | No. | Range | Mean | S. D. | V. | Significance with Total Yucatecans |
|---|---|---|---|---|---|---|
| Total Yucatecans .. | 880 | 26–50 | 37.65±.07 | 3.05±.05 | 8.10±.13 | |
| Group A ......... | 221 | 29–48 | 37.83±.13 | 2.92±.09 | 7.72±.25 | 1×pe D |
| Group B ......... | 199 | 26–50 | 37.80±.15 | 3.06±.10 | 8.09±.27 | 1×pe D |
| Group C ......... | 362 | 27–50 | 37.83±.11 | 3.14±.08 | 8.09±.20 | 2×pe D |
| Group D ......... | 52 | 31–45 | 36.38±.28 | 2.98±.20 | 8.19±.54 | 4×pe D |
| Group E ......... | 46 | 30–42 | 36.24±.28 | 2.81±.20 | 7.75±.54 | 5×pe D |
| Spanish ......... Barras, 1928 | 79 | 21–38 | 32.99±.23 | 3.08±.16 | 9.33±.50 | |
| Cacereños ........ Aranzadi, 1894*b* | 23 | ... | 34.00 | | | |
| Andalusian Moors . Coon, 1929 | 28 | ... | 35.64±.34 | 2.62±.24 | 7.36±.66 | |
| Mexicans ......... | 48 | ... | 37.65±.35 | 3.59±.25 | 9.54±.66 | |
| Chontals ......... | 80 | 32–47 | 39.00 | | | |
| Huaxtecs.......... | 100 | 28–44 | 38.10 | | | |
| *Mayas* ........... | 100 | 33–42 | 37.50 | | | |
| Tzotzils .......... | 100 | 33–46 | 40.50 | | | |
| Tzendals ......... | 100 | 33–50 | 39.90 | | | |
| Chols ............ Starr, 1902 | 100 | 31–48 | 37.10 | | | |
| Sioux, Pure........ | 540 | 32–50 | 39.90 | 3.22 | 8.07 | |
| Sioux, Half-Blood .. Sullivan, 1920 | 77 | 30–46 | 37.60 | 3.04 | 8.08 | |
| Hawaiians, Pure ... | 74 | ... | 44.22±.22 | 2.80±.15 | 6.32±.35 | |
| F₁ Hawaiian, North European ....... Dunn, Tozzer, 1928 | 10 | 40–49 | 43.10±.52 | 2.43±.37 | 5.64 | |

#### FEMALES

| | | | | | | |
|---|---|---|---|---|---|---|
| Total Yucatecans .. | 694 | 27–48 | 34.75±.08 | 2.96±.05 | 8.52±.15 | |
| Group A ......... | 154 | 29–43 | 35.34±.14 | 2.62±.10 | 7.41±.28 | 4×pe D |
| Group B ......... | 231 | 27–47 | 35.18±.13 | 2.86±.09 | 8.13±.26 | 4×pe D |
| Group C ......... | 201 | 27–44 | 34.55±.15 | 3.14±.11 | 9.09±.31 | 1×pe D |
| Group D ......... | 62 | 27–43 | 33.27±.26 | 2.98±.18 | 8.96±.54 | 6×pe D |
| Group E ......... | 46 | 27–42 | 33.46±.26 | 2.62±.18 | 7.83±.55 | 5×pe D |

TABLE 66.  (*Continued*)

| Group | No. | Range | Mean | S. D. | V. | Significance with Total Yucatecans |
|---|---|---|---|---|---|---|
| Mexicans ......... | 30 | 27–40 | 33.70 ± .33 | 2.70 ± .24 | 8.01 ± .70 | |
| Smith Coll. Students Steggerda *et al.*, 1929 | 100 | 27–37 | 32.28 ± .13 | 1.30 | 6.01 | |
| Smith Coll. Students Wilder and Pfeiffer, 1924 (Steggerda *et al.*, 1929) | 100 | ... | 32.18 | | | |
| Sioux, Pure........ | 157 | 32–48 | 37.40 | 2.91 | 7.77 | |
| Sioux, Half-Blood .. Sullivan, 1920 | 19 | 32–38 | 34.80 | 2.27 | 6.52 | |
| Hawaiians, Pure ... | 34 | 35–49 | 40.90 | | | |
| $\frac{3}{4}$ Hawaiian, $\frac{1}{4}$ North European ....... | 12 | 36–42 | 38.90 | | | |
| F₁ Hawaiian, North European ....... | 10 | 33–41 | 35.60 | | | |
| $\frac{1}{4}$ Hawaiian, $\frac{3}{4}$ North European ....... Dunn, Tozzer, 1928 | 6 | 30–35 | 32.50 | | | |

the two lengths demonstrates that in the case of the Yucatecans such an assumption is correct. For interpretation of the findings for nasal height, therefore, the reader is referred back to the discussion of upper face height. See also Plate 19.

**Nose Breadth.** The tables for breadth of the nose at the widest expansion of the alae show for both sexes distinctly smaller means in Groups D and E. The seriation curves (Plate 20) demonstrate the same tendency very nicely. Sullivan's and Dunn and Tozzer's material tell exactly the same story. It only needs to be added that the subgroup differences are greater in females than in males.

**Nasal Index.** The reader, after examination of the tables for nasal height and breadth, is fully prepared for the definite and significant differences that are apparent in the data for nasal index. Again the differences between the Indian and Whiter types of progeny are greater in males than in females. The phenomena of reduction of nasal breadth and lowering of the value of nasal index in the progeny of a broad-nosed type which has mixed with a

## TABLE 67. NASAL INDEX

### MALES

| Group | No. | Range | Mean | S. D. | V. | Significance with Total Yucatecans |
|---|---|---|---|---|---|---|
| Total Yucatecans .. | 880 | 48–94 | 64.28 ±.14 | 6.28 ±.10 | 9.77 ±.16 | |
| Group A ......... | 221 | 51–88 | 65.01 ±.28 | 6.12 ±.20 | 9.41 ±.30 | 3×pe D |
| Group B ......... | 199 | 51–88 | 64.85 ±.29 | 6.12 ±.21 | 9.44 ±.32 | 2×pe D |
| Group C ......... | 362 | 48–94 | 64.20 ±.22 | 6.10 ±.15 | 9.50 ±.24 | None |
| Group D ........ | 52 | 48–81 | 62.04 ±.68 | 7.26 ±.48 | 11.70 ±.77 | 3×pe D |
| Group E ......... | 46 | 49–75 | 61.37 ±.63 | 6.38 ±.45 | 10.40 ±.73 | 4×pe D |
| Spanish .......... Barras, 1928 | 79 | 35–72 | 59.85 ±.58 | 7.68 ±.41 | 12.83 ±.69 | |
| Spanish .......... Barras, 1923 | 206 | 39–83 | 61.62 ±.36 | 7.71 ±.26 | 12.51 ±.42 | |
| Andalusian Moors . Coon, 1929 | 28 | ... | 66.04 ±.87 | 6.82 ±.62 | 10.33 ±.93 | |
| Cacereños ........ Aranzadi, 1894b | 22 | ... | 62.30 ±.62 | 4.31 | 6.92 | |
| Mexicans ......... | 48 | ... | 65.81 ±.69 | 7.11 ±.49 | 10.80 ±.74 | |
| Athabascans (Tahltan) ......... Boas (Martin, 1914) | | | 62.60 | | | |
| Eskimo ..................... Duckworth (Martin, 1914) | | | 64.10 | | | |
| North French.................. Collignon (Martin, 1914) | | | 63.40 | | | |
| Anglo-Scots .................. Beddoe (Martin, 1914) | | | 65.10 | | | |
| Germans (Baden) ............. Fischer (Martin, 1914) | | | 65.70 | | | |
| Chols ............ | 100 | 59–107 | 76.40 | | | |
| Chontals ......... | 80 | 62–94 | 77.20 | | | |
| Huaxtecs.......... | 100 | 57–102 | 78.30 | | | |
| Tzentals .......... | 100 | 64–102 | 83.80 | | | |
| *Mayas* ........... | 100 | 63–93 | 77.50 | | | |
| Tzotzils .......... Starr, 1902 | 100 | 63–104 | 84.80 | | | |
| Sioux, Pure........ | 536 | 52–90 | 68.80 | 7.05 | 10.25 | |
| Sioux, Half-Blood .. Sullivan, 1920 | 77 | 56–86 | 69.20 | 7.08 | 10.23 | |
| Hawaiians, Pure ... | 74 | ... | 82.94 ±.61 | 7.73 ±.43 | 9.32 ±.52 | |
| F₁ Hawaiian, North European ....... Dunn, Tozzer, 1928 | 10 | 70–98 | 80.75 ±1.9 | 9.14 ±1.4 | 11.32 | |

TABLE 67.  *(Continued)*

FEMALES

| Group | No. | Range | Mean | S. D. | V. | Significance with Total Yucatecans |
|---|---|---|---|---|---|---|
| Total Yucatecans .. | 694 | 49–84 | 63.11±.16 | 6.12±.11 | 9.70±.18 | |
| Group A .......... | 154 | 51–79 | 63.72±.33 | 6.10±.23 | 9.57±.37 | 2×pe D |
| Group B .......... | 231 | 49–78 | 63.63±.24 | 5.52±.17 | 8.68±.27 | 2×pe D |
| Group C .......... | 201 | 49–82 | 62.96±.30 | 6.30±.21 | 10.01±.34 | None |
| Group D ......... | 62 | 49–84 | 61.21±.58 | 6.76±.41 | 11.04±.67 | 3×pe D |
| Group E .......... | 46 | 49–74 | 61.72±.65 | 6.50±.46 | 10.53±.74 | 2×pe D |
| Mexicans ......... | 30 | 53–76 | 63.37±.66 | 5.36±.47 | 8.46±.74 | |
| Smith Coll. Students Steggerda *et al.*, 1929 | 100 | 47–79 | 63.71±.39 | 5.74 | 9.01 | |
| Smith Coll. Students Wilder and Pfeiffer, 1924 (Steggerda *et al.*, 1929) | 100 | ... | 59.89 | | | |
| Athabascans (Tahltan) ......... Boas (Martin, 1914) | | | 62.20 | | | |
| Eskimo ..................... Duckworth (Martin, 1914) | | | 62.40 | | | |
| Nahua ..................... Ranke (Martin, 1914) | | | 71.70 | | | |
| Sioux, Pure........ | 157 | 52–86 | 68.00 | 7.09 | 10.42 | |
| Sioux, Half-Blood .. Sullivan, 1920 | 19 | 58–82 | 67.80 | 6.42 | 9.47 | |
| Hawaiians, Pure ... | 34 | 70–92 | 80.30 | | | |
| $\frac{3}{4}$ Hawaiian, $\frac{1}{4}$ North European ....... | 12 | 72–91 | 80.30 | | | |
| F₁ Hawaiian, North European ....... | 10 | 62–76 | 68.30 | | | |
| $\frac{1}{4}$ Hawaiian, $\frac{3}{4}$ North European ....... Dunn, Tozzer, 1928 | 6 | 51–79 | 62.50 | | | |

narrower-nosed variety of mankind, is so well known that further comment is unnecessary. The tables and the seriation curves (Plate 21) epitomize the situation.

**Observations on Nasal Wings.** The nasal wings of each Yuca-tecan examined were noted on the record sheet as "compressed," "medium," or "flaring." One of the criteria for admission to Group A was that the individual should possess medium or flaring, but never compressed alae. In sorting for members of Groups D and E, however, no stipulation was made concerning nasal wings. Group C, it will be recalled, was the residual group which remained after the other four subgroups had been sorted.

### TABLE 68. NASAL WINGS

#### MALES

|  | Compressed | Medium | Flaring | No. |
|---|---|---|---|---|
| Total Yucatecans | 36 | 267 | 577 | 880 |
|  | 4.1% | 30.3% | 65.6% |  |
| Group A | 0 | 78 | 143 | 221 |
|  | 0.0% | 35.3% | 64.7% |  |
| Group B | 2 | 44 | 153 | 199 |
|  | 1.0% | 22.1% | 76.9% |  |
| Group C | 19 | 96 | 247 | 362 |
|  | 5.2% | 26.5% | 68.2% |  |
| Group D | 8 | 23 | 21 | 52 |
|  | 15.4% | 44.2% | 40.4% |  |
| Group E | 7 | 25 | 14 | 46 |
|  | 15.2% | 54.3% | 30.4% |  |

#### FEMALES

|  | Compressed | Medium | Flaring | No. |
|---|---|---|---|---|
| Total Yucatecans | 32 | 306 | 356 | 694 |
|  | 4.6% | 44.1% | 51.3% |  |
| Group A | 0 | 60 | 94 | 154 |
|  | 0.0% | 39.0% | 61.0% |  |
| Group B | 1 | 90 | 140 | 231 |
|  | 0.4% | 39.0% | 60.6% |  |
| Group C | 15 | 92 | 94 | 201 |
|  | 7.4% | 45.8% | 46.8% |  |
| Group D | 9 | 34 | 19 | 62 |
|  | 14.5% | 54.8% | 30.7% |  |
| Group E | 7 | 30 | 9 | 46 |
|  | 15.2% | 65.2% | 19.6% |  |
| Mexicans | 1 | 24 | 5 | 30 |
|  | 3.3% | 80.0% | 16.7% |  |

Examination of the percentage table for the types of nasal wings shows progressively higher percentages of compressed and medium alae in Groups C, D, and E of both sexes than in Groups A and B. Since flaring and medium wings were, among other characters, used to select the more Indian of the Yucatecans for Groups A and B, it is to be expected that those subgroups should have more of the flaring variety than the others. It is evident, in the generally increasing percentages of medium wings from Group A to Group E, as well as in the relatively high proportion of compressed wings in Groups D and E, that these facts were so, not because the Whiter groups were sorted through use of those characters, but because

TABLE 69.  NASAL PROFILE

MALES

| | Concave | Straight | Convex | Concavo-Convex | No. |
|---|---|---|---|---|---|
| Total Yucatecans ............ | 13 | 100 | 677 | 90 | 880 |
| | 1.5% | 11.4% | 76.9% | 10.2% | |
| Group A ................... | 0 | 29 | 174 | 18 | 221 |
| | 0.0% | 13.1% | 78.7% | 8.2% | |
| Group B ................... | 2 | 31 | 153 | 13 | 199 |
| | 1.0% | 15.6% | 76.9% | 6.5% | |
| Group C ................... | 10 | 34 | 273 | 45 | 362 |
| | 2.8% | 9.4% | 75.4% | 12.4% | |
| Group D ................... | 1 | 1 | 43 | 7 | 52 |
| | 1.9% | 1.9% | 82.7% | 13.5% | |
| Group E ................... | 1 | 4 | 34 | 7 | 46 |
| | 2.2% | 8.7% | 73.9% | 15.2% | |

FEMALES

| | Concave | Straight | Convex | Concavo-Convex | No. |
|---|---|---|---|---|---|
| Total Yucatecans ............ | 28 | 118 | 399 | 149 | 694 |
| | 4.0% | 17.0% | 57.5% | 21.5% | |
| Group A ................... | 0 | 26 | 95 | 33 | 154 |
| | 0.0% | 16.9% | 61.7% | 21.4% | |
| Group B ................... | 6 | 36 | 144 | 45 | 231 |
| | 2.6% | 15.6% | 62.3% | 19.5% | |
| Group C ................... | 21 | 32 | 108 | 40 | 201 |
| | 10.5% | 15.9% | 53.7% | 19.9% | |
| Group D ................... | 1 | 13 | 31 | 17 | 62 |
| | 1.6% | 21.0% | 50.0% | 27.4% | |
| Group E ................... | 0 | 11 | 21 | 14 | 46 |
| | 0.0% | 23.9% | 45.7% | 30.4% | |
| Mexicans ................. | 6 | 5 | 10 | 9 | 30 |
| | 20.0% | 16.7% | 33.3% | 30.0% | |

certain definite linkages occur between those characters and the traits actually used for choosing members for the Whiter groups.

Other Observations on the Nose.  A summary of the judgments on *shape of nasal profile* demonstrates the presence of no findings sufficiently significant to require much consideration.  No individuals having concave noses were accepted for membership in Group A.  It appears that such a type of nasal profile is so rare among the Yucatecan males that the provision was scarcely necessary for that sex; but among the females, concave profiles showed a little higher incidence in general, but especially in Group C. That type of nasal curve is not typical either for Maya Indians or

TABLE 70.   NASAL ROOT DEPRESSION

MALES

|  | 0 | sm | + | ++ | +++ | No. |
|---|---|---|---|---|---|---|
| Total Yucatecans ....... | 20 | 360 | 393 | 102 | 5 | 880 |
|  | 2.3% | 40.9% | 44.7% | 11.6% | 0.6% |  |
| Group A .............. | 2 | 111 | 108 | 0 | 0 | 221 |
|  | 0.9% | 50.2% | 48.9% | 0.0% | 0.0% |  |
| Group B .............. | 5 | 83 | 87 | 24 | 0 | 199 |
|  | 2.5% | 41.7% | 43.7% | 12.1% | 0.0% |  |
| Group C .............. | 11 | 131 | 149 | 66 | 5 | 362 |
|  | 3.0% | 36.2% | 41.2% | 18.2% | 1.4% |  |
| Group D .............. | 1 | 19 | 24 | 8 | 0 | 52 |
|  | 1.9% | 36.5% | 46.1% | 15.4% | 0.0% |  |
| Group E .............. | 1 | 15 | 26 | 4 | 0 | 46 |
|  | 2.2% | 32.6% | 56.5% | 8.7% | 0.0% |  |

FEMALES

|  | 0 | sm | + | ++ | +++ | No. |
|---|---|---|---|---|---|---|
| Total Yucatecans ....... | 8 | 435 | 237 | 14 | 0 | 694 |
|  | 1.2% | 62.7% | 34.1% | 2.0% | 0.0% |  |
| Group A .............. | 0 | 109 | 45 | 0 | 0 | 154 |
|  | 0.0% | 70.8% | 29.2% | 0.0% | 0.0% |  |
| Group B .............. | 3 | 142 | 85 | 1 | 0 | 231 |
|  | 1.3% | 61.5% | 36.8% | 0.4% | 0.0% |  |
| Group C .............. | 1 | 123 | 66 | 11 | 0 | 201 |
|  | 0.5% | 61.2% | 32.8% | 5.5% | 0.0% |  |
| Group D .............. | 3 | 33 | 24 | 2 | 0 | 62 |
|  | 4.9% | 53.2% | 38.7% | 3.2% | 0.0% |  |
| Group E .............. | 1 | 28 | 17 | 0 | 0 | 46 |
|  | 2.2% | 60.9% | 36.9% | 0.0% | 0.0% |  |
| Mexicans .............. | 2 | 14 | 12 | 2 | 0 | 30 |
|  | 6.7% | 46.6% | 40.0% | 6.7% | 0.0% |  |

for Spanish Whites.   No definite linkage exists between that form of curve and other White characters, so that the residual group C received the great majority of the individuals so characterized.

The radiometric tables showed no definite differences in subgroups for *amount of nasal root depression*. The percentage tables for this observed trait have no features worthy of comment, save that Groups C and D of the males have higher frequencies of marked depression than any of the other groups presented for examination.

In discussion of radiometry it was pointed out that the tragion-rhinale protrusion index was very slightly less in the DE group of both sexes than in the others. The percentage table for *height of*

### TABLE 71.  HEIGHT OF NASAL ROOT

MALES

|  | sm | + | ++ | +++ | No. |
|---|---|---|---|---|---|
| Total Yucatecans | 42 | 520 | 294 | 24 | 880 |
|  | 4.8% | 59.1% | 33.4% | 2.7% |  |
| Group A | 12 | 149 | 57 | 3 | 221 |
|  | 5.4% | 67.4% | 25.8% | 1.4% |  |
| Group B | 14 | 120 | 64 | 1 | 199 |
|  | 7.0% | 60.3% | 32.2% | 0.5% |  |
| Group C | 16 | 205 | 128 | 13 | 362 |
|  | 4.4% | 56.6% | 35.4% | 3.6% |  |
| Group D | 0 | 26 | 23 | 3 | 52 |
|  | 0.0% | 50.0% | 44.2% | 5.8% |  |
| Group E | 0 | 19 | 23 | 4 | 46 |
|  | 0.0% | 41.3% | 50.0% | 8.7% |  |

FEMALES

|  | sm | + | ++ | +++ | No. |
|---|---|---|---|---|---|
| Total Yucatecans | 102 | 501 | 91 | 0 | 694 |
|  | 14.7% | 72.2% | 13.1% | 0.0% |  |
| Group A | 23 | 113 | 18 | 0 | 154 |
|  | 14.9% | 73.4% | 11.7% | 0.0% |  |
| Group B | 37 | 172 | 22 | 0 | 231 |
|  | 16.0% | 74.5% | 9.5% | 0.0% |  |
| Group C | 37 | 135 | 29 | 0 | 201 |
|  | 18.4% | 67.2% | 14.4% | 0.0% |  |
| Group D | 2 | 48 | 12 | 0 | 62 |
|  | 3.2% | 77.4% | 19.4% | 0.0% |  |
| Group E | 3 | 33 | 10 | 0 | 46 |
|  | 6.5% | 71.8% | 21.7% | 0.0% |  |

*nasal root* demonstrates that in the extreme "sm" or "very low" category, the Indians lead in frequency, while in the "++" or "+++" (high or very high) type, the Whiter subgroups have higher percentages. The data from radiometry and those from subjective observations appear to be at variance, but they probably are not, for the following reason: measurement of the radius from tragion to rhinale disregards the elevation of the nasal root

and bridge from the face itself. A rough measure of the height of
the nasal root and bridge relative to the facial level can be calculated by subtracting the average radii of prozygion from those of
rhinale. For the males the results so calculated are: A–30.7,
B–30.3, C–31.2, DE–32.0; for females they are: AB–24.2, C–26.1,

TABLE 72.  BREADTH OF NASAL ROOT

MALES

|  | sm | + | ++ | +++ | No. |
|---|---|---|---|---|---|
| Total Yucatecans | 43<br>4.9% | 334<br>38.0% | 487<br>55.3% | 16<br>1.8% | 880 |
| Group A | 7<br>3.2% | 90<br>40.7% | 120<br>54.3% | 4<br>1.8% | 221 |
| Group B | 8<br>4.0% | 83<br>41.7% | 104<br>52.3% | 4<br>2.0% | 199 |
| Group C | 19<br>5.2% | 128<br>35.4% | 210<br>58.0% | 5<br>1.4% | 362 |
| Group D | 6<br>11.5% | 16<br>30.8% | 29<br>55.8% | 1<br>1.9% | 52 |
| Group E | 3<br>6.5% | 17<br>37.0% | 24<br>52.2% | 2<br>4.3% | 46 |

FEMALES

|  | sm | + | ++ | +++ | No. |
|---|---|---|---|---|---|
| Total Yucatecans | 11<br>1.6% | 251<br>36.2% | 421<br>60.6% | 11<br>1.6% | 694 |
| Group A | 5<br>3.3% | 55<br>35.7% | 91<br>59.1% | 3<br>1.9% | 154 |
| Group B | 1<br>0.4% | 79<br>34.2% | 150<br>65.0% | 1<br>0.4% | 231 |
| Group C | 2<br>1.0% | 73<br>36.3% | 121<br>60.2% | 5<br>2.5% | 201 |
| Group D | 2<br>3.2% | 26<br>42.0% | 33<br>53.2% | 1<br>1.6% | 62 |
| Group E | 1<br>2.2% | 18<br>39.1% | 26<br>56.5% | 1<br>2.2% | 46 |

DE–25.0. These figures reconcile the seeming contradiction noted
above. The nasal roots and bridges of the Whiter subgroups are
probably on the average slightly higher from the facial levels than
in the Indian groups, but the latters' tendency to prognathism
makes the absolute value of the tragion-rhinale radius slightly
greater.

The two races which mixed to produce the Yucatecans are probably not characterized either by remarkable narrowness or extra-

ordinary *breadth of the nasal root.* The subgroups representing the descendants from the cross appear in the percentage table for nasal-root breadth to possess almost equal proportions in the medium to broad categories of that trait and practically no extreme gradations.

TABLE 73.  NASAL TIP — ELEVATION OR DEPRESSION

MALES

| | Depression | | Horizontal | Elevation | | No. |
|---|---|---|---|---|---|---|
| | ++, +++ | sm, + | | sm, + | ++, +++ | |
| Total Yucatecans ....... | 466 | 300 | 11 | 95 | 7 | 879 |
| | 53.0% | 34.1% | 1.2% | 10.8% | 0.8% | |
| Group A .............. | 112 | 85 | 3 | 20 | 1 | 221 |
| | 50.7% | 38.5% | 1.4% | 9.0% | 0.4% | |
| Group B .............. | 107 | 66 | 3 | 22 | 1 | 199 |
| | 53.8% | 33.2% | 1.5% | 11.1% | 0.5% | |
| Group C .............. | 120 | 194 | 2 | 41 | 4 | 361 |
| | 33.1% | 53.7% | 0.6% | 11.3% | 1.1% | |
| Group D .............. | 18 | 28 | 1 | 5 | 0 | 52 |
| | 34.6% | 53.8% | 1.9% | 9.6% | 0.0% | |
| Group E .............. | 12 | 24 | 3 | 6 | 1 | 46 |
| | 26.1% | 52.2% | 6.5% | 13.0% | 2.2% | |

FEMALES

| | | | | | | |
|---|---|---|---|---|---|---|
| Total Yucatecans ....... | 231 | 271 | 6 | 167 | 19 | 694 |
| | 33.3% | 39.0% | 0.9% | 24.1% | 2.7% | |
| Group A .............. | 50 | 68 | 1 | 32 | 3 | 154 |
| | 32.5% | 44.2% | 0.6% | 20.8% | 1.9% | |
| Group B .............. | 85 | 88 | 0 | 55 | 3 | 231 |
| | 36.8% | 38.1% | 0.0% | 23.8% | 1.3% | |
| Group C .............. | 65 | 75 | 3 | 49 | 9 | 201 |
| | 32.3% | 37.3% | 1.5% | 24.4% | 4.5% | |
| Group D .............. | 21 | 23 | 0 | 16 | 2 | 62 |
| | 33.9% | 37.1% | 0.0% | 25.8% | 3.2% | |
| Group E .............. | 10 | 17 | 2 | 15 | 2 | 46 |
| | 21.8% | 37.0% | 4.3% | 32.6% | 4.3% | |

Three types of factors must be considered as affecting the shape of a nose. They are: (1) the shape and size of the bony support, which includes the nasal bones and the frontal processes of the maxillae upon which they lie, as well as the bony skeleton of the face from which the two foregoing rise; (2) the shape and size of the various parts of the cartilaginous support, consisting of the septal cartilage, the lateral cartilages, and the greater alar car-

tilages; (3) the shape and size of the non-bony and non-cartilaginous
tissue of the nasal alae, which is principally fibrous in its structure.

It has been pointed out so far in the discussion of nasal form:
(1) that in nasal height the Whiter females are a little shorter than
the other subgroups, and that no definite difference is demonstrated

### TABLE 74.  NOSTRIL SHAPE

#### MALES

|  | Narrow Oval | Broad Oval | Round | No. |
|---|---|---|---|---|
| Total Yucatecans .......... | 140 | 737 | 3 | 880 |
|  | 15.9% | 83.8% | 0.3% |  |
| Group A.................. | 28 | 193 | 0 | 221 |
|  | 12.7% | 87.3% | 0.0% |  |
| Group B.................. | 19 | 179 | 1 | 199 |
|  | 9.5% | 90.0% | 0.5% |  |
| Group C.................. | 55 | 305 | 2 | 362 |
|  | 15.2% | 84.2% | 0.6% |  |
| Group D ................. | 19 | 33 | 0 | 52 |
|  | 36.5% | 63.5% | 0.0% |  |
| Group E.................. | 18 | 28 | 0 | 46 |
|  | 39.1% | 60.9% | 0.0% |  |

#### FEMALES

|  | Narrow Oval | Broad Oval | Round | No. |
|---|---|---|---|---|
| Total Yucatecans .......... | 114 | 580 | 0 | 694 |
|  | 16.5% | 83.5% | 0.0% |  |
| Group A.................. | 18 | 136 | 0 | 154 |
|  | 11.7% | 88.3% | 0.0% |  |
| Group B.................. | 19 | 212 | 0 | 231 |
|  | 8.2% | 91.8% | 0.0% |  |
| Group C.................. | 42 | 159 | 0 | 201 |
|  | 20.9% | 79.1% | 0.0% |  |
| Group D ................. | 18 | 44 | 0 | 62 |
|  | 29.0% | 71.0% | 0.0% |  |
| Group E.................. | 17 | 29 | 0 | 46 |
|  | 37.0% | 63.0% | 0.0% |  |

in the male groups; (2) that the Whiter groups in comparison to
the more Indian of the progeny have on the average in both sexes
slightly higher roots and bridges. These two statements sum up
the principal differences between subgroups that are due to differences in shape and relative size of the bony support.

When the point pronasale was considered under radiometric
measurements, it was found that the salient from subnasale of the

septal cartilage, with its superimposed greater alar cartilage, was progressively greater in both sexes from the A and B and AB groups through C to the DEs. That such shortening of the salient in the Indians is caused in part by stronger inferior and weaker anterior projection of the medial wings of the greater alar cartilages

TABLE 75.  FRONTAL VISIBILITY OF NOSTRILS

MALES

|  | 0 | sm | + | ++ | +++ | No. |
|---|---|---|---|---|---|---|
| Total Yucatecans ....... | 9 | 124 | 345 | 340 | 62 | 880 |
|  | 1.0% | 14.1% | 39.2% | 38.6% | 7.0% |  |
| Group A ............... | 0 | 24 | 91 | 92 | 14 | 221 |
|  | 0.0% | 10.9% | 41.2% | 41.6% | 6.3% |  |
| Group B ............... | 1 | 26 | 80 | 79 | 13 | 199 |
|  | 0.5% | 13.1% | 40.2% | 39.7% | 6.5% |  |
| Group C ............... | 5 | 54 | 134 | 138 | 31 | 362 |
|  | 1.4% | 14.9% | 37.0% | 38.1% | 8.6% |  |
| Group D ............... | 1 | 10 | 21 | 18 | 2 | 52 |
|  | 1.9% | 19.2% | 40.4% | 34.6% | 3.8% |  |
| Group E ............... | 2 | 10 | 19 | 14 | 1 | 46 |
|  | 4.3% | 21.7% | 41.3% | 30.4% | 2.2% |  |

FEMALES

|  | 0 | sm | + | ++ | +++ | No. |
|---|---|---|---|---|---|---|
| Total Yucatecans ....... | 5 | 107 | 300 | 237 | 45 | 694 |
|  | 0.7% | 15.4% | 43.2% | 34.2% | 6.5% |  |
| Group A ............... | 2 | 20 | 73 | 46 | 13 | 154 |
|  | 1.3% | 13.0% | 47.4% | 29.9% | 8.4% |  |
| Group B ............... | 0 | 33 | 97 | 86 | 15 | 231 |
|  | 0.0% | 14.3% | 42.0% | 37.2% | 6.5% |  |
| Group C ............... | 0 | 31 | 81 | 76 | 13 | 201 |
|  | 0.0% | 15.4% | 40.3% | 37.8% | 6.5% |  |
| Group D ............... | 0 | 11 | 30 | 19 | 2 | 62 |
|  | 0.0% | 17.7% | 48.4% | 30.7% | 3.2% |  |
| Group E ............... | 3 | 12 | 19 | 10 | 2 | 46 |
|  | 6.5% | 26.1% | 41.3% | 21.8% | 4.3% |  |

is suggested in the percentage table for amount of *depression or elevation of the nasal tip.* Over fifty per cent of the male Groups A and B have greatly depressed tips, while only twenty-six per cent of Group E is so characterized. A similar trend of milder degree is noted in the females, who have a greater proportion of elevated tips than do the males. The frequency values for moderately elevated tips are larger in the female Group E than in any of the others.

Since the Whiter groups of both sexes have longer septal salients than the Indian co-descendants, and more compressed nasal wings, the *nostril shape* should differ considerably between them. The percentage table for that subjective observation bears out this opinion: the Whiter groups of both sexes, in comparison to the

TABLE 76. LATERAL VISIBILITY OF NOSTRILS

MALES

| | 0 | sm | + | ++ | +++ | No. |
|---|---|---|---|---|---|---|
| Total Yucatecans ....... | 2<br>0.2% | 80<br>9.1% | 338<br>38.4% | 382<br>43.4% | 78<br>8.9% | 880 |
| Group A .............. | 0<br>0.0% | 14<br>6.3% | 80<br>36.2% | 107<br>48.4% | 20<br>9.0% | 221 |
| Group B .............. | 0<br>0.0% | 21<br>10.6% | 74<br>37.2% | 85<br>42.7% | 19<br>9.6% | 199 |
| Group C .............. | 2<br>0.5% | 31<br>8.6% | 136<br>37.6% | 161<br>44.5% | 32<br>8.8% | 362 |
| Group D .............. | 0<br>0.0% | 7<br>13.5% | 24<br>46.1% | 18<br>34.6% | 3<br>5.8% | 52 |
| Group E .............. | 0<br>0.0% | 7<br>15.2% | 23<br>50.0% | 13<br>28.3% | 3<br>6.5% | 46 |

FEMALES

| | 0 | sm | + | ++ | +++ | No. |
|---|---|---|---|---|---|---|
| Total Yucatecans ....... | 1<br>0.1% | 72<br>10.4% | 298<br>42.9% | 276<br>39.8% | 47<br>6.8% | 694 |
| Group A .............. | 0<br>0.0% | 15<br>9.8% | 71<br>46.0% | 53<br>34.4% | 15<br>9.8% | 154 |
| Group B .............. | 0<br>0.0% | 20<br>8.7% | 94<br>40.7% | 102<br>44.1% | 15<br>6.5% | 231 |
| Group C .............. | 0<br>0.0% | 22<br>10.9% | 81<br>40.3% | 85<br>42.3% | 13<br>6.5% | 201 |
| Group D .............. | 0<br>0.0% | 8<br>12.9% | 29<br>46.8% | 23<br>37.1% | 2<br>3.2% | 62 |
| Group E .............. | 1<br>2.2% | 7<br>15.2% | 23<br>50.0% | 13<br>28.3% | 2<br>4.3% | 46 |

more Indian groups, have greater proportions of nostrils of narrow oval shape.

A depressed nasal tip gives the observer a poorer view of the nostrils anteriorly than if the tip is elevated, providing in each case that alar flare is equal. However, depressed tips are often highly correlated with great alar flare, in which case the latter factor's presence in marked degree is more potent for marked *frontal and lateral nasal visibility* than the factor of depression of the nasal tip. The tables for these two observed traits indicate that the Indian's nostrils are more easily visible both from the front and from the side than are those of the Whiter progeny of the racial cross.

## THE EAR

Ear Length and Ear Breadth. The table for ear length of males clearly indicates smaller diameters as characteristic of the more Indian of the Yucatecan population. For females, the evidence shows a similar trend, although not so marked. Indeed, for the latter, the differences are not certainly significant. For small-statured people, the ear lengths are appropriately small.

TABLE 77.    EAR LENGTH

MALES

| Group | No. | Range | Mean | S. D. | V. | Significance with Total Yucatecans |
|---|---|---|---|---|---|---|
| Total Yucatecans .. | 706 | 50–78 | 60.60±.10 | 3.94±.07 | 6.50±.12 | |
| Group A ......... | 165 | 50–69 | 60.06±.19 | 3.59±.13 | 5.98±.22 | 3×pe D |
| Group B ......... | 158 | 51–71 | 59.99±.21 | 3.89±.15 | 6.48±.25 | 3×pe D |
| Group C ......... | 308 | 52–73 | 61.04±.15 | 3.95±.11 | 6.47±.18 | 3×pe D |
| Group D ........ | 38 | 54–69 | 61.34±.46 | 4.18±.32 | 6.81±.53 | 1×pe D |
| Group E ......... | 37 | 50–78 | 61.50±.55 | 4.94±.39 | 8.03±.63 | 1×pe D |
| Spanish ......... | 79 | 51–72 | 61.35±.30 | 3.96±.21 | 6.45±.35 | |
| Barras, 1928 | | | | | | |

FEMALES

| Total Yucatecans .. | 543 | 45–72 | 57.62±.12 | 4.25±.09 | 7.38±.15 | |
|---|---|---|---|---|---|---|
| Group A ......... | 126 | 47–72 | 57.54±.26 | 4.25±.18 | 7.39±.31 | None |
| Group B ......... | 184 | 48–71 | 57.82±.20 | 4.11±.14 | 7.11±.25 | 1×pe D |
| Group C ......... | 160 | 45–67 | 57.20±.23 | 4.32±.16 | 7.55±.28 | 2×pe D |
| Group D ........ | 42 | 46–68 | 58.86±.50 | 4.84±.36 | 8.22±.61 | 2×pe D |
| Group E ......... | 31 | 52–66 | 57.29±.43 | 3.57±.31 | 6.23±.53 | None |
| Smith Coll. Students | 100 | 51–68 | 58.87±.25 | 3.74 | 6.35 | |
| Steggerda et al., 1929 | | | | | | |
| Shoshoni ................... | | | 61.50 | | | |
| Boas (Martin, 1914) | | | | | | |
| Eskimo .................... | | | 63.60 | | | |
| Duckworth (Martin, 1914) | | | | | | |
| Germans ................... | | | 59.00 | | | |
| Schwalbe (Martin, 1914) | | | | | | |

As for breadth of ear, only one significant difference appears. The exception is that of the female Group B, in which case the ears are on the average broader than those of the group as a whole: on the other hand, there is a possibility that the mean of the Group A females is less. Indicated by only probably significant differences,

TABLE 78.  EAR BREADTH

MALES

| Group | No. | Range | Mean | S. D. | V. | Significance with Total Yucatecans |
|---|---|---|---|---|---|---|
| Total Yucatecans .. | 706 | 25–41 | 31.59 ±.06 | 2.53 ±.04 | 8.01 ±.14 | |
| Group A ......... | 165 | 26–38 | 31.36 ±.13 | 2.45 ±.09 | 7.81 ±.29 | 2×pe D |
| Group B ......... | 158 | 26–38 | 31.35 ±.13 | 2.44 ±.09 | 7.78 ±.30 | 2×pe D |
| Group C ......... | 308 | 25–41 | 31.68 ±.10 | 2.57 ±.07 | 8.11 ±.22 | 1×pe D |
| Group D ........ | 38 | 26–40 | 32.08 ±.30 | 2.75 ±.21 | 8.57 ±.66 | 1×pe D |
| Group E ......... | 37 | 27–41 | 32.36 ±.31 | 2.78 ±.22 | 8.59 ±.67 | 2×pe D |
| Spanish .......... Barras, 1928 | 79 | 25–42 | 34.11 ±.23 | 3.04 ±.16 | 8.91 ±.48 | |

FEMALES

| Group | No. | Range | Mean | S. D. | V. | Significance with Total Yucatecans |
|---|---|---|---|---|---|---|
| Total Yucatecans .. | 543 | 22–39 | 30.04 ±.07 | 2.58 ±.05 | 8.59 ±.18 | |
| Group A .......... | 126 | 22–37 | 29.70 ±.16 | 2.71 ±.12 | 9.12 ±.39 | 2×pe D |
| Group B .......... | 184 | 25–39 | 30.44 ±.12 | 2.43 ±.09 | 7.98 ±.28 | 3×pe D |
| Group C ......... | 160 | 24–38 | 29.86 ±.14 | 2.59 ±.10 | 8.68 ±.33 | 1×pe D |
| Group D ........ | 42 | 22–36 | 30.21 ±.29 | 2.80 ±.21 | 9.27 ±.68 | None |
| Group E .......... | 31 | 24–33 | 29.74 ±.26 | 2.13 ±.18 | 7.16 ±.61 | 1×pe D |
| Smith Coll. Students Steggerda et al., 1929 | 100 | 27–40 | 33.23 ±.17 | 2.50 | 7.52 | |
| Eskimo ....................... Duckworth (Martin, 1914) | | | 30.20 | | | |

the males show a tendency for broader ears in the Whiter sub-groups.

**Auricular Index.** The conclusions drawn for size of ear are somewhat indefinite. For males it would appear that the Whiter Yucatecans have absolutely longer ears and a tendency toward proportionately broader ones. But the mean indices of the diameters of the males show no significant variation from that of the whole group. For females, the same condition seems to obtain, except

TABLE 79.  AURICULAR INDEX

MALES

| Group | No. | Range | Mean | S. D. | V. | Significance with Total Yucatecans |
|---|---|---|---|---|---|---|
| Total Yucatecans .. | 706 | 40–65 | 52.28±.10 | 4.15±.07 | 7.94±.14 | |
| Group A .......... | 165 | 40–64 | 52.31±.23 | 4.36±.16 | 8.33±.31 | None |
| Group B .......... | 158 | 42–63 | 52.37±.22 | 4.12±.16 | 7.87±.30 | None |
| Group C .......... | 308 | 42–65 | 52.16±.16 | 4.20±.11 | 8.05±.22 | 1×pe D |
| Group D .......... | 38 | 43–62 | 52.66±.41 | 3.78±.29 | 7.18±.56 | None |
| Group E .......... | 37 | 45–60 | 52.64±.33 | 3.02±.24 | 5.74±.45 | 1×pe D |
| Spanish .......... Barras, 1928 | 79 | 41–68 | 55.42±.38 | 4.94±.26 | 8.91±.48 | |
| Spanish .......... Barras, 1923 | 206 | 41–76 | 54.42±.30 | 6.39±.21 | 11.74±.39 | |
| American Indians .............. Karutz (Martin, 1914) | | | 56.00 | | | |
| Colorado Indians............... Rivet (Martin, 1914) | | | 59.00 | | | |
| Eskimo ..................... Duckworth (Martin, 1914) | | | 53.00 | | | |
| Germans (Hamburg) ........... Karutz (Martin, 1914) | | | 54.60 | | | |
| Buriats ..................... Porotoff (Martin, 1914) | | | 56.40 | | | |
| Kalmucks ................... Koroljow (Martin, 1914) | | | 57.70 | | | |
| Negroes .................... Topinard (Martin, 1914) | | | 61.20 | | | |

FEMALES

| Group | No. | Range | Mean | S. D. | V. | |
|---|---|---|---|---|---|---|
| Total Yucatecans .. | 543 | 39–65 | 52.28±.13 | 4.54±.09 | 8.68±.18 | |
| Group A .......... | 126 | 39–65 | 51.83±.29 | 4.76±.20 | 9.18±.39 | 1×pe D |
| Group B .......... | 184 | 39–64 | 52.79±.21 | 4.16±.15 | 7.88±.28 | 2×pe D |
| Group C .......... | 160 | 41–65 | 52.31±.26 | 4.84±.18 | 9.25±.35 | None |
| Group D .......... | 42 | 43–62 | 51.45±.47 | 4.52±.33 | 8.78±.65 | 1×pe D |
| Group E .......... | 31 | 43–62 | 52.08±.48 | 3.94±.34 | 7.56±.65 | None |
| Smith Coll. Students Steggerda et al., 1929 | 100 | 44–66 | 56.31±.29 | 4.23 | 7.51 | |
| Colorado Indians............... Rivet (Martin, 1914) | | | 59.80 | | | |
| Eskimo ..................... Duckworth (Martin, 1914) | | | 47.40 | | | |

that the greater average breadth of Group B is responsible for a larger mean index, which is not certainly significant.

**Ear Protrusion.** Group A of the males and Groups A, B, and C of the females show higher frequencies of small amount of ear protrusion than do the remaining groups. The male groups, however,

TABLE 80.   EAR PROTRUSION

MALES

|  | 0 | sm | + | ++ | +++ | No. |
|---|---|---|---|---|---|---|
| Total Yucatecans ....... | 0<br>0.0% | 79<br>9.0% | 374<br>42.5% | 394<br>44.8% | 33<br>3.7% | 880 |
| Group A ............. | 0<br>0.0% | 39<br>17.6% | 85<br>38.5% | 91<br>41.2% | 6<br>2.7% | 221 |
| Group B ............. | 0<br>0.0% | 17<br>8.5% | 88<br>44.0% | 89<br>45.0% | 5<br>2.5% | 199 |
| Group C ............. | 0<br>0.0% | 20<br>5.5% | 166<br>45.9% | 162<br>44.7% | 14<br>3.9% | 362 |
| Group D ............. | 0<br>0.0% | 1<br>1.9% | 19<br>36.6% | 27<br>51.9% | 5<br>9.6% | 52 |
| Group E ............. | 0<br>0.0% | 2<br>4.3% | 16<br>34.8% | 25<br>54.4% | 3<br>6.5% | 46 |

FEMALES

|  | 0 | sm | + | ++ | +++ | No. |
|---|---|---|---|---|---|---|
| Total Yucatecans ....... | 1<br>0.1% | 128<br>18.5% | 435<br>62.7% | 129<br>18.6% | 1<br>0.1% | 694 |
| Group A ............. | 0<br>0.0% | 33<br>21.4% | 102<br>66.2% | 18<br>11.6% | 1<br>0.8% | 154 |
| Group B ............. | 1<br>0.4% | 44<br>19.0% | 145<br>62.8% | 41<br>17.8% | 0<br>0.0% | 231 |
| Group C ............. | 0<br>0.0% | 39<br>19.4% | 118<br>58.7% | 44<br>21.9% | 0<br>0.0% | 201 |
| Group D ............. | 0<br>0.0% | 8<br>12.9% | 35<br>56.5% | 19<br>30.6% | 0<br>0.0% | 62 |
| Group E ............. | 0<br>0.0% | 4<br>8.7% | 35<br>76.1% | 7<br>15.2% | 0<br>0.0% | 46 |

differ only slightly in percentages of marked protrusion, and the female Indian groups, as well as the Whiter ones, disagree among themselves as to proportion of great protrusion. The verdict must be that no great difference in subgroups can be pointed out in respect to protrusion of the external ear.

**Roll of Helix.** Group D of the males has a comparatively low proportion of slightly rolled helices, and Groups D and E a comparatively high percentage of greatly rolled ones. Among the female groups no definite variation is found.

TABLE 81. ROLL OF HELIX

MALES

| | 0 | sm | + | ++ | +++ | No. |
|---|---|---|---|---|---|---|
| Total Yucatecans | 1 | 274 | 481 | 124 | 0 | 880 |
| | 0.1% | 31.1% | 54.7% | 14.1% | 0.0% | |
| Group A | 0 | 65 | 127 | 29 | 0 | 221 |
| | 0.0% | 29.4% | 57.5% | 13.1% | 0.0% | |
| Group B | 0 | 65 | 113 | 21 | 0 | 199 |
| | 0.0% | 32.7% | 56.8% | 10.5% | 0.0% | |
| Group C | 0 | 121 | 190 | 51 | 0 | 362 |
| | 0.0% | 33.4% | 52.5% | 14.1% | 0.0% | |
| Group D | 1 | 10 | 30 | 11 | 0 | 52 |
| | 1.9% | 19.2% | 57.7% | 21.2% | 0.0% | |
| Group E | 0 | 13 | 21 | 12 | 0 | 46 |
| | 0.0% | 28.3% | 45.6% | 26.1% | 0.0% | |

FEMALES

| | 0 | sm | + | ++ | +++ | No. |
|---|---|---|---|---|---|---|
| Total Yucatecans | 0 | 156 | 386 | 152 | 0 | 694 |
| | 0.0% | 22.5% | 55.6% | 21.9% | 0.0% | |
| Group A | 0 | 42 | 81 | 31 | 0 | 154 |
| | 0.0% | 27.3% | 52.6% | 20.1% | 0.0% | |
| Group B | 0 | 48 | 129 | 54 | 0 | 231 |
| | 0.0% | 20.8% | 55.8% | 23.4% | 0.0% | |
| Group C | 0 | 43 | 115 | 43 | 0 | 201 |
| | 0.0% | 21.4% | 57.2% | 21.4% | 0.0% | |
| Group D | 0 | 15 | 34 | 13 | 0 | 62 |
| | 0.0% | 24.2% | 54.8% | 21.0% | 0.0% | |
| Group E | 0 | 8 | 27 | 11 | 0 | 46 |
| | 0.0% | 17.4% | 58.7% | 23.9% | 0.0% | |

**Attachment of Ear Lobes.** In both sexes, a definite difference in percentage incidence of attached and free lobes is noted. While three-quarters of each of the more Indian subgroups have attached lobes, the incidence of this variation is less in the Whiter. On the other hand, only approximately one-quarter of each of the Groups

### TABLE 82.  EAR LOBES

MALES

|  | Attached | Free | No. |
|---|---|---|---|
| Total Yucatecans ..................... | 635 <br> 72.2% | 245 <br> 27.8% | 880 |
| Group A ........................... | 169 <br> 76.5% | 52 <br> 23.5% | 221 |
| Group B ........................... | 150 <br> 75.4% | 49 <br> 24.6% | 199 |
| Group C ........................... | 258 <br> 71.3% | 104 <br> 28.7% | 362 |
| Group D ........................... | 34 <br> 65.4% | 18 <br> 34.6% | 52 |
| Group E ........................... | 24 <br> 52.2% | 22 <br> 47.8% | 46 |

FEMALES

|  | Attached | Free | No. |
|---|---|---|---|
| Total Yucatecans ..................... | 521 <br> 75.1% | 173 <br> 24.9% | 694 |
| Group A ........................... | 120 <br> 77.9% | 34 <br> 22.1% | 154 |
| Group B ........................... | 182 <br> 78.8% | 49 <br> 21.2% | 231 |
| Group C ........................... | 154 <br> 76.6% | 47 <br> 23.4% | 201 |
| Group D ........................... | 38 <br> 61.3% | 24 <br> 38.7% | 62 |
| Group E ........................... | 27 <br> 58.7% | 19 <br> 41.3% | 46 |

A, B, and C possess the free variety, but the percentage for the Groups D is greater in each sex, and that for the Groups E is upwards of one-half.

## CERTAIN SUBJECTIVELY OBSERVED TRAITS

Several physical traits which were not capable of measurement and which were observed subjectively have been discussed in appropriate parts of this study.  A few other characteristics of this kind could not be fitted into any other portion of the discussion, and so will be treated separately.

**The Hair and Beard.**  The typical form of head hair of American Indians and Mongoloids is straight.  Exceptions to this general rule are so rare that straight head hair was chosen as one of the traits to be used in sorting the progeny of the Yucatecan racial cross into subgroups. Possession of the character was required only in the cases of Groups A and B. When Groups C, D, and E were defined no stipulation was made in regard to form of the hair.

TABLE 83.  HAIR FORM

MALES

| | Straight | Low waves | Deep waves | Curly | Frizzly | No. |
|---|---|---|---|---|---|---|
| Total Yucatecans ....... | 635 | 172 | 33 | 38 | 1 | 879 |
| | 72.2% | 19.6% | 3.8% | 4.3% | 0.1% | |
| Group A .............. | 221 | 0 | 0 | 0 | 0 | 221 |
| | 100.0% | 0.0% | 0.0% | 0.0% | 0.0% | |
| Group B .............. | 172 | 16 | 7 | 4 | 0 | 199 |
| | 86.4% | 8.0% | 3.5% | 2.0% | 0.0% | |
| Group C .............. | 203 | 119 | 16 | 22 | 1 | 361 |
| | 56.2% | 33.0% | 4.4% | 6.1% | 0.3% | |
| Group D .............. | 19 | 19 | 6 | 8 | 0 | 52 |
| | 36.5% | 36.5% | 11.5% | 15.4% | 0.0% | |
| Group E .............. | 21 | 17 | 4 | 4 | 0 | 46 |
| | 45.7% | 36.9% | 8.7% | 8.7% | 0.0% | |

FEMALES

| | Straight | Low waves | Deep waves | Curly | Frizzly | No. |
|---|---|---|---|---|---|---|
| Total Yucatecans ....... | 513 | 160 | 13 | 4 | 4 | 694 |
| | 73.9% | 23.0% | 1.9% | 0.6% | 0.6% | |
| Group A .............. | 154 | 0 | 0 | 0 | 0 | 154 |
| | 100.0% | 0.0% | 0.0% | 0.0% | 0.0% | |
| Group B .............. | 208 | 19 | 3 | 0 | 1 | 231 |
| | 90.1% | 8.2% | 1.3% | 0.0% | 0.4% | |
| Group C .............. | 112 | 79 | 6 | 2 | 2 | 201 |
| | 55.7% | 39.3% | 3.0% | 1.0% | 1.0% | |
| Group D .............. | 23 | 35 | 2 | 1 | 1 | 62 |
| | 37.1% | 56.5% | 3.2% | 1.6% | 1.6% | |
| Group E .............. | 16 | 27 | 2 | 1 | 0 | 46 |
| | 34.8% | 58.7% | 4.3% | 2.2% | 0.0% | |
| Mexicans ............. | 19 | 10 | 1 | 0 | 0 | 30 |
| | 63.4% | 33.3% | 3.3% | 0.0% | 0.0% | |

Examination of the tables for hair form demonstrates that there is a high degree of association between other White traits and that of wavy hair. Curly hair, even in the Whiter groups, is rare, and especially so in the females. The incidence of the latter variation in the male Total Yucatecans is greater, however, than in the Half-Blood Sioux, as is the percentage for curly hair. The female Mexicans resident in Yucatan show a percentage distribution in hair form which compares well with that found for the Group C women. Concerning mixture of Chinese with Hawaiians, Dunn states: "The genetic relationship between the straight Mongoloid type of hair and the wavy European type has not been established, al-

TABLE 84.   HAIR TEXTURE

MALES

|  | Coarse | Medium | Fine | No. |
|---|---|---|---|---|
| Total Yucatecans ........... | 801 | 78 | 0 | 879 |
|  | 91.1% | 8.9% | 0.0% |  |
| Group A.................. | 221 | 0 | 0 | 221 |
|  | 100.0% | 0.0% | 0.0% |  |
| Group B.................. | 195 | 4 | 0 | 199 |
|  | 98.0% | 2.0% | 0.0% |  |
| Group C.................. | 320 | 41 | 0 | 361 |
|  | 88.6% | 11.4% | 0.0% |  |
| Group D .....:........... | 31 | 21 | 0 | 52 |
|  | 59.6% | 40.4% | 0.0% |  |
| Group E.................. | 16 | 30 | 0 | 46 |
|  | 34.8% | 65.2% | 0.0% |  |

FEMALES

|  | Coarse | Medium | Fine | No. |
|---|---|---|---|---|
| Total Yucatecans ........... | 572 | 120 | 2 | 694 |
|  | 82.5% | 17.2% | 0.3% |  |
| Group A.................. | 154 | 0 | 0 | 154 |
|  | 100.0% | 0.0% | 0.0% |  |
| Group B.................. | 226 | 5 | 0 | 231 |
|  | 97.9% | 2.1% | 0.0% |  |
| Group C.................. | 165 | 36 | 0 | 201 |
|  | 82.1% | 17.9% | 0.0% |  |
| Group D ................. | 19 | 42 | 1 | 62 |
|  | 30.7% | 67.7% | 1.6% |  |
| Group E.................. | 8 | 37 | 1 | 46 |
|  | 17.4% | 80.4% | 2.2% |  |
| Mexicans................. | 17 | 13 | 0 | 30 |
|  | 56.7% | 43.3% | 0.0% |  |

though the evidence of Bean and of other observers makes it appear probable that the Mongoloid type behaves as a dominant trait in inheritance. Our evidence partially corroborates this assumption in that the majority of the hybrids (60 per cent) had straight hair of the Mongoloid type."

A similar phenomenon seems to characterize the mixed Yucatecans, not only in hair form but also in hair texture. The proportions of the mixing groups in the various cases of mixture cited are probably in no two cases the same, but the general trend is similar in each group of progeny. It appears to the author that what is needed in the study of inheritance of hair form and texture is not a greater accumulation of subjective data but objective studies based on actual measurements.

The male Maya's comparative lack of facial hair was another of the sorting criteria used. The less heavily bearded Indians and the more heavily bearded Whiter offspring of the cross were concen-

TABLE 85.  BEARD (AND MOUSTACHE)

MALES

|  | 0 | sm | + | ++, +++ | No. |
|---|---|---|---|---|---|
| Total Yucatecans | 48 | 535 | 185 | 58 | 826 |
|  | 5.8% | 64.8% | 22.4% | 7.0% |  |
| Group A | 18 | 178 | 25 | 0 | 221 |
|  | 8.1% | 80.5% | 11.3% | 0.0% |  |
| Group B | 20 | 164 | 0 | 4 | 188 |
|  | 10.6% | 87.2% | 0.0% | 2.1% |  |
| Group C | 10 | 187 | 109 | 33 | 339 |
|  | 2.9% | 55.2% | 32.2% | 9.7% |  |
| Group D | 0 | 1 | 27 | 12 | 40 |
|  | 0.0% | 2.5% | 67.5% | 30.0% |  |
| Group E | 0 | 1 | 26 | 11 | 38 |
|  | 0.0% | 2.6% | 68.4% | 28.9% |  |

trated by the sorting method at either end of the gradation of racial subgroups. The table is therefore a biased one and deserves no further comment.

**Pigmentation.** Pigmentation has always been the most popular of all the differential racial criteria. So obvious a group of characters are comprised that any extended study of a race is incomplete without mention of them. Yet in many cases too much stress has been laid upon this group of traits. Such a situation was avoided in this study by use of these differential criteria in combination with other truly racial characteristics.

The most striking feature in the tables for hair color is the difference manifested in the two sexes. The so-called dominance of black over all other colors of hair is much more marked in the male group as a whole than in the female. As one compares the sexes subgroup by subgroup, one notes that the frequency of lighter hair

TABLE 86.  HAIR COLOR

### MALES

|  | Black | Dark Brown | Light Brown and Blond | No. |
|---|---|---|---|---|
| Total Yucatecans .......... | 791 | 82 | 6 | 879 |
|  | 90.0% | 9.3% | 0.7% |  |
| Group A.................. | 221 | 0 | 0 | 221 |
|  | 100.0% | 0.0% | 0.0% |  |
| Group B.................. | 194 | 5 | 0 | 199 |
|  | 97.5% | 2.5% | 0.0% |  |
| Group C.................. | 314 | 46 | 1 | 361 |
|  | 87.0% | 12.7% | 0.3% |  |
| Group D ................ | 49 | 3 | 0 | 52 |
|  | 94.2% | 5.8% | 0.0% |  |
| Group E.................. | 15 | 26 | 5 | 46 |
|  | 32.6% | 56.5% | 10.9% |  |

### MALES AND FEMALES

|  | Black | Dark Brown | Brown | Light Brown | Red-Brown | Yellow | No. |
|---|---|---|---|---|---|---|---|
| Hawaiians, Pure ...... | 91.6% | 5.8% | 0.6% | 0.0% | 1.3% | 0.0% | 154 |
| ¾ Hawaiian, ¼ North European .......... | 67.7% | 29.0% | 0.0% | 0.0% | 3.2% | 0.0% | 31 |
| F₁ Hawaiian, North European .......... | 44.0% | 32.0% | 20.0% | 0.0% | 3.7% | 0.0% | 25 |
| ¼ Hawaiian, ¾ North European .......... | 5.5% | 27.8% | 44.4% | 16.7% | 0.0% | 5.5% | 17 |
| Dunn, Tozzer, 1928 |  |  |  |  |  |  |  |

### MALES

|  | Black | Dark Brown | Brown | Light Brown | Red-Brown | Yellow | No. |
|---|---|---|---|---|---|---|---|
| Sioux, Pure .......... | 96.5% | 2.6% | 0.0% | 0.9% | 0.0% | 0.0% | 541 |
| Sioux, Half-Blood .... | 84.4% | 14.3% | 0.0% | 0.0% | 0.0% | 1.3% | 77 |
| Sullivan, 1920 |  |  |  |  |  |  |  |

### FEMALES

|  | Black | Dark Brown | Light Brown and Blond | Red-Brown | Yellow-Brown | No. |
|---|---|---|---|---|---|---|
| Total Yucatecans ....... | 500 | 171 | 15 | 7 | 1 | 694 |
|  | 72.1% | 24.6% | 2.2% | 1.0% | 0.1% |  |
| Group A .............. | 154 | 0 | 0 | 0 | 0 | 154 |
|  | 100.0% | 0.0% | 0.0% | 0.0% | 0.0% |  |
| Group B .............. | 209 | 20 | 2 | 0 | 0 | 231 |
|  | 90.5% | 8.6% | 0.9% | 0.0% | 0.0% |  |
| Group C .............. | 107 | 88 | 0 | 5 | 1 | 201 |
|  | 53.2% | 43.8% | 0.0% | 2.5% | 0.5% |  |
| Group D .............. | 27 | 29 | 6 | 0 | 0 | 62 |
|  | 43.5% | 46.8% | 9.7% | 0.0% | 0.0% |  |
| Group E .............. | 3 | 34 | 7 | 2 | 0 | 46 |
|  | 6.5% | 73.9% | 15.3% | 4.3% | 0.0% |  |
| Mexicans ............. | 18 | 11 | 0 | 1 | 0 | 30 |
|  | 60.0% | 36.7% | 0.0% | 3.3% | 0.0% |  |

in the subgroups B to E is much greater in the women than in the men. In the later discussion of variability it will be shown that in many measurable characters the females vary less than do the males of the same groups. There is not a great difference in hair color of the parental types in this case of mixture, but it cannot be

TABLE 87.  GRAYNESS

MALES

| | 0 | sm | + | ++ | +++ | No. |
|---|---|---|---|---|---|---|
| Total Yucatecans ....... | 660 | 95 | 63 | 53 | 9 | 880 |
| | 75.0% | 10.8% | 7.2% | 6.0% | 1.0% | |
| Group A .............. | 188 | 16 | 12 | 5 | 0 | 221 |
| | 85.1% | 7.2% | 5.4% | 2.3% | 0.0% | |
| Group B .............. | 165 | 19 | 10 | 4 | 1 | 199 |
| | 82.9% | 9.6% | 5.0% | 2.0% | 0.5% | |
| Group C .............. | 255 | 44 | 32 | 30 | 1 | 362 |
| | 70.4% | 12.1% | 8.8% | 8.3% | 0.3% | |
| Group D .............. | 26 | 8 | 5 | 9 | 4 | 52 |
| | 50.0% | 15.4% | 9.6% | 17.3% | 7.7% | |
| Group E .............. | 26 | 8 | 4 | 5 | 3 | 46 |
| | 56.5% | 17.4% | 8.7% | 10.9% | 6.5% | |

FEMALES

| | 0 | sm | + | ++ | +++ | No. |
|---|---|---|---|---|---|---|
| Total Yucatecans ....... | 534 | 46 | 53 | 47 | 14 | 694 |
| | 77.0% | 6.6% | 7.6% | 6.8% | 2.0% | |
| Group A .............. | 126 | 10 | 7 | 10 | 1 | 154 |
| | 81.8% | 6.4% | 4.5% | 6.4% | 0.9% | |
| Group B .............. | 177 | 15 | 21 | 13 | 5 | 231 |
| | 76.6% | 6.5% | 9.1% | 5.6% | 2.2% | |
| Group C .............. | 156 | 11 | 17 | 11 | 6 | 201 |
| | 77.6% | 5.5% | 8.5% | 5.5% | 2.9% | |
| Group D .............. | 36 | 6 | 7 | 11 | 2 | 62 |
| | 58.1% | 9.7% | 11.3% | 17.7% | 3.2% | |
| Group E .............. | 39 | 4 | 1 | 2 | 0 | 46 |
| | 84.8% | 8.7% | 2.2% | 4.3% | 0.0% | |

said concerning this trait that the females are less variable than the males. "Dominance" of black hair appears to affect the men more than the women.

In grayness of hair there is less sexual difference. The differences that occur are found at the Whiter extreme of the subgroup grada-tion rather than in the more Indian groups. Graying of hair with age has always been conceded to be a characteristic of the lighter races as opposed to the deeply pigmented varieties of mankind.

## TABLE 88.  EYE COLOR

### MALES

| | Black | Dark Brown | Light Brown | Yellow-Brown | Green-Brown | Blue-Brown | Blue | No. |
|---|---|---|---|---|---|---|---|---|
| Total Yucatecans. | 460 | 253 | 99 | 2 | 47 | 17 | 2 | 880 |
| | 52.3% | 28.8% | 11.2% | 0.2% | 5.3% | 1.9% | 0.2% | |
| Group A ....... | 152 | 69 | 0 | 0 | 0 | 0 | 0 | 221 |
| | 68.8% | 31.2% | 0.0% | 0.0% | 0.0% | 0.0% | 0.0% | |
| Group B ....... | 138 | 47 | 10 | 0 | 2 | 2 | 0 | 199 |
| | 69.4% | 23.6% | 5.0% | 0.0% | 1.0% | 1.0% | 0.0% | |
| Group C ....... | 157 | 105 | 69 | 2 | 23 | 6 | 0 | 362 |
| | 43.4% | 29.0% | 19.1% | 0.5% | 6.4% | 1.6% | 0.0% | |
| Group D ....... | 12 | 28 | 6 | 0 | 4 | 1 | 1 | 52 |
| | 23.1% | 53.8% | 11.5% | 0.0% | 7.7% | 1.9% | 1.9% | |
| Group E ....... | 1 | 5 | 13 | 0 | 18 | 7 | 2 | 46 |
| | 2.2% | 10.9% | 28.3% | 0.0% | 39.1% | 15.2% | 4.3% | |

### MALES AND FEMALES

| | Black | Dark Brown | Brown | Light Brown | Hazel | Blue | No. |
|---|---|---|---|---|---|---|---|
| Hawaiians, Pure ....... | | 43.9% | 43.2% | 11.6% | 0.6% | 0.6% | 155 |
| ¾ Hawaiian, ¼ North European .......... | | 27.3% | 48.5% | 21.2% | 3.0% | 0.0% | 33 |
| F₁ Hawaiian, North European .......... | | 8.0% | 48.0% | 36.0% | 4.0% | 4.0% | 25 |
| ¼ Hawaiian, ¾ North European .......... | | 17.6% | 23.5% | 17.6% | 5.9% | 35.3% | 17 |
| Dunn, Tozzer, 1928 | | | | | | | |

### MALES

| | Black | Dark Brown | Brown | Light Brown | Hazel | Blue | No. |
|---|---|---|---|---|---|---|---|
| Sioux, Pure .......... | 34.3% | 62.7% | 0.0% | 1.3% | 0.7% | 1.0% | 539 |
| Sioux, Half-Blood ..... | 18.2% | 50.6% | 0.0% | 18.2% | 9.1% | 3.9% | 77 |
| Sullivan, 1920 | | | | | | | |

### FEMALES

| Total | Black | Dark Brown | Light Brown | Yellow-Brown | Green-Brown | Gray-Brown | Blue-Brown | Blue | No. |
|---|---|---|---|---|---|---|---|---|---|
| Yucatecans.. | 452 | 164 | 53 | 1 | 14 | 2 | 7 | 0 | 693 |
| | 65.2% | 23.7% | 7.7% | 0.1% | 2.0% | 0.3% | 1.0% | 0.0% | |
| Group A .... | 130 | 24 | 0 | 0 | 0 | 0 | 0 | 0 | 154 |
| | 84.4% | 15.6% | 0.0% | 0.0% | 0.0% | 0.0% | 0.0% | 0.0% | |
| Group B .... | 175 | 50 | 5 | 0 | 0 | 0 | 1 | 0 | 231 |
| | 75.8% | 21.6% | 2.2% | 0.0% | 0.0% | 0.0% | 0.4% | 0.0% | |
| Group C .... | 114 | 49 | 33 | 0 | 4 | 1 | 0 | 0 | 201 |
| | 56.7% | 24.4% | 16.4% | 0.0% | 2.0% | 0.5% | 0.0% | 0.0% | |
| Group D .... | 30 | 29 | 1 | 0 | 1 | 0 | 0 | 0 | 61 |
| | 49.2% | 47.6% | 1.6% | 0.0% | 1.6% | 0.0% | 0.0% | 0.0% | |
| Group E .... | 3 | 12 | 14 | 1 | 9 | 1 | 6 | 0 | 46 |
| | 6.5% | 26.1% | 30.4% | 2.2% | 19.6% | 2.2% | 13.0% | 0.0% | |
| Mexicans ... | 16 | 11 | 2 | 0 | 0 | 0 | 1 | 0 | 30 |
| | 53.3% | 36.7% | 6.7% | 0.0% | 0.0% | 0.0% | 3.3% | 0.0% | |

On the other hand, the hair of blonds does not gray readily. It may be that the higher percentage of grayness in the members of Group D as compared to those of Group E may in part be due to the relative blondness of the latter group.

In eye color, unlike hair color, the females appear to be more homogeneous than the males. While 89 per cent of the females of the group as a whole are classifiable in the darker shades of black and dark brown, only 81 per cent of the males are so characterized. Also, seven per cent of the total males have green-brown or blue-brown eyes, but only three per cent of the females possess these eye colors. The Group A females are more uniformly black-eyed than the Group A members of the other sex. The women of Group E appear to be more strongly affected by the dominance of dark eye colors over light than the men, who show fairly equal proportions of the pure brown and the mixed varieties.

No great amount of lightness of eye color was introduced into the Yucatecan cross by the Spanish, but that which was brought in is without doubt linked with certain of the White traits which the author used for segregation of the Whiter subgroups. The Mendelian recessive character of lighter eye colors has been commented upon by many writers. Dunn remarks in connection with the occurrence of lighter colors of hair and eyes in Hawaiian-White crosses that "they are apparently behaving in this as in other crosses as recessives, although it is evident that dominance is not complete in respect to them." The lighter colors of certain Yucatecans are also best explained on the basis of their recessiveness. Segregation of pure blue eyes is a very rare phenomenon in Yucatan. The infrequency of blue eyes is due to their scarcity in the parent Spanish-White type, as well as to the disproportionate number of Indians to Whites in the racial cross. The table on relative homogeneity of the iris is to be considered as an integral part of and supplemental to the table for eye color. Raying of the iris was seen in most of the cases of mixed eye color as well as in some of the light browns. Comparatively few of the irises were zoned and practically all of these were found in members of Group E. Had the author desired so to refine his method as to consider separately the light-brown irises which were homogeneous and those which were rayed, zoned, or speckled, the results might have been interesting. This is suggested by the fact that the finer nuances of shade in eye

pigmentation have been shown to possess definite differential linkages with certain other anthropometric traits.  Reference to Table 2
demonstrates this point.  That table compares the various grades
of certain observed traits according to their linkages with mensurable characters.  It is demonstrated that while the men with lighter

TABLE 89.  IRIS

MALES

|  | Homogeneous | Rayed | Zoned | No. |
|---|---|---|---|---|
| Total Yucatecans .......... | 655 | 219 | 6 | 880 |
|  | 74.4% | 24.9% | 0.7% | |
| Group A................. | 196 | 24 | 1 | 221 |
|  | 88.7% | 10.9% | 0.4% | |
| Group B................. | 173 | 25 | 1 | 199 |
|  | 86.9% | 12.6% | 0.5% | |
| Group C................. | 247 | 114 | 1 | 362 |
|  | 68.2% | 31.5% | 0.3% | |
| Group D ................ | 30 | 21 | 1 | 52 |
|  | 57.7% | 40.4% | 1.9% | |
| Group E................. | 10 | 34 | 2 | 46 |
|  | 21.7% | 73.9% | 4.3% | |

FEMALES

|  | | | | |
|---|---|---|---|---|
| Total Yucatecans .......... | 587 | 103 | 2 | 692 |
|  | 84.8% | 14.9% | 0.3% | |
| Group A................. | 148 | 6 | 0 | 154 |
|  | 96.1% | 3.9% | 0.0% | |
| Group B................. | 214 | 17 | 0 | 231 |
|  | 92.6% | 7.4% | 0.0% | |
| Group C................. | 159 | 42 | 0 | 201 |
|  | 79.1% | 20.9% | 0.0% | |
| Group D ................ | 50 | 11 | 0 | 61 |
|  | 82.0% | 18.0% | 0.0% | |
| Group E................. | 16 | 27 | 2 | 45 |
|  | 35.6% | 60.0% | 4.4% | |

blue-brown irises have significantly longer heads than those of the
group of males as a whole, individuals having green-brown eyes
(or any darker shade) differ insignificantly from the total group.

Table 90 refers to skin color as observed on the inner surface of
the arms of the subjects.  In skin color, as in eye color, the females
vary less than the males.  In the more Indian subgroups they are
much more uniformly dark, no tint lighter than Von Luschan's

No. 19 appearing in the female Group A. Against this, one finds a considerable number of Group A men who are lighter than No. 19. Even the Whiter females have greater frequencies of the darker shades of skin color than the males of similar groups.

Table 2 shows the men with skin color lighter than Von Luschan's No. 17 to be characterized by taller stature, longer heads, less prominent cheek bones, and lower cephalic indices. The differences in stature and head length were only probably significant for Von Luschan's No. 16, but undoubtedly so for the shades of No. 14 and lighter. For this reason the arbitrary division between lighter and darker skin colors was set between Nos. 14 and 15.

That there is inheritance of skin color is demonstrated in the table and is a fact generally accepted. It might be thought that the greater exposure to the sun in the case of hacienda employes and of *milpa* farmers, many of whom are Indians, constitutes an argument against the purely hereditary origin of the darker skins of the more Indian part of the population. Such a factor is certainly operative. But it is also to be considered that more members of the Indian subgroups may engage in these occupations because they are constitutionally better fitted to withstand the direct exposure to the sun's rays than members of the lighter subgroups. The author recalls meeting with an albino Indian, who, except for his pigmentation, differed little from the generality of purer Indians encountered. The albino stated that his condition prevented him from doing any great amount of work in the sun. The parallel between this case and that of the Whiter Yucatecan is obvious. It also may be urged that the average woman of rural Yucatan spends more of her time in places sheltered from the sun than does the average man and should therefore show lighter skin color; but the fact is (as the table shows) that the females average a little darker in skin color than the males.

Certain observers have maintained that the presence of freckling is an indication of race mixture. This theory is substantiated by data which are again found in Table 2. There it is noted that the freckled members of the racial cross tend to have greater stature, longer heads, and cephalic indices of smaller value. The peculiar manifestation which the author has distinguished by the term "mass freckling" behaves in the same manner in its linkages as does the absence of freckling. Its identification with the more com-

## TABLE 90. SKIN COLOR (VON LUSCHAN'S SCALE)

### MALES

| | Very white | 10-11 | 12-14 | 15 | 16 | 17-18 | 19-20 | 21-22 | 23-25 | No. |
|---|---|---|---|---|---|---|---|---|---|---|
| Total Yucatecans | 7 | 7 | 71 | 43 | 41 | 38 | 232 | 380 | 61 | 880 |
| | 0.8% | 0.8% | 8.1% | 4.9% | 4.7% | 4.3% | 26.4% | 43.2% | 6.9% | |
| Group A | 0 | 0 | 0 | 9 | 6 | 10 | 57 | 115 | 24 | 221 |
| | 0.0% | 0.0% | 0.0% | 4.1% | 2.7% | 4.5% | 25.8% | 52.0% | 10.9% | |
| Group B | 0 | 0 | 3 | 7 | 5 | 11 | 61 | 95 | 17 | 199 |
| | 0.0% | 0.0% | 1.5% | 3.5% | 2.5% | 5.5% | 30.6% | 47.7% | 8.5% | |
| Group C | 0 | 0 | 24 | 23 | 18 | 14 | 101 | 162 | 20 | 362 |
| | 0.0% | 0.0% | 6.6% | 6.3% | 5.0% | 3.9% | 27.9% | 44.7% | 5.5% | |
| Group D | 1 | 3 | 16 | 2 | 9 | 2 | 11 | 8 | 0 | 52 |
| | 1.9% | 5.8% | 30.8% | 3.8% | 17.3% | 3.8% | 21.2% | 15.4% | 0.0% | |
| Group E | 5 | 4 | 28 | 2 | 3 | 1 | 2 | 1 | 0 | 46 |
| | 10.9% | 8.7% | 60.9% | 4.3% | 6.5% | 2.2% | 4.3% | 2.2% | 0.0% | |

### FEMALES

| | Very white | 10-11 | 12-14 | 15 | 16 | 17-18 | 19-20 | 21-22 | 23-25 | No. |
|---|---|---|---|---|---|---|---|---|---|---|
| Total Yucatecans | 3 | 8 | 53 | 7 | 45 | 9 | 323 | 228 | 18 | 694 |
| | 0.4% | 1.2% | 7.6% | 1.0% | 6.5% | 1.3% | 46.5% | 32.9% | 2.6% | |
| Group A | 0 | 0 | 0 | 0 | 0 | 0 | 82 | 67 | 5 | 154 |
| | 0.0% | 0.0% | 0.0% | 0.0% | 0.0% | 0.0% | 53.3% | 43.5% | 3.2% | |
| Group B | 0 | 0 | 3 | 1 | 8 | 3 | 120 | 87 | 9 | 231 |
| | 0.0% | 0.0% | 1.3% | 0.4% | 3.5% | 1.3% | 51.9% | 37.7% | 3.9% | |
| Group C | 0 | 0 | 18 | 3 | 17 | 4 | 99 | 57 | 3 | 201 |
| | 0.0% | 0.0% | 8.9% | 1.5% | 8.5% | 2.0% | 49.2% | 28.4% | 1.5% | |
| Group D | 0 | 4 | 9 | 1 | 15 | 2 | 16 | 14 | 1 | 62 |
| | 0.0% | 6.5% | 14.5% | 1.6% | 24.2% | 3.2% | 25.8% | 22.6% | 1.6% | |
| Group E | 3 | 4 | 23 | 2 | 5 | 0 | 6 | 3 | 0 | 46 |
| | 6.5% | 8.7% | 50.0% | 4.4% | 10.9% | 0.0% | 13.0% | 6.5% | 0.0% | |
| Mexicans | 0 | 1 | 1 | 2 | 8 | 2 | 7 | 9 | 0 | 30 |
| | 0.0% | 3.3% | 3.3% | 6.7% | 26.7% | 6.7% | 23.3% | 30.0% | 0.0% | |

176

## Broca Scale
### Males and Females

| | "Light" | 47 | 23 | 24 | 39 | 25 | 40 | No. |
|---|---|---|---|---|---|---|---|---|
| Hawaiians, Pure .................. | 0.0% | 22.7% | 18.7% | 38.7% | 6.6% | 4.0% | 9.3% | 75 |
| $\frac{3}{4}$ Hawaiian, $\frac{1}{4}$ North European ...... | 0.0% | 17.6% | 29.4% | 41.2% | 11.8% | 0.0% | 0.0% | 17 |
| F₁ Hawaiian, North European ...... | 0.0% | 0.0% | 100.0% | | 0.0% | 0.0% | 0.0% | 26 |
| $\frac{1}{4}$ Hawaiian, $\frac{3}{4}$ North European ...... | 22.2% | 0.0% | 66.7% | 11.1% | 0.0% | 0.0% | 0.0% | 9 |

Dunn, Tozzer, 1928

NOTE: The numbers of the Broca scale arrayed below are arranged in order of progressive darkness. The grades of Broca's scale have been placed opposite similar grades of Von Luschan's scale. The colors in the two are not of the same quality, and it is unwise to combine observations recorded on the two scales. (Dunn.)

| Von Luschan | | Broca |
|---|---|---|
| 11 | = | 47 |
| 12 | = | 23 |
| 14 | = | 24 |
| 15 | = | 39 |
| 16 | = | 25 |
| 17 | = | 40 |

monly observed phenomenon is therefore questionable and its significance must be considered as not yet determined.

Freckling is more common in Yucatecan women than in men, and Mexican women resident in Yucatan appear to have it more frequently than any subgroup of the Yucatecan females. This

### TABLE 91. FRECKLES

#### MALES

| | 0 | sm | + | ++, +++ | Mass | No. |
|---|---|---|---|---|---|---|
| Total Yucatecans ....... | 667 | 120 | 48 | 19 | 26 | 880 |
| | 75.8% | 13.6% | 5.5% | 2.2% | 3.0% | |
| Group A ............. | 211 | 0 | 0 | 0 | 10 | 221 |
| | 95.5% | 0.0% | 0.0% | 0.0% | 4.5% | |
| Group B ............. | 160 | 25 | 5 | 2 | 7 | 199 |
| | 80.4% | 12.6% | 2.5% | 1.0% | 3.5% | |
| Group C ............. | 232 | 73 | 36 | 13 | 8 | 362 |
| | 64.1% | 20.2% | 9.9% | 3.6% | 2.2% | |
| Group D ............. | 35 | 10 | 5 | 2 | 0 | 52 |
| | 67.3% | 19.2% | 9.6% | 3.8% | 0.0% | |
| Group E ............. | 29 | 11 | 3 | 2 | 1 | 46 |
| | 63.0% | 23.9% | 6.5% | 4.3% | 2.2% | |

#### FEMALES

| | 0 | sm | + | ++, +++ | Mass | No. |
|---|---|---|---|---|---|---|
| Total Yucatecans ....... | 342 | 155 | 96 | 54 | 47 | 694 |
| | 49.3% | 22.3% | 13.8% | 7.8% | 6.8% | |
| Group A ............. | 151 | 0 | 0 | 0 | 3 | 154 |
| | 98.0% | 0.0% | 0.0% | 0.0% | 2.0% | |
| Group B ............. | 86 | 72 | 40 | 12 | 21 | 231 |
| | 37.2% | 31.2% | 17.3% | 5.2% | 9.1% | |
| Group C ............. | 62 | 62 | 44 | 19 | 14 | 201 |
| | 30.8% | 30.8% | 21.9% | 9.5% | 7.0% | |
| Group D ............. | 28 | 9 | 9 | 11 | 5 | 62 |
| | 45.2% | 14.5% | 14.5% | 17.7% | 8.1% | |
| Group E ............. | 15 | 12 | 3 | 12 | 4 | 46 |
| | 32.6% | 26.1% | 6.5% | 26.1% | 8.7% | |
| Mexicans ............. | 8 | 5 | 7 | 10 | 0 | 30 |
| | 26.7% | 16.7% | 23.3% | 33.3% | 0.0% | |

peculiar variety of pigmentation can only be seen on fairly light skins. It is therefore appropriate that the Groups E, whose members were selected for lighter pigmentation, should show higher frequencies of marked freckling than the other groups.

**Eye-Folds.** The more Indian groups of the Yucatecans were required to manifest any type of eye-fold except the external; it was stipulated for the Whiter that they should have given proportions of certain traits, among which were listed either external folds or no folds at all. It should be noted that in the case of either set of groups, the absence of a fold was permitted. The sorting method has of course biased the distribution of the trait in the various sub-

TABLE 92.   EYE–FOLDS

MALES

| | Mongo-loid | Epicanthic ++, +++ | Epicanthic sm, + | No fold | External sm, + | External ++, +++ | No. |
|---|---|---|---|---|---|---|---|
| Total Yucatecans .... | 12 1.4% | 221 25.1% | 260 29.5% | 342 38.9% | 31 3.5% | 14 1.6% | 880 |
| Group A .......... | 6 2.7% | 87 39.4% | 70 31.7% | 58 26.2% | 0 0.0% | 0 0.0% | 221 |
| Group B .......... | 1 0.5% | 62 31.2% | 70 35.2% | 66 33.2% | 0 0.0% | 0 0.0% | 199 |
| Group C .......... | 5 1.4% | 71 19.6% | 114 31.5% | 148 40.9% | 20 5.5% | 4 1.1% | 362 |
| Group D .......... | 0 0.0% | 1 1.9% | 3 5.8% | 39 75.0% | 6 11.5% | 3 5.8% | 52 |
| Group E .......... | 0 0.0% | 0 0.0% | 2 4.3% | 31 67.4% | 6 13.0% | 7 15.2% | 46 |

FEMALES

| | Mongo-loid | Epicanthic ++, +++ | Epicanthic sm, + | No fold | External sm, + | External ++, +++ | No. |
|---|---|---|---|---|---|---|---|
| Total Yucatecans .... | 10 1.4% | 227 32.7% | 199 28.7% | 247 35.6% | 11 1.6% | 0 0.0% | 694 |
| Group A .......... | 2 1.3% | 64 41.6% | 53 34.4% | 35 22.7% | 0 0.0% | 0 0.0% | 154 |
| Group B .......... | 2 0.9% | 89 38.5% | 68 29.5% | 71 30.7% | 1 0.4% | 0 0.0% | 231 |
| Group C .......... | 6 3.0% | 72 35.8% | 66 32.8% | 53 26.4% | 4 2.0% | 0 0.0% | 201 |
| Group D .......... | 0 0.0% | 0 0.0% | 5 8.1% | 55 88.7% | 2 3.2% | 0 0.0% | 62 |
| Group E .......... | 0 0.0% | 2 4.3% | 7 15.2% | 33 71.8% | 4 8.7% | 0 0.0% | 46 |
| Mexicans .......... | 0 0.0% | 6 20.0% | 0 0.0% | 22 73.3% | 2 6.7% | 0 0.0% | 30 |

groups. Even so, it is interesting that epicanthic folds are a little more common in females than in males in the group as a whole, as well as in the various subgroups, while the converse is true for incidence of external eye-folds. That the internal eye-fold was a prevalent character in the ancient days of the Mayas is indicated by its frequent occurrence in representations of the face in the

ancient art. The incidence of it has probably been materially reduced by race mixture, but it is by no means in danger of disap-
pearing. If a homogeneous Yucatecan type is ever formed, it is to
be expected that the epicanthic eye-fold will be one of its fairly
constant characteristics.

## BLOOD GROUPING

Blood serum and corpuscles were collected for the purpose of
study of blood groups from people of four localities of Yucatan.
These are: from the native workmen at the ruins of Chichen Itza;
from the inhabitants of Hacienda Sacapuc; from the inhabitants of
Hacienda Canicab; and from patients in the Hospital O'Horan, a
general hospital in the city of Merida. Samples were also taken
from the insane patients of the Hospital Ayala of Merida, and are
included in the series described in Moss and Kennedy's article of
1929, but excluded from the Total Yucatecans group of either sex
here discussed. This exclusion was considered necessary for the
reason that inmates of the Hospital Ayala were not subjects for
any other of the data heretofore presented in this study. A considerable number of children gave specimens. They also are represented in Moss and Kennedy's study, but not here.

The sera and corpuscles were not typed on the spot, but pre-
served and forwarded for examination to Dr. W. L. Moss in Boston.
The method of preservation has been described in Moss and Kennedy's paper (1929) as follows: "Blood for serum was collected in
sterile Wright's tubes, and after coagulation the serum was taken
up in sterile capillary tubes and the ends sealed. Blood for corpuscles was taken in a preserving fluid recommended by Rous and
Turner. This preserving fluid consists of a mixture of two parts of
isotonic sodium citrate solution (3.8 per cent in water) and five
parts of isotonic dextrose solution (5.4 per cent in water). The two
isotonic solutions were sterilized separately, mixed in the above
proportions and introduced into U-shaped tubes, all with asceptic
precautions."

The total number of 738 specimens collected had the blood-group
distribution indicated in Table 93. The percentage for Group IV
in the larger population which includes children, insane, and a few
non-Yucatecans is somewhat less (76.6) than that of either the

## TABLE 93.  BLOOD GROUPS
(Iso–Agglutinins)

(The Moss Classification is here used)

MALES

| | I | II | III | IV | No. |
|---|---|---|---|---|---|
| Total Yucatecans ............ | 3<br>1.3% | 28<br>12.6% | 8<br>3.6% | 184<br>82.5% | 223 |
| Group A .................... | 0<br>0.0% | 1<br>2.5% | 1<br>2.5% | 38<br>95.0% | 40 |
| Group B .................... | 0<br>0.0% | 4<br>9.8% | 0<br>0.0% | 37<br>90.2% | 41 |
| Group C .................... | 0<br>0.0% | 12<br>12.8% | 2<br>2.1% | 80<br>85.1% | 94 |
| Group D ................... | 1<br>4.2% | 5<br>20.8% | 2<br>8.3% | 16<br>66.7% | 24 |
| Group E .................... | 2<br>8.3% | 6<br>25.0% | 3<br>12.5% | 13<br>54.2% | 24 |
| Yucatecans unselected for race, sex, or age ............... Williams (Moss, Kennedy, 1929) | 1.4% | 16.7% | 5.4% | 76.6% | 738 |

FEMALES

| | I | II | III | IV | No. |
|---|---|---|---|---|---|
| Total Yucatecans ............ | 0<br>0.0% | 17<br>14.0% | 4<br>3.3% | 100<br>82.7% | 131 |
| Group A .................... | 0<br>0.0% | 0<br>0.0% | 1<br>5.9% | 16<br>94.1% | 17 |
| Group B .................... | 0<br>0.0% | 2<br>5.7% | 0<br>0.0% | 33<br>94.3% | 35 |
| Group C .................... | 0<br>0.0% | 5<br>16.7% | 1<br>3.3% | 24<br>80.0% | 30 |
| Group D ................... | 0<br>0.0% | 5<br>20.0% | 1<br>4.0% | 19<br>76.0% | 25 |
| Group E .................... | 0<br>0.0% | 5<br>35.7% | 1<br>7.1% | 8<br>57.1% | 14 |
| North American Indians said to be pure .................. | 0.0% | 7.7% | 1.0% | 91.3% | 453 |
| Mixed and pure .............. | 0.9% | 16.4% | 3.4% | 79.1% | 1134 |
| Known to be mixed .......... | 2.4% | 25.6% | 7.1% | 64.8% | 409 |
| Americans (White) ............ Snyder, 1926 | 3.0% | 42.0% | 10.0% | 45.0% | 1000 |
| North American Indians ....... Coca and Diebert (Moss, Kennedy, 1929) | 0.0% | 20.2% | 2.1% | 77.7% | 862 |
| North American Indians ....... Nigg (Moss, Kennedy, 1929) | 0.3% | 27.2% | 1.6% | 70.9% | 316 |

TABLE 93.  (*Continued*)

| | | | | | |
|---|---|---|---|---|---|
| Navajo ....................... <br> Nigg (Moss, Kennedy, 1929) | 0.2% | 26.9% | 0.2% | 72.7% | 457 |
| Mexicans .................... | 0.0% | 21.4% | 10.7% | 67.9% | 28 |
| Mexicans (D. F.) .............. <br> Snyder, 1926 | 3.2% | 25.8% | 6.4% | 64.5% | 31 |
| Mexicans — Blue Ridge Prison <br> Farm (Texas)............... <br> Kelly (Moss, Kennedy, 1929) | 0.9% | 28.1% | 11.8% | 59.2% | 338 |
| Eskimo (Little White admixture) <br> Cape York .................. | 0.0% | 4.3% | 0.0% | 95.8% | 24 |
| Thule....................... | 8.8% | 15.8% | 5.3% | 70.2% | 57 |
| Northumberland Island ....... | 0.0% | 8.3% | 0.0% | 91.7% | 12 |
| Karma....................... | 0.0% | 16.1% | 0.0% | 83.9% | 31 |
| Eskimo Half-Breeds [1] ......... <br> Heinbecker and Pauli, 1927 | 10.3% | 40.2% | 8.3% | 41.2% | 97 |
| Americans.................... <br> Hektoen (Snyder, 1926) | 9.0% | 34.0% | 10.0% | 47.0% | ... |
| Americans.................... <br> Moss (Snyder, 1926) | 10.0% | 40.0% | 7.0% | 43.0% | 1600 |
| Americans.................... <br> Snyder, 1926 | 3.0% | 42.0% | 10.0% | 45.0% | 1000 |
| English ..................... | 3.0% | 43.4% | 7.2% | 46.4% | 500 |
| French...................... | 3.0% | 42.6% | 11.2% | 43.2% | 500 |
| Italians ..................... | 3.8% | 38.0% | 11.0% | 47.2% | 500 |
| Germans ................... <br> Hirszfelds (Snyder, 1926) | 5.0% | 43.0% | 12.0% | 40.0% | 500 |
| South Chinese ............... <br> Chi-Pan (Snyder, 1926) | 9.8% | 38.8% | 19.4% | 31.8% | 1296 |
| North Chinese .............. <br> Liu and Wang (Snyder, 1926) | 10.0% | 25.1% | 34.2% | 30.7% | 1000 |
| Japanese-Tokyo.............. <br> Nakajima (Snyder, 1926) | 8.0% | 38.5% | 22.4% | 31.5% | 501 |
| Filipinos .................... <br> Cabrera-Wade (Snyder, 1926) | 1.0% | 14.7% | 19.6% | 64.7% | 204 |

[1] Inhabitants of the following settlements "where the population is definitely half-breed": Godhavn, Proven, Block Island, Upernivik, and Pond Inlet.

male or the female group of Total Yucatecans (82–83 per cent). This may be attributed to the fact that a considerable number of the inmates of the insane institution were Whites or near-Whites. Even so, the percentage of Blood Group IV is higher than that found in any European population. The larger proportion of the remainder belong to Group II, the characteristic European blood group.

Group II is also the second in incidence in the Total Yucatecan population of either sex. Group I occurs very infrequently and not a single case appears in the table for females. Following the work of Coca and Deibert (1923) and that of Snyder (1926), one is led to look for a high percentage of Group IV in any North American Indian population, even in one that is not particularly pure. The Mayas are perhaps best described as Central Americans. Even in their racially mixed state they are seen to possess a high percentage of Blood Group IV.

These data on blood grouping of the Yucatecan population present an opportunity to test the trustworthiness of the method of racial subgroup sorting advocated in this study. Snyder, as well as Heinbecker and Pauli (see Table 93), present evidence based on genealogies and general observation that racially pure North American Indians and Eskimos tend toward uniform possession of Blood Group IV. They show a negative correlation to exist between amount of White blood in a mixed White-Indian or White-Eskimo group and the percentage of Group IV, and a positive correlation between amount of White blood and percentage of Group II. Group III also increases with mixture, but its proportion of the total is small. Exactly the same phenomena are observed in the Yucatecan subgroups of both sexes. The frequencies are tabulated separately for the sexes in order that the sorting for each sex might stand on its own merits. Although the trend in either case is that which Snyder and Heinbecker have demonstrated, the subgroup D of the females shows less difference from Group C than is noted in the case of the males.

Two points deserve special comment. The first is that throughout the foregoing discussion of other traits of the sorted subgroups, it has been emphasized that Groups D and E are not pure Whites, but only the nearest approximation to Whites that could be segregated from the group of Yucatecans as a whole. Comparison of the frequencies of Blood Groups II and IV in the subgroups D and E with those found in the various American White and European populations shows that the percentages approach each other but are not identical.

The second point is that Mexicans resident in Yucatan have been demonstrated in this study to be as White as the Whitest Yucatecan subgroups in certain characters. The blood group data are in harmony with this finding, as is shown in a comparison of the frequency of Blood Group IV in the male subgroup D and the author's Mexicans. According to the criterion of blood grouping, Kelly's Northern Mexicans have more White blood than either Snyder's or the author's Mexican groups.

It may be concluded that the blood group findings agree well with those relating to other physical traits of the sorted subgroups of the Yucatecans. These are among the most important of the data presented in justification of the racial subgroup sorting method advocated in this study.

## SOCIAL PHENOMENA

### OCCUPATION

As a routine part of the somatological examination, each individual was questioned as to his occupation. The table on which this discussion is based shows the numbers and percentages of the racial subgroups engaged in certain kinds of work. The biological factors determining these groups obviously have not conditioned the occupational distribution. The fact that some of these individuals are carrying on one kind of work, and some another, implies that certain psychological and social forces, class distinctions, and aptitudes have come into play. Among the hacienda and village Yucatecans, there are no great distinctions in mode of life between one person and another. Yet no visitor in Yucatan can doubt that those who are in business, those who work in trades and in skilled labor, or can afford to go into politics, have on the whole (and surely in times of economic stress) a richer and more abundant diet for themselves and their families than do the farmers of the *milpas* or small cornfields, and to somewhat less extent, the laborers on the haciendas. This is not to say that whatever differences have been found between the various subgroups are directly due to such favoring or unfavoring environmental influences for growth and nutrition. Rather should one say that in this case such influences are useful in fostering and perpetuating inborn differences.

Examination of the table indicates that Groups A, B, and C have fifty per cent or more of their members as hacienda laborers, while the proportion of such laborers in Groups D and E falls below that ratio. Yucatan is a great henequen-raising country, and all the hacienda laborers mentioned work on such plantations. As may be seen from the proportion of the Total Yucatecans so engaged, more than half of the total population here considered do such work. It is easy to understand, in view of the social factors concerned, why the Whiter groups are not so well represented in the

TABLE 94.  OCCUPATION

MALES

| Occupation | Group A | Group B | Group C | Group D | Group E | Total Yucatecans |
|---|---|---|---|---|---|---|
| | 221 | 188 | 340 | 40 | 39 | 828 |
| Farmers .................. | 102 | 70 | 108 | 12 | 7 | 299 |
| | 46.2% | 37.2% | 31.8% | 30.0% | 17.9% | 36.1% |
| [Farmers acting as archaeological laborers ........... | 28 | 13 | 16 | 2 | 0 | 59 |
| | 12.7% | 6.9% | 4.7% | 5.0% | 0.0% | 7.1%] |
| Laborers (Hacienda) ........ | 114 | 106 | 190 | 13 | 16 | 439 |
| | 51.6% | 56.4% | 55.9% | 32.5% | 41.0% | 53.0% |
| Men in trades [1] ............. | 3 | 6 | 23 | 5 | 6 | 43 |
| | 1.4% | 3.2% | 6.8% | 12.5% | 15.4% | 5.2% |
| Men in commerce .......... | 0 | 2 | 3 | 6 | 3 | 14 |
| | 0.0% | 1.1% | 0.9% | 15.0% | 7.7% | 1.7% |
| Foremen ................. | 0 | 1 | 4 | 1 | 2 | 8 |
| | 0.0% | 0.5% | 1.2% | 2.5% | 5.1% | 1.0% |
| Railroad Employes ......... | 0 | 0 | 2 | 0 | 3 | 5 |
| | 0.0% | 0.0% | 0.6% | 0.0% | 7.7% | 0.6% |
| School Teachers ............ | 0 | 0 | 1 | 1 | 1 | 3 |
| | 0.0% | 0.0% | 0.3% | 2.5% | 2.6% | 0.4% |
| Police (Municipal) .......... | 2 | 1 | 0 | 0 | 0 | 3 |
| | 0.9% | 0.5% | 0.0% | 0.0% | 0.0% | 0.4% |
| Municipal Officers.......... | 0 | 2 | 9 | 2 | 1 | 14 |
| | 0.0% | 1.1% | 2.6% | 5.0% | 2.6% | 1.7% |

[1] The term "trades" includes such occupations as mason, carpenter, baker, shoemaker, machinist, tinner, tailor, barber, cook, chiclero.

hacienda populations.  Group A is slightly less well represented than Groups B and C.  If that difference is significant, an explanation would be that the members of Group A tend to preserve to some extent their economic independence through independent farming of their own foodstuffs.

Thus through direct examination of the proportion of subgroups acting as independent farmers, it is noted that the highest ratio belongs to Group A; also that the proportion declines alphabetically with a value for Group E of only 17.9 per cent as compared with 46.2 per cent for Group A. Thirty-six per cent of the group as a whole are farmers by occupation, so that there is a rather clean-cut tendency between the values for Groups A and B on the one hand and those for Groups C, D, and E on the other.

The category "temporarily acting as archaeological laborers" refers to those employed as common laborers at the ruins of Chichen Itza. Each individual so classified is also counted under the head of one of the other categories. Most of the labor for the work at the ruins is recruited from the near-by villages, and the great majority of these men are ordinarily farmers. It is interesting (and after knowing the men, expected) that Group A is the best represented subgroup seen among the laborers at Chichen Itza. It is worth noting that when corn-planting time comes, one man after another absents himself from the work at the ruins or is represented by a substitute while the necessary work of the season is done on the *milpas*.

In trades, in business, as foremen, and as school teachers, Groups D and E apparently lead the more Indian types. About one-quarter of Groups D and E are in business or work at trades; only one-eighth of Groups A, B, and C are so employed, while Groups A and B alone show only six per cent. Municipal officers were not found among the Group A men but there seems to be a greater tendency toward equal distribution of the village public offices than is seen in trades or commerce.

## BIRTHPLACE

A question on birthplace was also a part of the routine of the physical examination. The tables show the percentage distribution of subgroups for birthplace in Mérida (the capital), in towns, in villages, and on haciendas.

Over ninety per cent of Groups D and E were born in towns or villages, as opposed to haciendas, and about eighty-five per cent of the female Groups D and E are similarly characterized. The Whiter types have four times the proportion born in Mérida than is noted for the more Indian groups. In the town and village births there are also proportionately more of Groups D and E than of the others, but the disproportion is in neither case as great as is seen for birthplace in Mérida. Considering only those born in towns or villages (excepting Mérida) the percentages for the male subgroups alphabetically are: 80, 77, 60, 49, and 44. For percentages of those born on haciendas the trend is quite the opposite. It is well to keep in mind that the births which are being discussed occurred in the great majority of cases from twenty to sixty years ago and that the conditions correlated with the findings made are past, not present ones.

TABLE 95.  BIRTHPLACE

MALES

| Birthplace | Group A | Group B | Group C | Group D | Group E | Total Yucatecans |
|---|---|---|---|---|---|---|
| | (221) | (199) | (362) | (52) | (46) | (880) |
| Mérida, population 1910, 62447 | 2 | 5 | 18 | 7 | 6 | 38 |
| | 0.9% | 2.5% | 5.0% | 13.5% | 13.0% | 4.3% |
| Towns over 3000, 1910 census | 9 | 21 | 37 | 12 | 6 | 85 |
| | 4.1% | 10.6% | 10.2% | 23.1% | 13.0% | 9.7% |
| Towns under 3000, 1910 census | 89 | 77 | 182 | 28 | 31 | 407 |
| | 40.3% | 38.7% | 50.3% | 53.8% | 67.4% | 46.2% |
| Haciendas.................. | 121 | 96 | 125 | 5 | 3 | 350 |
| | 54.8% | 48.2% | 34.5% | 9.6% | 6.5% | 39.8% |

FEMALES

| | (154) | (231) | (201) | (62) | (46) | (694) |
|---|---|---|---|---|---|---|
| Mérida, population 1910, 62447 | 9 | 5 | 10 | 12 | 5 | 41 |
| | 5.8% | 2.2% | 5.0% | 19.4% | 10.9% | 5.9% |
| Towns over 3000, 1910 census | 6 | 19 | 14 | 10 | 11 | 60 |
| | 3.9% | 8.2% | 7.0% | 16.1% | 23.9% | 8.6% |
| Towns under 3000, 1910 census | 73 | 105 | 109 | 30 | 23 | 340 |
| | 47.4% | 45.4% | 54.2% | 48.4% | 50.0% | 49.0% |
| Haciendas.................. | 66 | 102 | 68 | 10 | 7 | 253 |
| | 42.9% | 44.2% | 33.8% | 16.1% | 15.2% | 36.5% |

The percentage distribution with reference to birthplace for the various female subgroups parallels in general that for the males but the subgroup differences are less marked.

Comparison of the tables for occupation and birthplace indicates that the percentage of Group A born on haciendas is but little more than the percentage of Group A who now work as hacienda laborers. For all other subgroups, similar comparisons show that at some time during the growth of individuals now adults, there has occurred a movement from the towns to the haciendas. The number of men living in the small towns (where they were examined) may be summed up roughly for each subgroup by adding the respective percentages for farmers, business men, railroad employes, and those working at trades. These summed percentages are alphabetically for the subgroups: 48, 42, 40, 58, and 49. It is plain that these men of Groups D and E, and to a less extent those of Group C, were not born on haciendas, so that they must have been born in towns of the size of that in which they were found living, or in larger ones.

In summary it may be said that of the men and women of the more Indian subgroups now living in villages and on haciendas, the great majority were village- or hacienda-born, while in the case of the Whiter groups, most of them were born in villages or larger towns. It is to be expected that greater numbers of pure Whites live or have lived in the comparatively larger centers of population and that such localities tend to foster production of the racially mixed part of the population exemplified in Groups D and E.

### Birthplace Compared with Residence

Through comparison of the data for occupation with those for birthplace, evidence was brought forward to indicate that many of the male members of the Whiter subgroups and also of Group C have moved from their birthplaces in the towns to the haciendas. An opportunity is now presented to look into this situation more directly. Table 96 shows that of the male members of Group A living on haciendas, eighty per cent of them were born there. For the remaining subgroups, progressively smaller proportions were born where they now live and progressively increasing percentages had their birthplaces in the towns. Comparatively few individuals of any group had their origins in the larger towns or in Mérida, although eleven per cent of Group C and fifteen per cent of Group D claimed such birthplace. Why Group E of the hacienda dwellers possesses members born for the most part in the smaller towns, and born not at all in the larger ones, is obscure.

The percentages of small-town dwellers of Groups A and B who were born on haciendas is somewhat greater than the percentages for the remaining subgroups. More than one-quarter of the Indian inhabitants of villages and small towns were hacienda-born, as compared with one-twelfth and less for Groups C, D, and E. Until

only a few years ago, it is said, a large part of the Indian population
of the State of Yucatan lived as laborers on the henequen plantations. Now, as a result of political and social changes, not all of the
haciendas which were once cultivated are in operation. It seems
certain that at some time in the growth to adulthood of the
Yucatecans under consideration, those who are members of

TABLE 96.  BIRTHPLACE COMPARED WITH RESIDENCE

MALES

| Birthplace | *Hacienda Dwellers* | | | | | |
|---|---|---|---|---|---|---|
| | Group A | Group B | Group C | Group D | Group E | Total Yucatecans |
| | (110) | (103) | (177) | (13) | (11) | (414) |
| Hacienda .................. | 88 | 71 | 110 | 4 | 2 | 275 |
| | 80.0% | 68.9% | 62.1% | 30.8% | 18.2% | 66.4% |
| Towns of under 3000 ........ | 17 | 25 | 47 | 7 | 9 | 105 |
| | 15.4% | 24.3% | 26.5% | 53.8% | 81.8% | 25.3% |
| Towns of over 3000 ......... | 3 | 5 | 16 | 1 | 0 | 25 |
| | 2.7% | 4.8% | 9.0% | 7.7% | 0.0% | 6.0% |
| Mérida .................. | 2 | 2 | 4 | 1 | 0 | 9 |
| | 1.8% | 1.9% | 2.3% | 7.7% | 0.0% | 2.2% |
| | *Small-town Dwellers* | | | | | |
| | (111) | (85) | (163) | (27) | (28) | (414) |
| Hacienda .................. | 33 | 23 | 14 | 1 | 1 | 72 |
| | 29.7% | 27.1% | 8.6% | 3.7% | 3.6% | 17.4% |
| Towns of under 3000 ........ | 72 | 47 | 128 | 21 | 21 | 289 |
| | 64.9% | 55.3% | 78.6% | 77.8% | 75.0% | 69.8% |
| Towns of over 3000 ......... | 6 | 12 | 15 | 5 | 3 | 41 |
| | 5.4% | 14.1% | 9.2% | 18.5% | 10.7% | 9.9% |
| Mérida .................. | 0 | 3 | 6 | 0 | 3 | 12 |
| | 0.0% | 3.5% | 3.7% | 0.0% | 10.7% | 2.9% |

Groups D and E moved from the towns to the haciendas, and the
Group C Yucatecans imitated them to some extent. On the other
hand, individuals of Groups A and B evidently executed a smaller
retrograde movement from the haciendas to the smaller towns.
This may be understood when it is considered that certain of the
more Indian Yucatecans, as well as other peoples, prefer the more
independent, but (especially in times of drought and poor crops)
more precarious life of the *milpa* farmer to that of the better-housed
and better-fed hacienda worker.

Three-quarters of the members of Groups C, D, and E living in
small towns were born there. For Group C town dwellers it is

shown that of the remaining one-quarter, a few more recruits came from larger towns than from haciendas, while Groups D and E received their other quarter of population from the larger centers, and in the case of Group E, in part from Mérida.

Considering these facts in connection with the data for occupation, it is notable that most of the Group A and Group B population of the small towns are engaged in *milpa* farming and that certain individuals of these groups have left the haciendas to engage in such work. But the individuals of Groups C, D, and E, if they continue to live in town, or have come from larger centers, fail to take up that kind of occupation as frequently as do the Indians, and prefer trades and business. Otherwise they leave the town to do hacienda labor.

## MARRIAGE

In this study an attempt has been made to classify into racial subgroups the racially mixed men and women of rural Yucatan. These individuals are the progeny of mixed marriages which have occurred in both the remote and also the recent past. It will be interesting to investigate the marriages which have taken place between these racially mixed individuals who form the basis of this study, with special reference to the relative numbers of such alliances formed between individual members of the various subgroups.

There are five subgroups of each sex. Therefore a man of Group A has five possible subgroup choices or chances in selection of a mate. Since there are five male subgroups, there are twenty-five possible marriage combinations with reference to racial subgroups. (In the following discussion the particular marital combinations will be designated by use of such symbols as AA, which signifies that a man of Group A has married a woman of the same subgroup, or AE, which means that a Group A man is the husband of a Group E woman.)

Table 97 (I) considers marriages which have occurred in the combined locales of haciendas and villages of rural Yucatan. The gist of the table is that fewer BD and BE alliances are found than are expected by chance, but more CD, DD, DE, and EE unions have been made than the laws of chance predict. It is noteworthy that, statistically speaking, Group A men marry as many (but no more)

## TABLE 97. MARRIAGE

### I. (Haciendas and Villages)

| | | Group A | Group B | Group C | Group D | Group E | No. |
|---|---|---|---|---|---|---|---|
| MALES | Group A . | 28 | 30 | 24 | 2 | 4 | 88 |
| | | 22.1±6.12 | 30.2±7.06 | 26.4±6.64 | 4.6±2.88 | 5.1±3.02 | |
| | Group B . | 16 | 27 | 26 | 0 | 1 | 70 |
| | | 17.6±5.50 | 23.6±6.32 | 21.0±5.98 | 3.6±2.54 Signif. | 4.1±2.72 Signif. | |
| | Group C . | 32 | 46 | 38 | 11 | 7 | 134 |
| | | 33.7±7.42 | 45.2±8.42 | 40.3±8.02 | 7.0±3.54 Signif. | 7.8±3.72 | |
| | Group D . | 3 | 4 | 3 | 3 | 3 | 16 |
| | | 4.0±2.68 | 5.4±3.12 | 4.8±2.94 | 0.8±1.20 Signif. | 0.9±1.28 Signif. | |
| | Group E . | 3 | 3 | 7 | 1 | 4 | 18 |
| | | 4.5±2.84 | 6.1±3.30 | 5.4±3.10 | 0.9±1.28 | 1.0±1.34 Signif. | |
| No. . . . . . . . . . . | | 82 | 110 | 98 | 17 | 19 | 326 |

NOTE: In each square, three facts are presented which concern the marriage combination that has occurred. For example, in the square representing marriages of Group B men with Group E women, the figure 1 in the first line of the square shows that one such marriage actually did occur. The expression 4.1±2.72 indicates that four marriages plus or minus twice the probable error of the expected mean frequency of 4.1 may occur by the laws of chance. The expected chance frequency in this case lies somewhere within the range of values of 1.38 and 6.82 marriages. Since the actual frequency of 1 falls without the range of the expected chance values, significant difference is so designated in the third line of the square. See Goring, 1913, p. 108.

### II. (Haciendas)

| | | Group A | Group B | Group C | Group D | Group E | No. |
|---|---|---|---|---|---|---|---|
| MALES | Group A . | 14 | 15 | 11 | 0 | 3 | 43 |
| | | 10.8±4.28 | 15.3±5.04 | 11.8±4.46 | 2.3±2.04 Signif. | 2.8±2.24 | |
| | Group B . | 6 | 14 | 15 | 0 | 0 | 35 |
| | | 8.8±3.90 | 12.5±4.58 | 9.6±4.06 Signif. | 1.8±1.80 | 2.3±2.04 Signif. | |
| | Group C . | 22 | 27 | 18 | 7 | 5 | 79 |
| | | 19.9±5.66 | 28.2±6.54 | 21.7±5.86 Signif. | 4.2±2.72 | 5.1±3.00 | |
| | Group D . | 0 | 3 | 1 | 2 | 2 | 8 |
| | | 2.0±1.90 Signif. | 2.8±2.24 | 2.2±1.98 | 0.4±0.88 Signif. | 0.5±0.98 Signif. | |
| | Group E | 1 | 2 | 2 | 0 | 1 | 6 |
| | | 1.5±1.64 | 2.1±1.94 | 1.6±1.70 | 0.3±0.76 | 0.4±0.84 | |
| No. . . . . . . . . . . | | 43 | 61 | 47 | 9 | 11 | 171 |

TABLE 97.  (*Continued*)

III. (Villages)

| | | Group A | Group B | Group C | Group D | Group E | No. |
|---|---|---|---|---|---|---|---|
| | | | FEMALES | | | | |
| | Group A . | 14 | 15 | 13 | 2 | 1 | 45 |
| | | 11.3±4.38 | 14.2±4.84 | 14.8±4.94 | 2.3±2.02 | 2.3±2.02 | |
| | Group B . | 10 | 13 | 11 | 0 | 1 | 35 |
| | | 8.8±3.88 | 11.1±4.34 | 11.5±4.42 | 1.8±1.80 | 1.8±1.80 | |
| MALES | Group C . | 10 | 19 | 20 | 4 | 2 | 55 |
| | | 13.8±4.78 | 17.4±5.30 | 18.1±5.40 | 2.8±2.24 | 2.8±2.24 | |
| | Group D . | 3 | 1 | 2 | 1 | 1 | 8 |
| | | 2.0±1.90 | 2.5±2.12 | 2.6±2.16 | 0.4±0.84 | 0.4±0.84 | |
| | Group E . | 2 | 1 | 5 | 1 | 3 | 12 |
| | | 3.0±2.32 | 3.8±2.60 | 4.0±2.66 | 0.6±1.04 | 0.6±1.04 | |
| | | | Signif. | | | Signif. | |
| No. . . . . . . . . . | | 39 | 49 | 51 | 8 | 8 | 155 |

Group D and E women as expected; that although the CD marriages exceed the anticipated probability, the CE rate is not in excess; that while more Group E men take Group E women as mates than the laws of chance foretell, they espouse only the expected rate of the women of Group D and the other subgroups. All other marriages than those so far discussed occur no more nor less frequently than the expected rate shows.

In discussing occupation, residence, and birthplace, certain differential preferences were indicated for the Whiter and the more Indian types of the general rural population. For this reason, the material of Table 97 (I) was divided into the two tables 97 (II) and 97 (III) — one for residents of haciendas, the other for residents of villages. It is realized that some of the marriages of the hacienda men may have been contracted in towns and that marriages of village men may have occurred on haciendas. There is no way to avoid this situation; the tables must be considered as they stand.

On haciendas, AD, BE, and DA unions fall short of the prediction. On the other hand, BC, CD, DD, and DE marriages exceed the chance rates. In the villages, only the EB alliances are fewer than expected, and EE marriages in excess.

It is interesting that in each of the three tables Group A and B men are not found to procure more mates of any subgroup, not even of their own, than the laws of chance allow, with the one exception of the BC marriages of the haciendas. Group C males of the haciendas marry an excess of Group D females, and the DD and DE unions of the haciendas surpass chance predictions. In the villages, only the Group E men exercise a preference in mating, and then for wives of the same subgroup.

It would appear that on haciendas there exists a tendency toward preferential mating which shows itself in a desire on the part of the men to secure brides with as many White traits as themselves or more. In the latter case of such unions as BC, CD, and DE varieties, the children of such Whiter women will, on the average, tend to possess more Indian traits than their mothers. Thus, in the case of each variety of marriage, the racial *status quo* is not markedly disturbed.

The difference between the actual and the expected frequencies for AD and BE marriages is to be explained by the fact that the D and E women are taken in excess by the C and D men, leaving fewer for the males of the more Indian subgroups. It seems probable that life on the haciendas is somewhat patriarchal in nature, that there is some degree of respect shown for White blood, and that class distinctions tend to be fostered.

In the villages the situation is not at all the same. With the exception of the preference of Group E males for Group E females, the marriages occur between members of the various racial subgroups at the same rates of frequency that chance predicts. There is no more desire on the part of the men to choose Whiter than to choose more Indian wives. They marry at random. An individual's Whiteness (used in the racial sense), so far as marriage is concerned, is not held at so high a premium in the villages as on the haciendas. If such a tendency is not transient or temporary (and it probably is not), the villages are generally more efficient "melting pots" than are haciendas. It will be recalled that the great majority of the hacienda dwellers of Groups D and E were town-born and that more than half of all the Yucatecans of Groups C, D, and E named smaller or larger towns as their places of birth. If social class distinctions between Whiter and more Indian Yucatecans are less marked in towns than on haciendas, the towns should give origin to more mixed Yucatecans than do the haciendas.

Classification of Yucatecans by subgroups was made upon the basis of several characters, not by use of one. Although an individual of Group D possesses more White and fewer Indian traits than one of Group B, it does not necessarily follow that the former has lighter-colored skin than the latter. Since skin color is one of the more obvious of human physical traits, it will be interesting to check the conclusions just drawn from data on marriage as related to racial subgroups by examining tables relating marriage to skin color.

Table 98 (I) gives such data for Yucatecans of both haciendas and villages. Rather definite preferences are seen to be in effect. The darker men marry more dark and fewer light women, the medium, fewer dark and more women of medium color, and the light, fewer dark and more light women than expected. But these findings refer to both villages and haciendas, and differences between these two places of residence in respect to marriage have just been pointed out.

On the haciendas, excesses over the chance rates occur in the dark-dark, the medium-medium, and the light-light unions. Alliances between light men and dark women are evidently discouraged or not desired. This appears to substantiate the general thesis developed above — that on the haciendas social class distinctions based on racial differences tend to be fostered. In the villages, on the other hand, the only positive preference in mating demonstrated in Table 98 (III) is that of light-skinned men for light-skinned women. This bias in choice of a mate is evidently accomplished by the light men refraining from marriages with medium-colored women and taking more than their chance share of light ones; this in turn deprives the medium-colored men of their chance share of light-colored wives. The relations of marriage to skin color or of marriage to subgroup status of the participants are seen to be substantially the same. In either case, on haciendas and in villages, the light-skinned men or the men with more White traits show definite preference for similar women. The chief difference between marriage according to subgroup and marriage according to skin color is that while darker males of the haciendas prefer darker females, men with the most Indian traits do not marry their expected frequency of females so characterized. But both approaches to the question of who marries whom in racially mixed Yucatan

TABLE 98. MARRIAGE AS RELATED TO SKIN COLOR

I. (HACIENDAS AND VILLAGES)

Light — White to 14 of Von Luschan scale.
Medium — 15 to 20.
Dark — 21 to X.

FEMALES

| | | Dark | Medium | Light | No. |
|---|---|---|---|---|---|
| MALES | Dark ......... | 68[1] <br> 50.61 ±8.82 <br> Signif. | 74 <br> 83.74 ±10.64 | 8 <br> 15.64 ±5.20 <br> Signif. | 150 |
| | Medium ....... | 38 <br> 48.93 ±8.70 <br> Signif. | 95 <br> 80.95 ±10.52 <br> Signif. | 12 <br> 15.12 ±5.12 | 145 |
| | Light ......... | 4 <br> 10.46 ±4.28 <br> Signif. | 13 <br> 17.31 ±5.46 | 14 <br> 3.23 ±2.42 <br> Signif. | 31 |
| No. ................. | | 110 | 182 | 34 | 326 |

II. (HACIENDAS)

FEMALES

| | | Dark | Medium | Light | No. |
|---|---|---|---|---|---|
| MALES | Dark .......... | 64 <br> 54.18 ±5.20 <br> Signif. | 40 <br> 45.85 ±7.82 | 5 <br> 8.92 ±3.92 | 109 |
| | Medium ....... | 20 <br> 27.34 ±6.46 <br> Signif. | 30 <br> 23.16 ±6.04 <br> Signif. | 5 <br> 4.50 ±2.82 | 55 |
| | Light ......... | 1 <br> 3.48 ±2.50 | 2 <br> 2.95 ±2.30 | 4 <br> 0.57 ±1.02 <br> Signif. | 7 |
| No. ................. | | 85 | 72 | 14 | 171 |

III. (VILLAGES)

FEMALES

| | | Dark | Medium | Light | No. |
|---|---|---|---|---|---|
| MALES | Dark .......... | 4 <br> 6.61 ±3.40 | 34 <br> 29.10 ±6.56 | 3 <br> 5.29 ±3.04 | 41 |
| | Medium ....... | 18 <br> 14.52 ±4.90 | 65 <br> 63.87 ±8.26 | 7 <br> 11.61 ±4.42 <br> Signif. | 90 |
| | Light ......... | 3 <br> 3.87 ±2.62 | 11 <br> 17.03 ±5.24 <br> Signif. | 10 <br> 3.10 ±2.34 <br> Signif. | 24 |
| No. ................. | | 25 | 110 | 20 | 155 |

[1] See note under Table 97.

point out that the haciendas tend to preserve the existing racial types or at most foster desires to marry slightly lighter or Whiter women. The villages, in contrast, permit many marriages between individuals of differing types and differing skin colors.

Herskovits (1928) has studied this same phenomenon of preferential mating among American Negroes. He states (pp. 62–66): "That there is selective mating, I have not the slightest doubt. . . . Is it not true that the great majority of men want to marry women who will bring them prestige? . . . And why should it be any different with Negroes? Why should not skin color offer the invidious element necessary to confer distinction on an individual? I believe that this is exactly the state of affairs. . . . In the process of social selection of light women by dark men, we see the mechanism for the consolidation of the type which has been formed by the American Negro. What happens to the light men? They probably 'pass' over into the White group. . . . And what happens to the dark women? I must confess that I do not know. It may be that they become the wives in second marriages. . . . Then there is another consideration, that this variability of color is not fixed and that the term 'lighter woman' is also variable. A woman who is lighter than a very dark man may herself be dark indeed, while it is not easy for a very light man to find a wife lighter than himself. But, on the whole, this selective process is going on actively, and if it continues it will tend to stabilize the Negro type more and more firmly. Of course, it will make this type somewhat more Negroid than it is at present, since the offspring of the women will be darker than they, and the females (we may disregard the males in this consideration) will again be selected by men darker than themselves. But the type cannot revert to the African, because of White and American Indian blood that it contains."

The existence of strong prejudice in the United States against Negro-White marriage is well known. The relative lack of such objection to Indian-White unions in the United States has been remarked by Castle (1926). Herskovits believes that the fact that lighter American Negro women are made to bear darker children than themselves tends to stabilize the American Negro type. His low variability values for the American Negro appear to point toward relative stabilization. So far as marriage is concerned, it seems that the two cases of the American Negro and of the Yucatecan are not strictly parallel. It is probable that the factor conditioning marriage between Negro slaves on the Southern plantations of the United States were in some ways analogous to the affective factors on the haciendas of Yucatan. Class distinctions were fostered in either case. In a rough way, one may compare marriages among the village Yucatecans with those of the American Negroes of today. But in such comparisons, one must proceed with care. The color-bar which has always existed in the United States against the Negro has never been so effective against intermarriage with Indians; neither has it been a strong deterrent in Mexico. This situation permits in the towns of Yucatan the occurrence of many marriages between racially quite different individuals as well as racially similar ones. Widely varying types of progeny result and the family variability is surely high. The preceding discussion of physical measurements shows that statistically significant segregations have occurred for the generations now adults, and will probably continue to occur until the reservoirs of rather pure Maya Indians and pure or rather pure Whites are exhausted or cease to contribute to the mixture of the races; for no effective color-bar interferes with such procedure. The lack of such reservoirs in the case of the American Negro may help to explain his tendency toward formation of a stabilized type. In his melting pot, the American Negro is "stewing in his own juice."

It may be concluded that if conditions remain for some time as they now are, the haciendas will remain the habitat of the purest Maya Indians of rural Yucatan, that more of the progeny of race mixture will be found in the villages and towns, and that formation of a homogeneous Yucatecan type may have begun but as yet has not progressed far.

### THE FAMILY: ITS SIZE AND CONSTITUTION

To the author's wife fell the chief responsibility of conducting a questionnaire concerning the families of the villages and haciendas of Yucatan. Considering the delicacy of some of the questions asked, it was felt that an American woman was better fitted than an American man for such work. The plan of work consisted in house-to-house visits of the investigator, who was always accompanied by a Yucatecan of high standing in the community under

PART I

| | No. of families | Sex of children | Total children | | | | | Children per family | | | | |
|---|---|---|---|---|---|---|---|---|---|---|---|---|
| | | | Born | Born living | Living | Dead after birth | Still-born | Born | Born living | Living | Dead after birth | Still-born |
| 10+ children born; 20+ years married | 31 | Both sexes | 355 | 287 | 184 | 103 | 68 | 11.4 | 9.3 | 5.9 | 3.3 | 2.2 |
| | | Male | 203 | 163 | 101 | 62 | 40 | 6.6 | 5.3 | 3.3 | 2.0 | 1.3 |
| | | Female | 152 | 124 | 83 | 41 | 28 | 4.9 | 4.0 | 2.7 | 1.3 | 0.9 |
| 10+ children born; 15 to 19 years married | 3 | Both sexes | 33 | 16 | 7 | 9 | 17 | 11.0 | 5.3 | 2.3 | 3.0 | 5.6 |
| | | Male | 14 | 7 | 5 | 2 | 7 | 4.7 | 2.3 | 1.7 | 0.7 | 2.3 |
| | | Female | 19 | 9 | 2 | 7 | 10 | 6.3 | 3.0 | 0.7 | 2.3 | 3.3 |
| 5 to 9 children born; 20+ years married | 51 | Both sexes | 373 | 339 | 192 | 147 | 34 | 7.3 | 6.6 | 3.8 | 2.9 | 0.7 |
| | | Male | 207 | 190 | 115 | 75 | 17 | 4.1 | 3.7 | 2.3 | 1.5 | 0.3 |
| | | Female | 166 | 149 | 77 | 72 | 17 | 3.3 | 2.9 | 1.5 | 1.4 | 0.3 |
| 5 to 9 children born; 15 to 19 years married | 31 | Both sexes | 207 | 188 | 108 | 80 | 19 | 6.7 | 6.1 | 3.5 | 2.6 | 0.7 |
| | | Male | 114 | 100 | 56 | 44 | 14 | 3.7 | 3.2 | 1.8 | 1.4 | 0.5 |
| | | Female | 93 | 88 | 52 | 36 | 5 | 3.0 | 2.8 | 1.7 | 1.2 | 0.2 |
| 5 to 9 children born; 10 to 14 years married | 26 | Both sexes | 161 | 149 | 94 | 55 | 12 | 6.2 | 5.7 | 3.6 | 2.1 | 0.5 |
| | | Male | 83 | 74 | 46 | 28 | 9 | 3.2 | 2.8 | 1.8 | 1.1 | 0.3 |
| | | Female | 78 | 75 | 48 | 27 | 3 | 3.0 | 3.0 | 1.8 | 1.0 | 0.1 |
| 5 to 9 children born; 5 to 9 years married | 8 | Both sexes | 44 | 39 | 28 | 11 | 5 | 5.5 | 4.9 | 3.5 | 1.4 | 0.6 |
| | | Male | 28 | 25 | 20 | 5 | 3 | 3.5 | 3.1 | 2.5 | 0.6 | 0.4 |
| | | Female | 16 | 14 | 8 | 6 | 2 | 2.0 | 1.8 | 1.0 | 0.8 | 0.2 |
| 1 to 4 children born; 20+ years married | 19 | Both sexes | 46 | 44 | 32 | 12 | 2 | 2.4 | 2.3 | 1.7 | 0.7 | 0.1 |
| | | Male | 33 | 31 | 22 | 9 | 2 | 1.7 | 1.6 | 1.2 | 0.5 | 0.1 |
| | | Female | 13 | 13 | 10 | 3 | 0 | 0.7 | 0.7 | 0.5 | 0.2 | 0 |
| 1 to 4 children born; 15 to 19 years married | 8 | Both sexes | 21 | 21 | 14 | 7 | 0 | 2.6 | 2.6 | 1.8 | 0.8 | 0 |
| | | Male | 14 | 14 | 9 | 5 | 0 | 1.8 | 1.8 | 1.1 | 0.6 | 0 |
| | | Female | 7 | 7 | 5 | 2 | 0 | 0.9 | 0.9 | 0.6 | 0.2 | 0 |

| | |  | | | | | | | | | |
|---|---|---|---|---|---|---|---|---|---|---|---|
| 21 | 1 to 4 children born; 10 to 14 years married | Both sexes<br>Male<br>Female | 69<br>39<br>30 | 65<br>35<br>30 | 45<br>26<br>19 | 20<br>9<br>11 | 4<br>4<br>0 | 3.3<br>1.9<br>1.4 | 3.1<br>1.7<br>1.4 | 2.1<br>1.2<br>0.9 | 0.9<br>0.4<br>0.5 | 0.2<br>0.2<br>0 |
| 41 | 1 to 4 children born; 5 to 9 years married | Both sexes<br>Male<br>Female | 103<br>53<br>50 | 96<br>49<br>47 | 78<br>38<br>40 | 18<br>11<br>7 | 7<br>4<br>3 | 2.5<br>1.3<br>1.2 | 2.3<br>1.2<br>1.1 | 1.9<br>0.9<br>0.9 | 0.5<br>0.3<br>0.2 | 0.2<br>0.1<br>0.1 |
| 29 | 1 to 4 children born; 1 to 4 years married | Both sexes<br>Male<br>Female | 37<br>24<br>13 | 36<br>24<br>12 | 28<br>19<br>9 | 8<br>5<br>3 | 1<br>0<br>1 | 1.3<br>0.8<br>0.5 | 1.2<br>0.8<br>0.4 | 1.0<br>0.7<br>0.3 | 0.2<br>0.2<br>0.1 | 0.03<br>0<br>0.03 |
| 2 | No children born; 15 to 19 years married | | 0 | | | | | | | | | |
| 2 | No children born; 10 to 14 years married | | 0 | | | | | | | | | |
| 7 | No children born; 5 to 9 years married | | 0 | | | | | | | | | |
| 26 | No children born; 1 to 4 years married | | 0 | | | | | | | | | |

199

## Part II
### Regardless of number of children

| | |  | | | | | | | | | |
|---|---|---|---|---|---|---|---|---|---|---|---|
| 101 | 20+ years married | Both sexes<br>Male<br>Female | 774<br>443<br>331 | 670<br>384<br>286 | 408<br>238<br>170 | 262<br>146<br>116 | 104<br>59<br>45 | 7.7<br>4.4<br>3.3 | 6.6<br>3.8<br>2.8 | 4.0<br>2.4<br>1.7 | 2.6<br>1.4<br>1.1 | 1.0<br>0.6<br>0.4 |
| 44 | 15 to 19 years married | Both sexes<br>Male<br>Female | 261<br>142<br>119 | 225<br>121<br>104 | 129<br>70<br>59 | 96<br>51<br>45 | 36<br>21<br>15 | 5.9<br>3.2<br>2.7 | 5.1<br>2.7<br>2.4 | 2.9<br>1.6<br>1.3 | 2.2<br>1.2<br>1.0 | 0.8<br>0.5<br>0.3 |
| 49 | 10 to 14 years married | Both sexes<br>Male<br>Female | 230<br>122<br>108 | 214<br>109<br>105 | 139<br>72<br>67 | 75<br>37<br>38 | 16<br>13<br>3 | 4.7<br>2.5<br>2.2 | 4.3<br>2.2<br>2.1 | 2.8<br>1.5<br>1.4 | 1.5<br>0.8<br>0.8 | 0.3<br>0.2<br>0.1 |

# TABLE 99. — PART II (Continued)

| | No. of families | Sex of children | Total children | | | | | Children per family | | | | |
|---|---|---|---|---|---|---|---|---|---|---|---|---|
| | | | Born | Born living | Living | Dead after birth | Still-born | Born | Born living | Living | Dead after birth | Still-born |
| 5 to 9 years married | 56 | Both sexes | 147 | 135 | 106 | 29 | 12 | 2.6 | 2.4 | 1.9 | 0.5 | 0.2 |
| | | Male | 81 | 74 | 58 | 16 | 7 | 1.4 | 1.3 | 1.0 | 0.3 | 0.1 |
| | | Female | 66 | 61 | 48 | 13 | 5 | 1.2 | 1.1 | 0.9 | 0.2 | 0.1 |
| 1 to 4 years married | 55 | Both sexes | 37 | 36 | 28 | 8 | 1 | 0.7 | 0.7 | 0.5 | 0.1 | 0.02 |
| | | Male | 24 | 24 | 19 | 5 | 0 | 0.4 | 0.4 | 0.3 | 0.1 | 0 |
| | | Female | 13 | 12 | 9 | 3 | 1 | 0.3 | 0.2 | 0.2 | 0.1 | 0.02 |
| *Regardless of years married* | | | | | | | | | | | | |
| 10+ children born | 34 | Both sexes | 388 | 303 | 191 | 112 | 85 | 11.4 | 8.9 | 5.6 | 3.3 | 2.5 |
| | | Male | 217 | 170 | 106 | 64 | 47 | 6.4 | 5.0 | 3.1 | 1.9 | 1.4 |
| | | Female | 171 | 133 | 85 | 48 | 38 | 5.0 | 3.9 | 2.5 | 1.4 | 1.1 |
| 5 to 9 children born | 116 | Both sexes | 785 | 715 | 422 | 293 | 70 | 6.8 | 6.2 | 3.6 | 2.5 | 0.6 |
| | | Male | 432 | 389 | 237 | 152 | 43 | 3.7 | 3.4 | 2.0 | 1.3 | 0.4 |
| | | Female | 353 | 326 | 185 | 141 | 27 | 3.0 | 2.8 | 1.6 | 1.2 | 0.2 |
| 1 to 4 children born | 118 | Both sexes | 276 | 262 | 197 | 65 | 14 | 2.3 | 2.2 | 1.7 | 0.5 | 0.1 |
| | | Male | 163 | 153 | 114 | 39 | 10 | 1.4 | 1.3 | 1.0 | 0.3 | 0.1 |
| | | Female | 113 | 109 | 83 | 26 | 4 | 0.9 | 0.9 | 0.7 | 0.2 | 0.03 |
| No children born | 37 | | 0 | | | | | | | | | |
| *Regardless of number of children and of years married* | | | | | | | | | | | | |
| | 305 | Both sexes | 1449 | 1280 | 810 | 470 | 169 | 4.8 | 4.2 | 2.7 | 1.5 | 0.5 |
| | | Male | 812 | 712 | 457 | 255 | 100 | 2.7 | 2.3 | 1.5 | 0.8 | 0.3 |
| | | Female | 637 | 568 | 353 | 215 | 69 | 2.1 | 1.9 | 1.2 | 0.7 | 0.2 |

*Regardless of number of children*

| | No. of families | Sex of children | Percentage of living-born | | Percentage of total born | Sex ratio of: | | | | |
|---|---|---|---|---|---|---|---|---|---|---|
| | | | Living | Dead after birth | Still-born | Born | Living-born | Living | Dead after birth | Still-born |
| 20+ years married | 101 | Both sexes | 60.9 | 39.1 | 13.4 | 134 | 134 | 140 | 126 | 131 |
| | | Male | 62.0 | 38.0 | 13.3 | | | | | |
| | | Female | 59.4 | 40.6 | 13.6 | | | | | |
| 15 to 19 years married | 44 | Both sexes | 57.3 | 42.7 | 13.8 | 119 | 116 | 119 | 113 | 140 |
| | | Male | 57.9 | 42.1 | 14.8 | | | | | |
| | | Female | 56.7 | 43.3 | 12.6 | | | | | |
| 10 to 14 years married | 49 | Both sexes | 65.0 | 35.0 | 7.0 | 113 | 104 | 107 | 97 | 433 |
| | | Male | 66.1 | 33.9 | 10.7 | | | | | |
| | | Female | 63.8 | 36.2 | 2.8 | | | | | |
| 5 to 9 years married | 56 | Both sexes | 78.5 | 21.5 | 8.2 | 123 | 121 | 121 | 123 | 140 |
| | | Male | 78.4 | 21.6 | 8.6 | | | | | |
| | | Female | 78.7 | 21.3 | 7.6 | | | | | |
| 1 to 4 years married | 55 | Both sexes | 77.8 | 22.2 | 2.7 | 185 | 200 | 211 | 167 | |
| | | Male | 79.2 | 20.8 | 0.0 | | | | | |
| | | Female | 75.0 | 25.0 | 7.7 | | | | | |

*Regardless of number of years married*

| | No. of families | Sex of children | Living | Dead after birth | Still-born | Born | Living-born | Living | Dead after birth | Still-born |
|---|---|---|---|---|---|---|---|---|---|---|
| 10+ children born | 34 | Both sexes | 63.0 | 37.0 | 21.9 | 127 | 128 | 125 | 133 | 124 |
| | | Male | 62.4 | 37.6 | 21.7 | | | | | |
| | | Female | 63.9 | 36.1 | 22.2 | | | | | |
| 5 to 9 children born | 116 | Both sexes | 59.0 | 41.0 | 8.9 | 122 | 119 | 128 | 108 | 159 |
| | | Male | 60.9 | 39.1 | 10.0 | | | | | |
| | | Female | 56.7 | 43.3 | 7.6 | | | | | |
| 1 to 4 children born | 118 | Both sexes | 75.2 | 24.8 | 5.1 | 144 | 140 | 137 | 150 | 250 |
| | | Male | 74.5 | 25.5 | 6.1 | | | | | |
| | | Female | 76.1 | 23.9 | 3.5 | | | | | |

*Regardless of number of children and number of years married*

| | No. of families | Sex of children | Living | Dead after birth | Still-born | Born | Living-born | Living | Dead after birth | Still-born |
|---|---|---|---|---|---|---|---|---|---|---|
| | 305 | Both sexes | 63.3 | 36.7 | 11.7 | 127 | 125 | 129 | 119 | 145 |
| | | Male | 64.2 | 35.8 | 12.3 | | | | | |
| | | Female | 62.1 | 37.9 | 10.8 | | | | | |

observation. The assistant, prompted by the investigator, put the questions either in Spanish or in the Mayan tongue as the occasion demanded. Knowledge of Maya is necessary for such work because it is the only language understood by a considerable number of rural Yucatecans, especially women. Mothers of the families were in all cases the persons queried. In each village and hacienda, the native assistant was chosen not only for his knowledge of languages, but also because of his particular knowledge of the community. The assistant was able to verify many of the recorded answers from his own familiarity with the family in question.

The strict accuracy of data collected by means of questionnaires is never certain. Yet the method is often the only available tool of the investigator. The greatest pains were taken in collecting the material about to be presented. Obviously questionable cases were thrown out of the series. Of a total of 329 families surveyed, material from 305 of them are presented in Table 99 for examination and discussion.

In the preparation of the raw data for Table 99 it was considered that the families should first be distributed into like groups on the basis of two criteria; i. e. (1) according to number of children born (including stillborn), and (2) according to the number of years of the marriage duration. The detailed findings are shown in Part I of the table. These minutiæ are given here not with the idea of using them as a basis for discussion as much as for the purpose of presenting data which will be available to other workers in the same general field.

Part II of Table 99 considers first the findings for the families sorted according to years married, regardless of number of children. The number of cases in each group is fairly well distributed, except for a preponderance of unions which had endured twenty or more years; the latter circumstance is due in great part to answers of older widows. The percentage and sex-ratio portion of Part II epitomizes the raw figures and averages per family first shown. The average number of children born per family (including stillborn) drops from about eight in the oldest marriages to one in the youngest. The average numbers of living children born in these two extreme groups are respectively approximately seven and one. In proportion to the average number of living children born, the alliances of fifteen or more years' duration kept alive until the time of the questionnaire about sixty per cent of them; the ten to fourteen group, about sixty-five per cent, and all younger marriages, over seventy-five per cent. It is of course unfair to compare these families in this fashion, for the offspring of the older families, having lived more years, have exposed themselves to more of the various vicissitudes of life. The "dead after birth" column of the table is of course the complement of the "living" column.

A great many more births are designated as stillborn in the older marriages than in the younger. It is possible that stillborn births include a certain number of miscarriages and abortions. Considering the general reticence regarding the whole subject of expulsion of both the younger and the more mature products of conception, it is remarkable that any questionnaire should reveal in any section of a population that for every six living births, one stillbirth occurs. Thirteen per cent of all births in marriages of twenty or more years' duration are stillbirths. Woodbury (1925) bases the following remarks upon data from eight cities of the United States: "When the stillbirths in the age group (of mothers) "40 and over" were analyzed, it was found that the rate for ages 40 to 44 was only 5.1 per cent and that for ages 45 and older (based on very few cases) was more than three times as high (15.4 per cent). The lowest proportion of stillbirths was found in the group of births to mothers who were 20 to 24 years of age." Since there is a high correlation between age of the mother and long duration of marriage, the proportion of thirteen per cent above mentioned does not seem as exorbitantly high as at first sight.

The drop in the stillbirth rate in the younger marriages may possibly be attributed to better prenatal care of the prospective mother in the earlier years of her marriage, to her better health at that time as compared to that of later years, and to the probability that her share of the family food is greater when there are fewer mouths to feed.

At this time it is appropriate to look into the subject of age of mothers at birth of first child. Table 100 is based upon answers returned in the questionnaire and refers to age at birth of first child regardless of whether it was living or dead. It is impossible to provide information regarding age at birth of first living child. From the data presented, two important conclusions result. They are: (1) Women with a greater number of White characteristics tend to begin their childbearing at a little later age than those possessing more Indian traits. (2) For 269 Yucatecan women of the villages and haciendas, the average age for birth of the first child is about sixteen years. It has often been stated that the girls of warm climates begin menstruation at an earlier age than those of cooler climates. Physicians of Yucatan, in answer to a question upon this point, agreed that the age of beginning of the function averaged in their experience from eleven to twelve years. They also stated that there appeared to be no difference in age of onset between the racially purer and the more mixed girls of the population. An average of twelve years for inception of the menstrual cycle was

TABLE 100. AGE OF MOTHER AT BIRTH OF FIRST CHILD

|  | Age | | | | |
|---|---|---|---|---|---|
|  | X–14 | 15–16 | 17–18 | 19–X | No. |
| Group A .......... | 10–26.3% | 19–50.0% | 8–20.5% | 1– 2.6% | 38 |
| Group B .......... | 10–15.9% | 37–58.7% | 14–22.2% | 2– 3.2% | 63 |
| Group C .......... | 22–27.8% | 34–43.0% | 18–22.8% | 5– 6.3% | 79 |
| Groups D and E ... | 2– 6.9% | 15–51.7% | 8–27.6% | 4–13.8% | 29 |
| Total Yucatecans .. | 44–21.1% | 105–50.2% | 48–23.0% | 12– 5.7% | 209 |

Average age at birth of first child for 269 Yucatecan women = 15.9 years.

given by the superintendent of a girls' school; which school had among its students various degrees of White-Indian racial mixture. The time of sexual maturity among Yucatecan women is without doubt early. The strict accuracy of the mean of sixteen years for age at birth of first child is not certain, but it is safe to assume that many first children are born before the mother reaches the age of twenty years.

If younger marriages mean at the same time younger mothers, the lower stillbirth rate in Yucatecan marriages of short duration is at variance with the findings for cities of the United States of both Woodbury (1925) and Rochester (1923). The former (quoted above) found that "the stillbirth rates varied with the age of the mother, being relatively high for the babies both of mothers under 20 and of those 40 years of age and over. For the infants of mothers who were under 18 the rate was 5.2 per cent, only slightly less than that (5.6 per cent) for those of mothers who were 40 and over." Rochester, after a study of conditions in Baltimore for the year

1915, found that "premature births were most prevalent among the youngest mothers. . . . Stillbirths, on the other hand, were most prevalent among the oldest mothers, although the stillbirth rate among mothers under 20 was also above the average. This (latter) variation was true for native and foreign-born white mothers; it did not appear among the colored mothers, but the colored groups were too small to afford basis for any deductions."

Why should the stillbirth rate for young colored mothers and for Yucatecan marriages of short duration (which probably means young mothers) be relatively lower than among young White mothers of Baltimore? Woodbury writes that colored mothers of all ages show the extremely high rate of eight per cent in the years 1911 to 1916, which is probably due to the great prevalence of syphilis among them. It is understandable how syphilis might be more common in older than in very young colored women, but that does not yet explain why a relatively higher rate should prevail among very young White women than in the same age group of American Negroes and Yucatecans. The following hypotheses are put forward in partial explanation: (1) There is apt to be more frankness in answering questions relating to stillbirth among older than among younger Yucatecan women; (2) the heads of White children are relatively large and therefore liable to greater birth trauma; (3) the pelves of the harder-working young Negroes and Yucatecans may be relatively larger and conducive to easier labor than those of the younger White women.

A comparison of the sex ratios in the various groups of marriages segregated according to duration, shows that the 20+ group has the lowest stillbirth ratio. (The 1 to 4 group is not considered because of the small number of children involved.) It is generally stated that the larger heads of boys cause greater birth trauma than is seen in the case of girl babies. It is consistent then to expect that the larger birth canals of women who have borne several children should differentiate less between the sexes than those of younger women. Conversely, it is fitting that the sex ratio of the living born should be greater in older Yucatecan marriages than in younger; but the ratio for the 1 to 4 group does not agree with this tendency, being highest of all. However, the small number of children of this group probably does not warrant computation of the proportion in this case. Further detailed discussion would not seem to be justified, considering that Schultz (1921) has pointed out that sex ratio varies greatly with age of the fetus, a factor which is not controlled in the data here presented.

The material is now to be considered from the viewpoint of number of children born, regardless of number of years of duration of the marriage. In the families in which ten or more children were born, the stillbirth rate reaches the extraordinary value of twenty-two per cent of all children born. As previously shown, however, the rate for mothers over the age of forty-five years in certain cities of the United States is about fifteen per cent, in comparison to thirteen per cent in Yucatecan women who were married over twenty years. By no means all of the mothers married twenty years bore ten children in that time, and it is logical to assume that those who did had poorer health and cared less well for themselves and their prospective children than those who had fewer pregnancies. The rate drops sharply to nine stillbirths in the group which bore five to nine children, while that which had one to four shows a rate of five.

But the most interesting feature of the stillbirth statistics concerns the sex ratio. The sex ratio of the "1 to 4 children born" group is highest of all at 250; that of the "5 to 9" group is 159, while the "10+" group has a value of only 124. Stated in another way, the male and female ratios of stillborn to total born in the same three groups are: 6.1 and 3.5, 10.0 and 7.6, and 21.7 and 22.2. That stillborn children are more apt to be males than females is well known. These figures just given are explainable in the following fashion. Male babies with large heads, passing through the birth canals of mothers who have borne few or no children, are more liable to injury than female babies with smaller heads. As the birth canals become better adapted to their function, there is less danger to the larger-headed boys, until, after ten or more children are born, the chances of injury become equal in the two sexes. Meanwhile, for reasons before mentioned, the factors for good nutrition and care of the intrauterine child become less and less effective, and the rate for both sexes rises.

The explanation for the greater stillbirth rate of males so far brought forward in this discussion has been based on injury occurring in the process of labor. Schultz (1918) quotes Dutton as expressing the opinion that at the time of birth the bones of the male skull are as a rule more firmly ossified than those of the female; and also that with the advance of civilization, the pelvic development in women is not proportionate to the cephalic development which is taking place in infants. Ladame is quoted as saying that those children dying during labor amounted to 36.4 per cent of all the stillborn in Switzerland in 1900. Schultz cites the following hypotheses explanatory of the greater mortality of males due to other causes than that of labor itself:

(1) Carvallo and Auerbach believe the male fetus to be less resistant.

(2) Rauber explains that the larger fetuses of males make greater demands upon the mother than females.

(3) Lillie offers the suggestion that the greater mortality among male fetuses is a result of disturbance of the equilibrium that protects the male from the sex-hormones of the mother.

There is no way of knowing how many of the Yucatecan children in question died before birth and how many during birth. Unfortunately no worth while data on prematurity are available. That deliveries are not always easy among the Yucatecan women, the author can be certain, for he was called upon for assistance in the case of a woman who was bearing her ninth child. Labor lasted several hours and for four after his arrival, after which time a large living baby was born.

If the 305 families are considered without regard to number of children born or the time of duration of the marriage, it is found that an average of five children are born to each family. The sex ratio of children born (including stillborn) is 127. The sex ratio of the living-born among the Yucatecans is 125. For European countries Schultz gives the average as 105 or 106. The ratio in Japan for more than a million births is about the same as that of Europe. Excepting Japan, Schultz states, "Concerning countries outside of Europe, there is little information." The figure given above (125) is based on 1280 children — too small a number to give very definite conclusions. Discussion of the sex ratio of the living-born will again be taken up when the statistics for the State of Yucatan are considered.

The stillbirth percentage of total births for the 305 families is 11.7, and for every 100 living births, 13.2 stillbirths occur. The

Negroes of Florida in 1925 had almost as high a rate as that quoted for Yucatecans, a percentage of 12.1. The comparable figure in the United States registration area for 1918 was 3.6. Of this large proportion of stillbirths in the Yucatecan families, many were boys, for the sex ratio is 145. Schultz' table, from Morgan, shows European ratios which vary from 125 to 135. It would appear that among the Yucatecan families of both villages and haciendas, the stillbirth rate and the stillbirth sex ratio are both higher than commonly seen among peoples of wholly European origin.

The sex ratio of the living children will next be discussed. It is slightly higher than that for the living-born, and has a value of 129. Conversely the ratio for children dead after birth is a little lower. In the more detailed discussion of the mortality rate for infants and children of the whole state of Yucatan, an opportunity will be afforded to compare the sex ratios just stated with ratios based upon considerably larger numbers. At this time, however, one may compare the ratios of children dead after birth in the five groups of families classified on the basis of duration of marriage. The children of these groups are necessarily of various ages, and the age means of the groups of children rise, of course, with duration of the marriage. The trend of the sex ratios from the families of the "1 to 4" group through the others up to the "20+" group is from 167 through 97 to 126. This seems to indicate that at some time after the first years of life, and before adulthood, the risk of life to boys as compared with the risk to girls, becomes for a time relatively less than in the earlier and later years of growth. This suggestion can be tested in the light of other statistics to be presented.

## THE FAMILY: MODIFYING FACTORS OF ITS SIZE AND CONSTITUTION

The population among whom the bulk of the family statistics were collected live within or near to the town of Dzitas, near the ruins of Chichen Itza. Dzitas is the reporting center for vital statistics of a subdepartment of the same name, which is a part of the larger department of the state of Yucatan called Espita. Since the population of the subdepartment of Dzitas is not large, vital statistics based upon a single year are almost worthless. Therefore there are presented in Table 101 a summary of the mortality statistics for that subdepartment for the twenty years from 1907 to 1926 inclusive. The choice of those years has the advantage of being the period in which many of the children of the 305 families were born and were growing to maturity or died.

The stillbirth rate per hundred live births is somewhat less than is found in the averages from the questionnaire, but yet exceeds the general average for the United States. It is in the mortality of children during the first year of life that a strikingly high rate ap-

TABLE 101. DEATHS FROM ALL CAUSES DURING THE 20 YEARS 1907–1926 IN THE SUB–DEPARTMENT OF DZITAS, DEPART-MENT OF ESPITA, STATE OF YUCATAN[1] (CENSUS SUB-DEPARTMENT OF DZITAS, 1910, 2005; 1921, 2703)

| | DZITAS | | | | | | | |
| Age | Number of deaths | | Percentage of total deaths | | | Deaths per 100 live births [2] | | |
| | No. | Sex Ratio | M | F | M + F | M | F | M + F |
|---|---|---|---|---|---|---|---|---|
| Stillborn . . . . . . . . . . . | 92 | 124 | 6.5 | 5.1 | 5.8 | 5.1 | 4.1 | 4.6 |
| 0–1. . . . . . . . . . . . . . | 357 | 109 | 23.6 | 21.1 | 22.4 | 18.8 | 17.1 | 17.9 |
| 2–5. . . . . . . . . . . . . . | 296 | 83 | 17.0 | 20.1 | 18.6 | 13.5 | 16.2 | 14.9 |
| 6–10. . . . . . . . . . . . . | 96 | 134 | 7.0 | 5.1 | 6.0 | 5.5 | 4.1 | 4.8 |
| 11–20. . . . . . . . . . . . | 113 | 59 | 5.3 | 8.8 | 7.1 | 4.2 | 7.1 | 5.7 |
| 21–X . . . . . . . . . . . . | 640 | 99 | 40.5 | 39.8 | 40.2 | 32.2 | 32.0 | 32.1 |
| Total Dzitas deaths for 20 years . . . . . . . | 1594 | 98 | . . | . . | . . | 79.4 | 80.5 | 80.0 |

[1] From records of Registro Civil, Dzitas, Yucatan, Mexico.
[2] Total live births in subdepartment Dzitas in 20 years were 1993.

pears. Twenty-three per cent of all deaths in the twenty-year period occurred in the first year of life and only a slightly smaller proportion in the second to fifth years of life. From the ages of six to twenty the mortality is comparatively less, which may be due in part to the possession of high resistance against disease in the children and adolescents who successfully passed through the trying first five years. The sex ratios of children dead at the various ages are most interesting. From the data on the families sorted according to duration of marriage, it was guessed that at some time in the middle years of growth of Yucatecan children, the sex ratios for the dead after birth were lower than formerly. Table 101 shows the girls of the 2 to 5 and the 11 to 20 groups to have been in greater danger of death than the boys.

Further investigation of the deaths between the ages of eleven and twenty shows that of the 113 deaths in twenty years 71 were of girls and 42 of boys. Malaria accounted for a considerable number, in the proportion of fourteen males to twenty-four females; the female disproportion was greater in the years past seventeen. Five males died of diarrhoea in comparison to fifteen females; the deaths were fairly equally distributed through the age groups. To respiratory diseases, including terminal pneumonia of measles and influenza, eighteen girls succumbed, and only eight boys. Several of these girls were over seventeen years of age. Six females died in childbirth, two at the age of sixteen, two at eighteen and two at twenty. These deaths formed a proportion of about eight per cent of the total 11 to 20 mortality of females. Other causes were responsible for the deaths of fifteen boys and eight girls. There seems to be no doubt that adolescent girls have lower resistance to prevalent diseases of Yucatan than boys of the same age.

In Table 102 published vital statistics for the state of Yucatan and its departments are presented for comparison with those of other countries. One of the first phenomena that attracts attention is that of birthrate for each thousand inhabitants. The birthrate for Yucatan and its departments is seen to be about twice as high as the corresponding figure for the United States Registration area in 1917. The rate given is a little higher than those for British India, Jamaica, and Japan. The figure for Chile approaches the Yucatecan rate most closely. The sex ratio for living births is not much different from that for the United States in 1918, but the proportion in the department of Espita, where many of the 305 families investigated live, is higher than the average for the state. The sex ratio for stillbirths in the state as a whole (120) is lower than the United States in 1918 (137), but for four of the departments is about the same or higher. The number of stillbirths for every hundred live births in the state (4.2) is low in comparison to the rate for the 305 families previously discussed (11.7), but it is interesting to observe that a rate of 7.8 is quoted for the Department of Espita, where many of the 305 families live.

For the year 1917, the mortality at all ages for the Department of Espita surpassed all others with a rate of 65 per thousand inhabitants; for the state as a whole in that year the rate was 41. It is true that an accurate census of the state is difficult to obtain, yet

TABLE 102.  STATE OF YUCATAN: BIRTHS, STILLBIRTHS, AND DEATHS

| | Annual live births per 1000 inhabitants | Sex ratios living births | Stillborn per 100 live births | Sex ratio stillborn | Annual total deaths per 1000 inhabitants | Deaths in first year per 100 total deaths | Deaths in first 5 years per 100 total deaths | Deaths in first year per 100 live births |
|---|---|---|---|---|---|---|---|---|
| State of Yucatan, 1917 | 48.6 | 107 | 4.2 | 120 | 40.8 | 27.5 (1918—9 mos.) | 48.6 | 20.9 (1918—9 mos.) |
| Departments of the state of Yucatan: Merida | 50.0 | 107 | 4.1 | 118 | 38.2 | ... | 45.3 | ... |
| Acanceh | 53.8 | 101 | 4.3 | 159 | 42.2 | ... | 57.7 | ... |
| Espita | 40.5 | 112 | 7.8 | 150 | 64.6 | ... | 44.8 | ... |
| Izamal | 45.8 | 107 | 3.4 | 131 | 47.0 | ... | 50.1 | ... |
| Maxcanu | 43.6 | 130 | 4.2 | 78 | 38.3 | ... | 45.9 | ... |
| Motul | 53.9 | 99 | 4.7 | 81 | 40.3 | ... | 52.2 | ... |
| Vallodolid | 50.3 | 103 | 3.4 | 133 | 42.9 | ... | 43.5 | ... |
| Sub-department Dzitas | 42.3 | 99 | 4.6 | 124 | 35.1 | 22.3 | 41.0 | 17.9 |
| U. S. Reg. Area, 1917 | 24.7 | 106 | 3.6 (1918) | 137 (1918) | 14.3 | 16.0 | 22.8 | 9.3 |
| U. S. Reg. Area, 1923 (colored) | 26.3 | ... | 7.5 (1927) | ... | 17.7 | 15.8 (1920) | 21.6 (1920) | 11.7 |
| Florida (colored), 1925 | 22.9 | ... | 12.1 | ... | 16.6 | ... | ... | 10.5 |
| British India, 1925 | 33.7 | ... | ... | ... | 27.9 | ... | ... | 17.4 |
| Chile, 1925 | 40.0 | ... | ... | ... | 29.2 (1924) | ... | ... | 25.8 |
| Jamaica, 1925 | 34.6 | ... | ... | ... | 21.4 | ... | ... | 17.4 |
| Japan, 1925 | 34.9 | ... | ... | ... | 20.3 | ... | ... | 14.2 |
| Uruguay, 1925 | 25.4 | ... | ... | ... | 11.8 | ... | ... | 11.5 |

Yucatecan data from *La Higiene*, 1918, Vol. I, No. 1.
Other data from *Birth, Stillbirth, and Infant Mortality Statistics*, 1927, Part II, and *Mortality Statistics* 1925, Part II, Department of Commerce, Bureau of the Census, U. S. Government Printing Office, Washington, 1929.

211

the rates for any of the departments are high even in comparison with India, Chile, and Jamaica. One circumstance which has a bearing on the discussion is that the years from 1910 to 1921 were a time of revolution in Yucatan and in Mexico in general.

It has already been shown that in the subdepartment of Dzitas, infant deaths play a large part in the generally high total mortality. This fact is borne out by the high proportion (27.5 per cent) of deaths in the first year of life as compared with deaths at all ages

TABLE 103.  STATE OF YUCATAN

First Nine Months of 1918.[1]  (Last Three Months Omitted because of Beginning of Influenza Epidemic)

(Of 9449 deaths at all ages from all causes, 60.9 per cent were due to the following four groups of diseases)

| Age | Percentage of 9449 deaths due to: | | | | |
|---|---|---|---|---|---|
| | Malaria | Whooping cough | Pneumonia, broncho-pneumonia, bronchitis, influenza | Diarrhoea | The four disease groups |
| 0–1.............. | 2.1 | 4.7 | 1.4 | 7.7 | 15.9 |
| 1–2.............. | 1.1 | 1.9 | 1.0 | 6.2 | 10.2 |
| 2–5.............. | 1.4 | 2.7 | 1.2 | 4.6 | 9.9 |
| Total: 0–5...... | 4.6 | 9.3 | 3.6 | 18.5 | 36.0 |
| 5–X .... | 7.3 | 0.9 | 6.9 | 9.8 | 24.9 |
| 0–X .... | 11.9 | 10.2 | 10.5 | 28.3 | 60.9 |

[1] *La Higiene*, 1918, Vol. I, No. 1.

in the same period. The comparative figure for the United States registration area for 1917 is 16.0 per cent. Calculating the proportion of deaths in the first year for every 100 live births, the state of Yucatan and the subdepartment of Dzitas possess rates of the same magnitude as those of India and Jamaica, higher rates than either Japan or the United States, and lower ones than that of Chile. That the first year is not the only dangerous time for the children of Yucatan is demonstrated by the fact that mortality in the first five years of life constitutes from 43 to 57 per cent of all deaths, while in the United States, less than one-quarter of the total annual mortality occurs in this period of childhood.

Table 103 indicates that, of all deaths in a given period, both those of children and adults, 61 per cent were attributable to four groups of diseases; i. e. malaria, respiratory diseases, whooping cough (which should probably be included with the latter group), and diarrhoea.  Of the 61 per cent, 36 per cent occurred in children under the age of five years, and the remaining 25 per cent in children over five and in adults.  It is notable that diarrhoea takes a greater toll among children under the age of five than does any other disease.  Furthermore, it has been shown in the Yucatecan

TABLE 104.  DEATHS UNDER ONE YEAR OF AGE
PER 1000 LIVE BIRTHS

| Cause of death | Yucatan, 1918 First nine months [1] | | | Reg. area Continental U. S. | | | |
| | | | | 1927 | | | 1922 |
| | M+F | M | F | M+F | M | F | M+F |
| All causes  ............... | 209.0 | | | 64.6 | | | |
| Measles  ................. | 6.5 | 6.8 | 6.2 | 0.4 | 0.5 | 0.4 | 0.6 |
| Whooping cough ........... | 36.0 | 31.5 | 40.8 | 1.9 | 1.9 | 2.0 | 1.4 |
| Pneumonia, broncho-pneumonia, bronchitis, influenza . | 17.5 | 18.0 | 16.9 | 10.1 | 11.1 | 9.0 | 13.7 |
| Diarrhoea and enteritis....... | 58.4 | 53.8 | 63.5 | 7.8 | 8.6 | 6.9 | 11.7 |
| Tuberculosis (all forms) ...... | ... | ... | ... | 0.6 | 0.6 | 0.6 | 0.9 |
| Convulsions ............... | 15.7 | 16.6 | 14.7 | 0.5 | 0.6 | 0.4 | 0.8 |
| Congenital malformations .... | ... | ... | ... | 5.6 | 6.1 | 5.1 | 6.3 |
| Congenital debility  ......... | 25.8 | 30.1 | 21.2 | 4.8 | 5.4 | 4.1 | 6.4 |
| Premature birth ........... | ... | ... | ... | 16.8 | 18.5 | 15.0 | 18.1 |
| Malaria  ................. | 16.3 | 17.2 | 15.2 | ... | ... | ... | ... |
| Other causes ............. | 32.8 | ... | ... | 16.1 | ... | ... | 16.3 |

[1] Last three months omitted because of beginning of influenza epidemic.  Data from *La Higiene*, 1918, Vol. I, No. 1.

publication *La Higiene* for 1918 (Vol. I, p. 248) that 65 per cent of the deaths at all ages in 1917, due to gastro-intestinal diseases, occurred in the four months of July to October inclusive; that 51 per cent of deaths from a similar cause in persons over the age of five happened in this period; and that 73 per cent of similarly caused deaths in children under five took place in those months.

.  In Table 104, a comparison is made between causes of infant deaths in Yucatan and in the registration area of the United States in 1927.  It is immediately apparent that tuberculosis, congenital malformations, and premature births are not given as important causes in the Yucatecan statistics.  It may be that since cow's milk is almost unknown as an infant food in Yucatan, the opportunity for contraction of bovine tuberculosis in infancy is not present. As to congenital malformations, the author saw very few during his stay in the country. Many of the premature births are probably included among the stillbirths. The four groups of transmissible diseases discussed above again appear as important causes of death. To the list are here added measles, convulsions, and congenital debility. It is easily understood why the latter is an important factor in infant mortality, for rigorous selection begins at the moment in which a child is born. Those who are not born with superior or at least normal physical equipment soon drop out of the race.

It is evident from the foregoing discussion of infant and child mortality in Yucatan that if coöperation on the part of the people can be obtained by public health workers, the high death rate among children under the age of five years will be materially reduced. It is at the same time highly probable that the strong and hardy — if not necessarily robust — constitutions of adult Yucatecans may be attributed to the rigorous selection to which they have been subjected from their earliest childhood.

## VARIABILITY

Boas and Herskovits have emphasized in various writings a very important point in connection with physical variability in human groups. (See Boas, 1928 and Herskovits, 1926 and 1928.) It is that low variability or homogeneity does not necessarily mean racial purity. The author wishes to add to the statement the qualification that low variability does not necessarily mean racial purity *in the sense of purity of previously known races or subraces.* Low variability does signify that isolation and inbreeding have occurred, and that old races are being perpetuated in relative purity or new subraces are being formed. Examples which seem to justify this opinion are those of Fischer's Rehobother Bastaards of South Africa and Carter's Tennessee Mountaineers. In both cases low variability is found; both are inbred populations. But the former are the progeny of a racial cross between Dutch and Hottentots, while the latter are all descendants of one branch of the White race.

Herskovits believes that the American Negro, because of inbreeding due to certain social restrictions against his marriage with

Whites, is well into the process of formation of a new somatic type. This belief he bases on a study of the relative variability of that group in certain measurements. As a test of the homogeneity of eight groups of American Negroes, sorted according to genealogical information, Herskovits added the measures of variability for thirty traits. Of the eight sums obtained, he found the smallest to be not the "unmixed Negro" group, but the class who described themselves as having more Negro than White blood, with Indian mixture in addition; also he discovered that "though the unmixed Negro class is next in lowness in the scale of the summated variabilities, it is almost identical in this respect with another class which represents large mixture."

Table 105 quotes freely from Herskovits (1928) and shows the standard deviations in various measurements of certain groups of American Negroes, of Yucatecans considered as a group, and of other populations (all males). Examination of the table indicates that the two groups — the mixed American Negro and the mixed Yucatecan — are somewhat similar in magnitude of the variability shown in certain measurements and indices. The general thesis that isolation (either geographical or social) and inbreeding tend to create populations of low variability is borne out by the low figures in cephalic index for Fischer's Bastaards, for the Tennessee Mountaineers, and for East European Jews. It is therefore apparent that before deciding as to whether the low variability of a given group means the refinement of an old racial type or the existence of a new one, hitherto unknown, one must investigate its history, its customs, its physical environment, and especially its relations with other peoples. Also, in evaluating variability of a measurement or index, one must take into account particular factors which affect certain body dimensions and indices and which have no effect on others. Breadth dimensions do not necessarily behave like those of length, and one can be sure that differences in available food may affect an adaptive character such as weight and make no change at all in eye color.

Too few characters are compared in Table 105 to justify a decision on the relative variabilities of the racially mixed American Negroes and Yucatecans, but the table does show that certain genealogically sorted and local subgroups of the American Negroes have in sitting height, cephalic index, and nose breadth, lower

TABLE 105. STANDARD DEVIATIONS IN VARIOUS
HUMAN GROUPS

*(Based upon Tables from Herskovits' "The American Negro," 1928)*

MALES

| Stature | Standard Deviation |
|---|---|
| Total Yucatecans | 5.46 cm. |
| American Negroes, Davenport and Love | 6.9 |
| American Negroes, Herskovits | 6.4 |

| Sitting Height | |
|---|---|
| Total Yucatecans | 3.44 cm. |
| American Negroes, Davenport and Love | 3.5 |
| American Negroes, Herskovits | 3.5 |
|    Of unmixed Negro blood | 3.1 |
|    Of more Negro than White blood | 3.3 |
|    Of same amount Negro and White blood | 3.3 |
|    Of more White than Negro blood | 3.2 |
| Kajiji (West Africa) | 3.94 |
| Ekoi (West Africa) | 3.07 |
| Kagoro (West Africa) | 3.00 |
| Whites, Davenport and Love | 3.51 |

| Bi-iliac Diameter | |
|---|---|
| Total Yucatecans | 1.44 cm. |
| American Negroes, Davenport and Love. | 2.35 |
| American Negroes, Herskovits. | 1.83 |

| Cephalic Index | |
|---|---|
| Total Yucatecans | 3.22 per cent |
| American Negroes, Herskovits | 3.45 |
| American Negroes (New York City), Herskovits | 1.85 |
| Ekoi (West Africa) | 3.27 |
| Kajiji (West Africa) | 3.07 |
| Vai (West Africa) | 2.96 |
| Bastaards, Fischer | 1.26 |
| White skulls, Todd | 4.74 |
| Old Americans, Hrdlička | 3.01 |
| Blue Ridge Mountaineers, Carter | 1.85 |
| Delaware Indians | 3.50 |
| Chippewa Indians | 1.77 |
| Central Italians | 2.39 |
| Bohemians | 2.37 |
| East European Jews | 2.29 |

TABLE 105.  (*Continued*)

| Face Height | Standard Deviation |
|---|---|
| Total Yucatecans | 6.22 mm. |
| American Negroes, Herskovits | 6.31 |
| Kagoro (West Africa) | 7.52 |
| Ekoi (West Africa) | 6.82 |
| Vai (West Africa) | 5.84 |
| Old Americans, Hrdlička | 6.72 |
| English Criminals, Goring | 7.70 |

| Nose Breadth | |
|---|---|
| Total Yucatecans | 3.05 mm. |
| American Negroes, Herskovits | |
| Of unmixed Negro blood | 2.8 |
| Of more Negro than White blood | 3.4 |
| Of same amount Negro and White blood | 3.0 |
| Of more White than Negro blood | 3.9 |

| Ear Length | |
|---|---|
| Total Yucatecans | 3.94 mm. |
| American Negroes, Herskovits | 4.32 |
| Ekoi (West Africa) | 3.96 |
| Marquesan Islanders | 5.72 |
| Old Americans, Hrdlička | 5.72 |
| English Criminals, Goring | 4.88 |

standard deviations than do the Yucatecans considered as a unit group.  In the cases of the American Negroes and the Yucatecans, as among all populations, tendency toward formation of a type or types is present.  How successful these tendencies are depends upon how much inbreeding, due to social or geographical isolation, is permitted.  Among both the compared groups there are certain localities in which such type formations are going forward rapidly, and others in which the attempts are being constantly frustrated. The designation of a group of individuals as a racial type, according to the definition of race used in this paper, depends not at all upon their common possession of adaptive characters, but rather upon their holding in common certain non-adaptive traits.  That the Yucatecans cannot yet be said to constitute a racial type is apparent from the fact that truly racial subgroups can with ease be selected from the group as a whole.  Certain Negroid characters mark almost every descendant of a White-Negro cross; blending certainly occurs, but the Negroid character of certain traits generally persists in some degree. This phenomenon is not so common in White-Indian crosses; the Indian traits differ less from certain White ones than do Negroid characters. In comparison of White-Negro and White-Indian crosses, attention should also be called to the fact that while comparatively few new White-Negro crosses now occur in the United States, there are in Yucatan large reservoirs of both fairly pure Indians, and Whites and near-Whites, who may possibly add to the mixed population already present. Herskovits has good evidence that the American Negro is in the process of forming a new racial type. Eventually the Yucatecans may obtain greater homogeneity in non-adaptive traits than they now possess as a group. But before discussion of the variability of the Yucatecans as a group can be concluded, comparisons should be made with the measures of variability of Spanish groups representative of those with whom the Maya Indians mixed and with those of other groups who are also the progeny of White-Indian crosses.

An explanation of the symbolism used is necessary before Table 106 can be properly read. The coefficient of variation of a measurement or index represents the percentage relation existing between the standard deviation of a series and its mean. Since it is a proportion, and not an absolute number of millimeters or index units as is the standard deviation, it is capable of being directly compared with any other coefficient of variation. The coefficient of variation of a given measurement with its probable error is generally stated in the form: 3.00 ± .10. This expression means that the chances are even that the constant's value lies somewhere between 2.90 and 3.10. It has been assumed in Table 106 that two coefficients may be of the same general magnitude when the value of one of them lies within the range of plus or minus three times the probable error of the other. For example, a coefficient of 3.20 lies within the range of 3.00 ± .30 or from 2.70 to 3.30. In Table 106 coefficients of variation of various groups have been compared with those of the Total Yucatecans or Yucatecans considered as a group. Such a *similar* value for the coefficient as just given is designated in the table by the letter s, meaning similar. If a given coefficient has a value *lower* or *less* than that of the minimum of the range, it is shown in the table by a letter L, signifying less variability than is found in the Total Yucatecans. If, on the other hand, a given value

TABLE 106.  COMPARISON OF COEFFICIENTS OF VARIATION OF
CERTAIN GROUPS AND SUBGROUPS WITH THOSE OF THE
UNIT GROUP OF TOTAL YUCATECANS

LEGEND

L = Coefficients of variation *lower* than those of Total Yucatecans; variability is less.

s = Coefficients of variation *similar* to those of Total Yucatecans; variability is similar.

G = Coefficients of variation *greater* than those of Total Yucatecans; variability is greater.

PART I.  *Dimensions of Body Length*

MALES

| Groups | A | B | C | D | E | Andalu-sian Moors | Mexi-cans | Sioux Pure | Sioux Half-Blood |
|---|---|---|---|---|---|---|---|---|---|
| Stature | L | L | s | G | G | L | G | L | G |
| Acromial height | L | L | s | G | G | L | . | L | G |
| Sternal height | L | L | s | G | G | . | . | . | . |
| Sitting height | s | L | s | s | s | L | s | L | G |
| Tibiale-Spherion | s | s | s | s | s | . | . | . | . |
| Acromion-Radiale | s | s | s | s | s | . | . | . | . |
| Radiale-Dactylion | s | s | s | s | L | . | . | . | . |
| Span | s | s | s | L | L | s | . | s | s |

FEMALES

| Groups | A | B | C | D | E | Mexi-cans | Smith students | Sioux Pure | Sioux Half-Blood |
|---|---|---|---|---|---|---|---|---|---|
| Stature | s | L | s | L | s | G | s | L | s |
| Acromial height | s | s | s | s | s | . | s | L | s |
| Sternal height | L | L | s | s | s | . | . | . | . |
| Sitting height | G | L | s | L | s | G | L | s | G |
| Tibiale-Spherion | . | . | . | . | . | . | . | . | . |
| Acromion-Radiale | L | s | s | L | G | . | L | . | . |
| Radiale-Dactylion | s | s | s | G | s | . | . | . | . |
| Span | L | s | s | . | . | . | G | s | G |

PART II.  *Dimensions of Length of Head and Face*

MALES

| Groups | A | B | C | D | E | Spanish (Barras) | Andalu-sian Moors | Mexi-cans | Sioux Pure | Sioux Half-Blood |
|---|---|---|---|---|---|---|---|---|---|---|
| Head length | s | L | s | s | G | G | s | s | s | G |
| Face height | L | s | s | G | s | G | L | L | s | s |
| Upper face height | s | s | s | s | s | G | L | L | G | s |
| Nose height | s | G | G | s | L | G | s | s | s | s |
| Ear length | L | s | s | s | G | s | . | . | . | . |

FEMALES

| Groups | A | B | C | D | E | Mexi-cans | Smith students | Sioux Pure | Sioux Half-Blood |
|---|---|---|---|---|---|---|---|---|---|
| Head length | s | L | G | L | G | G | L | L | L |
| Face height | L | L | G | s | L | G | s | s | L |
| Upper face height | s | L | G | L | s | G | . | . | . |
| Nose height | s | L | G | s | L | L | s | L | L |
| Ear length | s | s | s | G | L | . | L | . | . |

TABLE 106. (*Continued*)

PART III. *Expressions of Breadth and Bulk of the Body*

MALES

| Groups | A | B | C | D | E | Andalusian Moors | Sioux Pure | Sioux Half-Blood | U.S. Army Whites, 1919 |
|---|---|---|---|---|---|---|---|---|---|
| Biacromial diameter | S | S | S | S | S | G | G | S | . |
| Bi-iliac diameter | L | G | S | S | L | G | . | . | . |
| Chest breadth | S | S | S | L | L | G | . | . | . |
| Chest depth | S | G | S | S | S | . | . | . | . |
| Chest girth | S | S | S | G | G | . | . | . | . |
| Weight | L | S | L | G | G | . | . | . | S |

FEMALES

| Groups | A | B | C | D | E | Smith students | Sioux Pure | Sioux Half-Blood | Mexicans |
|---|---|---|---|---|---|---|---|---|---|
| Biacromial diameter | L | S | L | S | G | L | G | G | . |
| Bi-iliac diameter | S | S | S | . | . | L | . | . | . |
| Chest breadth | L | L | S | S | . | L | . | . | . |
| Chest depth | S | S | L | G | . | L | . | . | . |
| Chest girth | L | L | G | G | G | . | . | . | L |
| Weight | L | L | G | G | G | G | . | . | . |

PART IV. *Dimensions of Breadth and Depth of the Head and Breadth of the Face*

MALES

| Groups | A | B | C | D | E | Spanish (Barras) | Andalusian Moors | Mexicans | Sioux Pure | Sioux Half-Blood |
|---|---|---|---|---|---|---|---|---|---|---|
| Head breadth | S | S | S | G | S | L | S | G | S | S |
| Head height | S | L | S | S | G | G | G | G | . | . |
| Bizygomatic diameter | L | S | G | G | G | G | L | G | G | G |
| Bigonial diameter | L | S | S | S | G | G | G | G | . | . |
| Minimum frontal diameter | S | S | S | G | L | G | G | S | . | . |
| Nose breadth | S | S | S | S | S | G | L | G | S | S |
| Ear breadth | S | S | S | G | G | G | . | . | . | . |

FEMALES

| Groups | A | B | C | D | E | Mexicans | Smith students | Sioux Pure | Sioux Half-Blood |
|---|---|---|---|---|---|---|---|---|---|
| Head breadth | S | L | G | S | S | G | L | S | L |
| Head height | S | L | S | G | S | G | S | . | . |
| Bizygomatic diameter | L | L | G | G | S | G | L | S | L |
| Bigonial diameter | G | S | S | L | L | S | L | . | . |
| Minimum frontal diameter | S | S | S | S | S | G | . | . | . |
| Nose breadth | L | S | G | S | L | L | L | L | L |
| Ear breadth | S | L | S | G | L | . | L | . | . |

PART V. *Length-length Indices*

MALES

| Groups | A | B | C | D | E | Andalusian Moors | Mexicans | Sioux Pure | Sioux Half-Blood |
|---|---|---|---|---|---|---|---|---|---|
| Relative shoulder height | L | S | S | G | S | G | . | . | . |
| Relative sitting height | S | S | S | G | S | L | G | G | G |
| Relative span | S | S | S | . | . | . | . | G | S |
| Intermembral | G | S | L | S | G | . | . | . | . |

TABLE 106.  (*Continued*)

FEMALES

| Groups | A | B | C | D | E | Mexi-cans | Smith students | Sioux Pure | Sioux Half-Blood |
|---|---|---|---|---|---|---|---|---|---|
| Relative shoulder height ... | S | S | S | G | S | . | . | . | . |
| Relative sitting height ..... | L | S | G | L | G | G | G | G | G |
| Relative span ........... | L | S | S | . | . | . | L | S | L |
| Intermembral ........... | S | S | S | L | S | . | . | . | . |

PART VI.  *Length-breadth Indices*

MALES

| Groups | A | B | C | D | E | Spanish (Barras) | Andalu-sian Moors | Mexi-cans | Sioux Pure | Sioux Half-Blood |
|---|---|---|---|---|---|---|---|---|---|---|
| Relative shoulder breadth .. | L | S | S | S | G | . | G | . | G | S |
| Cephalic ................ | S | S | S | L | G | G | L | G | G | L |
| Facial.................. | L | S | S | G | G | G | L | L | G | G |
| Upper facial ............. | L | S | S | G | G | G | S | L | . | . |
| Nasal .................. | S | S | S | G | G | G | G | G | S | S |
| Auricular ............... | S | S | S | L | L | G | . | . | . | . |

FEMALES

| Groups | A | B | C | D | E | Mexi-cans | Smith students | Sioux Pure | Sioux Half-Blood |
|---|---|---|---|---|---|---|---|---|---|---|
| Relative shoulder breadth .. | L | S | S | S | G | . | . | G | G |
| Cephalic ................ | S | L | S | G | L | G | S | L | L |
| Facial.................. | S | S | G | L | S | G | S | S | L |
| Upper facial ............. | S | S | G | L | S | G | . | . | . |
| Nasal .................. | S | L | S | G | G | L | L | G | S |
| Auricular ............... | S | L | G | S | L | . | L | . | . |

PART VII.  *Breadth-breadth Indices*

MALES

| Groups | A | B | C | D | E | Spanish (Barras) | Andalu-sian Moors | Mexi-cans | Sioux Pure | Sioux Half-Blood |
|---|---|---|---|---|---|---|---|---|---|---|
| Hip-shoulder............. | S | G | S | L | L | . | . | . | . | . |
| Cephalo-facial ........... | S | G | S | G | L | G | G | G | G | G |
| Fronto-parietal........... | L | G | S | S | L | G | G | . | . | . |
| Zygo-frontal ............. | S | G | S | L | L | G | G | G | . | . |
| Fronto-gonial ............ | S | S | S | S | L | . | . | . | . | . |
| Zygo-gonial ............. | S | S | S | S | L | G | . | L | . | . |

FEMALES

| Groups | A | B | C | D | E | Mexi-cans | Smith students | Sioux Pure | Sioux Half-Blood |
|---|---|---|---|---|---|---|---|---|---|---|
| Hip-shoulder............. | G | S | S | . | . | . | L | . | . |
| Cephalo-facial ........... | L | L | S | G | G | G | . | G | L |
| Fronto-parietal........... | S | S | S | S | G | G | . | . | . |
| Zygo-frontal ............. | L | L | S | S | G | L | . | . | . |
| Fronto-gonial ............ | G | G | S | L | L | . | . | . | . |
| Zygo-gonial ............. | G | S | S | L | L | L | . | . | . |

TABLE 106. (*Continued*)

PART VIII. *Other Indices*

MALES

| Groups | A | B | C | D | E | Spanish (Barras) | Andalusian Moors |
|---|---|---|---|---|---|---|---|
| Thoracic | S | S | S | L | L | . | . |
| Relative chest girth | S | L | S | G | G | . | . |
| Index of build | S | S | S | G | G | . | . |
| Length-height | S | L | S | S | G | G | S |
| Breadth-height | S | L | S | L | G | G | G |

FEMALES

| Groups | A | B | C | D | E | Smith students |
|---|---|---|---|---|---|---|
| Thoracic | S | S | S | . | . | . |
| Relative chest girth | L | L | G | S | G | . |
| Index of build | L | L | G | G | L | . |
| Length-height | S | L | G | S | S | S |
| Breadth-height | S | S | S | S | S | S |

is *greater* than the maximum of the range, the symbol G is used, showing that the variability of the given group for the measurement or index in question is greater than that of the Total Yucatecans.

Part I of Table 106 shows that the Andalusian Moors of Coon have three out of four length dimensions of the body which are less variable than those of the Total Yucatecans. These people are of Spanish descent and live in Morocco. Because of the latter fact, they probably intermarry and live together in the same restricted physical environment; which facts would account for their low variability in certain greater body lengths. Mexican males as well as females, resident in Yucatan, tend to vary more than the Yucatecans. The pure Sioux appear to be more homogeneous in certain length measurements than the Indian-White mixture of Southern Mexico, while the mixed Sioux tend to be more variable, and never less.

In lengths of the head and face, the inbred Andalusian Moors are again seen to be relatively homogeneous, while Barras' Spanish sample (probably not an inbred group) is on the other hand comparatively heterogeneous. The male Mexicans are less and the female Mexicans more variable than Yucatecans of the respective sexes. The pure and mixed Siouan groups of the male sex are alike in exhibiting in three-fourths of the cases coefficients similar to those possessed by male Yucatecans, while those of the two Siouan female groups are less.

The Andalusian Moors, who previously have shown low variability, in dimensions of body breadth show high coefficients. In biacromial diameter high values are found in the male and female pure Sioux and in the female half-breeds.

Barras' Spanish are almost uniformly high in variability of breadth of head and face, and the variability of the Moors in this respect can only be described as extreme. The Mexicans, both males and females, resemble the Spanish in their frequently high coefficients of variation. It should be remarked, however, that the coefficients for nose breadth of the Moors and of the female Mexicans, and those for head breadth of the Spanish males, are definitely lower than the ones found in the Maya-Spanish progeny. The pure and mixed Sioux males have variabilities in head breadth and nose breadth of the same magnitude as the Yucatecans, as do the pure Sioux women, while the half-breed females possess lower coefficients.

Relative sitting height is the best representative of the length-length indices shown. Except in the case of the Andalusian Moors, the Yucatecans have lower variability than any of the other groups of either sex. In relative span, three out of four Siouan coefficients are not excessive.

A résumé of the foregoing discussion is that, in body lengths, the Andalusian Moors, an inbred Spanish group, and the pure Sioux, representative of unmixed Indians, are less variable than the Yucatecans. In lengths of the head and face the Moors and the pure Sioux tend to exhibit less variability. The Mexicans, who represent various mixtures of Spanish-White and Indian vary more than their southern neighbors in this respect, while the Half-Blood Sioux vary considerably more in the body lengths, if less in the smaller lengths of head and face. The Moors and the pure Sioux, who were homogeneous in lengths, show much more variability in body breadths. Breadths of head and face are better stabilized among the Yucatecans than are lengths of the same parts, but even so, Spanish head breadth, the Moors' face breadth and nose breadth, the pure Siouan females' nose breadth, and the Half-Blood Siouan females' head, face, and nose breadths all represent a lower order of variability.

In view of the conclusions of the résumé, it is not surprising that relative shoulder breadth should be more variable in four out of five of these groups than in Yucatecans. In cephalic and facial indices the Moors, having slightly variable component dimensions, have also small indicial variabilities. The Sioux males fail to exhibit the expected low coefficients, but the females do. In general, it may be said that length-breadth proportions, especially of the head and face, have greater or smaller coefficients of variation in the groups cited, not because of the direct action of certain hereditary or environmental factors, but because of the action of those factors on the component dimensions themselves. If both length and breadth of head are stabilized as in the case of the Andalusian Moors, prediction of the variability of cephalic index may be made with some certainty. Evidently, neither the pure Sioux nor the Yucatecans have sufficiently stabilized head length or breadth or both to be assured of low variability of the resulting index.

If the Yucatecans are not too stable in their length-breadth proportions, they do not vacillate to any great extent in the breadth-breadth indices. The coefficients are less among the Yucatecans in all breadth-breadth indices except for one case in the male groups. The Mexican and Sioux Half-Blood women have between them three lower coefficients than the Yucatecans while the Yucatecan females possess three higher ones than the others.

One may assume from the discussion that while the Yucatecans as a group are not excessively variable in their physical characteristics, they are less homogeneous in dimensions of length than in those of breadth. Consequently, measures of variation in the breadth-breadth indices are less variable than those calculated between breadths and lengths.

The Yucatecans as a single group have been compared with various others. They were sorted, as shown in the earlier part of this study, into subgroups which were to represent various grades of mixture between Spanish Whites and Maya Indians. In comparison with the Yucatecan group as a whole, are these subgroups more or less variable? A continued examination of Table 106 will answer this query.

In length dimensions of the body, Groups A and B of both sexes are more homogeneous than the group as a whole. Groups D and E of the males are less so, but the female Group D possesses as many low coefficients as do the female Groups A and B. The smaller length dimensions of the head and face are least variable in the Group A males and in the Group B females. The female groups D and E have more low coefficients than has Group A, while the male Groups D and E have on the whole slightly higher variability than the others.

Body breadths vary most among the males in Groups B and C, but among the females most in Groups D and E. The latter observation may not be entirely justified, for data are lacking for bi-iliac diameter in both groups and for chest breadth in Group E. Chest girth and body weight vary more in Groups D and E of both sexes than in any of the others.

Variability in breadths of the head and face appear to increase with the Whiteness of the subgroups in the males. Among the females, Groups C and D exhibit higher coefficients than do Groups A and B but Group E possesses as many low values as do the two Indian subgroups. In bizygomatic diameter, it may be remarked, Groups A and B of both sexes are less variable than the others. In head height, E varies most among the male and D among female subgroups, while Group B of both sexes varies least of all.

The Whiter subgroups are slightly less homogeneous in length-length indices than the others among the males, but the female groups A and D vary less than the others of their sex. Length-breadth indices are without doubt less variable among the more Indian groups of the male sex than among the Whiter. Taking all length-breadth indices into account, the more Indian subgroups of both sexes are more homogeneous than the others. It should be noted, however, that the coefficient for cephalic index of the male Group D is lower than that of any other, and that the female Group D's values for facial and upper facial indices, and Group E's for cephalic and auricular indices, are lower than those for the group as a whole.

The coefficients of variation in breadth-breadth indices are most interesting. Among the male subgroups, Groups D and E vary less than any of the others, while among the females, Groups A and E share honors for the greatest number of high coefficients. In cephalo-facial and zygo-frontal indices, however, the two female Indian groups are homogeneous, while in fronto-gonial and zygo-gonial indices, the female Groups D and E are less variable than the others.

In relative chest girth and index of build, as well as in weight, the male Groups D and E are most variable. The same is true for the females, except that in index of build the women of Group E are as homogeneous as are those of Groups A and B. In length-height and breadth-height indices of the head, the only notable feature is that the Group E males vary more than other male subgroups.

In the foregoing discussion much has been said about Groups A, B, D, and E, but little about Group C. When the Yucatecan group as a whole was sorted into subgroups, Groups A and B were first selected, then Groups D and E. The residual subgroup — Group C — remained. Throughout Table 106 Group C is noted to possess variability of the same order as, or higher than, the variability of the unselected group of Total Yucatecans. If Group C represents those individuals who tend toward neither the White nor the Indian types, and who partake in some degree of the characteristics of both, it seems reasonable to assume that the existence of this sub-group signifies that a Yucatecan type, different from its parental races, is in the process of creation. Unlike Herskovits' American Negroes, Group C has not yet been permitted to attain any great degree of homogeneity, because new crosses are continually being made between fairly pure Indians and fairly White Yucatecans. Especially is this true in the villages, as opposed to the haciendas of the country, as was shown in the discussion of marriage. Among all peoples, certain environmental and hereditary factors are always at work which tend to place the stamp of uniformity upon all members of the group. This is true in Yucatan as elsewhere. But in that country, up to the present time, the centrifugal almost balance the centripedal forces, and the nascent state of equilibrium is upset again and again.

One of the very interesting features of this tendency toward formation of a new Yucatecan type is the difference between the sexes. Of the male Total Yucatecans, Group C forms about forty per cent; of the female group as a whole, Group C constitutes only about thirty per cent. The females, it appears, tend to be segregated into the Whiter or more Indian types to a greater extent than do the males, who blend more in their non-adaptive characteristics.

If one type can not be formed from a population, then two or more types must be existent. The most Indian subgroups of the Yucatecan population have been defined as Groups A and B; the

Whitest — Groups D and E. In males, low variability in body lengths is confined to Groups A and B, but in females, Groups A, B, and D are so characterized. In cephalic and facial lengths, a similar phenomenon is observed, for the greatest homogeneity seen among male subgroups is that of Group A, and Groups D and E are relatively variable, while the female types B, D, and E share several low coefficients. The body breadths of the men exhibit, like the females of the two former cases, low variability at either end of the Indian-White scale, and the females run true to form in cephalic and facial breadths in the possession of low coefficients by Groups A and B, as well as by Group E. In these smaller breadths, however, the males are relatively homogeneous only in the subgroups A and B, and quite variable in Groups D and E.

If a table were made, based upon the statements of the preceding paragraph, it would show that while both the Whiter and the more Indian subgroups of the females tend toward a lower grade of variability than the Yucatecan group as a whole, only the Indian male types accurately can be so described. It should be noted, however, that the heterogeneity of the Whiter males is more marked in breadths of the head and face than in the lengths. This difference in relative variabilities between lengths and breadths of the male Groups D and E as well as the generally higher variabilities of these two subgroups results in the heterogeneity found in their length-breadth indices. The Whiter females, being more homogeneous than the males in length and breadth of the face and head, are also more homogeneous than the males in indices calculated from these dimensions. But if the Whiter males are variable in certain other respects, it must be admitted that in breadth-breadth indices they vary but little. In the case of the male Group E it is a peculiar fact, but true, that although in absolute breadths the members differ greatly one from the other, the proportions between those breadths in individuals are strikingly uniform. The opposite condition prevails in Group B, but in Group A the variability is neither particularly high nor particularly low. In the females, the extreme groups which were only mildly variable in absolute breadths exhibit in the relations of breadths to breadths a tendency toward greater variation than is seen in the Whiter males.

Out of the foregoing involved discussion of relative variability in Yucatecan types emerges one point of considerable interest to students of race mixture. It is that the females of the Yucatecan progeny, when sorted into subtypes, by means of non-adaptive traits, appear to be less variable within those groups than are the males of corresponding groups. The one exception to this generalization lies in the proportional relation existing between breadths of the head or face. In expressions of size, the males are as a rule the more variable. Also, in the Yucatecan group as a whole, relatively fewer women than men are found who can not be classified as being more Indian than White or more White than Indian. These pronouncements bring to mind the famous controversy once carried on by Karl Pearson and Havelock Ellis concerning the relative variability of men and women. The data presented here agree with Ellis's conclusion that males are the more variable of the two sexes. The fact is all the more interesting because it relates to conditions in a mixture between two quite different races of mankind.

One last comment deserves consideration. It is that selective mating of like with like on the haciendas of Yucatan, plus the lower variability of the female sex, tends to create a very homogeneous set of mothers in each of the various types and so works toward perpetuation of those types. The probability is that the haciendas of Yucatan have always performed that very function. But if selective mating disappears on haciendas, or the purer Indians leave the haciendas for the villages, the random matings which are practiced there will soon remove the greatest obstacle to formation of a homogeneous Yucatecan type and the Maya Indian of Yucatan will become as extinct as the Tasmanian.

## CONCLUSION

The data presented in this study have been considered mainly from the viewpoint of the student of race. The term "race" is sometimes loosely interpreted as referring to national, habitat, linguistic, or religious groups of mankind, so that it has been necessary to state the definition of the term as it is here used. The definition adopted is that of Hooton (1926). He gives the following interpretation: "A race is a great division of mankind, the members of which, though individually varying, are characterized as a group by a certain combination of morphological and metrical features, principally non-adaptive, which have been derived from their common descent."

Races, both primary and secondary, have arisen because of in-breeding in isolated human groups. The isolation is sometimes geographical, sometimes social. Improved facilities for travel and changed ideas regarding social status have modified the tendencies toward isolation of certain human groups again and again through-out history. The last few hundred years have seen more and more examples of mixture between widely differing racial groups.

Draper (1924) spoke for many students of similar belief when he wrote:

It may well be that the conception of race as we have so far held it is no longer tenable on account of the almost universal admixture which modern means of transportation have brought about. The increasing facilities for migratory movements during the last hundred years have forever shattered the biologic isolation of the sub-species of man.

If the social barriers against intermarriage of quite racially different individuals were completely broken down, and if random mating were the rule, the biological entities known as races or subraces might well fear for their continued existence as such. However, the most common occurrence is the participation in a racial mixture of only parts of the whole groups involved, so that through dispropor-tion in numbers of one racial group over the other, or through prejudice against intermixture, reservoirs of the pure races remain outside the mixture. Such reservoirs work toward the continuance of existence of the pure or nearly pure races, and against the for-mation of a new secondary race. Inbreeding in isolation is neces-sary for the formation of such a new composite subrace. Since the reservoirs of pure stocks and frequent lack of random mating work against the formation of a homogeneous new racial type of com-posite character, it follows that not one new type but several are created. This is due to the fact that the racial characteristics of one or the other mixing groups are not inherited on the "all or none" principle but independently, with "linkage" existing be-tween certain of them.

In the case of Yucatecan race mixture, Spanish-White and Maya-Indian reservoirs of a fair degree of purity exist; random mating is not a universal phenomenon. Cursory observation of the rural Yucatecan population shows that the mixed progeny are not homogeneous in racial type, but that they vary greatly in possession of White and Indian non-adaptive traits. Using non-adaptive White and Indian traits as criteria, advantage was taken of this state of affairs by sorting the racially mixed progeny into groups which approximate in greater and less degree to each of the parent groups of the mixture. Each individual of the cross is said to possess a definite racial status. An individual is a member of a pure racial group because he possesses certain non-adaptive traits derived from common descent of the group's members. Why is not a prodduct of race mixture classifiable through use of a sorting method such as that suggested above? If it can be proven that subgroups of such progeny of race mixture differ significantly (in the statistical sense) from the group of mixed progeny as a whole in several important respects, the assumption that the subgroups are racial in character will be justified, and the hopelessness of such a view as Draper's is unwarranted.

Table 107 epitomizes the statistical significance or insignificance of differences which exist between the means of the male and female Total Yucatecans and the various male and female subgroups. The reader should be reminded that significance of mean differences depends to great extent upon smallness of standard deviations of the subgroups, and hence upon their relative homogeneity.

In body lengths, both males and females show many means that differ significantly from those of the group as a whole. It appears that trunk lengths tend to differ significantly more frequently than extremity lengths. The smaller lengths of the head and face exhibit the same trends seen in the greater lengths. Head length follows the lead of the body lengths closely, but the heights of the face differ significantly from those of the Total Yucatecans less frequently. It will be recalled that the subgroups differ greatly among themselves in respect to prognathism. If the facial contour lines are thus different from one another in the various subgroups, projective distances between face height or its parts are really not comparable.

Body breadth and depth diameters of the males, like body lengths, differ significantly from the total groups in Groups A, C, and E. Expression of significance of differences is hindered here, as in the females, by small numbers in the Groups D and E. Body weight averages differ significantly in the extreme groups A and E.

TABLE 107.  COMPARISON OF MEANS OF CERTAIN GROUPS
AND SUBGROUPS WITH THOSE OF THE UNIT GROUP
OF TOTAL YUCATECANS

LEGEND

G = Means *significantly greater* than those of the Total Yucatecans.
g = Means *probably significantly greater* than those of the Total Yucatecans.
s = Means *insignificantly different* from those of the Total Yucatecans; similar.
l = Means *probably significantly less* than those of the Total Yucatecans.
L = Means *significantly less* than those of the Total Yucatecans.

PART I.  *Dimensions of Body Length*

MALES

| Groups | A | B | C | D | E | Andalusian Moors | Mexicans |
|---|---|---|---|---|---|---|---|
| Stature | L | l | G | G | G | G | G |
| Acromial height | L | l | G | s | G | G | . |
| Sternal height | L | L | G | G | G | . | . |
| Sitting height | L | s | g | g | G | G | |
| Tibiale-Spherion | l | L | G | s | s | . | . |
| Acromion-Radiale | L | l | G | g | s | . | . |
| Radiale-Dactylion | L | s | g | s | s | . | |
| Span | l | s | G | s | s | G | . |

FEMALES

| Groups | A | B | C | D | E | Mexicans | Smith College students |
|---|---|---|---|---|---|---|---|
| Stature | L | L | g | G | G | G | G |
| Acromial height | L | L | G | G | g | . | c |
| Sternal height | L | L | g | G | G | . | |
| Sitting height | L | L | g | G | G | G | G |
| Acromion-Radiale | L | s | s | g | s | . | G |
| Radiale-Dactylion | s | s | s | s | s | . | . |
| Span | s | s | l | . | . | . | G |

PART II.  *Dimensions of Length of Head and Face*

MALES

| Groups | A | B | C | D | E (Barras) | Spanish | Andalusian Moors | Mexicans |
|---|---|---|---|---|---|---|---|---|
| Head length | L | L | g | G | G | G | G | G |
| Face height | l | l | G | s | s | s | g | s |
| Upper face height | s | s | s | s | s | L | L | s |
| Nose height | l | s | L | s | s | L | L | L |
| Ear length | L | L | G | s | s | g | . | . |

TABLE 107. (Continued)

### FEMALES

| Groups | A | B | C | D | E | Mexicans | Smith College students |
|---|---|---|---|---|---|---|---|
| Head length | L | s | s | s | G | g | G |
| Face height | s | s | s | L | l | s | L |
| Upper face height | s | s | s | l | L | l | . |
| Nose height | g | s | s | l | l | L | L |
| Ear length | s | s | l | g | s | . | G |

### PART III. Expressions of Breadth and Bulk of Body

#### MALES

| Groups | A | B | C | D | E | Andalusian Moors |
|---|---|---|---|---|---|---|
| Biacromial diameter | L | s | G | s | s | s |
| Bi-iliac diamter | L | s | G | s | G | G |
| Chest breadth | s | s | g | s | s | s |
| Chest depth | L | s | G | G | G | . |
| Chest girth | L | s | G | g | s | . |
| Weight | L | s | g | s | G | . |

#### FEMALES

| Groups | A | B | C | D | E | Smith College students | Mexicans |
|---|---|---|---|---|---|---|---|
| Biacromial diameter | s | s | g | s | s | G | . |
| Bi-iliac diameter | s | s | s | . | . | . | . |
| Chest breadth | s | L | s | G | . | L | . |
| Chest depth | s | s | s | G | . | g | . |
| Chest girth | s | s | s | s | s | . | L |
| Weight | s | L | s | s | g | G | . |

### PART IV. Dimensions of Breadth and Depth of the Head and Breadth of the Face

#### MALES

| Groups | A | B | C | D | E | Spanish (Barras) | Andalusian Moors | Mexicans |
|---|---|---|---|---|---|---|---|---|
| Head breadth | s | l | s | s | s | L | L | L |
| Head height | s | l | s | s | s | G | G | G |
| Bizygomatic diameter | s | s | g | s | l | L | L | L |
| Bigonial diameter | s | s | s | s | s | L | l | s |
| Minimum frontal diameter | l | s | G | s | s | s | s | s |
| Nose breadth | s | s | g | L | L | L | L | s |
| Ear breadth | l | l | s | s | g | G | . | . |

## TABLE 107. (*Continued*)

### FEMALES

| Groups | A | B | C | D | E | Mexicans | Smith College students |
|---|---|---|---|---|---|---|---|
| Head breadth | s | s | l | s | g | L | L |
| Head height | s | g | s | s | s | s | G |
| Bizygomatic diameter | g | s | s | L | l | L | L |
| Bigonial diameter | s | s | g | s | s | s | g |
| Minimum frontal | l | s | s | s | g | s | . |
| Nose breadth | G | G | s | L | L | L | L |
| Ear breadth | l | G | s | s | s | . | G |

### PART V. *Length-Length Indices*

#### MALES

| Groups | A | B | C | D | E | Andalusian Moors | Mexicans |
|---|---|---|---|---|---|---|---|
| Relative shoulder height | s | s | g | L | s | L | . |
| Relative sitting height | s | g | s | s | s | s | s |
| Relative span | s | s | s | . | . | . | . |
| Intermembral | g | s | l | s | s | . | . |

#### FEMALES

| Groups | A | B | C | D | E | Mexicans | Smith College students |
|---|---|---|---|---|---|---|---|
| Relative shoulder height | s | s | s | s | s | . | . |
| Relative sitting height | l | s | s | s | s | s | s |
| Relative span | s | g | s | . | . | . | L |
| Intermembral | s | G | s | L | l | . | . |

### PART VI. *Length-Breadth Indices*

#### MALES

| Groups | A | B | C | D | E | Spanish (Barras) | Andalusian Moors | Mexicans |
|---|---|---|---|---|---|---|---|---|
| Relative shoulder breadth | s | s | s | s | s | . | L | . |
| Cephalic | G | s | s | L | L | L | L | L |
| Facial | l | s | s | s | g | G | G | G |
| Upper facial | s | s | s | s | s | g | s | g |
| Nasal | G | g | s | L | L | L | s | s |
| Auricular | s | s | s | s | s | G | . | . |

#### FEMALES

| Groups | A | B | C | D | E | Mexicans | Smith College students |
|---|---|---|---|---|---|---|---|
| Relative shoulder breadth | G | s | s | L | l | . | . |
| Cephalic | G | s | L | L | L | L | L |
| Facial | s | s | s | s | s | G | G |
| Upper facial | s | s | s | s | s | g | . |
| Nasal | g | g | s | L | l | s | s |
| Auricular | s | g | s | s | s | . | G |

TABLE 107. (*Continued*)

PART VII. *Breadth-Breadth Indices*

MALES

| Groups | A | B | C | D | E | Spanish (Barras) | Andalusian Moors | Mexicans |
|---|---|---|---|---|---|---|---|---|
| Hip-shoulder | l | s | s | s | g | . | . | . |
| Cephalo-facial | s | s | g | L | L | L | s | s |
| Fronto-parietal | s | s | g | l | l | G | G | . |
| Zygo-frontal | l | s | s | s | g | G | G | G |
| Fronto-gonial | s | s | s | s | s | . | . | . |
| Zygo-gonial | s | s | s | s | G | G | . | G |

FEMALES

| Groups | A | B | C | D | E | Mexicans | Smith College students |
|---|---|---|---|---|---|---|---|
| Hip-shoulder | s | s | s | . | . | . | l |
| Cephalo-facial | s | s | G | L | L | s | . |
| Fronto-parietal | L | s | s | s | s | G | . |
| Zygo-frontal | L | s | s | G | G | G | . |
| Fronto-gonial | s | s | g | L | l | . | . |
| Zygo-gonial | l | s | s | g | s | G | . |

PART VIII. *Other Indices*

MALES

| Groups | A | B | C | D | E | Spanish (Barras) | Andalusian Moors |
|---|---|---|---|---|---|---|---|
| Thoracic | s | s | s | s | s | . | . |
| Relative chest girth | s | s | s | s | l | . | . |
| Index of build | s | s | s | s | G | . | . |
| Length-height | G | G | s | L | L | L | l |
| Breadth-height | s | s | s | L | l | G | G |

FEMALES

| Groups | A | B | C | D | E | Smith College students |
|---|---|---|---|---|---|---|
| Thoracic | G | s | s | . | . | . |
| Relative chest girth | g | s | s | L | L | . |
| Index of build | l | s | s | s | G | . |
| Length-height | s | g | s | L | l | L |
| Breadth-height | s | g | s | s | s | G |

The real differences in body breadths and bulk among the female subgroups are fewer than among the male. The two bony breadths — bi-iliac and bi-acromial — differ insignificantly in all subgroups, but chest breadth and depth, both of which measure thickness of bony-covered viscera, show significant variation in averages in Groups B and D. Weight is significantly less in Group B and probably greater in Group E.

In head breadth, neither male nor female subgroups really vary from the general average of the whole group. In head height and in bigonial diameter, the same tendency is manifested. In minimum breadth of the forehead, probably significant differences indicate the presence of a trend toward smaller breadths in the more Indian groups and larger ones in the Whiter. The male averages in face breadth show a tendency in the opposite direction, which tendency is more clearly depicted in the seriation curves for the male bizygomatic diameter. Subgroup differences in female face breadth are even more evident than in males. But the only mean differences that are consistently significant throughout the subgroups in breadths of face are those of breadth of nose. It is interesting and suggestive to compare this finding with that of the significant differences which were found in female chest breadth and depth.

The following hypothesis is suggested by the above findings: that the progeny of mixture between stocks which differ in lengths and breadths tend to segregate toward the extremes of the parent body lengths and soft-part breadths, but that dominance or relative dominance of the greater bony breadths occurs.

Relations of lengths to lengths show no significant change, except in the proportion of lengths of the upper and lower extremities. The proportionately longer arms of the Indians and relatively shorter ones of the Whiter subgroups differ to a significant degree among the female groups. Of the male length-breadth indices, cephalic and nasal really differ from those of the Total Yucatecans, while facial index varies to only a probably significant degree in the extreme subgroups. Among the female groups, the three of six length-breadth indices which differ significantly are relative shoulder breadth, cephalic, and nasal. Differential inheritance of breadths is found among the males, as manifested in breadth-breadth indices, in certainly two, and probably five of six cases. The female subgroups differ significantly in two-thirds of the breadth-breadth indices. In thoracic index, a real difference occurs in the female Group A. In relative chest girth, Group A probably varies from the whole group and Groups D and E certainly do. Index of build is significantly greater in Group E of both sexes. Length-height index of the head is dissimilar in various groups of both sexes, while breadth-height index differs significantly only in the males.

The proportions of significant and probably significant subgroup differences to the total number of measurements and indices considered are summarized in the appended table.

Groups A, D, and E, the extreme subgroups, vary more consistently than the others from the averages of the total groups. In the discussion of variability, it was pointed out that the females of the Yucatecan progeny, when sorted into subtypes, appear to be less variable within those groups than are the males of the corresponding groups. It was also found that there are fewer Yucatecan women than men who can not be classified as being more Indian than White or more White than Indian. Consistent with these

| Subgroup | Total number measurements and indices | | Significant differences | | Significant and probably significant differences | |
|---|---|---|---|---|---|---|
| | Male | Female | Male | Female | Male | Female |
| Group A ................. | 47 | 46 | 16 | 12 | 26 | 21 |
| Group B ................. | 47 | 46 | 4 | 9 | 13 | 15 |
| Group C ................. | 47 | 46 | 14 | 3 | 25 | 12 |
| Group D ................. | 46 | 41 | 11 | 18 | 15 | 23 |
| Group E ................. | 46 | 39 | 15 | 11 | 23 | 23 |

generalizations is the fact that the females of Group C have fewer significant and probably significant differences from the Total Yucatecans' average than the males. Compensation for this is found to some extent in the tendency toward expression of more mean differences in the female Groups B, D, and E than in their male counterparts.

Certainly the numbers of statistically significant differences between means of the sorted subgroups and those of the Total Yucatecans are too great to be called mere chance variations. That the subgroups are racially dissimilar is also shown by the differences in many non-mensurable traits, in blood-group affinities, in facial profile, and in certain social respects such as occupation, birthplace, and preferential mating.

This study has demonstrated the practicability of a method for resolving a racially mixed and heterogeneous population into racial subtypes. It is hoped that the results of the application of the method used in this study will help to do away with ill-defined ideas concerning the nature of race and will assist in making the study of race of practical utility in prosecution of the problems confronting mankind.

# APPENDIX

# APPENDIX

## TEETH

**Denture Measurements.** To Sr. Dr. Rafael Cervera L. of Mérida, Yucatan, the author is indebted for invaluable assistance
in procuring denture reproductions of Yucatecans. On returning
to the United States, the casts were turned over to Dr. Adelbert
Fernald of Boston, Mass., who further prepared the reproductions
for study and made the measurements here presented. Those on
the Eskimo and Pecos Indians are kindly lent by Dr. Fernald. The
denture measurements on American Whites were obtained by the
author from reproductions belonging to Dr. O. W. Brandhorst of
St. Louis. The dentures are for the most part those of dental
students carefully selected for normality.

Dr. Fernald chose the following list of measurements of dentures
as particularly significant: (The items refer to either upper or lower
dentures, except in the case of palate height.)

Breadth at M 1 and at M 2: transverse distance between buccal grooves of
    the molars in question.
Intercanine breadth: transverse distance between cutting edges of canines.
Palate height: distance from vault to dental occlusal surfaces between the
    second premolar and first permanent molar.
Incisor-M 1 and Incisor-M 2 lengths: antero-posterior distance from labial
    surface of central incisors to transverse line connecting buccal grooves of
    the molars in question.
Canine-M 1 and Canine-M 2 lengths: antero-posterior distance from trans-
    verse line connecting cutting edges of canines to transverse line connecting
    buccal grooves of the molars in question.
Incisor-Canine length: antero-posterior distance from labial surface of the
    central incisors to a transverse line connecting the cutting edges of the
    canines.

The table compares the means of these measurements in Yucatecans, American Whites, Eskimos, and in Pecos Indians. For only
the two former peoples are the numbers of cases involved sufficiently large to justify use of statistical constants. It is noteworthy
that the Yucatecan males exceed or are similar to the American
White males in all measurements of the upper denture except in

# APPENDIX

## DENTURE MEASUREMENTS
### MALES

| Upper | | Yucatecans | American Whites (Brandhorst) | Eskimos (Fernald) | Pecos (Fernald) |
|---|---|---|---|---|---|
| Breadth at M 1 | Mean | (16) 57.44 [1] | (37) 55.38 | (4) 58.0 | (10) 60.3 |
| | S. D. | 2.76 | 2.48 | | |
| | V. | 4.80 | 4.48 | | |
| Breadth at M 2 | | (14) 61.07 | (36) 61.03 | . . . | . . . |
| | | 1.79 | 2.53 | | |
| | | 2.93 | 4.15 | | |
| Intercanine breadth | | (31) 36.94 [1] | (37) 34.14 | (2) 38.5 | (10) 41.4 |
| | | 2.99 | 1.70 | | |
| | | 8.09 | 4.98 | | |
| Palate height | | (32) 20.16 | (37) 20.92 | (4) 18.2 | (10) 13.7 |
| | | 2.59 | 2.19 | | |
| | | 12.85 | 10.47 | | |
| Incisor, M 1 length | | (16) 30.25 | (37) 29.76 | (4) 29.0 | (10) 32.8 |
| | | 2.95 | 1.87 | | |
| | | 9.75 | 6.28 | | |
| Incisor, M 2 length | | (11) 41.73 | (36) 40.14 | . . . | . . . |
| | | 2.99 | 2.25 | | |
| | | 7.17 | 5.61 | | |
| Canine, M 1 length | | (16) 21.56 | (37) 21.62 | (4) 21.8 | (10) 24.1 |
| | | 1.41 | 1.30 | | |
| | | 6.54 | 6.01 | | |
| Canine, M 2 length | | (11) 33.45 | (36) 32.03 | . . . | . . . |
| | | 2.54 | 1.76 | | |
| | | 7.59 | 5.49 | | |
| Incisor, Canine length | | (30) 8.47 | (37) 8.14 | (4) 7.2 | (10) 8.7 |
| | | 1.88 | 1.45 | | |
| | | 22.20 | 17.81 | | |
| **Lower** | | | | | |
| Breadth at M 1 | Mean | (15) 51.00 | (37) 49.65 | (4) 51.0 | (10) 54.2 |
| | S. D. | 3.37 | 2.44 | | |
| | V. | 6.61 | 4.91 | | |
| Breadth at M 2 | | (14) 57.14 | (37) 55.92 | . . . | . . . |
| | | 3.98 | 2.73 | | |
| | | 6.97 | 4.88 | | |
| Intercanine breadth | | (33) 27.39 [1] | (37) 24.86 | (4) 29.5 | (10) 32.2 |
| | | 2.80 | 1.37 | | |
| | | 10.22 | 5.51 | | |
| Incisor, M 1 length | | (15) 24.47 | (37) 25.57 | (4) 26.5 | (10) 25.7 |
| | | 2.34 | 1.60 | | |
| | | 9.56 | 6.26 | | |

[1] Difference between Yucatecans and American Whites statistically significant.

## DENTURE MEASUREMENTS. (*Continued*)

| Lower | Yucatecans | American Whites (Brandhorst) | Eskimos (Fernald) | Pecos (Fernald) |
|---|---|---|---|---|
| Incisor, M 2 length | (14) 35.79 | (37) 36.24 | . . . | . . . |
| | 5.60 | 1.98 | | |
| | 15.71 | 5.46 | | |
| Canine, M 1 length | (16) 19.38 [1] | (37) 20.60 | (4) 18.8 | (10) 18.4 |
| | 1.65 | 1.37 | | |
| | 8.51 | 6.65 | | |
| Canine, M 2 length | (14) 30.21 | (37) 31.27 | . . . | . . . |
| | 4.70 | 1.80 | | |
| | 15.56 | 5.76 | | |
| Incisor, Canine length | (32) 5.44 | (37) 4.97 | (4) 7.8 | (10) 8.3 |
| | 1.37 | 1.17 | | |
| | 25.18 | 23.54 | | |

### FEMALES

| Upper | Yucatecans | American Whites (Brandhorst) | Eskimos (Fernald) |
|---|---|---|---|
| Breadth at M 1 | (5) 60.2 | (10) 52.9 | (4) 56.2 |
| Breadth at M 2 | (8) 60.8 | (8) 56.8 | . . . |
| Intercanine breadth | (12) 35.6 [1] | (10) 32.3 | (4) 38.5 |
| Palate height | (13) 19.5 | (10) 18.9 | (4) 18.8 |
| Incisor, M 1 length | (5) 31.2 | (10) 28.9 | (4) 30.2 |
| Incisor, M 2 length | (8) 41.8 | (8) 38.6 | . . . |
| Canine, M 1 length | (5) 23.2 | (10) 20.8 | (4) 23.2 |
| Canine, M 2 length | (7) 33.0 | (8) 30.8 | . . . |
| Incisor, Canine length | (13) 8.5 | (10) 8.1 | (4) 7.0 |
| **Lower** | | | |
| Breadth at M 1 | . . . | (10) 47.8 | (4) 51.0 |
| Breadth at M2 | (11) 55.0 | (9) 52.8 | . . . |
| Intercanine breadth | (13) 27.7 [1] | (10) 23.6 | (4) 33.2 |
| Incisor, M 1 length | . . . | (10) 24.8 | (4) 24.2 |
| Incisor, M 2 length | (10) 34.9 | (9) 34.7 | . . . |
| Canine, M 1 length | . . . | (10) 20.1 | (4) 16.2 |
| Canine, M 2 length | (10) 28.9 | (9) 30.1 | . . . |
| Incisor, Canine length | (13) 5.8 | (10) 4.7 | (4) 8.0 |

[1] Difference between Yucatecans and American Whites statistically significant.

palate height. However, the only statistically significant differences occur in breadth at M 1 and in intercanine breadth. The lower denture shows uniform excess in breadths on the part of the Yucatecans just as in the case of the upper, but of the breadths only the transverse diameter between the canines is statistically superior in the Yucatecans. It is interesting to note that the incisor-molar and canine-molar lengths of the lower denture are in all cases of lower value in the Yucatecan males; only the canine-M 1 length is significantly lower by statistical standards. Palate height differs insignificantly between the two groups.

The finding of broader dentures in Yucatecan males than in American White males is not unexpected, for previously there has been demonstrated a similar difference in breadth of face between Yucatecans and Spanish Whites. The various lengths of the upper and lower dentures are, however, statistically similar except in the lower canine-M 1 length, in which case the Whites are superior. It will also be recalled that head length is significantly greater in Spanish Whites than in the Yucatecans. It is reasonable to assume that some measure of positive correlation should occur between head length and denture length. The data on protrusion indices of facial points (Table 45) have no bearing on the actual length of denture, for the prognathism of the Yucatecans which causes greater protrusion in their case is the result of protrusion anteriorly of the denture as a whole rather than a lengthening of it.

The dentures of female Yucatecans and American Whites differ in the same way as do the males. Only in intercanine breadths of both uppers and lowers are the differences statistically significant. This occurs in spite of the small number in each series. In comparison with the other groups, the female Eskimos have broader dentures, but the lengths are of the same order of magnitude as those of the Whites and the Yucatecans. The same statement holds true for the males as well. The Pecos males exceed the other groups in all upper denture measurements and in the breadth dimensions of the lower denture. The length dimensions of the lower denture of the Pecos Indians are of approximately the same value as those of the compared groups. Compensation is effected in possession by the Pecos of the lowest average palate height given in the table. This may be due in some small degree to the great amount of wear which the Pecos dentures so frequently show. No great difference exists in palate heights of the Yucatecans and Whites of either sex.

One may summarize the preceding discussion of denture measurements by stating that intercanine breadth of the Yucatecans is significantly greater than in American Whites in both the upper and lower dentures of both sexes; that breadth at M 1 is greater in the upper denture of the Yucatecan males than in the Whites; that canine-M 1 length is significantly smaller in the lower denture of Yucatecan males than in the Whites. The numbers on which these statements are based are small, but, in absence of more extensive data, it may be concluded that Yucatecans have broader dentures than American Whites and a tendency toward shorter ones in the lower jaw. The table also suggests that the upper denture of the White males flares more at the second molars (in comparison to breadth at first molars) than in the case of the Yucatecans; this phenomenon in the table may however be accidental.

### TEETH MISSING

#### Males and Females

| Age | None | 1–3 | 4–8 | 8+ | No. |
|---|---|---|---|---|---|
| 18–20 | 51 | 7 | 2 | 0 | 60 |
| | 85.0% | 11.7% | 3.3% | 0.0% | |
| 21–29 | 55 | 23 | 11 | 0 | 89 |
| | 61.8% | 25.8% | 12.4% | 0.0% | |
| 30–39 | 21 | 22 | 13 | 3 | 59 |
| | 35.6% | 37.3% | 22.0% | 5.1% | |
| 40–54 | 10 | 16 | 27 | 14 | 67 |
| | 14.9% | 23.9% | 40.3% | 20.9% | |
| 55–χ | 3 | 4 | 9 | 13 | 29 |
| | 10.3% | 13.8% | 31.0% | 44.8% | |
| Total | | | | | 304 |

**Dental Caries and Missing Teeth.** On 304 individuals, both males and females, data are available concerning number of missing teeth. Presumably, the great majority of these teeth are missing because of dental caries. Various observers of the meat-eating Eskimos have noted the fine condition of the teeth of these people. More recently, it has been reported that those Eskimos who are living close to White settlements and who have access to the White man's food and especially to the canned variety, are showing a much higher incidence of caries than are other Eskimos of more remote districts. The Maya Indians of Yucatan have long been in contact with the White man. Whatever may have been the condition of the teeth of the pre-Columbian Mayas, it is certain that the teeth of present-day Yucatecans do not compare with the sound dentures of isolated Eskimos.

Even at the age of eighteen or twenty, only eighty-five per cent of Yucatecans have lost no teeth. With progressive age, the number of missing teeth increases until, at the age of fifty-five or older, more than seventy-five per cent have lost four or more, and forty-five per cent have missing eight or more.

From the forty-five denture reproductions made by Sr. Dr. Cervera L. and examined by Dr. Fernald, one may glean certain information concerning the association of caries and missing teeth. In the case of each individual shown in the table, the number of missing teeth were added to the number of teeth possessing cavities. It is

### MISSING TEETH + CAVITIES

#### MALES AND FEMALES

| Age | None | 1–3 | 4–8 | 8+ | No. |
|---|---|---|---|---|---|
| 18–20 | 3 | 2 | 1 | 1 | 7 |
| | 43 % | 29 % | 14 % | 14 % | |
| 21–29 | 4 | 4 | 6 | 1 | 15 |
| | 27 % | 27 % | 40 % | 7 % | |
| 30–39 | 2 | 4 | 5 | 2 | 13 |
| | 15 % | 31 % | 38 % | 15 % | |
| 40–54 | 2 | 0 | 2 | 2 | 6 |
| | 33 % | 0 % | 33 % | 33 % | |
| 55–χ | 0 | 0 | 2 | 2 | 4 |
| | 0 % | 0 % | 50 % | 50 % | |
| Total | | | | | 45 |

assumed that the number of missing teeth represents the number rendered functionless by caries, while the number of teeth with cavities represents the number of teeth of impaired function well on their way to become totally functionless. Thus the combined number of missing teeth plus teeth with cavities gives an index of the number of teeth affected by caries at the time of examination or in the past. The trend of the table is similar to that which refers only to missing teeth, except that fewer sound teeth are found in any age group. Instead of eighty-five per cent of sound teeth in the 18–20 age group of the preceding table, only forty-three per cent are now found; rather than seventy-five per cent with four or more teeth missing in the 55–X group, there are now seen one hundred per cent of that age group who have four or more missing or carious teeth. The number of cases here considered is indeed small, yet the indication of high incidence of dental caries and the consequent loss of teeth is certain.

Pickerill (1912) makes the following statements concerning dental caries:

> Mummery and Miller believed that a larger consumption of meat explained the difference (of groups in relative immunity to caries). This theory, although a factor, must *per se* fall to the ground, since both Mummery's and Patrick's figures show that several meat-eating races have a higher incidence of caries than non-meat-eating. Also it is of the very highest significance that in Patrick's list the great rice-eating, almost vegetarian races of South-Eastern Asia should show the least incidence of caries: out of 2000 teeth, only 2 per cent were carious. . . . The number of individuals affected by dental caries (among the colonials of Australia and New Zealand, who eat enormous quantities of meat) is estimated to be from 90 to 95 per cent (by the Australian and New Zealand Dental Associations). . . .
>
> There are two general principles to be found running through the dietaries of all the natural races. They are — firstly, *variety*, and secondly, *sapidity*. The constant inclusion of articles in the food which have a direct stimulating effect upon the salivary glands is the one and only link which connects up all the races showing a relative immunity to caries. It is common alike to dwellers in the Arctic and Equatorial regions, it is found in meat-eating and in vegetarian tribes, it is present in both low and high types of uncivilized man. Although a variety of sapid substances are used, the ones most frequently recurring are acid in reaction, chiefly fruits and berries: these are the very stimulants which produce the most profuse and the most alkaline flow of saliva, and to this latter I think we are justified in ascribing the relative immunity found in the races which have been considered.

Whether or not Pickerill's thesis is generally accepted, his theory fits the case of the rural Yucatecans. For only a small part of each year is a variety of foods available for consumption. The *tortilla* made of corn is for many the only article of diet for considerable periods. That the diet of rural Yucatecans is not a balanced one is indicated by the prevalence of pellagra in the population. Furthermore, fruits and berries are not easily available at all times of year. They are rather occasional delicacies, not constantly used articles of diet. Meat is eaten, but not daily.

It appears that the physical environment works against the possibility for the inhabitants of Yucatan of Pickerill's two requirements of variety and sapidity of food. Yucatan lies within the Tropic of Cancer, but is far from typically tropical in its vegetation. It is a dry country for six months of the year. It may very

well be that the climatic effect on the food supply has a great deal
to do with the high incidence of dental caries in Yucatan.

**Wear of Teeth.** Concerning this phenomenon, Hrdlička (1920)
states:

> A valuable indication as to advancing age is furnished to us by the wear of
> the teeth. In Whites, this seldom commences before the thirty-fifth or is
> marked before the fiftieth year of age, and in many individuals of the more
> cultured classes it may remain slight up to old age; but among grain-eating,
> primitive peoples, such as American Indians, wear may commence even before
> the adult life has been reached, be very marked at fifty, and reach an extreme
> grade after sixty-five.

### WEAR OF TEETH

#### MALES AND FEMALES

| Age | None | sm | + | ++, +++ | No. |
|---|---|---|---|---|---|
| 18–20 | 0 | 43 | 9 | 1 | 53 |
| | 0.0% | 81.1% | 17.0% | 1.9% | |
| 21–29 | 3 | 30 | 36 | 5 | 74 |
| | 4.1% | 40.5% | 48.6% | 6.8% | |
| 30–39 | 0 | 9 | 22 | 15 | 46 |
| | 0.0% | 19.6% | 47.8% | 32.6% | |
| 40–54 | 0 | 3 | 16 | 42 | 61 |
| | 0.0% | 4.9% | 26.3% | 68.9% | |
| 55+ | 0 | 1 | 0 | 24 | 25 |
| | 0.0% | 4.0% | 0.0% | 96.0% | |
| Total | | | | | 259 |

In many American-Indian groups, wear has been attributed principally to the presence, in the ground grain used for food, of stone
fragments from the grinding stones. The use of manual stone
grinders in Yucatan is fast giving way to the use of food-choppers
and community power mills, but it is probable that many of the
present generation in rural Yucatan (especially the older individuals) have eaten much stone-ground corn. In any case, in wear of
teeth the Yucatecans more than fulfill Hrdlička's generalization
quoted above, for in the age groups of forty or older, approximately
seventy per cent exhibit marked wear of teeth.

**Shovel Incisors.** Hrdlička has noted that the "ventral surface
of upper incisors may be marked by shovel-shaped concavity with
pronounced rim, which is characteristic of the American Indian,
occurs occasionally in other yellow-brown people, but is rare or less

## SHOVEL INCISORS

### MALES AND FEMALES

| Age | 0 | sm | + | ++, +++ | No. |
|---|---|---|---|---|---|
| 18–20 .................... | 2 | 1 | 5 | 45 | 53 |
| | 3.8% | 1.9% | 9.4% | 84.9% | |
| 21–29 .................... | 3. | 7 | 16 | 48 | 74 |
| | 4.1% | 9.4% | 21.6% | 64.9% | |
| 30–39 .................... | 1 | 4 | 11 | 29 | 45 |
| | 2.2% | 8.9% | 24.4% | 64.4% | |
| 40–54 .................... | 3 | 12 | 15 | 27 | 57 |
| | 5.3% | 21.1% | 26.3% | 47.4% | |
| 55+ ..................... | 3 | 4 | 7 | 8 | 22 |
| | 13.6% | 18.2% | 31.8% | 36.4% | |
| Total | | | | | 251 |

frequent in other races." The Maya Indians and Yucatecans of mixed blood show frequent incidence of this condition, and thus indicate their relation to other American Indian groups. Aside from confirming this expected finding, the most interesting suggestion from the table is the indication that the character in its moderate or pronounced form tends to become less marked with age. The regular trend of decreasing incidence of the " + + " and " + + + " category with increasing age does not appear to be an accidental phenomenon.

# BIBLIOGRAPHY

# BIBLIOGRAPHY

ARANZADI, T. DE and HOYOS SAINZ, L.
  1894 a. "Vorläufige Mittheilung zur Anthropologie von Spanien," *Archiv für Anthropologie*, Bd. XXII, S. 425.

ARANZADI, T. DE.
  1894 b. "Observaciones antropomètricas en los Cacereños," *Actas de la Sociedad Española de Historia Natural*, segunda serie, t. III (XXIII), Sesion de Enero.

BARRAS DE ARAGON, FRANCISCO DE LAS.
  1923. "Notas sobre indices obtenidos de medidas tomadas en vivo, de sujetos naturales de la provincia de Sevilla y sus limitrofes," *Memorias de la Sociedad Española de Antropologia*, t. II, Memoria XIII, Sesion 12, p. 21. Madrid.
  1925. "Sobre indices de varias provincias de España, obtenidos con medidas tomadas del vivo," *Asociacion Española para el Progreso de las Ciencias*, t. VI, p. 115. Congreso de Coimbra.
  1928. *Personal Communication.* (Anthropometric data from Spain in general.)

BEAN, R. B.
  1911. "Heredity of Hair Form among the Filipinos," *American Naturalist*, Vol. XLV.

BENEDICT, F. G.
  1928. "Basal Metabolism Data on Normal Men and Women with Some Considerations on the Use of Prediction Standards," *American Journal of Physiology*, Vol. LXXXV, No. 3, July.

BOAS, FRANZ.
  1928. *Anthropology and Modern Life.* W. W. Norton and Co., Inc. New York.

CASTLE, W. E.
  1920. *Genetics and Eugenics.* Harvard University Press, Cambridge.
  1926. "Biological and Social Consequences of Race Crossing," *American Journal of Physical Anthropology*, Vol. IX, No. 2, p. 145.

CHARNAY, D.
  1887. *The Ancient Cities of the New World.* Translation by Gonino and Conant. Chapman and Hall, Ltd. London.

COCA, A. F. and DEIBERT, F. O.
  1923. "Blood groups among American Indians," *Journal of Immunology*, Vol. VIII, No. 6, p. 487.

COLE, LEON J.
 1910. "The Caverns and People of Northern Yucatan," *Bulletin of the American Geographical Society*, Vol. XLII, May, p. 321.

COON, C. S.
 1929. *Personal Communication.* (Metric data on the Andalusian Moors.)

DAVENPORT, C. B.
 1913. *Heredity of Skin Color in Negro-White Crosses.* Carnegie Institution of Washington, Washington.

DAVENPORT, C. B. and LOVE, A. G.
 1921. *The Medical Department of the United States in the World War, Vol. XV, Part I, Army Anthropology.* Government Printing Office, Washington.

DENIKER, J.
 1900. *The Races of Man.* Walter Scott, Ltd., London.

DIAZ DEL CASTILLO, BERNAL.
 1916. *The True History of the Conquest of New Spain* Edited by Genaro Garcia. Translated by A. P. Maudslay. Hakluyt Society, London.

DONNISON, C. P.
 1929. "Blood Pressure in the African Native. Its Bearing on the Etiology of Hyperpiesia and Arteriosclerosis," *The Lancet*, Vol. CCXVI, No. 5497, January 5, p. 6.

DRAPER, GEORGE.
 1924. *Human Constitution.* W. B. Saunders Co., Philadelphia.

DREYER, GEORGES.
 1921. *The Assessment of Physical Fitness.* Paul B. Hoeber, New York.

DUNN, L. C.
 1923. "Some Results of Race Mixture in Hawaii," *Eugenics in Race and State*, Vol. II, Scientific Papers of the Second International Congress of Eugenics. Williams and Wilkins Co., Baltimore.

DUNN, L. C. and TOZZER, A. M. (Data collected by latter.)
 1928. "An Anthropometric Study of Hawaiians of Pure and Mixed Blood," *Papers of the Peabody Museum of American Archaeology and Ethnology*, Harvard University, Vol. XI, No. 3. Published by the Museum, Cambridge.

FLEMING, H. C.
 1924. "Medical Observations on the Zuñi Indians," *Contributions from the Museum of the American Indian*, Heye Foundation, Vol. VII, No. 2. Published by the Museum, New York.

GORING, CHARLES.
 1913. *The English Convict.* His Majesty's Stationery Office, London.

HERSKOVITS, MELVILLE J.
  1926. "Correlation of Length and Breadth of Head in American Negroes," *American Journal of Physical Anthropology*, Vol. IX, No. 1, p. 87.
  1928. *The American Negro.* Alfred A. Knopf, New York.

HOOTON, E. A.
  1923. "Observations and Queries as to the Effect of Race Mixture on Certain Physical Characteristics," *Eugenics in Race and State,* Vol. II, Scientific Papers of the Second International Congress of Eugenics. Williams and Wilkins Co., Baltimore.
  1926. "Methods of Racial Analysis," *Science*, Vol. LXIII, No. 1621, January 22, p. 75.

HRDLIČKA, ALEŠ.
  1908. *Physiological and Medical Observations among the Indians of Southwestern United States and Northern Mexico.* Government Printing Office, Washington.
  1909. "On the Stature of the Indians of the Southwest and of Northern Mexico," *Putnam Anniversary Volume*, p. 405.
  1920. *Anthropometry.* The Wistar Institute of Anatomy and Biology, Philadelphia.

HUNTLEY, L. G.
  1928. "Geological and Archaeological Records of the Yucatan Peninsula," *Science*, Vol. LXVIII, No. 1760, September 21, p. 264.

JOYCE, THOMAS A.
  1927. *Maya and Mexican Art*, p. 162. The Studio, London.

MACLEOD, G., CROFTS, E. E., and BENEDICT, F. G.
  1925. "The Basal Metabolism of Some Orientals," *American Journal of Physiology*, Vol. LXXIII, No. 2, July.

MARTIN, RUDOLF.
  1914. *Lehrbuch der Anthropologie.* Gustav Fischer, Jena.

MORLEY, S. G.
  1915. *An Introduction to the Study of Maya Hieroglyphs.* Bulletin 57, Bureau of American Ethnology. Government Printing Office, Washington.

MOSS, W. L. and KENNEDY, J. A.
  1929. "Blood Groups in Peru, Santo Domingo, Yucatan, and among the Mexicans at the Blue Ridge Prison Farm in Texas," *Journal of Immunology*, Vol. XVI, No. 2, February.

OLORIZ Y AGUILERA, D. FEDERICO.
  1894. *Distribucion Geografica del Indice Cefalico en España.* Madrid. (Also in *Boletin de la Sociedad Geografica*, XXXVI, 389.)
  1896. *La Talla Humana en España.* Discursos leidos en la Real Academia de Medicina. Madrid.

254 BIBLIOGRAPHY

PEARSON, KARL.
1906. "Note on the Significant or Non-Significant Character of a Sub-sample Drawn from a Sample," *Biometrika*, Vol. V, p. 181.

PICKERILL, H. P.
1912. *The Prevention of Dental Caries and Oral Sepsis.* Bailliere, Tindall and Cox, London.

PIGNET.
1901. "Du coefficient de robusticité," *Le Bulletin Medical*, Vol. XV, No. 33. Paris.

ROCHESTER, ANNA.
1923. *Infant Mortality: results of a field study in Baltimore, Maryland, based on births in one year.* United States Department of Labor, Children's Bureau, Publication No. 119. Government Printing Office, Washington.

SAPPER, KARL.
1905. "Der gegenwärtige Stand der ethnographischen Kenntnis von Mittelamerika," *Archiv für Anthropologie*, Neue Folge, Bd. III, S. 1.

SCHULTZ, ADOLF H.
1918. "Studies in the Sex-Ratio in Man," *Biological Bulletin*, Vol. XXXIV, No. 4.
1921. "Sex Incidence in Abortions." Publication 275, Carnegie Institution. Washington.

SHAPIRO, H. L.
1926. *A Study of Race Mixture as Exemplified in the Descendants of Tahitians and the English Mutineers of the Bounty.* Doctor's thesis, Harvard University.

SINNOTT, E. W. and DUNN, L. C.
1925. *Principles of Genetics.* McGraw-Hill Book Co., New York.

SNYDER, LAWRENCE H.
1926. "Human Blood Groups: Their Inheritance and Racial Significance," *American Journal of Physical Anthropology*, Vol. IX, No. 2, p. 233.

SPINDEN, H. J.
1913. "A Study of Maya Art," *Memoirs of the Peabody Museum of American Archaeology and Ethnology*, Vol. VI. Harvard University. Published by the Museum, Cambridge.
1921. "Yellow Fever First and Last," *World's Work*, XLIII, 169.
1928. "The Population of Ancient America," *Geographical Review*, Vol. XVIII. October, p. 641.

STARR, FREDERICK.
1902. *Physical Characters of Indians of Southern Mexico.* University of Chicago Press, Chicago.
1908. *In Indian Mexico.* Forbes and Co., Chicago.

STATE OF YUCATAN, MEXICO, DIRECCION GENERAL DE SALUBRIDAD E HIGIENE.
1918. *La Higiene,* Año I, Num. 1. Mérida, Yucatan, Mexico.

STEGGERDA, M. and BENEDICT, F. G.
1928. "The Basal Metabolism of Some Browns and Blacks in Jamaica," *American Journal of Physiology,* Vol. LXXXV, No. 3, July.

STEGGERDA, M., CRANE, J., and STEELE, M. D.
1929. "One hundred measurements and observations on one hundred Smith College students," *American Journal of Physical Anthropology,* Vol. XIII, No. 2, p. 189.

STEPHENS, JOHN L.
1843. *Incidents of Travel in Yucatan.* Two volumes. Harper and Brothers, New York.

SULLIVAN, LOUIS R.
1920. "Anthropometry of the Siouan Tribes," *Anthropological Papers of the American Museum of Natural History,* Vol. XXIII, Part III. New York.

TOZZER, ALFRED M.
1907. *A Comparative Study of the Mayas and Lacandones.* Macmillan Company, New York.

UNITED STATES DEPARTMENT OF COMMERCE, BUREAU OF THE CENSUS.
1929. *Birth, Stillbirth, and Infant Mortality Statistics: 1927, Part II.* Government Printing Office, Washington.
1929. *Mortality Statistics: 1925, Part II.* Government Printing Office, Washington.

WILLIAMS, G. D., and BENEDICT, F. G.
1928. "The Basal Metabolism of Mayas in Yucatan," *American Journal of Physiology,* Vol. LXXXV, No. 3, July.

WOODBURY, ROBERT MORSE.
1925. *Causal Factors in Infant Mortality: a statistical study based on investigations in eight cities.* United States Department of Labor, Children's Bureau, Publication No. 142. Government Printing Office, Washington.

## BIBLIOGRAPHIC NOTE

To two investigators in the field of physical anthropology I owe special thanks for comparative material.

Sr. Profesor Francisco de las Barras de Aragon, of the Universidad Central at Madrid, lent me unpublished somatological data on Spanish males. Complete metrical records of Spanish subjects are comparatively rare. I wish to take this means of expressing my gratitude to the man who has made this invaluable material available to me. The loaned records consist of cephalic and facial measurements of seventy-nine Spanish university students. Fifty-seven of them are eighteen years of age or older. Twenty-two, aged seventeen, whose means do not vary significantly from those of the older age group, were added to the former series. All parts of Spain are represented in the nativity of the subjects, but the majority of the young men come from that country's western provinces.

Dr. Carleton S. Coon of Harvard University was kind enough to supply me with unpublished material on the Andalusian Moors of Sheshawen, a city of Morocco. Dr. Coon states: "The inhabitants of Sheshawen are for the most part descendants of refugees from Granada who were expelled from Spain in the time of Ferdinand and Isabella. It is likely that the Granadan Moors had more Arab than Berber blood in them. I enquired very carefully into genealogies and found only one of the group measured to have had a grandparent from outside — in this case a Riffian. If there has been any race mixture, it has been with Riffians rather than with Jeballys or Arabs, since the Riffians come nearer to their self-imposed social standards."

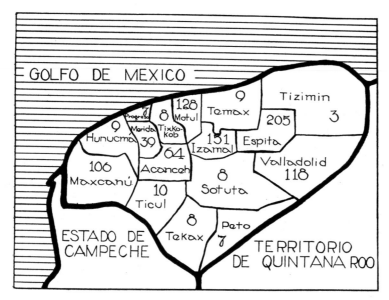

Map of the state of Yucatan showing birthplace of members of the Yucatecan male series

## Plate II

**HARVARD UNIVERSITY**                                    **ANTHROPOMETRY**

No .............. Sex ..... ........... Race, Nationality, or Tribe ..............................................................

Age ............ Date ............ Birthplace ..................................................................................

Time of day ......................... Name .......................................................................................

Occupation ........................ Race, Nationality, or Tribe of Father ................................................

Married ........ .......................... Race, Nationality, or Tribe of Mother ...........................................

Father or Mother of .......................................................................................................

Son or Daughter of.................................................................. Brother or Sister of...........................

### MEASUREMENTS

**(1–6: anthropometer)**
1. Stature ............................. ..
2. Acromial ht.............................................
3. Sternal ht. ......... ...... ........
4. Sitting ht............................ ............
5. Sternal ht. sitting ...............................
6. (Span) ................................................

**(7–13: large sliding caliper)**
7. Acromion-radiale ..............................
8. Radiale-dactylion .............................
9. Tibiale-sphyrion ................................
10. Biacromial ......................................
11. Bi-iliac ......................................
12. Chest breadth ..................................
13. Chest depth ...................................

**(14–15: steel tape)**
14. (Chest girth) ..............................
15. (Head circum.) ............................

**(16–20: spreading compass)**
16. Head-length ...............................
17. Head-breadth .............................
18. Bizygomatic ...............................
19. Bigonial ....................................
20. Min. frontal ...............................

**(21–26: sliding caliper)**
21. Total facial ht. ..........................
22. Upper facial ht. ........................
23. Nose height ...............................
24. Nose breadth .............................
25. (Ear length) .............................
26. (Ear breadth) ............................

### INDICES

2/1 Rel. shoulder ht. ............................
10/1 Rel. shoulder br. ...........................
4/1 Rel. sitting ht. ...............................
7+8/1–4 Intermembral
11/10 Hip-shoulder .............................
6/1 Rel. span ......................................
17/16 Cephalic ..................................
31/16 Length-height ............................
31/17 Breadth-height ..........................
20/17 Fronto-parietal .........................
18/17 Cephalo-facial ..........................
21/18 Total facial ..............................
22/18 Upper facial .............................
24/23 Nasal .......................................
20/18 Zygo-frontal .............................
19/18 Zygo-gonial ..............................
40/36 Oral protrusion .........................
42/36 Gnathic .....................................

| | radius | angle | |
|---|---|---|---|
| 27. Inion | radius...................... | angle........................ | |
| 28. 90° | radius...................... | angle........................ | |
| 29. Opisthocranion | radius...................... | angle........................ | |
| 30. ca. Lambda | radius...................... | angle............. . ........ | |
| 31. Vertex. | radius...................... | angle........................ | |
| 32. ca. Bregma | radius...................... | angle........................ | |
| 33. Crinion | radius...................... | angle........................ | |
| 34. Metopion | radius...................... | angle........................ | |
| 35. Glabella | radius...................... | angle........................ | |
| 36. Nasion | radius...................... | angle........................ | |
| 37. Rhinale | radius...................... | angle........................ | |
| 38. Pronasale | radius...................... | angle........................ | |
| 39. Subnasale | radius...................... | angle........................ | |
| 40. Labrale sup. | radius...................... | angle........................ . ..... | |
| 41. Labrale inf. | radius...................... | angle........................ | |
| 42. Prosthion | radius...................... | angle........................ | |
| 43. Inf. incis. pt. | radius...................... | angle........................ | |
| 44. Bromentale | radius...................... | angle........................ | |
| 45. Menton | radius...................... | angle........................ | |
| 46. Prozygion | radius...................... | angle........................ | |

**(27–50: radiometer)**

### PHYSIOLOGICAL

Weight.............................. Pulse .........................
Temperature...................... Respiration .................
Blood pressure.................... Basal metab. ...............
Squeeze: r............................... l.........................
Skin color no........................... Blood group...............

### PSYCHOLOGICAL

.............................................................................
.............................................................................
.............................................................................
.............................................................................
.............................................................................
.............................................................................
.............................................................................
.............................................................................
.............................................................................
.............................................................................
.............................................................................
.............................................................................

lat. distance ......................................................

### ASYMMETRY

| | breadth | half br. | mid. face line |
|---|---|---|---|
| 47. Head-breadth | breadth...................... | half br. ............ ........ | mid. face line............................. |
| 48. Min. frontal | breadth...................... | half·br. ............. _...... | mid. face line............................ |
| 49. Bizygomatic | breadth...................... | half br. .......... ........ | mid. face line............................ |
| 50. Bigonial | breadth...................... | half br. ............ ....... | mid. face line...... .................... |

*Underscore following if data have been obtained:*
Photographs: frontal, profile; hair sample, mouth cast, blood sample, face cast, foot-print, hand-print.

Record Blank

## Plate II

### OBSERVATIONS

(To be graded according to average values in adult male Europeans.  Underscore and use following symbols: — = absent, undeveloped, none; sl. = slight, very small; sm. = submedium, small, few; + = average, medium, several; + + = above average, large, pronounced, many; + + + = great, very many, extraordinary development; ? = not observable.)

SKIN: Color: forehead..................... breast..................... volar surface of forearm...... ........ .....

Texture: coarse, medium, fine; dry, medium, oily

Freckles: no................................ size.... ................................. location.................................

Moles: pigmented, hairy: no.......................... size.......................... . location...........................

HAIR: Form: straight, low waves, deep waves, curly, frizzly, woolly

Texture: coarse, medium, fine; dry, medium, oily

Quantity: head..................... moustache . . .............. beard..................... body.......................

Color: dark: black, dark brown; medium: reddish brown, light brown; light: ash-blond, golden, red; grayness: degree.......................white.

Whorls: number.................................... .................................. location..................................

EYES: Color: dark: black, dark brown, light brown; mixed: blue-brown, gray-brown, green-brown, yellow-brown; light: light blue, dark blue.

Iris: homogeneous, rayed, zoned, speckled; arcus senilis...................................................

Sclera: clear, speckled, yellow, blood-shot

Folds: complete Mongoloid......................... epicanthus..................... median....................

external.........................

Palpebral opening: height................................. obliquity..................................

EYEBROWS: thickness.................. concurrency.................. lateral extension ....................

BROW–RIDGES: median, continuous: size.................. prominence of glabella..................

FOREHEAD: height .............. breadth ............. slope.............bosses, med. eminence..............

NOSE: Nasion depression........................... Nasal root: ht...................... br............................

Nasal profile: concave, straight, convex, concavo-convex

Nasal tip: thickness......................................... elevation, depression .......................................

Nasal wings: compressed, medium, flaring

Septum: str., convex, concavo-convex; inclination: up, down.........deflection: r., l.,............

Nostrils: angle: acute, obtuse; narrow oval, broad oval, round: frontal visibility..................

lateral visibility........................

LIPS: Integumental: thickness........................... Membranous: thickness.........................

eversion..................... Lip seam............ . ........

PROGNATHISM: Alveolar.......................... facial......................... dental....................

CHIN: prominence............... .... median, bilateral    MALARS: prominence........ ..........

CHEEKS: fullness............................ GONIAL ANGLES: prominence............................

WRINKLING.........................

TEETH: Eruption: complete, unerupted....................................................................

Wear...................... Caries.......................... Lost..........................................

Shovel incisors....................... Cusp formulae..........................................................

Bite: under, edge-to-edge, slight over, marked over

Anomalies: number.................................................... form..............................

PALATE: shape............................................. .......... br.............................................. ht............................

EARS: Lobe: size.............. attached, free.  Roll of helix............. Darwin's point................

Antihelix: prominence.................. . ......................... Ear protrusion.........................

TEMPORAL FULLNESS........................... OCCIPITAL PROTRUSION......................

LAMBDOID FLATTENING.................... ASYMMETRY: Cranial, r., l., .......................

Facial: r., l.,......................... NECK: length........................ thickness......................

SHOULDERS: slope..................... SCAPULAE: Vertebral borders: str., concave, convex

CHEST DEVELOPMENT....................... BREASTS IN WOMEN: Shape: disk, cone, hemisphere, pendent. Size.................. BACK: Skoliosis................ Lumbar curve..............

ABDOMEN: prominence..................... BUTTOCKS.................... THIGHS...............

CALVES........................ FOOT ARCH..................... HEEL PROJECTION....................

HALLUX: Size.................. Interval.................. GENERAL MUSCULATURE................

FATTY DEPOSITS.......................

STATE OF HEALTH..................................................................................................

ANOMALIES ....... . . ....................................................................................................

PATHOLOGICAL ................................................................................................................

Record Blank

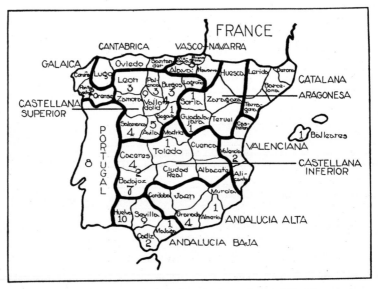

Map of the Spanish peninsula showing the provenience of some of Cortes' companions
in the conquest of Mexico

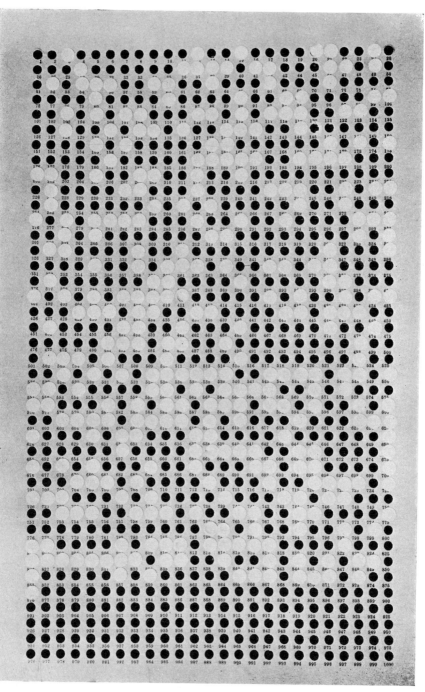

Sorting card

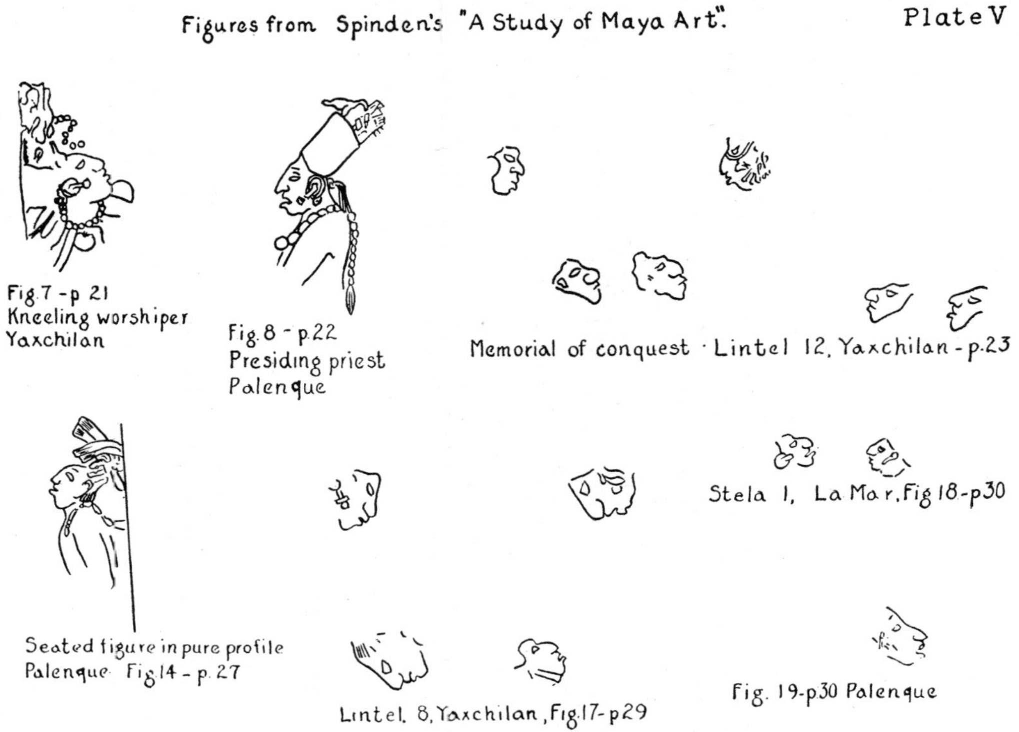

## Figures from Spinden's "A Study of Maya Art".

### Plate V

Fig 7 - p 21
Kneeling worshiper
Yaxchilan

Fig. 8 - p.22
Presiding priest
Palenque

Memorial of conquest · Lintel 12, Yaxchilan - p.23

Stela 1, La Mar, Fig 18-p.30

Fig. 19-p30 Palenque

Seated figure in pure profile
Palenque Fig.14 - p. 27

Lintel. 8, Yaxchilan, Fig.17-p29

Figures from Spinden's *A Study of Maya Art.*

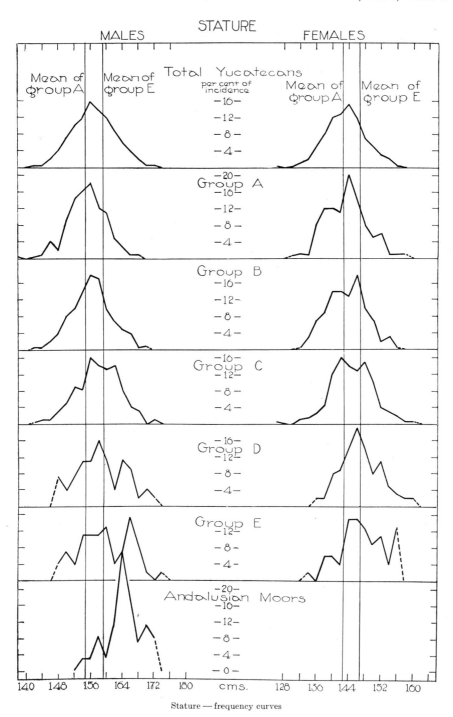

Stature — frequency curves

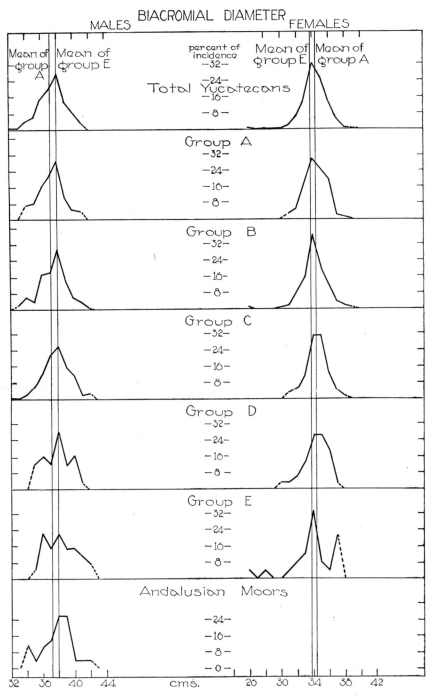

Biacromial diameter — frequency curves

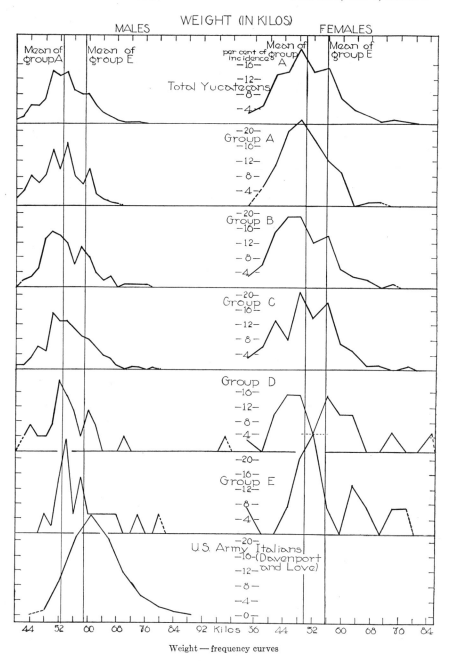

Weight — frequency curves

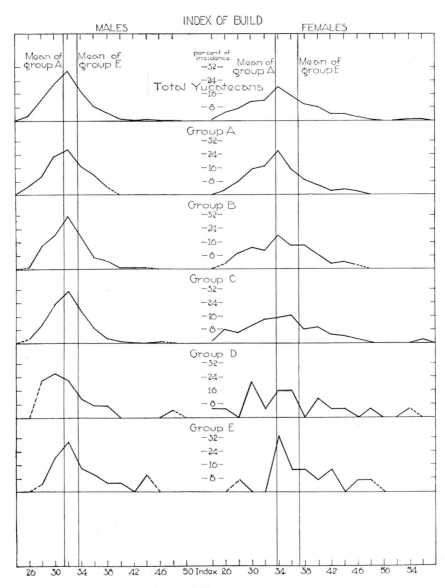

Index of build — frequency curves

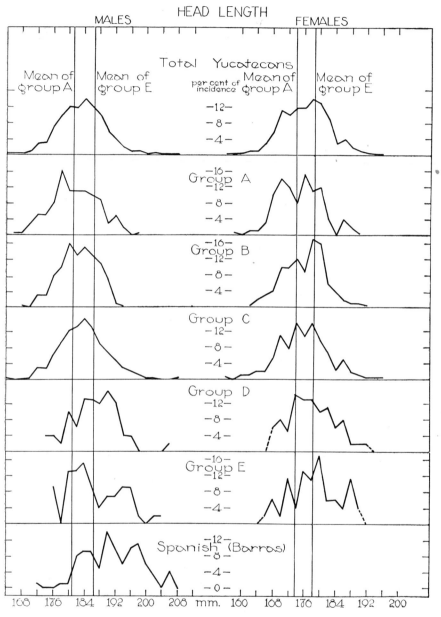

Head length — frequency curves

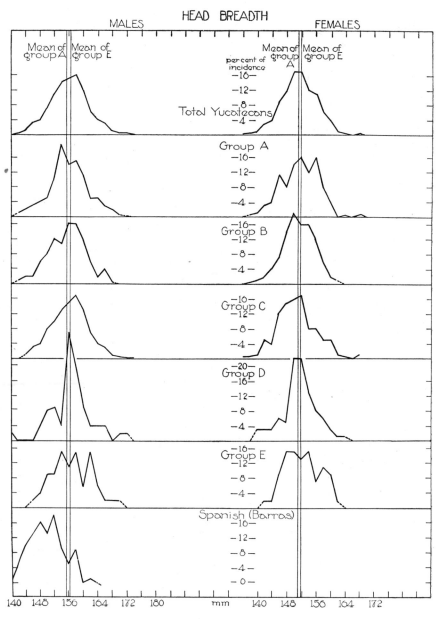

Head breadth — frequency curves

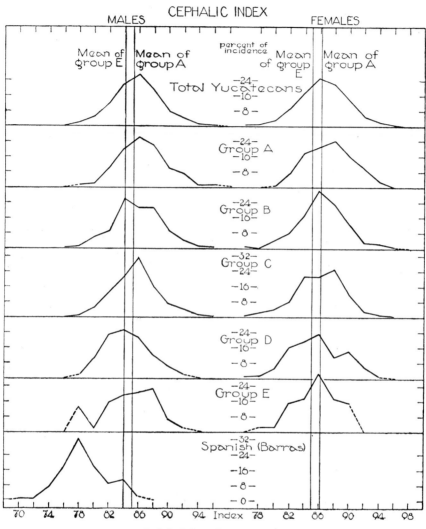

Cephalic Index — frequency curves

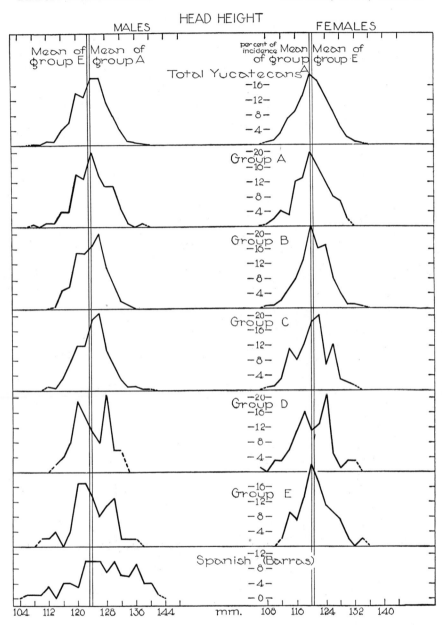

Head height — frequency curves

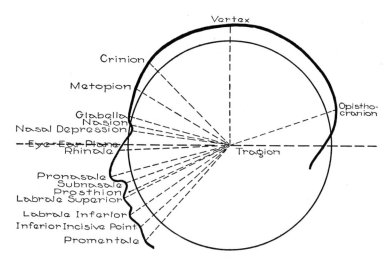

Radii used in calculation of protrusion indices of cephalic and facial points

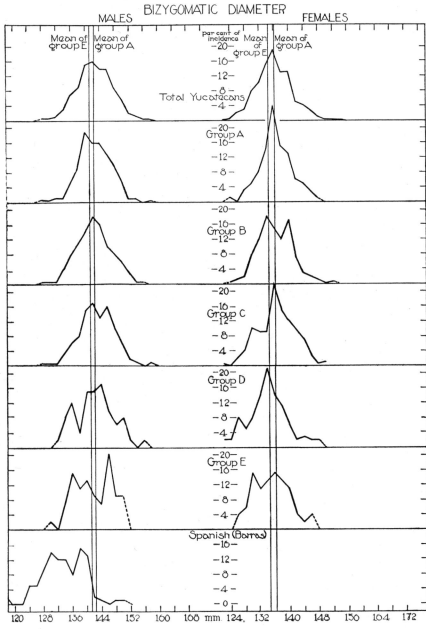

Bizygomatic diameter — frequency curves

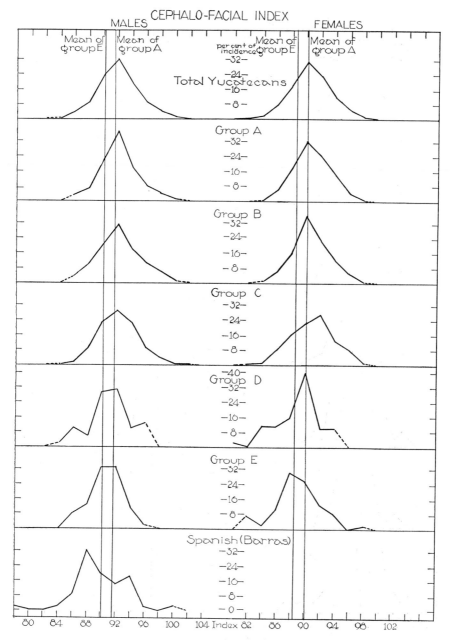

Cephalo-facial Index — frequency curves

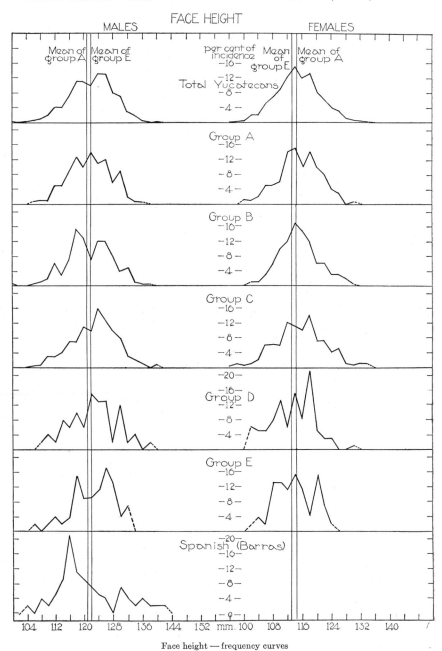

Face height — frequency curves

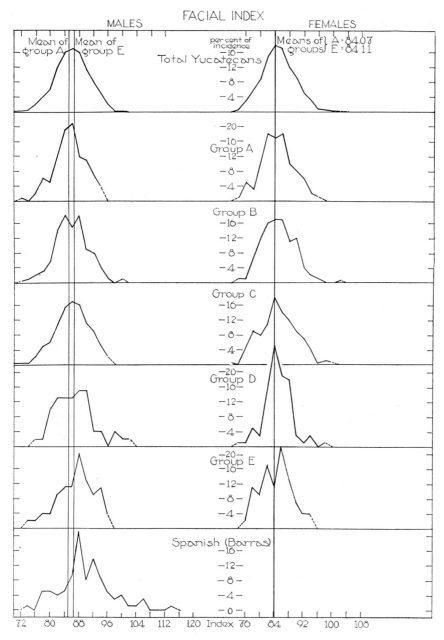

FACIAL INDEX

MALES

FEMALES

Mean of Group A | Mean of Group E

per cent of incidence

Total Yucatecans

Means of A = 84.07 groups E = 84.11

Group A

Group B

Group C

Group D

Group E

Spanish (Barras)

72  80  88  96  104  112  120  Index  76  84  92  100  108

Facial Index — frequency curves

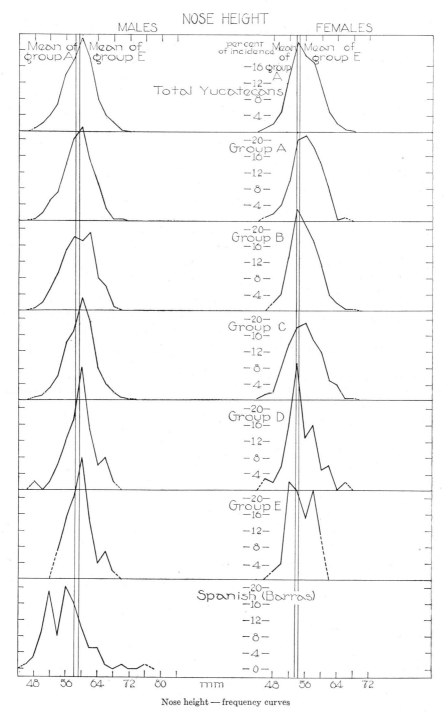

Nose height — frequency curves

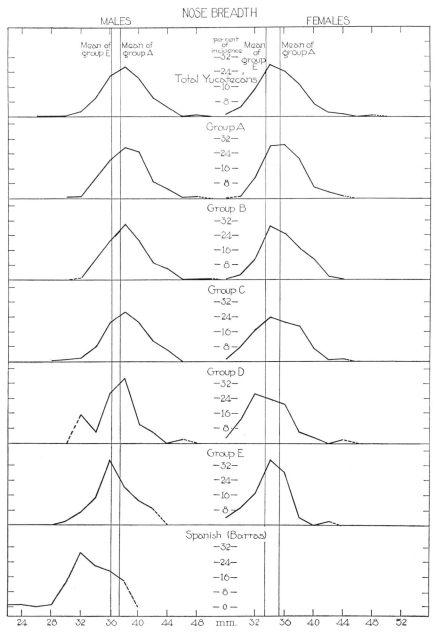

Nose breadth — frequency curves

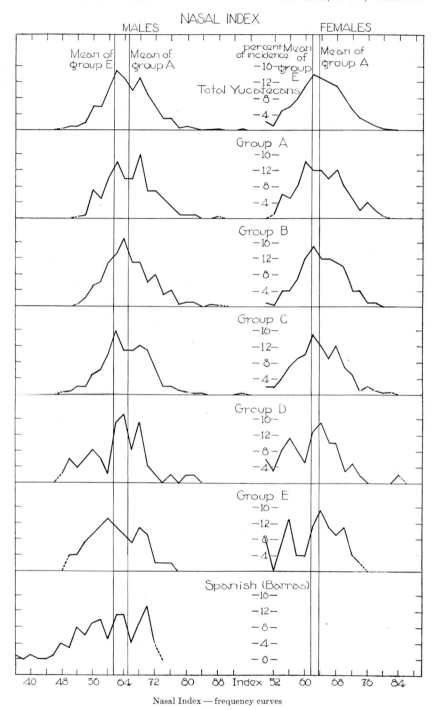

Nasal Index — frequency curves

PEABODY MUSEUM PAPERS

Bureau of International Research
Harvard University and Radcliffe College

No..................

## QUESTIONNAIRE

**Sociological Data**

| | Father | Mother | Children in Order of Age |
|---|---|---|---|

1. NAME ............ F............ M............ 1................ 2................ 3................ 4................

2. AGE (Indicate age at death by parentheses)

    F............ M............ 1................ 2................ 3................ 4................

3. OCCUPATION ............ F............ M............ 1................ 2................ 3................ 4................

4. Amounts earned (monthly) ............ F............ M............ 1................ 2................ 3................ 4................

5. ............ F............ M............ 1................ 2................ 3................ 4................

6. ............ F............ M............ 1................ 2................ 3................ 4................

7. ............ F............ M............ 1................ 2................ 3................ 4................

8. ............ F............ M............ 1................ 2................ 3................ 4................

9. ............ F............ M............ 1................ 2................ 3................ 4................

10. EDUCATION (State number of years of schooling, and highest grade of institution attended. $P$ = primary, $G$ = grammar school, $H$ = high school, $C$ = college.)

    F............ M............ 1................ 2................ 3................ 4................

11. SPECIAL INTERESTS ............ F............ M............ 1................ 2................ 3................ 4................

12. DISEASES ($wh$ = whooping cough, $me$ = measles, $mu$ = mumps, $ch$ = chicken pox, $sc$ = scarlet fever, $dip$ = diphtheria, $sm$ = small pox, $ma$ = malaria, $pn$ = pneumonia, $br$ = bronchitis, $fu$ = influenza, etc.).

    F............ M............ 1................ 2................ 3................ 4................

13. ANY CONVICTIONS FOR ANTI-SOCIAL ACTS (State nature of offence and penalty)

    F............ M............ 1................ 2................

**Physiological Data — Females**

MOTHER. — Present age............ Age at onset of puberty............ Age at marriage............ Date of marriage............ Date of birth of each child............

............ Number of miscarriages............ Still-born children............ Duration of suckling without supplementary feeding for each child............

Use of contraceptive measures............ Age of menopause............ Uterine troubles............

Previous marriages ............

UNMARRIED DAUGHTERS. — Present age............ Age at onset of puberty............ Age at menopause............

Sacral spots at birth or during infancy; size and duration............

SEX DATA (diseases) ............

Family questionnaire

PEABODY MUSEUM PAPERS

Bureau of International Research
Harvard University and Radcliffe College

No.......................

QUESTIONNAIRE — Mixed Blood & Pure Families

| Genealogical Data | Father | Father's Father | Father's Mother | Mother | Mother's Father | Mother's Mother |
|---|---|---|---|---|---|---|
| 1. NAME | 1. | 2. | 3. | 4. | 5. | 6. |
| 2. AGE (Indicate age at death by parentheses) | 1. | 2. | 3. | 4. | 5. | 6. |
| 3. BIRTHPLACE | 1. | 2. | 3. | 4. | 5. | 6. |
| 4. LEGITIMATE | 1. | 2. | 3. | 4. | 5. | 6. |
| 5. Proportion INDIAN BLOOD | 1. | 2. | 3. | 4. | 5. | 6. |
| 6. Proportion WHITE BLOOD (State what stock) | 1. | 2. | 3. | 4. | 5. | 6. |
| 7. Proportion OTHER BLOOD | 1. | 2. | 3. | 4. | 5. | 6. |
| 8. CAUSE OF DEATH if dead | 1. | 2. | 3. | 4. | 5. | 6. |
| 9. NUMBER and SEX of CHILDREN now surviving | 1. | 2. | 3. | 4. | 5. | 6. |
| 10. NUMBER and SEX of CHILDREN now deceased | 1. | 2. | 3. | 4. | 5. | 6. |
| 11. OCCUPATION | 1. | 2. | 3. | 4. | 5. | 6. |
| 12. EDUCATION | 1. | 2. | 3. | 4. | 5. | 6. |
| 13. Estimated SKIN COLOR if absent or deceased | 1. | 2. | 3. | 4. | 5. | 6. |
| 14. Estimated HAIR COLOR and FORM if absent or deceased | 1. | 2. | 3. | 4. | 5. | 6. |
| 15. Estimated TYPE OF FEATURES if absent or deceased | 1. | 2. | 3. | 4. | 5. | 6. |
| 16. MISCELLANEOUS | 1. | 2. | 3. | 4. | 5. | 6. |

Family questionnaire

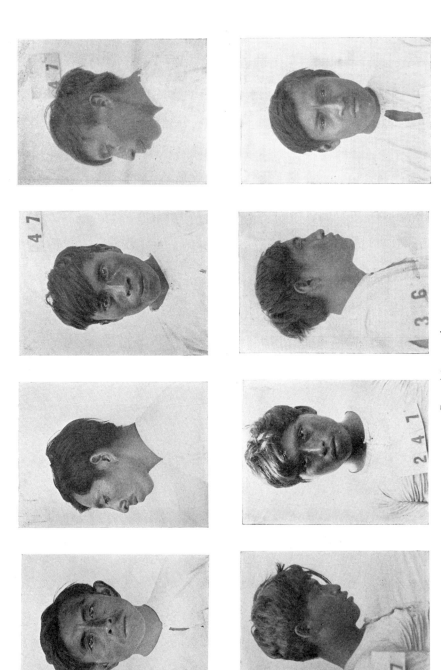

Group A types, males

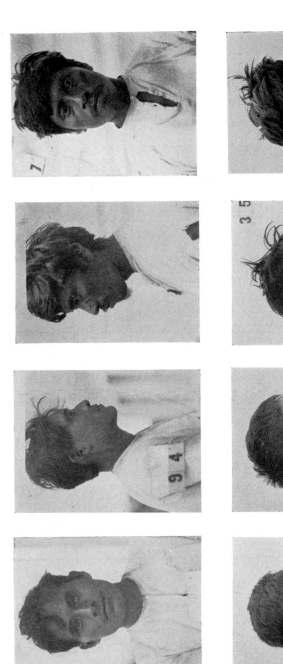
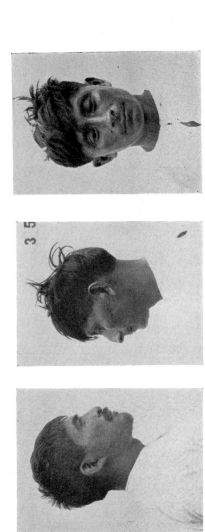
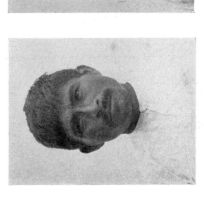

Group B types, males

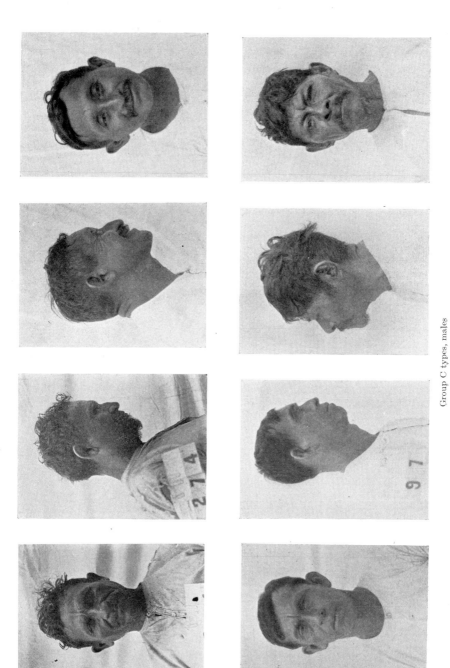

Group C types, males

Group D types, males

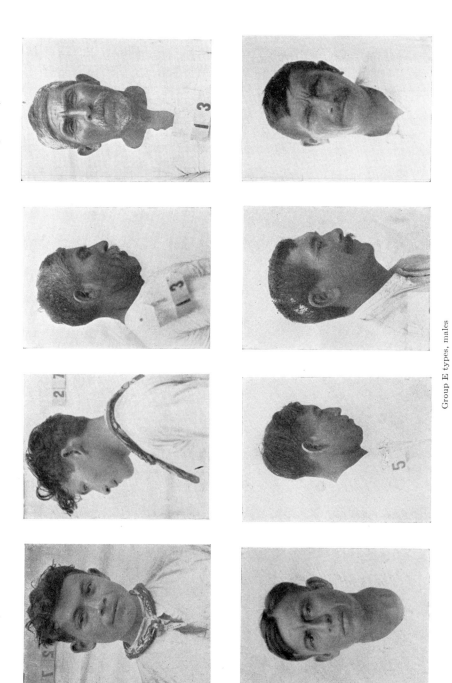

Group E types, males

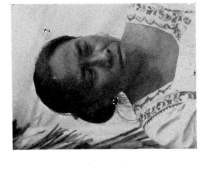

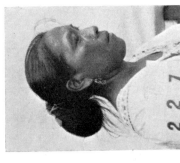

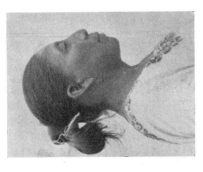

Group A types, females

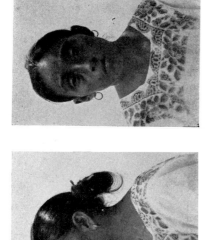

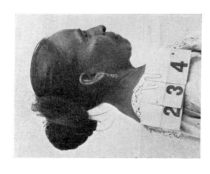

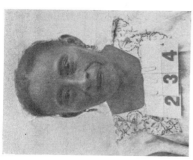

Group B types, females

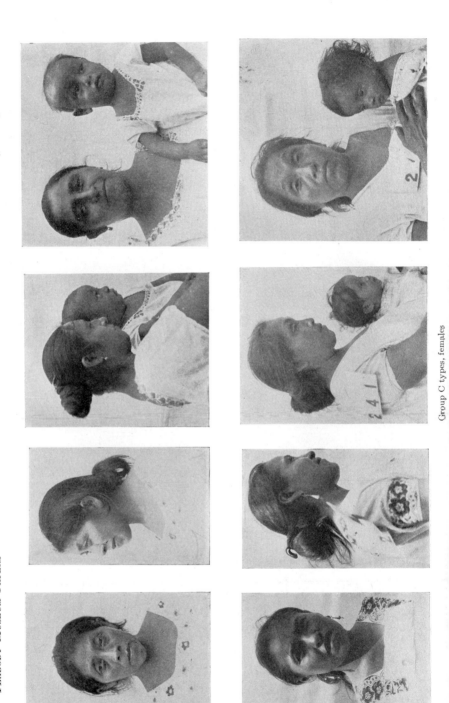

Group C types, females

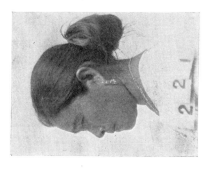

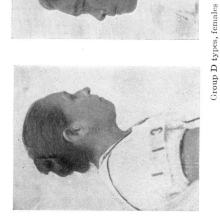

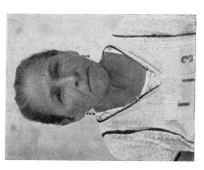

Group D types, females

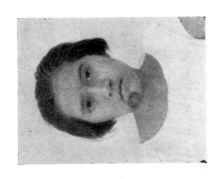

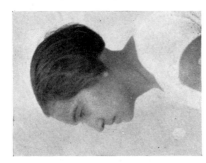

Group E types, females

Typical rural Yucatecan families

(*Above*) A rural Yucatecan family. (*Below*) A Yucateco-Mexican family. Note the difference in costume between the older woman and the two younger ones.

(*Above*) Hacienda laborers. The dress is typical. (*Below*) Hacienda woman. She is
bringing home corn paste ground at the hacienda mill

(*Above*) A village church.  (*Below*) A hacienda chapel

(*Above*) Street and plaza of a Yucatecan town of 1400 population. (*Below*) Hacienda
street. Note windmill base at right and track for hauling of henequen at left

(*Above*) A hacienda laborer's house of the better kind.  (*Below*) Houses of poor villagers

(*Above*) *Casa principal* of a hacienda
(*Below*) Mayor and school teachers of a Yucatecan town

(*Above*) A village school.  (*Below*) A hacienda school

(*Above*) Water storage tank on a hacienda. There are no streams in Yucatan and water is precious. Note windmill in the distance. (*Below*) Irrigation system for a hacienda garden. A tank like that shown above supplies the troughs

(*Above*) Village women at a well. (*Below*) A hacienda pump. Water is brought to
the surface by moving the stick in a horizontal circle

(*Above*) Pulling water from a well by horse power. The horse's harness is made of henequen. (*Below*) A Yucatecan beehive. Hollowed logs are plugged at the ends and a hole bored on the circumferences of the cylinder for ingress and egress of the insects

(*Above*) Cutting henequen on a Yucatecan hacienda.  (*Below*) Drying henequen fibre

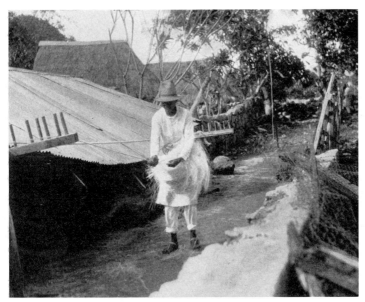

(*Above*) Villager making twine from henequen fibre
(*Below*) Making rope from henequen fibre

(*Above*) Thatching.  (*Below*) Masons at work

(*Above*) Baking wheat bread; a delicacy. (*Below*) Washing. Note the "tub" of hollowed log